Helping Skills

Helping Skills

Facilitating Exploration, Insight, and Action

Clara E. Hill
Karen M. O'Brien

American Psychological Association

Washington, DC

Published by
American Psychological Association
750 First Street, NE
Washington, DC 20002

Copies may be ordered from
APA Order Department
P.O. Box 92984
Washington, DC 20090-2984

In the U.K., Europe, Africa, and the Middle East, copies may be ordered from
American Psychological Association
3 Henrietta Street
Covent Garden, London
WC2E 8LU England

Typeset in Stone Serif by TechBooks, Fairfax, VA

Printer: United Book Press, Inc., Baltimore, MD
Dust jacket designer: Minker Design, Bethesda, MD
Technical/Production Editor: Amy J. Clarke

On the cover: *Breton Girls Dancing, Pont-Aven* (1888, oil on canvas) by Paul Gauguin, from the Collection of Mr. and Mrs. Paul Mellon, © 1999 Board of Trustees, National Gallery of Art, Washington, DC. Reprinted with permission.

Library of Congress Cataloging-in-Publication Data
Hill, Clara E.
   Helping skills : facilitating exploration, insight, and action / Clara E. Hill and Karen M. O'Brien.—1st ed.
     p. cm.
   Includes bibliographical references and index.
   ISBN 1-55798-572-3 (acid-free paper)
   1. Counseling.   2. Helping skills behavior.   I. Hill, Clara E.   II. O'Brien, Karen M.   III. Title
BF637.C6H46   1999
158'.3—dc21
                                           98-33121
                                              CIP

British Library Cataloguing-in-Publication Data
A CIP record is available from the British Library.

Printed in the United States of America
First Edition

To my husband, Jim Gormally, my fellow traveler in the process of learning helping skills; to my children, Kevin and Katie, who have tested my helping skills; and to my students who have taught me how to teach helping skills—Clara E. Hill

To my parents, Eileen and John O'Brien, who provided the love, encouragement, and education that enabled their children to become effective helpers, and to my aunt, Sister Nora O'Brien, who has served as an exemplary role model for helping others—Karen M. O'Brien

Contents

Part II: Exploration Stage

Labs

Acknowledgments

We are very grateful for the many people who have read selected chapters or all of the book and provided valuable feedback: Lisa Flores, Suzanne Friedman, Julie Goldberg, Jim Gormally, Allison Grolnick, Debby Herbenick, Pam Highlen, Merris Hollingworth, Ian Kellems, Sarah Knox, Misty Kolchakian, Jim Lichtenberg, John Norcross, David Petersen, Eric Spiegel, Linda Tipton, Terry Tracey, and Elizabeth Nutt Williams. Several colleagues in Taiwan listened to an early presentation of our ideas for several of the chapters and provided excellent feedback. We profited considerably from the editorial feedback, guidance, and encouragement of Beth Beisel, Amy Clarke, and Linda McCarter. In addition, we were most fortunate to work with a great editor, Margaret Schlegel, who provided guidance and encouragement throughout the process.

I (Clara E. Hill) want to acknowledge Bill Anthony (who studied with Robert Carkhuff), from whom I first learned helping skills many years ago in graduate school. I clearly recall the heady times of coming to believe that I could help clients if I applied the helping skills.

I (Karen M. O'Brien) would like to acknowledge the unending support and valuable assistance provided by my partner in helping and in life, David Petersen. David believed in the importance of this book and contributed (and sacrificed) much to enable me to concentrate on the creation of this text.

We also are most indebted to the many students in our undergraduate course in helping skills and in our graduate courses in theories and strategies of counseling over the last several years. They have taught us a tremendous amount about how to teach helping skills with their willingness to challenge our ideas, offering thoughtful perspectives on the process of becoming helpers and providing ideas for examples in the text. We thank our clients who provided us with challenges to grow as helpers and with numerous case illustrations for our book. Finally and with much gratitude, we recognize and acknowledge our therapists and supervisors, who served as wonderful models for how to use helping skills and who provided much encouragement throughout our process of becoming helpers.

Preface

The purpose of this book is to teach readers basic helping skills and to assist them in becoming more effective in their professional and personal interactions. Our interest in training helpers developed from teaching basic helping skills classes to undergraduate and graduate students. As we developed our courses, we experienced frustration in finding the right textbook that would embody our philosophy of helping and address the needs of our students. Few, if any, helping skills texts integrate the importance of affect, cognition, and behavior in the process of change. Some concentrate on feelings while disregarding the role of challenge and action in facilitating critical life changes, whereas others highlight insight at the expense of affective exploration and behavioral change. Several popular texts focus solely on a problem-solving approach, which neglects the critical role of affect in helping clients express, understand, and alter that with which they are dissatisfied in their lives. To address these limitations, we used the knowledge generated from our experiences as students, teachers, counselors, supervisors, and researchers to write a book that teaches helpers to assist clients in exploring their feelings and thoughts, gaining new insights about their problems, and moving toward positive behavioral changes. Note that the names have been changed in the examples throughout the book to protect the identity of those involved.

Our Philosophy of Helping

This text introduces the three-stage model of helping, an integrated model that is grounded in research and theory. We liken the production of our text to the creation of a skyscraper in which we have employed two qualified groups of professionals: first, the architects (the researchers) who have formulated (after extensive thought and research) an innovative design that meets all of the building, site, and cultural requirements and who have subsequently produced the construction documents from which to build; second, the construction contractors (the theorists) who have lain a strong, deeply rooted foundation from which we construct our model of helping skills. With this solid grounding (theory) and empirically tested plans (research), we hope that you find our helping skills model to be structurally sound, aesthetically pleasing, and effective.

Grounding our model in theory is important because we built on the work of accomplished clinicians and theoreticians who have articulated a rich theoretical knowledge base. Rogers, Freud, Erikson, Mahler, Skinner, Ellis, Beck, and others have provided brilliant insights into the nature of human beings, the mechanisms of change in counseling, and the techniques for assisting individuals to achieve their potential and accomplish their goals. Our three-stage model is grounded in the contributions of these sage theorists, and readers are introduced to the salient aspects of their work.

Grounding our model in research is also important. Research educates helpers about the effective (and ineffective) use of helping skills. Our confidence in promoting the helping skills is strengthened by the knowledge that these skills have been tested empirically and found to be useful to clients. Moreover, because research in helping skills is still in its infancy, we provide ideas for studies to encourage others to do research.

We also conceptualize the helping process as comprising moment-by-moment interactional sequences. Using a tested theory of the interactions between helpers and clients (Hill, 1992), we postulate that at any moment in the helping process, helpers develop intentions for how they want to help clients. These intentions are based on what they know about clients and what they hope to accomplish with clients at a given time. With these intentions in mind, helpers select verbal and nonverbal skills with which to intervene. In turn, clients react to the interventions in ways that influence how they then choose to behave with helpers. Thus, helping involves not only the overt behaviors but also the cognitive processes of helpers (i.e., intentions) and clients (i.e., reactions). Awareness of intentions assists helpers in selecting effective interventions. In addition, attention to the clients' reactions to the interventions can aid helpers in planning future interventions.

Finally, we sought to write a book that both supports students' development as helpers and provides challenges to facilitate the development of helping skills. Becoming an effective helper is an exciting and challenging process. For some, this undertaking can be life changing. Many of our students are fascinated by the process of becoming helpers, and they pose thoughtful questions as they struggle to learn the skills and develop confidence in their ability to assist others. Because the focus of this book is on helpers (not clients), we pose many questions that relate to the helpers' development and concomitant feelings and thoughts. Thus, we ask our readers to try to understand themselves better and to think carefully about the process of becoming effective helpers.

Some of our students have made difficult but appropriate decisions not to pursue careers in helping as a result of the self-exploration that accompanies this process. Others have become passionate in their pursuit of careers in nursing, medicine, social work, psychology, and other human service fields. We encourage our readers to become actively involved by thinking about the questions and practicing the experiential exercises provided in this helping skills text.

What Our Text Does Not Provide

It seems necessary to clarify the focus of this book by also indicating what our text does not provide. We do not provide important additional information needed to counsel children, families, or clients who have serious emotional or psychological difficulties. Although helping skills form the foundation for work with children, families, or adults with serious emotional disorders, additional, more advanced therapeutic interventions also are needed to work with these populations.

Furthermore, we do not address the diagnosis of psychological problems or identify characteristics of psychopathology, which are two important topics that require extensive additional training. We encourage helpers to pursue further training in assessment and psychopathology after developing a working knowledge of basic helping skills. We believe that all helpers, even those working with healthy populations, should be able to recognize serious psychological disorders. This level of knowledge aids helpers in making appropriate referrals and working only with clients who they have been trained to assist.

In addition, this book does not fully address the myriad of cross-cultural issues related to helping. We believe that the influence of culture is pervasive and is reflected in the helping process through the client's and helper's worldviews and the interaction between them. Clients need to be viewed in the context of the multitude of influences that have an impact on their lives (e.g., family and friends, support systems, racial and cultural background, work experiences, life transitions, socioeconomic status). We strongly encourage helpers to educate themselves about multicultural theory and research (e.g., Atkinson, Morten, & Sue, 1993; Helms & Cook, 1999; Ponterotto, Casas, Suzuki, & Alexander, 1995; Sue & Sue, 1999).

Our Goals for This Book

We have several goals for readers who read this book and complete the exercises. Readers should be able to articulate the principles of the integrated three-stage model of helping as well as the theoretical and research foundations underlying this model. They should demonstrate an understanding of the interactional sequences of helping, including the intentions that helpers have for interventions with clients, the helping skills that are commensurate with these intentions, the possible reactions and behaviors demonstrated by clients, and the means by which helpers, evaluate the interventions used. In addition, readers should gain a better understanding of themselves relative to becoming helpers, including their thoughts about helping as well as their strengths and areas for continued growth. Finally, we hope to instill enthusiasm for the process of learning to help others— an enterprise that is certain to provide countless challenges and rewards throughout a lifetime.

OVERVIEW

1 Becoming an Effective Helper

> Nothing in life is achieved without effort, daring to take risks, and often some suffering.
>
> *Erich Fromm*

Angeli was a stellar student and athlete. She was president of her high school class and had been accepted into an elite eastern university. By any standard, she was an exceptional and talented individual with much promise. After arriving at college, Angeli began to exhibit much sadness and inactivity. Much to the dismay of her family, teachers, and friends, she lost interest in interacting with others, studying for her classes, and attending track practice. Angeli's track coach encouraged her to meet with a helper who used helping skills to assist Angeli in exploring her feelings and understanding the underlying issues related to her sadness and inactivity. Angeli felt supported, cared for, and challenged by her helper. The helping relationship that she developed enabled her to express, understand, struggle with, and overcome the feelings of inadequacy, loneliness, and loss that emerged when she left for college.

MOST PEOPLE need assistance at some point in their lives to deal with troublesome issues that stifle their personal growth and limit their potential. Many of you may be interested in learning the skills that would enable you to help someone like Angeli. The work of a helper offers a powerful and rewarding opportunity to make a difference in people's lives and to learn and grow personally and professionally. As you read these words and reflect on the process of becoming a helper, you may have contradictory thoughts and feelings. Beginning helpers initially may exhibit much confidence in their ability to help others (Hill, O'Brien, et al., 1998) because they often have listened and advised friends and family members about their pressing concerns. However, research suggests that less positive feelings and questioning thoughts also accompany the process of learning helping skills (i.e., concern about performing well, anxiety about saying the right thing in sessions, and hesitation about whether or not helping others is a desirable role). Thus, our purpose in this book is twofold. First, we present a three-stage model of helping that can be used to assist individuals who are struggling with emotional or life transition difficulties. Second, we accompany you on a journey toward self-discovery about the role of helping in your life by providing opportunities for you to practice beginning helping skills and reflect on the process of becoming an effective helper.

The purpose of the first chapter is to provide an overview of this book and to articulate our definition of helping. We want you to learn about the goals of helping and the limitations associated with helping. We address the question of why people seek help from others, review relevant research about the outcomes of helping, describe the process of becoming a helper, and discuss what motivates people to help. Finally, we describe the layout of this book and provide suggestions for how to use the exercises in the text. Being a helper has been one of the most rewarding aspects of our personal and professional lives, and we welcome you to discover the role of helping in your life.

WHAT IS HELPING?

Throughout the text, we use the terms *helper* to describe the individual providing assistance and *client* to indicate the person receiving support. *Helping* can be defined as assisting clients in exploring feelings, gaining insight, and making positive changes in their lives. Helpers and clients work together to achieve these outcomes with helpers facilitating the process of change and clients deciding what and how they want to change. Helping is often an effective means for clients to obtain relief from emotional pain, discover a direction for their lives, and receive feedback that can facilitate change. Furthermore, the process of helping enables clients to experience healthy relationships, work toward personal growth, address existential concerns, and learn valuable skills.

Helping skills encompass both verbal and nonverbal forms of communication. These interventions include attending and listening behaviors, closed and open questions, restatements, reflections of feelings, challenges, interpretations, self-disclosures, approval and reassurance, immediacy, information, and direct guidance. These skills have been shown by researchers to be effective in developing helping relationships with clients and assisting clients in improving their lives. Prior to focusing on the development of these skills, we believe it is important to articulate the similarities and differences among helping, counseling, and psychotherapy.

Helping Versus Counseling Versus Psychotherapy

At times, the distinction among helping, counseling, and psychotherapy can be confusing. *Helping* is a broad and generic term that includes the assistance provided by a variety of individuals including physicians, nurses, counselors, psychotherapists, and human service providers. Beginning helpers differ from counselors and psychotherapists in three ways: the goals of the intervention, the people providing and receiving assistance, and the skills and education required.

First, the goals of helping for beginning helpers are to listen well, promote growth, and assist with transitions. In addition to sharing these goals, counselors and psychotherapists remedy personal problems, facilitate personality change, and intervene with severe psychological malfunctioning. Hence, counseling and psychotherapy go beyond basic helping skills to address more complicated and serious concerns.

Second, beginning helpers tend to work most effectively with people who are relatively psychologically healthy. These individuals may need assistance to address crises or pressing concerns, or they may want to maximize their potential in all aspects of their lives. For example, college students who are searching for direction or well-functioning couples who want to enhance their relationships or improve their communication skills can benefit from working with beginning helpers.

Third, beginning helpers are not professionals with advanced training and cannot consider themselves to be counselors or therapists. Counselors and psychotherapists have completed many years of training, whereas helpers have only received instruction in the basic helping skills. These basic skills must be integrated with advanced training for helpers to become more advanced human service providers (e.g., rabbis, counselors, nurses, therapists). Helpers often aspire to become counselors and psychotherapists, extending their education to receive advanced training and eventual licensure as mental health professionals.

A final note relates to the differences between counseling and psychotherapy. At times, the two are differentiated by length of treatment (counseling may have fewer sessions than therapy), clientele (counseling often is used with more healthy individuals), qualifications of the provider (counselors may have masters or doctoral degrees, whereas therapists tend to be doctoral-level practitioners), and types of problems presented in sessions (counseling may deal with development and life transition issues, whereas therapy may address more serious psychological disturbances). However, we operate from the perspective that counseling and psychotherapy are very similar, that helping skills form the foundation for both counseling and therapy, and that most individuals can benefit from learning basic helping skills.

We also believe that although helping, counseling, and psychotherapy tend to be of great benefit to clients, these processes also can inhibit personal growth. The following sections address the facilitative and problematic aspects of helping.

Facilitative Aspects of Helping

For people in emotional pain, effective helping can provide necessary support and relief. For example, Jillian and Jesse came to counseling because Jillian had been involved in a sexual relationship with a senior colleague at work. Both individuals were extremely hurt and felt very angry with each other. Months of working on communication skills and receiving assistance in exploring feelings, understanding the factors related to the affair, and learning how to work proactively to improve their relationship resulted in positive changes for the couple. Jillian and Jesse were able to communicate their feelings openly, grieve the loss of trust in their relationship, and move toward rebuilding their lives together as a cohesive and caring couple.

In addition to facilitating emotional healing, helping can assist individuals in determining the direction of their lives. Sometimes, people seek assistance believing that helpers provide answers to complicated questions and future plans. The most effective helpers have the ability to assist individuals in determining goals for themselves that are consistent with their dreams, values, and abilities. For example, Mai Lin came to counseling because she was uncertain about whether she should move far away from her family and end her relationship with her live-in boyfriend. She described her current situation and asked the helper to tell her what seemed like the best path for her. After dealing with her anger and frustration at the helper for not providing the answers, Mai Lin was able to explore her unwillingness to take responsibility for the direction of her life and her reluctance to address the questions that plagued her. She contemplated her fear of taking action and making the wrong decisions and connected this with feelings of helplessness that she had experienced as a child of a battered woman. Further exploration of thoughts, feelings, and behaviors provided her with the desire to begin to make small decisions with the support and encouragement of her helper. Soon, Mai Lin was able to progress to more challenging decisions (e.g., ending her romantic relationship and moving across the country on her own to explore her independence and to understand her self better).

An additional facilitative aspect of helping involves helpers providing feedback about how clients appear to others, information that others might hesitate to provide. For example, a client who is having difficulty maintaining relationships may be able to hear (from the helper) that he appears very dependent and needy in sessions and may want to examine whether these behaviors are present in other relationships. Although helpers should phrase their comments in a gentle manner, honest feedback can be extremely helpful in motivating individuals to change.

Helping also can enable clients to experience a healthy, nondamaging relationship with another person. Sometimes, the helping process is described as "reparenting" in that a caring relationship with a helper alleviates some of the previous hurtful and unhealthy interactions experienced with important figures early in life. For example, Kondja came to helping because she felt depressed and lacked direction for her life. She believed that her mother did not want her as a child, and she cried when she saw mothers and daughters who were connected and loving with one another. Kondja had been in a series of relationships in which she felt ignored, alone, uncared for, and discounted. During the helping process, Kondja experienced the helper as unconditionally accepting, actively listening, and genuinely caring. The development of a supportive relationship with a helper assisted Kondja in healing past wounds, drinking less alcohol to numb her feelings, and developing healthy relationships in which she valued herself enough to ensure that her needs were met.

Moreover, clients can learn skills needed to live more effectively and attain their potential. These skills might include learning how to communicate with others, practicing ways to resolve conflicts, identifying decision-making strategies, or changing unhealthy habits (e.g., rarely exercising; having unprotected, anonymous sex). Clients sometimes need to learn assertiveness skills to express their feelings and needs in a respectful yet firm manner. Often, these skills can alleviate the powerlessness that individuals feel when they are unable to communicate their emotions directly and can assist clients in engaging more fully in their lives.

Helping can assist individuals in dealing with existential concerns (i.e., who am I, where am I going, and what do I want out of life). As often stated, "the unexamined life is not worth living" (Socrates). Helping can promote proactive involvement in life when these questions are asked, reflected on, and answered. For example, helping adolescents sometimes involves identifying the direction in which they are headed. Max was referred for helping because of failing grades, poor peer relationships, and generalized sadness. After several sessions, Max began to address critical questions regarding how he might live his life, the fears he often confronts within himself, and the salience of his relationships with others. Helping provided him with an opportunity to look within himself, discover what felt important, and then make some decisions about how to change his unhealthy behaviors.

Finally, effective helping results in teaching valuable skills to clients so that they can leave helping relationships having learned how to explore feelings and thoughts, trust their insights, and motivate themselves to proactive living. Similar to how children need to grow up and leave their parents, clients also need to leave their helpers. Perhaps some of you have tried to teach others the art of in-line skating; you hold them up, and they hang on while they make their first attempt at skating. In time, they begin to skate by themselves. The steps that they make on their own are rewarding not only for the beginning skater, but also for the teacher. The same is true with helping: Providing the initial support and teaching the viable skills are most effective when individuals internalize the message and "roll" on their own.

Problematic Aspects of Helping

Despite the positive aspects of helping, providing assistance to others has potential liabilities. Sometimes, helping can provide just enough relief to enable people to stay in maladaptive situations or relationships. For example, battered women's shelters provide needed safety and security to abused women and their children. However, shelter workers have observed that occasionally shelters provide just enough assistance to enable women to return to the abusive situation. When the helpers in one shelter confronted this "enabling" in themselves and discussed these behaviors with the residents, some of the battered women were able to identify their pattern of seeking shelter during the abusive periods and returning home in the "honeymoon period." Without this insight, helping could have enabled some of the women to continue in a potentially deadly cycle.

Helping can create dependency in clients who rely on their helpers for support and feel as if they are unable to process feelings or make changes in their lives without assistance from others. For example, Kathleen might decline a spontaneous invitation to join her new partner's family on Cape Cod for a week, because she felt like she needed to process the decision with her therapist (who herself was on vacation for 2 weeks).

Helpers may facilitate dependency by providing clients with "the answers" to their problems. Effective helpers understand that providing the answers does not truly help others; rather, clients need to participate actively in a process where they uncover new insights and discover which actions feel best for themselves. This strategy works because only clients fully know the situations, experience the associated feelings, and have the best answers to the presenting problems. In addition, advising others may be problematic when the solution that we provide does not fit with their needs. Many of us have made suggestions to family members or friends about how to handle difficult situations, only to find that our advice was not exactly what they wanted to hear. For example, a helper told a close friend to stay away from the boyfriend who broke up with her because he was not good enough for her. After they got back together, the friend resented the helper's critical words about her sweetheart. Although challenging, empowering clients to make their own decisions is critically important.

Sometimes, helpers' personal issues place them at risk for encouraging dependency in those they assist. For helpers who are lonely and isolated, being needed by their clients may fulfill personal needs that are not being met elsewhere. Helpers who have not developed a network of social support and personal relationships may be at special risk for encouraging their clients to rely extensively on them.

Another problematic aspect of helping emerges when helpers impose personal or societal values onto their clients (McWhirter, 1994). For example, some helping professionals have attempted to alter the sexual orientation of people who were lesbian, gay, or bisexual. Other helpers have advised parents to raise their children in a certain religion because the helper believed that problems in families result from children not having a strong religious foundation. One of the challenges of being a helper involves recognizing how our personal values influence our work with clients. Because the values we hold undeniably have an influence on the helping process, becoming an effective helper entails learning more about yourself and your values to ensure that they do not affect the helping process negatively. For example, an older male client working with a feminist female helper once stated that women should not work outside the home because they take jobs away from qualified men who have families to raise. In this case, the helper's and client's values differed, yet challenging the client about his belief system did not seem to be an effective means of developing a therapeutic relationship. Fortunately, the helper was able to separate her values from the client's values and reflect an underlying message of concern about his fears about the stability of his job.

WHEN DO PEOPLE SEEK HELP FROM OTHERS?

People may seek assistance from others when they become aware that they are in pain or are facing a difficult situation, perceive their feelings or situation as problematic, and believe that help could assist them in alleviating their distress (Gross & McMullen, 1983). People seek help when the pain they feel is greater than the perceived or actual barriers to seeking professional assistance. Sometimes the barriers involve practical considerations such as the time or money required to obtain help, but often the obstacles are emotional and can include fears about deeply exploring problems and concerns about the opinions of others regarding people who seek therapy.

For example, Conchita came to her first helping session because she was experiencing multiple stressors. She had discovered that her sister was diagnosed with depression (her mother had committed suicide 3 years earlier), she was failing all of her courses (previously she had been an "A" student), her first serious boyfriend broke up with her, and she was pregnant. Conchita recognized that her situation and feelings were problematic, and she felt that she could no longer cope with the problems she was experiencing. For some time, Conchita had felt that she should handle her problems by herself because she feared what others might think of her if they knew that she needed to see a helper. Moreover, she was on a limited budget and was reluctant to pay for helping. However, her brother had felt better after talking with a helper, and she perceived that her feelings and problems would be amenable to assistance from a mental health professional. Thus, Conchita sought help because she believed the costs associated with helping (e.g., financial expense and perceived stigma) were less important than the potential benefits (e.g., emotional support and assistance with coping).

Others may engage in a helping relationship because they are having trouble adjusting to a particular stage in life or because they want to maximize their potential. For example, Donnell came to therapy because he wanted to revitalize his life. Although successful in many ways (e.g., he owned his own business, had a loving relationship with his partner and child, and played in a band for fun), he knew that he had unresolved issues that limited him from living his life fully. He was afraid of looking at some of these issues because it might mean making some big changes in his life. He addressed these issues with a helper and moved from anger and disappointment about his childhood to acceptance of the limitations of his parents. This movement freed him to be more open with others and more accepting of himself.

Many people, however, hesitate to seek professional help (Gross & McMullen, 1983). They feel embarrassed or ashamed about asking for assistance or believe that going for help constitutes emotional weakness or inadequacy (Shapiro, 1984). Many Americans, for example, believe that individuals should rely solely on themselves and that all problems should be solved individually. Given these beliefs, it is not surprising that researchers have found that people seek help first from friends and family members and only last from professionals (Tinsley, de St. Aubin, & Brown, 1982; Webster & Fretz, 1978).

Some people are also concerned about talking with others because they feel that no one could possibly understand their situation. Others fear a punitive response or a value judgment regarding their thoughts, feelings, or actions. Furthermore, individuals may be concerned that they will be labeled *mentally ill* and thus be subject to the many negative stereotypes and stigma associated with this label (Sue, Sue, & Sue, 1994). Some clients may be hesitant to seek therapy because they rely on their insurance companies to pay for therapy, and they are concerned that the stigma associated with being in therapy could have negative ramifications for obtaining insurance or employment in the future.

Clearly, many people experience distress about seeking professional help. Individuals in considerable pain who admit their need for psychological assistance have made significant progress toward obtaining the help they need. Support from friends and family can provide the necessary encouragement for these individuals to contact trained helpers (Gourash, 1978). For example, Joe was reluctant to seek help after his wife of 40 years died. His friends and children encouraged him to attend a support group for adults who have lost their partners. Although initially reluctant, Joe was so upset about his loss that he agreed to participate in the group sessions if his daughters would accompany him. The support that his family and friends provided enabled Joe to access the help that he needed.

In addition, helpers need to work to change negative attitudes about seeking professional psychological assistance in our society. We might begin by stressing the belief that people are courageous when they recognize that they need help and then access that assistance from trained helpers. Ideally, helping would be considered a valuable and standard service for people experiencing normal life transitions or crisis situations. Only then can we ensure that individuals contact skilled professionals when they need assistance to address their problems and maximize their potential.

DOES HELPING WORK?

In this section, we focus on research about the effectiveness of psychotherapy. In 1952, Eysenck compiled the results of 24 studies that investigated the outcome of therapy interventions in an attempt to answer the important question "Does psychotherapy work?" Although this early compilation of studies questioned the efficacy of psychotherapy, later investigators with more sophisticated research designs have overwhelmingly concluded that counseling and therapy are helpful and that most clients improved by the end of therapy at a greater rate than those in need who did not receive therapeutic interventions (Smith, Glass, & Miller, 1980). Specifically, Smith et al. found that the average client who received therapy was psychologically healthier than 80% of untreated individuals.

Why the discrepancy between Eysenck's work and the investigation of subsequent researchers? Reviewers have criticized Eysenck's (1952) conclusions because they were based on a faulty research design. In addition, Eysenck used different guidelines for evaluating the outcome of the control and treatment groups, applying more stringent criteria for determining improvement in the treatment group. For example, at the beginning of the study, clients in the treatment group had more serious psychological disturbances than those in the control group. One would expect the healthiest individuals to demonstrate the highest level of functioning at the end of the study because they had the fewest problems at the start of the study. Moreover, people in the control group did, in fact, receive treatment: They were often the recipients of helping behaviors from friends, family members, clergy, and medical personnel. Finally, Eysenck did not account for differences in the level of experience among those providing treatment. Typically, we would expect that experienced therapists would provide the most effective treatment, and thus this variable should be controlled for in any study of therapy effectiveness.

When researchers established that psychotherapy in general is indeed helpful, they began to ask about the relative effectiveness of different types of therapy. To date, hundreds of studies have been conducted comparing client-centered, psychodynamic, cognitive–behavioral, experiential, and other therapies. Wampold et al. (1997) performed a meta-analysis of psychotherapy outcome studies and concluded that no one type of therapy is more effective than another. Although one might conclude that therapy sessions are similar across theoretical orientations, a large body of research points to significant differences in therapist and client behaviors among the different orientations to therapy (see review in Hill & Corbett, 1993). Hence, we can conclude that although various approaches to therapy use different techniques, most therapies are equally effective, and no one type of therapy works best with every client in every counseling situation. The findings from this area of research have been humorously summarized using the Dodo bird verdict from *Alice in Wonderland*: "Everyone has won and all must have prizes" (Carroll, 1865/1962, p. 412). Additional research is needed, however, because the measures available to assess outcome in psychotherapy are unrefined and may not detect differences among approaches.

One line of psychotherapy research has examined how many psychotherapy sessions are needed to reduce psychological distress and return the client to normal psychological functioning (e.g., Howard, Lueger, Maling, & Martinovich, 1993; Kopta, Howard, Lowry, & Beutler, 1994). In their review of a large number of studies, these researchers found that clients who had experienced significant emotional pain improved fairly quickly, whereas clients with chronic characterological problems (i.e., innate, severe, ongoing, and difficult to treat disorders) required the greatest number of sessions to return to normal functioning. It is interesting to note that they suggested that most clients need 1 year of therapy for a 75% chance of recovery. Furthermore, change in psychotherapy seemed to occur in a stepwise function, with improvements in subjective well-being occurring first, reduction in symptoms related to the emotional problems following, and enhancements in life functioning occurring last for most clients.

In summary, therapy has been shown to be an effective means of helping people cope with emotional pain and interpersonal problems (Strupp, 1996). Furthermore, researchers have identified myriad factors that relate to positive outcome in therapy and have described the difficulty in studying factors related to client change (Lambert & Hill, 1994). Additional research is needed and thus, throughout this book, suggestions for studies that could inform and advance the helping process are provided.

ON BECOMING A HELPER

Helping seems to be a natural tendency in many people, and most people have an innate desire to assist others. For many of us, our natural inclination toward helping must be complemented by learning and practicing helping skills until they become an integral part of who we are. Helpers who have integrated helping skills into their way of being tend to have several characteristics in common: They listen carefully, encourage exploration of thoughts and feelings, assist clients in gaining new perspectives on the problem, and motivate clients to take actions to improve their lives. Furthermore, effective helpers work from a clearly articulated theoretical foundation and remain knowledgeable about the recent research findings related to helping interventions.

Many people can become effective helpers if they are motivated to learn helping skills and practice these new behaviors (even when those behaviors initially feel awkward and forced). Many effective helpers have stories of their initial attempts at assisting others. For example, when one helper first started studying helping behaviors, her father was undergoing heart surgery. She spoke to him every day and asked him how he was feeling. Finally, after weeks of this, he asked her if she really wanted to know how he was feeling. "Finally!" she thought, "he'll share his innermost feelings with me." Her dad said that he was feeling like he liked her a lot more before she began studying helping skills. Many of your friends and family may have similar reactions as you begin to learn helping skills. Initially, this may be discouraging, but it may help to know that most effective helpers practice these behaviors for many years before comfortably integrating them into their way of being. In fact, many helpers discover that during the process of becoming a helper, their helping skills and confidence seem to deteriorate before they improve, perhaps because beginning helpers often learn how difficult it is to use helping skills in an integrated and comfortable manner.

Healthy Motivators

The process of becoming a helper might begin profitably with helpers trying to understand what motivates them to want to help others. Many people aspire to help others for healthy reasons. Some are altruistic and want to make a difference in people's lives. For example, helpers might want to provide support to those in need by volunteering to work in a shelter for homeless women or by becoming a buddy to a gerontology patient who is confined to a nursing home. People who are motivated to use helping skills in situations like these provide others with supportive relationships in which clients feel listened to, cared for, and understood. Some helpers also choose to make a difference in children's lives by mentoring or tutoring young students, using the foundation of helping skills to develop encouraging relationships. Others hope to make life less painful for those in troubled situations. For example, helpers can provide an important function by assisting teens who think they might be gay or lesbian and fear retribution from family and friends.

In addition, individuals may also recognize a special talent in themselves for listening and supporting others. Perhaps you are the person that friends and family talk with when they are hurt or upset. Others may have role models (e.g., parents, aunts, cousins) who have dedicated their lives to the service of others. Some people view helping as consistent with their cultural values and thus seek careers that enable them to assist others. Furthermore, some people aspire to be helpers because they experienced therapy as helpful when they were struggling with painful issues. For example, Kendra was 12 years old when she lost her mother and had to assume the role of mother to her five siblings. She received therapy to help her cope with her loss and her new responsibilities. Kendra now aspires to help children who have experienced loss in their lives. Another example involves rape survivors who become crisis counselors after receiving supportive counseling that helped them resolve disturbing issues related to the rape.

For many individuals, the helping environment is attractive because it allows them to work with many people who are striving toward actualization of their potential. Helpers who work in group practice settings may have the opportunity to interact with smart, capable colleagues who value personal growth and helping others. Many helpers receive support from their colleagues to actively examine their own issues and improve themselves to ensure their continued success in the helping role. Furthermore, helpers are often excited by their contribution to the process of change in clients' lives and are energized by their clients' hard work and striving toward personal growth.

Finally, people may enter helping fields to work for social change. Helping affords a unique opportunity to make a difference in the lives of individuals and sometimes to influence social policies. Helpers who work with adolescents in at-risk environments may provide them with skills, hope, and encouragement to overcome obstacles and graduate from high school and college. Other helpers may draft legislation or testify on behalf of policies that fight discrimination (e.g., sexual harassment) or encourage funding for social services (e.g., child care). Contributions to social change also occur through research that helpers undertake to evaluate the effectiveness of helping interventions (e.g., studying the efficacy of training undergraduate students to be effective helpers for battered women who have entered the criminal justice system).

Unhealthy Motivators

Unfortunately, helpers might also sometimes be motivated to work with people for less healthy reasons (Bugental, 1965). Individuals sometimes fashion themselves as saviors for the less fortunate or as wise distributors of knowledge and advice. Unconsciously, people may want to help others because they are needy themselves and view helping as a way to develop relationships. Others may use helping as a way to feel better about what they have by comparing themselves to those who are less fortunate. For some people, helping others enables them to feel superior to those whom they are helping. Many of us have heard of helpers who enter helping fields to work through unresolved personal issues or to change situations that they found unchangeable in their past (e.g., an unhappy childhood). All helpers have unresolved issues in their lives, and problems can emerge when helpers use their work primarily to address their own concerns.

Multiple Motivators

Most of us probably aspire to help others for a combination of healthy and un-healthy reasons. The key is to understand our motivations and to monitor them in the helping process. We recommend that helpers seek therapy to learn more about themselves and their motivation for becoming helpers and to resolve personal problems. Helpers also should have some form of supervision available to them when they are learning and later practicing helping skills. We believe that the more aware helpers are of themselves and their issues, the less they allow unconscious influences to disrupt the process of helping.

ORGANIZATION OF THIS BOOK

The first section of this book provides an overview of this text, the integrated three-stage approach to helping, and the theoretical rationale from which this helping model emerges. Unlike many other helping texts, we also have provided a chapter on ethics and confidentiality at the beginning of this book because we believe that beginning helpers need to be aware of ethical concerns that may emerge throughout the process of becoming helpers and practicing helping skills.

The next three sections contain the skills necessary to assist clients in progressing through the exploration, insight, and action stages. In each section, an overview chapter highlights the theoretical foundation and the goals of the stage. The problems that helpers face, as well as discussion questions to facilitate the helper's understanding of each stage, are presented. The skills chapters follow the overview chapters and include sections describing the definition of and the rationale for each skill and the helper intentions and client reactions associated with the skill. We also provide empirical evidence that supports the use of the skill and a discussion of how to apply the skill in a helping session. Helpers then are taught how to determine the effects of the skill on clients, as well as to be aware of problems that helpers may encounter when learning and using the skill. A case example of how the skill can be used effectively is provided, and the skills chapters conclude with helpful hints for implementing the skill. Readers are encouraged to become actively involved by answering the discussion questions and by participating in practice exercises and lab experiences formulated to assist them in trying to learn and perform the skill.

At the end of each stage, a chapter addresses the integration of the skills taught for that stage. We also provide research ideas to advance the empirical investigation of the effectiveness of helping skills. In addition, an extended clinical example is included to illustrate the skills used in the stage. Finally, the last chapter reviews techniques related to managing helping sessions and addresses issues related to integrating the helping skills in the three stages. We close with two examples of how the skills are interwoven in a helping session and concluding comments about your journey to becoming an effective helper.

USING THE PRACTICE ELEMENTS OF THIS BOOK

Reading about helping skills is important, but reading alone does not make you an effective helper. Having extensive knowledge about helping, although important, is only the first step on your journey toward helping others. We believe that the best way for you to learn the skills is first to read and study the text and then to apply what you have learned by answering questions about the material and by participating in practice helping exercises and lab experiences. The following sections describe the ways in which you can use this book to maximize your growth as a helper.

Practice Exercises

At the end of each skills chapter, we provide practice exercises in which statements made by clients are presented. These exercises provide readers with the opportunity to think about and formulate responses to hypothetical client situations prior to practicing the skills in the lab setting. We ask that you generate an intention for your reply and write down your intervention for each client situation. Then, compare your answers with our suggestions for possible responses, found immediately following the practice exercises.

What Do You Think?

In addition to the practice exercises, several questions are provided at the end of each chapter to stimulate your thinking about the material presented in the text. We suggest that you contemplate each question and discuss your responses with your classmates. Professors may elect to assign these questions as homework assignments or include them in their examinations.

Lab Experiences

Throughout this book, we provide lab exercises to assist beginning helpers in practicing helping skills in dyads or small groups. These experiences are a critical component of learning to become an effective helper. Repeated practice is necessary to go beyond understanding the skills to integrate the skills into one's repertoire as a helper. During scheduled class periods, helpers are asked to practice the skills with peers who act as clients while presenting real problems. Observers take careful notes and attend to the helper's ability to deliver a particular skill, so that they can provide feedback to the helper. Everyone has an opportunity to experience the roles of helper, client, and observer for each skill. We also involve students who have successfully completed the helping skills course as lab leaders to facilitate the lab experiences and provide feedback to the beginning helpers. After the lab experiences, readers are asked to complete the "personal reflections" section in which they contemplate questions of importance to their development as skilled helpers and discuss their responses with their classmates.

The success of the lab experiences depends partly on the participants' willingness to reveal information about personal topics. We ask participants to discuss personal topics rather than fabricate problems for two reasons. First, helpers have difficulty learning what is effective when students are not responding genuinely. Second, students often are unable to provide useful feedback to helpers about what is helpful and how the interventions feel if they are not discussing real problems. When role-playing, students are often more involved in trying to think of how the person they are pretending to be might feel or behave than immersing themselves in the immediate experience.

As clients, students are not equally comfortable disclosing personal information with different helpers. We encourage students to come to each lab section prepared with two or three different topics representing different levels of disclosure that they are willing to discuss on a given day. Students might start with the safest topic and only share more if they feel comfortable doing so. Students are not expected to disclose more than they feel comfortable discussing and are encouraged to address only those issues that they feel safe sharing with others.

At times, students might disclose an issue that they initially think is safe but after exploration become uncomfortable, either because of the depth of the topic or because they do not feel comfortable with the helper. We emphasize that students always have the right (without jeopardy or prejudice) to indicate that they choose not to explore a particular issue further. We do not recommend that students discuss very deep or very troublesome topics because helpers are not trained to handle intense disclosures. However, a student who is unwilling to disclose any personal information may have difficulty being an effective client in the lab exercises and may want to consider studying helping skills at some later date.

Exhibit 1.1 provides topics that students in our courses have discussed. Again, the student's issues do not have to be major "problems" but should include current concerns

---

▬▬ EXHIBIT 1.1. CLIENT TOPICS FOR LAB EXPERIENCES

Ideal Topics

> Career—future plans
>
> Choosing a major or graduate program
>
> Problems at work
>
> Roommate issues
>
> Romantic relationships
>
> Studying and school issues

Relatively Safe Topics

> Minor family issues
>
> Autonomy–independence struggles
>
> Minor relationship concerns
>
> High school experiences
>
> Personal views on alcohol and drugs
>
> Existential concerns (e.g., who am I?)
>
> Happy childhood memories
>
> Hobbies and extracurricular activities

Topics That Could Be Too Disclosing

> Traumas (e.g., sexual or physical abuse, rape, victimization, child abuse, serious medical condition)
>
> Serious problems in romantic relationships
>
> Shameful feelings
>
> Serious family disputes

and issues about which the student has some feelings. Although we indicate that a topic may be "safe" for many people, it may not be comfortable for an individual student, so each person selects an issue to discuss. Students may want to refer to this list throughout the semester when a topic is needed for the lab exercises.

Although practice sessions might seem somewhat artificial, the information shared is at times personal and should be treated in a confidential manner. Helpers should not disclose information shared in practice sessions without the permission of the client. Specifically, helpers should only discuss the material presented in helping sessions with their supervisors and classmates, and then only when it relates to developing their helping skills. When one respects clients, they respond by sharing personal information and delving deeply into their thoughts and feelings. Confidentiality of shared information provides a foundation for respectful interactions with others.

The focus of the lab experiences is on the helper and teaching the helping skills. However, students have reported that it was beneficial to talk about their concerns as they played the client role and that the experience of being clients provided them with firsthand exposure to how it feels to receive the various helping skills. Moreover, students often develop empathy with their clients after having experienced the amount of courage it takes to share concerns with a helper.

We also recognize that problems can occur when practicing helping skills with classmates who are friends or acquaintances. During helping sessions with friends, we suggest that helpers pretend that they know nothing about them and respond only to what clients actually reveal during helping sessions. Although challenging to discount relevant information, students in our classes have found the lab exercises easier to perform if they consider only information provided in the practice helping session. For example, Nancy was practicing her helping skills with her friend, Katrina. Katrina was bemoaning the fact that her partner had not called her in 2 weeks. Although Nancy knew the reasons for her partner not calling (Katrina had dated someone else the previous weekend), she focused on Katrina's feelings related to not having contact with her partner.

Providing Feedback to Your Peers

Providing feedback is an essential component of training. Helpers need to learn what they did well and what behaviors were most helpful to the clients. Equally importantly, they need to know what behaviors were not effective so that they can improve their helping skills.

The best sources of feedback are the clients who have experienced the helper's interventions firsthand. The next best sources of feedback are the observers who have watched the practice sessions and imagined how the interventions might feel if they were the client. It is also beneficial for helpers to hear that different people had different responses to the same intervention, emphasizing that there is no one right way to intervene and that different people have different reactions.

We believe that helpers need feedback about what they did well and how they might improve their helping skills. Helpers appreciate positive feedback because learning helping skills is challenging and they appreciate encouragement that they are on the right track. However, some of the most valuable feedback that helpers receive are suggestions to guide them in how to change and improve their helping skills. We enjoyed working with supervisors who told us that we were doing a terrific job as helpers, but we feel most fortunate to have had exceptional supervisors who were not afraid to point out our errors and provide concrete recommendations for how we might improve our skills. Likewise, students often feel cheated if they consistently receive only positive feedback, yet also may feel wounded if critical comments are provided exclusively.

We recommend providing only one piece of feedback for improvement at a time because it is less overwhelming and more feasible to focus on making one change in a given lab experience. All feedback should be stated in behavioral terms to have the greatest impact. A broad and nonspecific statement (e.g., "You did not connect with the client") does not provide direction for changes in future helping sessions. In contrast, a concrete behavioral statement (e.g., "You did not make any eye contact") gives a helper a better idea of what to change to facilitate the process of helping.

Being a client in practice helping sessions should not be a substitute for seeking counseling or therapy. Students experiencing personal distress should arrange to be seen by a counselor or therapist. University counseling centers often provide counseling services for students at little or no cost. For many students, university counseling centers offer an excellent opportunity to learn more about themselves and to address salient issues. Being a participant in counseling allows students to experience "the other side" of helping and gain respect for the courage clients exhibit when they share their concerns with their helpers. Moreover, beginning helpers often report that watching their counselors provide helping skills can teach them about effective (and ineffective) helping techniques. Hence, we want to encourage people to seek counseling when needed. We firmly believe that helpers should work through their problems, so that their issues do not exert a negative influence on the helping process. We also encourage helpers to experience the many benefits that result from a careful exploration of their thoughts and feelings.

IS THIS BOOK RIGHT FOR YOU?

The material presented in this book can be applied to countless helping situations involving both professional and lay helpers. Perhaps the most obvious audiences for this book are students who are training to become mental health professionals. Individuals who plan to provide psychological services to others benefit from learning the basic helping skills that serve as the foundation for most psychological interventions. Specifically, students enrolled in counseling classes at the undergraduate, masters, and doctoral level could use this text to learn basic helping skills that can be applied to their work with clients. For example, students in counseling psychology, clinical psychology, social work, and psychiatry may be interested in this book. In addition, counselors who work with specific types of clients (e.g., alcohol and drug counselors, rehabilitation counselors, and marriage and family counselors) would add specialized knowledge to these basic helping skills to work effectively with their clients.

A less obvious (but equally important) reason for learning helping skills involves improving relationships with friends, significant others, and family members. After learning the attending and listening skills, students often report that they now realize how often they have not really listened to people whom they love. Although difficult, using listening skills while a significant other is complaining about one of your irritating behaviors could help in resolving the issue. Improvements in listening often result in more open and healthy communication with significant others.

Relatedly, helping skills can be used to assist friends and family members who are struggling with important choices or painful issues. At times, friends may ask for help from friends when they experience significant losses (e.g., the ending of a relationship, the death of a family member). Family members may request assistance when they encounter an important decision (e.g., which job to pursue, whether to relocate for a romantic relationship). In addition, helping skills are used when people experience a crisis in their significant relationships (e.g., close friends strongly disagree about an important topic, two members of a couple feel differently about having children). Although using basic helping skills in our relationships is appropriate (e.g., listening carefully to the feelings of others), acting as a skilled helper with a friend or family member as a client is not appropriate because it is impossible to be objective. Furthermore, relationships may be less satisfying and less mutual when one person is a helper and the other a client. Thus, it seems timely to note that the use of helping skills with friends, family members, and co-workers should be undertaken cautiously, and one should never take on the role of the helper with these individuals. Professionals always should be contacted when the needs of the individual require an experienced helper or counselor.

The helping skills taught in this book are also applicable to people who assist clients in helping professions other than psychology. For example, volunteers and staff members in nonprofit agencies often are required to practice effective helping skills. Hot line volunteers benefit from applying basic helping skills to communicate empathy and understanding to the many clients with diverse problems whom they encounter over the phone. Crisis workers assisting battered women and their children use basic helping skills to ensure the safety of their clients. Hospice workers can learn how to respond empathically to individuals struggling with despair, loss, loneliness, and pain. Furthermore, hospice workers often use basic helping skills when interacting with the patients' family members and close friends. Being able to listen empathically and reflect feelings appropriately can assist significant others in resolving issues related to the illness and death of patients.

Another application of helping skills in professional interactions involves allied health professionals. Recently, a physician inquired whether our university provided basic helping skills courses. She explained that about 60% of her clients presented with emotional concerns as well as physical complaints. She felt that her medical training did not prepare her to deal effectively with the personal problems presented by her patients. Many medical professionals and health service providers could enhance their effectiveness by using helping skills. Doctors, dentists, and nurses could learn to respond effectively to clients who fear invasive procedures or want additional information about sick loved ones. In fact, researchers have found that breast cancer patients who interacted with a surgeon who had been trained to either use basic helping skills or chat with them on the night before surgery evidenced less anxiety and depression 1 year after their operation (Burton, Parker, & Wollner, 1991). Furthermore, there is probably no greater need for effective helping skills in the medical profession than the time at which medical personnel must notify significant others of a death. Using the skills taught in this book could enable helpers to respond empathically toward the families and significant others in these situations. Finally, volunteers in medical settings encounter many instances where helping skills are warranted (e.g., when worried families become frustrated while waiting to hear about the results of surgery or when visiting with a patient who has been unable to leave the hospital for weeks).

In addition, training in helping skills could assist nuns, priests, rabbis, ministers, and lay clergy in working with individuals who question their faith, celebrate important events, or struggle with loss and grief. Because many people turn to religious leaders in times of crisis, training in basic helping skills could prepare these leaders for responding empathically at critical moments in people's lives.

Professionals pursuing business and law careers that involve working with others also could benefit from learning to communicate effectively. Many people would rather do business with and make referrals to an accountant who listens patiently and understands their fears related to paying taxes. Helping skills also can be useful to attorneys when confronting hostile couples filing for divorce or when helping personal injury clients make decisions about whether or not to accept a settlement. The ability to listen effectively and understand nonverbal behavior could assist lawyers in uncovering important material in depositions to further positive outcomes for their clients. The importance of helping skills in the legal profession is demonstrated by the inclusion of a basic counseling skills course in the curriculum of some law schools.

Some of our students have suggested that all professors be required to learn basic helping skills. Imagine if every teacher was trained to be an effective helper! Although they still might not believe outlandish excuses for late assignments, professors might be able to respond more caringly to questions posed or personal struggles faced by students.

CONCLUDING COMMENTS

You are about to embark on an exciting and challenging journey toward becoming an effective helper. Although learning helping skills takes time, knowledge, and lots of practice, the rewards for integrating helping skills in your personal and professional repertoire are plentiful. We hope to help you reach your destination of learning helping skills by focusing on the development of these skills while providing a theoretical and research foundation for helping behaviors, as well as exercises to practice these skills. Unfortunately, attaining the information is not sufficient to make you an effective helper. Effective helping requires practice, and even experienced helpers often return to the basics to review and refresh skills. We hope this book assists you in learning helping skills and exploring your potential for, and interest in, becoming an effective helper. Bon voyage!

What Do You Think?

- Think of a time when you felt helped by someone. What did that person do that was helpful to you?
- Now remember a time when you needed help and the person you turned to was not at all helpful. What did she or he do to make this experience unhelpful?
- Describe the way in which society perceives those who seek professional help. How could you help society decrease the stigma attached to help-seeking?
- Write a brief job description for a helper. Include personal characteristics, required training, and job responsibilities. Now, evaluate yourself in comparison to the description that you developed.
- What would it take for you to seek professional help? Address the benefits and costs you associate with seeking assistance.
- Discuss the reasons (both healthy and unhealthy) that motivate you to learn helping skills.
- Identify several current situations in your life where helping skills could be used.
- In your opinion, what are the top three characteristics of an effective helper?

2 Theoretical Foundation of the Three-Stage Model of Helping

To be where we are, and to become what we are capable of becoming, is the only end in life.

Robert Louis Stevenson

Monci had been a placement counselor for many years and enjoyed interpreting tests and sharing resources with clients who were contemplating job changes, but she was learning new things in her helping skills class. She was introduced to the theories of counseling, and she began to develop a theoretical orientation to helping others. She was challenged to identify her assumptions about human nature, the role of the environment in shaping human behavior, the methods by which people change (and maintain those changes), and the model that she would use to help others. She felt excited about thinking about theoretical and philosophical issues that would enable her to become a better helper.

THE HELPING process involves taking clients "down and into" understanding themselves more and then "up and out" into the world better able to cope with problems (Carkhuff, 1969; Carkhuff & Anthony, 1979). To accomplish this, helpers act as collaborators and facilitators. Helpers have no special knowledge or wisdom about how clients ought to live their lives. What they bring to the helping relationship are empathy and specific helping skills to guide clients in exploring their feelings and values, understanding their problems, making choices, and implementing changes in thoughts, affect, and behaviors.

Our three-stage model for helping (exploration, insight, action) is a framework for using helping skills to lead clients through the process of exploring concerns, coming to greater understanding of problems, and making changes in their lives. It is based on our clinical and teaching experiences, and it is influenced by client-centered, psychoanalytic, and cognitive–behavioral theories. Each of these theoretical orientations has contributed valuable insights into our entire formulation of the helping process, and each is the primary influence for one of the three stages of the model. In this chapter, we lay the foundation for our model by describing our assumptions about human nature, providing a brief overview of the three stages (which are expanded on in subsequent chapters), and then we discuss three key components of the model: empathic collaboration, schematic changes, and covert processes.

ASSUMPTIONS UNDERLYING THE THREE-STAGE MODEL

Because our assumptions about human nature form the philosophical foundation for this model, we think it is important to let the reader know our thinking about these

19

issues. We discuss these assumptions only briefly because our focus is on explicating the helping process rather than creating a theory of personality development.

We believe that people are born with varied potential in the psychological, intellectual, physical, and interpersonal domains. Thus, some people are genetically more intelligent, attractive, physically strong, active, verbally articulate, and mechanically adept than other people. Temperamental differences among infants at birth carry over to adulthood (e.g., some children are active whereas others are phlegmatic). These potentials unfold as children develop, and there exists a strong biological pull toward growing and developing one's potential. We do not believe that people are either inherently good (as Carl Rogers postulated) or inherently governed by instinctual urges (as Sigmund Freud postulated) at birth. Instead, as stated above, we believe that people have certain biological predispositions at birth and have a tendency toward fulfilling these potentials. How they are developed depends largely on the environment, to which we turn next.

The environment can enhance or thwart the innate movement toward survival and development. Healthy environments provide basic biological needs (such as food and shelter) and emotional needs (such as relationships characterized by acceptance, love, support, encouragement, recognition, and appropriate challenges). When infants and children are provided with a "good enough" environment that meets their basic needs, their potential unfolds naturally. No environment is perfect, but the environment needs to be at least adequate to allow children to prosper. Either too much gratification or too much deprivation stunts children's growth, but an adequate amount of support allows children to develop naturally to fulfill their potential.

Early experiences, particularly in terms of attachment and self-esteem, are crucial in laying the foundation for personality. People continue, however, to change and adapt throughout their lives within the limits of their biological predispositions and early experiences. Thus, although a foundation is laid, there is still a wide range within which people can grow and develop. They cannot transform their personalities completely, but they can come to accept who they are and make the most of their potential.

We also believe that people develop defenses to cope with anxiety, particularly during childhood when they tend to have less control over their personal destinies (e.g., a child might learn to withdraw to defend against dominating parents). At a moderate level, these defenses are adaptive because all of us need strategies to cope with life. These defenses became maladaptive, however, when the individual uncritically uses the defenses in all situations or is no longer able to use the defenses effectively to cope with the demands of living.

External circumstances also influence a person's behavior. A person living in the midst of a bloody revolution and political chaos has different constraints on his or her behavior than does a person living in a benign democracy where freedom of expression is allowed. Furthermore, we believe that although people are influenced by past learning and external circumstances, they have some degree of control over their lives and choice about how they behave. We believe that we act partially on the basis of personality and previous experience, but also that we make choices and have the ability to alter somewhat the course of our existence. For example, although friendliness is influenced by personality (e.g., introversion vs. extroversion) and previous experiences with meeting people, a person still has some range of choices about how she or he acts to others in a new situation. Thus, determinism is balanced by free will.

We also propose that emotions, cognitions, and behaviors are all key components of personality. All are intertwined and operate in combination with one another. How we think influences how we feel and behave. How we feel has an impact on how we think and behave; how we behave affects how we think about ourselves and how we feel. Thus, any treatment approach must focus on all three aspects of human existence (emotions, cognitions, and behaviors) in helping people change.

In summary, we believe that people are influenced by both their biology and environment, particularly early experiences that contribute to the development of attachment to others and self-esteem. Furthermore, although people are influenced by past experiences, they have some choice and free will. It is also important to recognize that people develop defenses as strategies for coping with the demands of the world. In addition, personality is composed of feelings, thoughts, and behaviors, all of which are intertwined. These assumptions lead us to have an optimistic, but cautious, view about the possibility of change. We believe that people can change within limits. People cannot discard their past learning or biological predispositions, but they can learn to live with themselves and accept themselves. They can develop more adaptive behaviors, thoughts, and feelings. In short, people can adjust to their inner potentials, make the best of what they have, and make choices about how they want to live their lives within the limits imposed by biology, early experiences, and external circumstances.

THREE-STAGE MODEL

As Figure 2.1 illustrates, the helping process involves three stages: an exploration stage (helping clients explore their thoughts, feelings, and actions); an insight stage (helping clients come to understand their thoughts, feelings, and actions); and an action stage (helping clients decide what action to take on the basis of their exploration and insight).

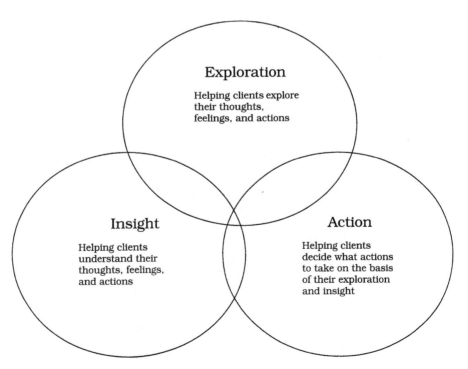

FIGURE 2.1. The three-stage model of helping.

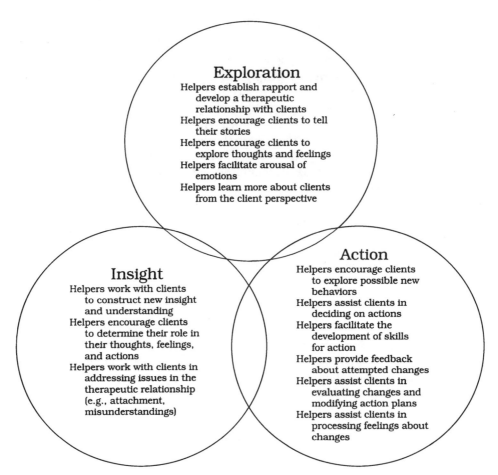

FIGURE 2.2. Tasks of the helping skills model. The helper and client cycle through all of the stages for each problem that the client presents for discussion.

Before focusing on specific skills, we introduce helpers to the philosophy and theory underlying the model. Helpers need to be aware of the tasks and goals for each of the stages (see Figure 2.2) and be clear on what they are trying to accomplish with clients. When helpers understand the general philosophy and the underlying theories, they can more easily learn the skills required for each stage of the process.

Exploration Stage

In the exploration stage, helpers seek to establish rapport, develop a therapeutic relationship with clients, encourage clients to tell their stories, help clients explore their thoughts and feelings, facilitate the arousal of client emotion, and learn about their clients. They accomplish these things through attending nonverbally to clients, listening carefully to everything clients say verbally and nonverbally, restating the content of what clients say, reflecting feelings, and asking open-ended questions to encourage clients to explore.

Exploration is crucial to give clients an opportunity to express their emotions and to think through the complexity of their problems. Having another person act as a sounding board or mirror is often extremely helpful because it is difficult to examine one's concerns objectively without external feedback. When thinking about issues by themselves, clients often become blocked by their own defenses and anxieties, which can make them feel that they are going around in circles rather than generating insight and making changes.

The exploration stage also provides helpers with an opportunity to learn more about their clients from the client's perspective. Helpers cannot assume that they know clients' feelings or problems. Helpers might be imposing their own standards and values on clients if they assume that they know how clients feel about problems or what solutions clients should choose. Even when clients are the same age, race, and gender as helpers, helpers cannot assume that clients have similar problems and feelings. For example, Jennifer, who was similar in age, race, and gender to her helper, disclosed that she had just become engaged. Because the helper had just recently gotten married and was very happy, she assumed that the client felt similarly and started congratulating her. Jennifer broke down in tears and ran out of the room. Fortunately, the helper realized her mistake, called Jennifer, and asked her to return for a session. It turned out that Jennifer felt pressured to get engaged and, in fact, felt quite ambivalent about the relationship. When the helper could listen without assumptions, she was able to learn how Jennifer truly felt.

The exploration stage is informed primarily by Rogers's client-centered theory (Rogers, 1942, 1951, 1957, 1967, 1980). Rogers believed that people are inherently good but do not achieve their potential because they try to please other people instead of following their own internal experiencing. He believed that if helpers could accept clients completely and communicate empathy, respect, and genuineness to the clients, clients could come to accept themselves. This acceptance would allow clients to unblock their natural potential and, hence, to live fully and productively.

Insight Stage

In the insight stage, helpers collaborate with clients to achieve new insight or understandings about their inner dynamics, attain new awareness of their role in perpetuating their problems, and deal with the therapeutic relationship. Insight is important because it helps clients see things in a new light. Thus, we believe that insight is crucial for a greater sense of self-understanding and for taking appropriate responsibility. Insight helps clients understand why they behave, think, and feel as they do. When clients have some awareness about their behavior, it is easier for them to change. Although behaviorally oriented theorists do not believe that insight is necessary for people to change, we believe that having an explanation for feelings and behaviors allows people to feel a sense of responsibility and control in their lives. Understanding, however imperfect, seems to guide future changes. Insight may also lead to longer lasting change because it provides clients with a template for making sense out of events and helps them make better choices. Although people can and certainly do come to insight on their own, hearing new ideas and receiving feedback from a caring helper who has a different perspective often can enable clients to develop a deeper level of awareness and understanding.

In contrast to only focusing on providing listening-type responses as in the exploration stage, helpers in the insight stage also challenge perspectives, offer their own ideas, and use their own experiences in the service of helping clients see things in a new way. Helpers actively work with clients in the insight stage to construct meanings and reframe experiences. The insight stage involves brainstorming, in which helpers and clients work together to learn new things about the client. Clients need the external perspective of the helper to give them new ideas and feedback, especially when they are stuck or blocked. Of course, helpers do not necessarily have the "right" perspective, but they may have alternative perspectives that clients can consider. It is also important to stress that although helpers use their own perspectives in this stage, the relationship remains collaborative and focused on coming to shared understandings rather than on helpers imposing insight on clients.

In addition, many issues arise in the therapeutic relationship that need to be addressed in the insight stage. Hence, the relationship itself is a focus of learning and change. Helpers provide clients with feedback about their behaviors in sessions and assist them in understanding how these behaviors have developed and what function they now serve. By understanding how they are perceived by their helpers, many clients are better able to understand how other people react to them.

The insight stage is informed by psychoanalytic theory, particularly by theorists such as Freud, Erikson, Mahler, Bowlby, Kohut, and Greenson. An important feature of psychoanalytic theory for this model is the emphasis on early development (particularly attachment and individuation) as the foundation of personality. The need to survive often requires that children form defenses to cope with the world. These defenses, while adaptive at the time, can prevent people from functioning well as adults. For example, a person who has formed a defense of avoiding all adults because they might punish him could have a hard time relating to adults as equals when he becomes an adult. In therapy, clients need to dig deep into themselves and come to understand how these defenses developed so that they can reduce the defenses and change maladaptive behavior patterns. They also need to understand what currently helps them maintain defenses and maladaptive behavior patterns. Thus, a key to changing is gaining insight into the origins and maintenance of behavioral patterns.

Action Stage

In the action stage, helpers guide clients in moving toward making decisions and changes that reflect their new understanding of themselves. Helpers and clients together explore the idea of changing. They try to determine whether clients want to change and explore the meaning of change in clients' lives. They might brainstorm possible changes and help clients make decisions about which changes to pursue. In some cases, helpers teach the skills that clients need to have to make changes in their lives. They also might help to develop strategies to assist clients in trying new behaviors and asking for feedback from others outside the helping relationship. In addition, helpers and clients continually evaluate the outcome of action plans and make modifications to assist clients in obtaining the desired outcomes. As in the first two stages, the process is collaborative. Helpers continue to ask about clients' feelings about changing and the change process. Again, helpers are not experts but are guides who assist clients in exploring thoughts and feelings about action and making positive changes in their lives.

By putting their new ways of thinking into practice, clients are able to consolidate the changes in their thinking. Without action, changes in thinking from the insight stage are typically short lived. Psychoanalytic theorists assume that insight naturally leads to action and, thus, helpers do not have to be concerned with encouraging clients to think about making specific changes. For some clients, this may be true. However, several things can block clients from moving to action after they attain insight. First, clients might not have the skills to make the desired changes. For example, although Jamilla now realizes that she is unassertive because of being raised by controlling parents and accepts responsibility for changing, she might have a hard time becoming more assertive unless she has assertiveness skills in her repertoire. She may need to learn to make eye contact and state her needs directly. Second, even though a person might attain insight during the helping process, change is difficult because old habits are hard to break and people are often willing to settle for what they know rather than risking change and the unknown. For example, Candy might realize that she needs to be more assertive with her husband but is unwilling to make the changes because she is afraid of her husband's anger and of upsetting the status quo. The role of a helping relationship here might be to prepare Candy for thinking about possible changes. Third, significant others often have strong reactions to changes made by clients, and clients need assistance in figuring out how to deal with interpersonal obstacles to change. Continuing our previous example, Candy's husband may have difficulty adjusting to her new requests for assistance with household chores and may insist that Candy return to her previous ways. Hence, clients often need help in learning more appropriate skills and in overcoming obstacles to change.

Exploration and insight provide the foundation for clients to understand their motivations and take responsibility for changing. Both helpers and clients need an adequate basis of understanding the scope and dynamics of the client's problem prior to developing an action plan. Unlike the radio talk show psychologist who listens for three sentences and then advises the client, helpers rely on careful, thoughtful listening and probing to help clients fully explore their problems and gain new insights.

The theoretical foundation for the action stage is behavioral and cognitive–behavioral theory, particularly as articulated by B. F. Skinner, Wolpe, Lazurus, Bandura, Ellis, and Beck. These theorists believed that behaviors (including thoughts) are learned according to learning principles (e.g., reinforcement, punishment, shaping, generalization, extinction, modeling, thoughts mediating actions) and thus can be changed using these same learning principles. Hence, they view helping as an application of behavioral and cognitive principles to specific problems. They help clients assess current behaviors, teach new behaviors, reinforce changes, and help to modify action plans that are not working effectively.

ESSENTIAL COMPONENTS OF ALL THREE STAGES

Empathic Collaboration

Empathic collaboration is a major feature of all three stages of the model and, hence, merits attention as we describe the stages. Helpers need to try to understand their clients as much as possible, realizing that it is never possible to understand another person fully. Empathy implies understanding clients at both a cognitive level (what they are thinking and saying) and an affective level (what they are feeling; Duan & Hill, 1996). Although helpers sometimes feel the same emotions as their clients, empathy requires that they recognize that the pain, anger, frustration, joy, or other emotions belong to the client and not the helper. Empathy is sometimes confused with a certain type of response to clients (such as reflection of feelings), but we assert that empathy is not a specific response type or skill; rather, it is an attitude or manner of responding with genuine caring and a lack of judgment. Empathy involves a deep respect for the client and for the clients' willingness and courage to explore their problems, gain insights, and make changes. This attitude is typically implemented through a variety of helping skills depending on what helpers perceive that clients need at specific times.

Furthermore, the whole helping process is collaborative, in that helpers serve as guides or coaches for clients in working through problems. Helpers are not the experts in how clients ought to live their lives, but they are experts at facilitating the process of exploring feelings and values, achieving understanding, and making choices and changes. Rather than giving answers to clients, helpers try to teach clients how to think through problems, make decisions, and implement changes. This model is client-centered in that clients are helped to determine their own solutions to the problems they face. A good metaphor is the parable about teaching a person to fish rather than just giving her or him a fish: Giving a person one fish feeds the person for one meal, whereas teaching her or him to fish enables the person to eat for a lifetime.

Although both empathy and collaboration are crucial components of the helping process, they are not specific skills that can be taught directly. Rather, they are outcomes of the successful implementation of helping skills and a reflection of the way the helper feels about the client. We as helpers can be knowledgeable about our implementation of verbal and nonverbal behaviors, aware of how we come across when using these interventions, aware of our intentions for using different interventions, and aware of client reactions to these interventions, but we cannot always control the outcome of the helping session. We can strive toward empathy and collaboration but cannot always attain these goals because much depends on the client and how well we "match" or "click" with clients. Even so, however, through knowledge, awareness, and a genuine desire to understand, respect, and work with another person, empathic collaboration is more likely to emerge and be experienced by helpers and clients.

Schematic Change

A second major feature of the three-stage model is schematic change. A schema is an "abstract structure that comprises and/or generates patterns or themes of experience" (Mahoney, 1991, p. 78). In other words, a schema is a cluster of related thoughts, feelings, sensations, memories, and actions (Cartwright, 1990; Cartwright & Lamberg, 1992; Glass & Holyoak, 1986; L. S. Greenberg, Rice, & Elliott, 1993; Medin & Ross, 1992; Stein, 1992). We store everything we experience or learn in schemas.

Only those details of events to which a person pays attention are stored in memory, such that insignificant events (e.g., a person sneezing or a momentary burst of cold air) are not typically stored unless the event is particularly meaningful for some reason. Events are not stored "accurately" but are stored according to one's perceptions of the events, which explains why people often have varying recollections of the same situation. In addition, people do not retain information within schemas to the same degree. Memories that are brought into awareness and thought about again remain prominent in the schema, whereas unused memories fade away. Some memories also become distorted or changed over time so that memories are not always accurate (Glass & Holyoak, 1986; Loftus, 1988).

Information is stored (encoded) in one or more schemas (Caspar, Rothenfluh, & Segal, 1992; Medin & Ross, 1992; Rummelhart & McClelland, 1986). Within each schema, individual elements are interconnected and are also linked to elements in other schemas. Elements that are closely related for an individual have positive or excitatory connections (e.g., the elements of dreams and nightmares may be closely connected for a person), whereas others that are minimally related or unrelated for an individual have negative or inhibitory connections (e.g., the elements of dreams and trucks may be negatively connected for a person). Furthermore, these connections can change with use or disuse, such that the continual activation of a connection strengthens it, whereas a lack of use weakens the connection. Hence, people who think about and practice helping skills after they learn them are more likely to remember them than people who never think about them or practice them again.

Schemas are idiosyncratic for different individuals. For example, Joe has a schema for parties that involves thoughts about how people might not like him, feelings of anxiety and panic, bodily sensations of heart palpitations and sweaty palms, memories of specific situations in which he was anxious during parties, and specific ways that he typically behaves during parties. In addition, Joe's party schema has positive or excitatory connections with his schema for dates, so that the two schemas share many elements (e.g., memories of being lonely, feelings of being isolated, feelings of shame, and missed opportunities). Each schema also has unique elements, such that Joe's party schema includes various escape or avoidance strategies whereas his date schema includes thoughts about how to ask someone out. In contrast, Cindy's party schema has positive or excitatory connections with her fun and friendship schemas, so Cindy expects that parties are opportunities to have a good time and meet people. Hence, in contrast to Joe, Cindy has positive thoughts and eager anticipation when she thinks about going to parties.

Thinking about changes in schemas is a useful way of conceptualizing how change occurs through helping. Much of what occurs in the helping process is reorganizing and reframing our thinking into more adaptive patterns. These changes in thinking help us see the world in a different way, which can lead to changes in behaviors and affect. Hence, the helping process involves a fundamental change in the ways clients think. Schemas are brought to the surface during the exploration stage and changed during the insight stage. These changes are consolidated during the action stage. Thus, changes in thinking are just as important as changes in overt behavior.

Covert Processes

Another essential component of this model is the notion that a great deal of what occurs in interpersonal relationships occurs on a covert level. All of us operate at several levels simultaneously—we present one face to the world and yet have other reactions that we keep to ourselves. In fact, we learn from an early age to hide these covert reactions, particularly if they are negative and could displease others. For effective helping, helpers have to be aware of their own internal processes so that they can be aware of their motivations, distractions, and intentions for behaving as they do in sessions. In addition, helpers also have to be aware of, respectful of, and curious about client reactions. Helpers who are aware that clients often have hidden reactions and secrets that can have an enormous influence on the helping process can try to get beneath the surface of the "polite" mask that clients present and discover how they really feel. When clients identify and experience their feelings fully, they can accept feelings that have been deemed unacceptable previously.

With each intervention, it is useful for helpers to stop and reflect about their covert processes and where they are in the helping process (e.g., "Where am I now and what am I trying to accomplish?"). Ivey (1994) labeled this as being *intentional* or being aware of reasons for intervening and conscious about what one wants to accomplish with each intervention. In addition, it is important for helpers to observe the client's reactions to each of their interventions. The ultimate test of the utility of any intervention is how the client responds and uses the intervention. Hence, both helper intentions and client reactions are important constructs that we focus on throughout this book.

CONCLUDING COMMENTS

Each of the three stages is important in the helping process, and helpers should not shortchange one stage to rush to the next. The first stage lays the foundation for the next two stages. Hence, the foundation for insight comes from a thorough exploration of problems. Similarly, action is based on an in-depth understanding of the problems, an understanding that is necessary to assist clients in moving from insight to positive change.

Although it sounds straightforward to move from exploration to insight to action, things do not always flow quite so smoothly with most clients, and stages are not always as differentiated and sequential as they appear when reading about them. Within sessions, helpers and clients sometimes move back and forth among the stages. For example, helpers often have to return to exploring new facets of a client's problem during the insight and action stages. In addition, attaining insight often forces a client to explore newly recognized feelings and thoughts. Similarly, realizing that a client is reluctant to change might necessitate more exploration and insight about obstacles. Sometimes action needs to be taken before much exploration has taken place, such as when a client is in crisis and needs help immediately. For example, a client who has medical problems caused by anorexia might first need to learn to eat in a healthy manner and only later might be ready and able to explore motives underlying her eating disorder. In some cases, clients cannot really explore until they have been taught to relax. Other clients cannot handle insight and are resistant to having anyone "poke around in their heads"; they only want guidance about very specific problems. With such clients, helpers may need to move more quickly to the action stage. However, we caution helpers to explore enough to make sure that they know what is going on, what actions have been tried, and what help is needed before they rush to generate possible actions. Finally, throughout the process of helping, helpers might focus more on the exploration stage in early sessions, whereas they might focus more on the action stage in later sessions.

In summary, the three-stage model provides an overall plan and philosophy for the helping process, but helpers must attend to individual needs of clients and environmental pressures before determining how to respond at any given moment. We do not provide a simplistic cookbook of what to do at each moment in helping because that would not be possible given the infinite number of situations that could arise with different helpers and clients. Instead, we hope to collaborate with readers to help you think about what skills to use at different points in the helping process.

What Do You Think?

- What are your assumptions about human nature? Specifically, discuss the role of genetics, temperament, environment, early experiences, attachment, individuation, self esteem, defenses, determinism, free will, and the balance of emotions, cognitions, and behaviors.

- What view of development (client centered, psychoanalytic, or cognitive–behavioral) seems most appealing to you? Provide several reasons for your choice.

- Discuss the roles of collaboration, empathy, insight, and action in helping.

- Describe the types of clients who would be most suited for client centered, psychoanalytic, or cognitive–behavioral approaches to helping.

- If you were to choose a therapist for yourself, would you choose someone who was client centered, psychoanalytic, cognitive–behavioral, or integrative (combining all three approaches as we do in this book)? Provide your rationale for this choice.

- Do you think that action needs to follow exploration and insight or do you think that a person can move directly to action without exploration and insight? Provide a rationale for your opinion.

3 Process of Helping

> We ought to respect the effect we have on others. We know by our own experience
> how very much others affect our lives, and we must remember that we in turn must
> have the same effect on others.
>
> *George Eliot*

James, a 21-year-old European American, beginning helper who tentatively felt an affinity
for a Rogerian theoretical orientation, was in the middle of his first session with an 18-year-
old Japanese American male college student who was having problems with shyness and was
contemplating whether he wanted to become less shy. At a particular moment in the session,
James noticed that the client was feeling down. He formulated an intention to help the client
identify and express his feelings and chose to use a reflection of feelings to implement that
intention. The client felt understood by the helper, perceived the helper as trying to help
him, and so revealed more about his feelings of isolation. James then wanted to help the client
explore more about his feelings and so asked an open question about how he felt about making
friends. The process continued with James carefully watching the client and reassessing what
skills to use at each moment in the changing process.

MUCH OF what happens in helping situations is so complex that it is often difficult for
helpers, especially beginning helpers, to have a full awareness of the process. Furthermore,
the helping process occurs at lightning speed, without helpers giving conscious thought
to the many components and decisions that accompany interactions. Helpers must learn
to react quickly because clients constantly present new needs and challenges.

Initially, analyzing each part of the helping process often feels uncomfortable and
cumbersome because helpers are not used to breaking their interactions down and examining them so carefully. Furthermore, most beginning helpers are not used to thinking
about their reasons for doing things and are not used to examining the reactions of others.
In this chapter, we break the helping process down into what happens moment by moment. By slowing the process down, helpers can begin to understand their reactions and
responses in different situations and learn about client reactions to their interventions.
Having more self-awareness, helpers can be more psychologically available for clients and
more intentional in their behaviors.

We begin by examining background variables that influence the helping process.
Then we focus on context variables that set the stage for the moment-by-moment interaction. Next, we move to discussing the moment-by-moment interactional sequence and
how interactions with the external world influence the helping process. Finally, we discuss
how all of these variables lead to the outcome of the helping process. Figure 3.1 summarizes
the variables that are involved in the helper–client interaction.

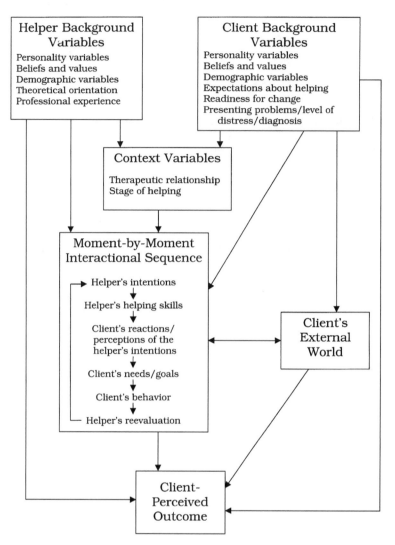

FIGURE 3.1. Factors influencing the helping process.

BACKGROUND VARIABLES

Background variables are what helpers and clients bring to the helping process.

Helper Background

Helpers bring unique ways of viewing the world to the helping process. They contribute their personalities, beliefs, assumptions about the world, values, experiences, and cultural and demographic characteristics. In addition, helpers bring their theoretical orientation (beliefs about how to help) and their previous experiences in helping (both informal and formal). For example, one could imagine that an introverted, young, European American female helper with a psychodynamic theoretical orientation would have a very different impact on the helping process than an extroverted, middle-aged, Iranian American male helper with a cognitive–behavioral theoretical orientation.

Client Background

A young, bright, attractive college student who is away from home for the first time and is feeling lonely and homesick would be very different to work with than a substance-abusing older man who has been court-ordered to attend counseling sessions because he batters his wife. Clients bring unique ways of viewing the world to the helping process in terms of their individual personalities, beliefs, assumptions about the world, values, experiences, and cultural and demographic characteristics. Furthermore, clients bring their expectations about what the helping process should entail, their readiness to change, their presenting problems, level of distress, and diagnoses. In this section, we focus on readiness to change and presenting problems because of the centrality of these variables to the helping process.

Client Readiness for Change

Clients are at various stages of readiness for change; some are reluctant to participate in any form of helping, others are eager to learn more about themselves, and yet others are ready to make changes in their behaviors. Prochaska, Norcross, and DiClemente (1994) identified six stages of change: precontemplation, contemplation, preparation, action, maintenance, and termination.

In the precontemplation stage, clients are unaware of the need to change or have no desire to change. Precontemplators lack information about their problems, engage in denial about their problems, and often blame other people or society for their problems. Other people are typically more bothered by the precontemplator's behavior than is the precontemplator.

In the contemplation stage, clients are aware of and accept responsibility for problems. They are beginning to think about changing but have not yet actively decided to change. Fear of failure often keeps clients stuck at this stage. Clients in this stage often spend time thinking about the causes of their problems and what it would be like to change.

In the preparation stage, clients have made a commitment to change and are preparing themselves to begin the change process. Some clients make public announcements that they plan to change (e.g., "I plan to lose 30 lbs"). Some clients prepare themselves mentally for how their lives will be different (e.g., "When I begin studying more, I won't be able to go out and party all the time").

In the action stage, clients actively begin to modify their behaviors and their surroundings. They might stop smoking cigarettes, begin studying at regularly specified times, start taking more time for themselves, or decide to get married. The commitment and preparation done in the contemplation and preparation stages seem to be crucial for success in this stage, in that prepared clients are more aware of what they are striving for and why.

In the maintenance stage, clients have changed and are trying to consolidate their changes and deal with lapses. The process of change does not end, then, with the action stage. It has been estimated to take 21 days or more for a change to become incorporated into one's lifestyle, suggesting that it is not easy to make changes that stick. This stage is very challenging and can last a long time, because permanent change is difficult and often requires major lifestyle alterations.

In the termination stage, people no longer are threatened by the original temptations, the problem behaviors do not return, and people have confidence that they can cope without relapse. The effort to change and maintain the changes is no longer salient for people in this stage. In other words, the person does not have to think as much about changing or maintaining changes, and other things become more central.

Clients can be at different stages of change for different problems. For example, a client could be in the maintenance stage for stopping smoking, but still be at a precontemplation stage in terms of resolving spiritual issues in his life.

Our goal as helpers is to assist clients in moving through the stages so that they become aware of problems, take responsibility for their behaviors, make decisions about how to change, make the actual changes, and then work on consolidating their changes. Movement through the stages can often take considerable time such that a person might be in one of the stages for a given problem for several months or even years.

Working with precontemplative clients can be very difficult because they often come to helping under duress (e.g., court referral) rather than because they genuinely want to change. In contrast, working with clients in the contemplation, preparation, action, and maintenance stages tends to be easier because such clients tend to be eager to work on themselves. We can compare precontemplative clients to carts with square wheels; it is more difficult to push a cart with square wheels than to push a cart with round wheels—the cart with square wheels does not budge no matter what the helper does. The process works better when clients are interested in rather than resistant to change.

Helping skills also vary with clients who are at different stages of readiness for change. Helpers typically spend more time in the exploration and insight stages of the helping process with clients in the precontemplation, contemplation, and preparation stages of readiness for change, whereas they spend more time in the action stage of helping with clients in the action, maintenance, and termination stages of readiness for change.

Presenting Problems, Level of Distress, and Diagnoses

Clients come to the helping process with various problems. Issues that can often be dealt with by beginning helpers using this model involve problems with identity, relationships, educational and career concerns, existential issues, spiritual issues, and maladaptive thoughts, feelings, and behaviors. Clients who present relatively straightforward problems in adjustment and living (e.g., career issues, relationship problems) typically need someone to listen empathically, help them sort out and understand their thoughts and feelings, and decide what actions to pursue. A number of issues, however, cannot be dealt with very productively in a helping process focused exclusively on skills learned in this model. People who have problems with serious mental illness, poverty, medical problems, or legal problems typically need helpers who use advanced skills in addition to the basic helping skills. Others who have longstanding psychological or organic problems (such as schizophrenia) typically require more intensive treatment from experienced therapists. We recommend that beginning helpers work only with clients who have problems with adjustment and living and refer severely disturbed clients to more experienced and qualified therapists.

CONTEXT VARIABLES

Context variables form the backgorund within which helping takes place. The two that we discuss in this section are the therapeutic relationship and stages of helping.

Therapeutic Relationship

A strong working alliance is necessary for successful helping (Gelso & Carter, 1985, 1994). Bordin (1979) suggested that the working alliance has three aspects: the bond (i.e., the connection between the helper and client), an agreement on goals (a consensus about changes the client needs to make), and an agreement on tasks (a consensus about what is to take place during the helping process to meet the goals). Hence, a strong working alliance might involve a helper and client genuinely liking and respecting each other, deciding together to work on exploration and insight in the sessions, and agreeing about their goals to help the client develop better interpersonal relationships. This bond is similar to what one might experience in a close relationship with a friend—one feels connected and has shared understandings of what is going to happen in the relationship. In contrast, helping relationships have specific tasks and goals to accomplish to help clients resolve problems. Furthermore, different clients have different needs, and so different kinds of therapeutic relationships are needed (see Bachelor, 1995). For example, one client might need a lot of warmth, whereas another client might be put off by too much warmth and prefer a helper who is objective and businesslike.

Research has found that the relationship is the best predictor of the outcome of therapy (Horvath & Symonds, 1991; Orlinsky, Grawe, & Parks, 1994). Clients have consistently reported that the most helpful aspect of therapy was feeling understood and supported. For some people, the relationship itself is curative and they need nothing else from the helper. Others need more in the way of helper skills.

Although most researchers agree that a good therapeutic relationship facilitates the helping process and most of us can recognize when we are involved in a good re-lationship, researchers are much less clear on how to establish good relationships with clients. We postulate that helpers establish good therapeutic relationships by attending and listening carefully to clients, using the appropriate helping skills at the right times, treating clients according to their individual needs, being aware of their own feelings and limitations, being aware of the client's reactions to their interventions, and being open to feedback from clients.

We think the therapeutic relationship works as follows. Clients often come to helpers feeling that no one listens to them or cares about them. Helpers try to pay full attention to their clients and communicate an understanding of the client's feelings and experiences. They are empathic and nonjudgmental, accepting their clients as they are, which allows the clients to feel safe enough to express their hurt and pain. Under this influence, clients begin to feel that if their helpers accept them for who they are, they must be okay. It also allows them to see that not all people are like significant others with whom they experience difficulty. Furthermore, it helps to reduce their anxiety and thus increases their capacity for facing interpersonal pain and anxiety. The clients slowly begin to build self-esteem, which is the foundation for change. They also feel safe to explore thoughts and feelings, come to new understandings, and make changes.

Helpers cannot establish relationships with all clients. Establishing relationships with some clients is difficult because the clients are not motivated or ready to be helped. For example, an adolescent might be forced by her parents to go for helping but not want to be there. Moreover, some clients have been so hurt and their capacity to trust so seriously impaired that they cannot benefit from a facilitative relationship. One therapist used a metaphor that some clients are like leaky gas tanks—you can never fill them up. Clients who have been seriously damaged in relationships cannot attach to therapists.

The fault sometimes lies with the helpers, however. All helpers have limitations related to their backgrounds and personal problems. We like to think of helpers as wounded healers who have personal issues that they have not resolved completely. All of us have issues, but most of us can set them aside most of the time when we are helpers. If the personal issues are too salient, helpers are less likely to go beyond their needs and focus on clients' needs. For example, a helper who has just had a major fight with his spouse may not be able to concentrate on listening to the client's problems with studying.

Some matches between helpers and clients are not ideal and do not result in positive therapeutic relationships. For example, a female client who has been raped recently might not be able to talk to any male helper because she is terrified of all men. An alcoholic client might not want to see a helper who has never had problems with alcoholism because he fears that such a helper could not understand his struggle to stay sober. Helpers who have not resolved their experiences of traumatic sexual or physical abuse might not be able to hear a client's story of sexual abuse without having strong emotional reactions or being distracted by their own pain.

No one can fully understand another person. We can try to empathize and imagine how the other person feels, but we can never fully remove ourselves from our own experiences to understand another person completely. Similarly, although we might try to have unconditional positive regard (caring for, understanding, and appreciating clients for who they are regardless of how they behave), our regard for clients often has conditions (e.g., that they allow us to help them, that they talk openly about their problems, or that they not get angry at us). Unfortunately, we are not always fully aware of all of our personal issues and the conditions that we place on clients. Helpers need to do their best to form positive therapeutic relationships with clients, and they need to deal with their issues in their own therapy.

Stages of Helping

As discussed in chapter 2, helpers have specific tasks during each of the stages of helping for what they want to accomplish (see Figure 2.2). During the exploration stage, the tasks are to establish rapport and develop a therapeutic relationship, to enable clients to tell their stories, to facilitate clients in exploring their feelings and thoughts, to arouse emotions, and to learn about the clients. The typical skills used to facilitate these exploration tasks are open question, restatement, and reflection of feelings. In the insight stage, the tasks are to assist clients in developing greater understanding of their particular concerns and insight into the ways in which they contribute to problems and to deal with the therapeutic relationship. In addition to continuing to use the exploration skills, helpers also use challenge, interpretation, self-disclosure, and immediacy to facilitate insight. In the action stage, the tasks are to assist clients in deciding how they want to change and to help them figure out how to implement these changes in their lives. In addition to continuing to use the exploration and insight skills, helpers use information and direct guidance to facilitate action.

The stages provide a blueprint or structure for how helpers proceed through sessions. Remembering the philosophy behind the model and the stage-specific tasks is crucial so that helpers remain focused on what they are trying to accomplish with their clients. Learning and practicing the skills can aid helpers in accomplishing the tasks that accompany each stage. We discuss these tasks and skills in detail throughout this book.

MOMENT-BY-MOMENT INTERACTIONAL SEQUENCE

Given the background variables and the specific context, the helper needs to act at a given moment in the session. How does the helper select an intervention? We hypothesize the following sequence of events: Helpers formulate intentions on the basis of their assessment of the current situation. These intentions lead to the choice of specific helping skills. In turn, clients react to the helper interventions, which lead them to reevaluate their needs and goals and decide how to behave with the helper. In turn, helpers assess client reactions and reevaluate what they need to do for their next intervention. The process thus continually unfolds with each person reacting both overtly and covertly, trying to determine the intentions of the other and deciding how to interact. The process thus changes depending on the perceptions, needs, and intentions of the moment. We describe each of these steps more completely in the sections that follow.

Helper's Intentions

On the basis of everything the helper knows at the time, she or he thinks about what is possible to accomplish with the next intervention. The helper develops an intention for how to influence the client to respond. For example, a helper might intend to get or give information, to focus on feeling, or to deal with problems in the relationship (see the helper intentions list in Appendix A). The intentions guide the helper's choice of verbal and nonverbal interventions. Thus, the helper's intention is the reason behind the intervention. The helper might have several intentions for a single intervention.

Intentions are covert and are not necessarily apparent to clients. In fact, helpers are not always aware of their intentions at the time of delivery. For example, beginning helpers sometimes inadvertently self-disclose to make themselves feel better rather than to be helpful to clients. As helpers become more experienced, however, they typically become more aware of their intentions and more intentional in their actions. Going back over videotapes after sessions and thinking about one's intentions for each intervention is an excellent way to increase awareness of what one is trying to accomplish. By slowing the process down and examining it piece by piece, helpers can discover the different layers of feelings, thoughts, and actions. After much experience with examining intentions during videotape replays, helpers are often able to gain an awareness of intentions while they are in sessions with clients. We encourage beginning helpers to become intentional in their interventions and to think about what they are trying to accomplish during each intervention.

Research has shown that therapists from different theoretical orientations used intentions differently (Hill & O'Grady, 1985; Stiles et al., 1996). For example, psychodynamic therapists used more intentions aimed at feelings and insight, whereas behavioral therapists used more intentions directed at examining behaviors and cognitions and for promoting change. Therapists are able to identify intentions pretty easily when they go through tapes of sessions within at least 24 hr of the session and put themselves back into how they were feeling and reacting at the time in the session (rather than how they currently feel about their interventions).

Helping Skills

Moment by moment, helpers make decisions about which helping skills to use. They might ask an open question to encourage the client to talk more about the problem or challenge the client to become more aware of discrepancies. The helping skills system

(HSS), shown in Appendix B, lists a variety of helping skills that can be used in helping. (Appendix C presents guidelines for using the HSS in research.)

Matching the helping skill to the helper's intention at a given moment is important. An open question may be the optimal choice if the helper's intention is to encourage the client to talk about problems, but it would not be as good a choice as reflection of feelings if the intention is to support the client, build the relationship, or communicate an understanding of the client's feelings. Hill and O'Grady (1985) and Hill, Helms, Tichenor, et al. (1988) found that therapist intentions were connected consistently to their helping skills. For example, when therapists wanted to encourage their clients to express and experience feelings, they used open question, reflection, or interpretation. In contrast, when therapists wanted to give information to clients, they used information, direct guidance, or self-disclosure. These results suggested that therapists' intentions influenced which skills they used but that therapists did not always pair each intention with a particular response mode. Rather, they thought about what was needed at the moment and how best to achieve the intention at that time.

Applying the helping skills in sessions with clients is both an art and a science. In addition to matching the skill to the intention, helpers should bear in mind that there are verbal and nonverbal components to the skills and that the same intervention can have a totally different impact depending on the manner of delivery. If the helper says, "You seem to be feeling anxious" in a supportive, gentle tone and makes appropriate eye contact, the client has a different reaction than if the helper uses a critical, judging tone and does not look at the client. Appropriate nonverbal behaviors vary across clients, so helpers need to use nonverbal behaviors carefully and intentionally (see chapter 6).

The choice of intervention is limited to those skills in the helper's repertoire. Most helpers use the skills that are familiar to them and that fit their style. For example, some helpers feel uncomfortable challenging clients, so they use only supportive interventions. As was found in the research on intentions, helpers use skills that fit their theoretical orientation (Elliott et al., 1987; Hill, Thames, & Rardin, 1979; Mahrer, Sterner, Lawson, & Dessaulles, 1986; Stiles, 1979; Stiles, Shapiro, & Firth-Cozens, 1988; Strupp, 1955, 1957). In these studies, psychoanalytic therapists used more interpretation, behavioral therapists used more information and direct guidance, and Rogerian therapists used more reflection of feelings. In addition, helpers in different roles used different helping skills in ways that were consistent with what they were required to do in their roles. For example, psychotherapists in brief psychotherapy used mostly information and paraphrase (Hill, 1989). Radio psychology talk show hosts and career counselors used mostly information and direct guidance (A. Levy, 1989; Nagel, Hoffman, & Hill, 1995). Family practice lawyers used mostly information, whereas mental health professionals (e.g., counselors, social workers) used mostly information and closed questions (Toro, 1986). Nonprofessional group leaders used mostly information and self-disclosure (Toro, 1986). School counselors working with children used mostly closed question and information, whereas the same school counselors working in a consultation with teachers used mostly information, paraphrase, and closed question (Lin, Kelly, & Nelson, 1996).

Hill, Helms, Tichenor, et al. (1988) examined the effects of helping skills on immediate outcome (defined by client and therapist ratings of helpfulness, client reactions, and client experiencing levels). They found that helping skills had a small but significant effect on immediate outcome. It was actually surprising that they found any such overall effect given the large number of uncontrolled background and situational variables. Specifically, interpretation, self-disclosure, paraphrase (restatement and reflection), and approval were very helpful interventions. Open question, confrontation, and information were moderately helpful interventions. In contrast, direct guidance and closed question were not perceived as being very helpful. In a number of studies that have investigated the effects of helping skills, interpretation is the only one that has consistently been found to be helpful (Elliott, 1985; Elliott, Barker, Caskey, & Pistrang, 1982; Hill, Carter, & O'Farrell, 1983; O'Farrell, Hill, & Patton, 1986).

In addition, Hill, Helms, Tichenor, et al. (1988) found evidence for a more complex process such as is posited in this chapter. Specifically, *preceding client behavior* (client experiencing levels in the turn preceding the helper's intervention), therapist intentions, and therapist helping skills were all important in predicting immediate outcome. When clients were at low levels of experiencing (i.e., telling stories rather than expressing their feelings), the most helpful interventions involved intentions of exploring feelings and behaviors, with the associated helping skills of paraphrase (restatement and reflection of feelings), interpretation, and confrontation. The least helpful interventions involved the intentions of setting limits, giving information, and attending to helper needs, with the associated helping skills of closed questions, open questions, and direct guidance. In contrast, when clients were at moderate to high levels of experiencing (experiencing their feelings and having some insight), almost anything helpers did was perceived as helpful. Hence, helper skills had the most differential effect on the process when clients were at low levels of experiencing.

Client's Reactions

An intervention is met by one or more client reactions. When helpers are successful, the client reactions match the helper's intentions and helping skills. For example, if the helper's intention is to provide emotional support, and the helping skill used is an encourager such as "I understand what you're going through," the client's reaction might be feeling understood and supported. However, if the intervention is not successful, the client might react by feeling that the helper did not really hear what was being expressed or that the helper made incorrect assumptions.

Hill, Helms, Spiegel, and Tichenor (1988) developed a measure of client reactions by asking clients about how they felt about therapist interventions. About 60% of the reactions were positive (e.g., felt understood), although clients also reported many negative reactions (e.g., "felt worse"). The client reactions system is presented in Appendix D.

Clients are sometimes consciously aware of their reactions, whereas at other times they might be unaware of their reactions. In addition, clients sometimes have difficulty admitting to having reactions that are not socially acceptable (e.g., feeling angry at a helper's intervention). Admitting negative feelings about helpers can be difficult if clients respect and need the helpers or if clients cannot allow themselves to have negative emotions. For example, a client might react negatively to something a helper says because it is similar to something her parents said, but the client might not allow herself to express these negative feelings for fear of hurting the helper. Instead, this client might smile politely but feel somewhat distant and unengaged, not understanding consciously why she withdrew from the interaction.

Client reactions are sometimes covert (i.e., not displayed). We have evidence from research that clients often hide negative reactions from their therapists out of fear of retaliation or out of deference to the helper's authority (e.g., Hill, Thompson, Cogar, & Denman, 1993; Hill, Thompson, & Corbett, 1992; Rennie, 1994). For example, clients who feel angry at or misunderstood by their helpers are not likely to reveal those feelings if they feel unsafe in the therapeutic relationship.

In addition to hiding negative reactions during sessions, Regan and Hill (1992) and Hill et al. (1993) found that clients left at least one thing unsaid during sessions. Clients indicated that they left things unsaid because the emotions felt overwhelming, they wanted to avoid dealing with the disclosure, and they feared that the helpers would not understand. Furthermore, about half of the clients had major life secrets that they had not told their helpers (Hill et al., 1993; Kelly, 1998). They typically did not disclose these secrets, even in long-term therapy, because they felt ashamed or embarrassed or thought that either they or the helpers could not handle the disclosure. These results are important because they remind us that helpers cannot "read" clients' minds and hence cannot assume that they know how clients are reacting.

Given that clients have negative reactions (and often hide them), it seems crucial to see whether one can detect these hidden negative reactions. Hill and Stephany (1990) looked at whether specific client nonverbal behaviors were associated with client reports of positive and negative reactions. The only result they found was that clients had fewer head nods when they were experiencing negative reactions. Clients seemed to become more still and less animated when they did not like what helpers were doing. These results suggest that helpers need to look closely at client lack of nonverbal movements as a possible sign of dissatisfaction or distress.

What Influences Client Reactions?

A number of factors influence the reactions clients have to helper interventions. First, clients' reactions are influenced by their needs at the time. For example, clients in severe crisis might tolerate almost any intervention because they are desperately in need of help. In contrast, a high-functioning client might have a specific need to make a decision about a career and therefore demand that the helper be knowledgeable about careers to help him with this decision.

We also speculate that clients' reactions are moderated by the therapeutic relationship. In generally positive relationships, clients might tolerate some mistakes from helpers without an adverse reaction because they feel that helpers are genuinely trying to be helpful. If the relationship is problematic or rocky, however, anything helpers do might elicit negative reactions from disgruntled clients.

In addition, clients' reactions seem to be influenced by their impressions of the helper's intentions. For example, if clients think that their helpers were acting out of their own personal needs and not in the best interest of the clients (regardless of what the helpers' actual intention was), clients might have negative reactions. If clients think that therapists want to extend therapy to make more money rather than because their clients need help, clients might become quite angry and be uncooperative. In contrast, clients who think that their helpers are beginners who are struggling to be helpful (perhaps with limited success), they might feel sympathetic and have positive reactions. Clients' perceptions, even though they might not match the "reality" of helpers' intentions, seem to influence clients' reactions.

Helper Awareness of Client Reactions

In two studies (Hill, Thompson, & Corbett, 1992; Thompson & Hill, 1991), helpers were found to be better at detecting positive client reactions (e.g., felt supported, therapeutic work) than negative reactions (e.g., no reaction, challenged). One could postulate that helpers could not detect the negative reactions because clients did not express these reactions. Indeed, Hill, Thompson, et al. (1992) and Hill, Thompson, Cogar, and Denman (1993) found evidence that clients hid negative reactions more often than positive reactions. One would also postulate that some helpers are better than others at decoding reactions, as was found in the above studies and has been shown in the emotion literature (J. A. Hall, Rosenthal, Archer, DiMatteo, & Rogers, 1978; Rosenthal, Hall, DiMatteo, Rogers, & Archer, 1979). Hence, not detecting client reactions can be due either to clients hiding their reactions, particularly the negative ones, or to helpers having difficulty in perceiving reactions, particularly the negative ones.

The findings from the research about reactions are sobering for helpers, who need to be aware that they might not know when clients have negative feelings or are hiding things in sessions. We would speculate that the more helpers can become aware of what clients are feeling, the better they perform as helpers. Furthermore, helpers need to be trained to understand and work with negative affect, especially when that negative affect is directed toward them. Such training is useful to enable helpers to deal more effectively with clients during sessions, to enable clients to experience a relationship in which negative feelings can be expressed and responded to in a healthy manner, and to provide a model for clients of how to deal effectively with conflict in their lives.

Client's Needs or Goals

Clients decide what they need and want from the interaction and what it is possible to obtain from helpers at a particular time. Clients are not passive recipients of helpers' interventions, but are actively involved in getting what they need from interactions. For example, one client might feel a need to retreat to avoid further confrontation. Another client might decide that he wants to reveal more because his helper is accurate in understanding him and can be trusted with secrets.

Clients also want to have an impact on their helpers. They might want to impress or please their helpers by doing whatever the helpers suggest. For example, Sam wanted to please his helper and so kept telling her what a good job she was doing. Other clients might decide not to reveal shameful secrets because they do not want to tarnish the helper's opinion of them.

We do not mean to imply that clients consciously plot the reactions they want to elicit from their helpers. Rather, we believe that clients act on the basis of their past experiences in ways that maximize the probability of getting their needs met. Most of this decision process about what they need from the interaction and what impact they want to have on helpers is intuitive rather than consciously planned. Some of these client goals are influenced by transference, which occurs when clients project how significant people in their lives (such as parents) behaved onto how they expect their helpers to behave (see Gelso & Hayes, 1998; Gelso, Hill, Mohr, Rochlen, & Zack, 1999). For example, if a client feels that no one listened to her as a child, she might not be able to believe that anyone could possibly want to listen to her now. Hence, even though the helper is attentive, the client might want the helper to "prove" that he really wants to listen to her or she will not talk in the session. Rather than recognizing that the helper is silent because he does not know what to say, this client might perceive the silence as occurring because the helper is bored by her. Another example is the client who believes that all older men are critical like his father was; it may be hard for him to believe that an older male helper could be any different.

Client's Behaviors

Clients engage in specific behaviors on the basis of their reactions, feelings about the therapeutic relationship, needs in the interaction, and goals for a desired impact. The client behavior system, shown in Appendix E, indicates that clients can resist, agree, make an appropriate request, recount, engage in cognitive–behavioral or affective exploration, come to insight, or discuss therapeutic changes. Clients' behaviors are determined not only by the interaction, but also by their communication ability, awareness of needs, level of pathology, and personality structure. Hence, one client might be very articulate and insightful about describing the causes of his pain, whereas another client might be unskilled at communicating feelings and be unaware of what she is feeling in the moment.

Helper's Assessment of Client's Reactions

Helpers, in turn, try to assess the clients' reaction to their interventions. For example, they observe whether clients felt supported and understood or confused and misunderstood. Unfortunately, helpers are not always accurate in determining clients' reactions. A popular perception is that helpers can read clients' minds. In fact, our research suggests that helpers are not particularly adept at perceiving negative client reactions to their interventions, although they are somewhat more accurate at perceiving positive client reactions (Hill, Thompson, et al., 1992). The lesser ability to perceive negative client reactions might occur because, as we noted earlier, clients hide negative reactions from helpers. People often learn as young children not to show negative reactions for fear of evoking displeasure or being punished (e.g., imagine what would happen if an elementary school student told her teacher that she or he did not like what the teacher said). Hence, helpers have to be vigilant not to assume that clients have positive reactions just because the clients are not displaying negative reactions.

In addition, helpers might be reluctant to recognize when clients have negative reactions. Just as client perceptions may be distorted by transference, helper perceptions are sometimes distorted by their own past experiences, a phenomenon that has been called *countertransference* (see Gelso & Hayes, 1998; Hayes et al., 1998). For example, many helpers have a hard time with clients' anger directed at them. They want everyone to like them, and having clients get angry at them feels scary and upsetting. When clients are angry, these helpers might misinterpret the anger as a rejection of them personally rather than appreciating that clients are able to express their anger (as they might other feelings). Other helpers might have difficulty allowing clients to become upset and cry because they feel obligated to make everything better and have all clients be happy. Again, this is why it is critical for people considering a career as a helper to explore their own issues, needs, and limitations.

Unfortunately, not all helpers have received skills training or have been trained to examine the effects of their interventions on clients. Hence, they use interventions that feel comfortable rather than ones that match the needs of particular clients in specific situations. In addition, there is a danger that over time helpers can become insensitive to the influence of their behavior on clients and assume that they know how the clients are reacting internally. Helpers, even when they are experienced, must strive to be aware of their reactions and the impact of their interventions on clients.

Helper's Reevaluation: An Ongoing Process

On the basis of their perceptions of the client's reactions (whether accurate or not) and observation of the overt behaviors, helpers reevaluate and devise new intentions and accompanying skills for the next intervention. If a helper perceives that the last intervention was successful and thinks that a similar intervention would be appropriate, she might continue with the same intention–skill combination. For example, if a reflection resulted in the client talking about sadness, the helper might use another reflection to help the client delve even deeper into these feelings. If a helper perceives that the last intervention was helpful but that something new is needed, he might choose a different intention–skill combination. For example, if a helper had reflected feelings and the client responded by talking about deep feelings but seemed to have a sense of completion, the helper might decide to use an open question to find out more about other aspects of problems.

If a helper perceives that the last intervention was not received well by the client, the helper tries to determine why the intervention was not successful. If the timing was bad, the helper might decide not to continue that intervention but to go back to a more exploratory intervention to learn more about the problem. In contrast, if the helper decides that the intentions for an intervention were on target but the wrong skill was used, the helper might use a different skill to implement the same intention. For example, a beginning helper might implement the intention of getting the client to talk about feelings by asking a closed question such as "Did you have any feelings about that?" By observing the client's response to this closed question (e.g., the client might respond, "No"), the helper might realize that the format of the closed question stopped rather than facilitated exploration. Hence, the helper might choose to use a reflection of feeling (e.g., "Perhaps you feel scared right now") in the next intervention and observe how the client responds. Thus, by paying attention to client reactions, helpers can devise new interventions to fit the immediate need.

The ultimate criterion for the effectiveness of the helper's intervention is always the client's response. Therefore, helpers need to monitor client reactions to determine whether their interventions are helpful, and they need to make adjustments when clients respond negatively. Of course, such constant awareness demands that helpers be open to feedback, have the skills in their repertoires to try something different, and have a good enough relationship with their clients to allow for misunderstandings. Unfortunately, many helper issues can interrupt this process: a bad day, a lack of openness and awareness, a lack of skills, or a lack of a good enough relationship with the client. Training and supervision are necessary to enable helpers to deal with obstacles to their effectiveness.

There is rarely an objectively "right" helper intervention. The criterion for a helpful intervention is how the client feels and responds. We like to think of helpers as personal scientists, investigating the effects of each intervention on clients, testing what works and what does not work, and then deciding what needs to be done next. Helpers have to be very attentive to what works with individual clients. Even if a helper finds that certain helping skills work well with one client, those same skills might not work with the next client.

No helper can ever be perfect because there is no such concept as perfection in helping. One could argue that being a perfect helper would not be helpful for clients because it would not present a realistic relationship—everyone makes mistakes, and learning how to deal with mistakes can be very therapeutic. Helpers who recognize their mistakes, apologize, and process the event can provide a powerful example for clients about how to deal with problems in relationships. Helpers should relax, do the best they can, and try to learn from their experiences.

EXTERNAL WORLD

Typically helping sessions last only 1 hr or so a week for a few weeks, whereas clients live the rest of their lives outside of the helping sessions. As helpers, we hope that clients take what they have learned from helping sessions and try to apply it to "real life." In one case of brief psychotherapy presented in Hill (1989), the therapist confronted the client with the fact that she did not seem to need him or listen to anything he said. The client was very surprised because she had never viewed herself this way. She thought that she was working intensely on the relationship. She went out and asked her friends, who agreed with the therapist's assessment that she seemed self-possessed and not in need of anything from them. Hearing this feedback from both the therapist and her friends forced the client to look at her behavior. In this case, the client successfully used the feedback from the friends to validate what she was learning in therapy. Ideally, clients think about what helpers have said and keep working on issues between sessions.

In intensive psychotherapy, clients sometimes form images, or what have been called *internal representations*, of their therapists to remind them of their helpers in between sessions (Farber & Geller, 1994; Geller, Cooley, & Hartley, 1981; Geller & Farber, 1993; Knox, Goldberg, Woodhouse, & Hill, in press; Orlinsky & Geller, 1993). For example, some clients might hold imaginary discussions with their helpers to figure out what they would suggest they do in difficult situations. Others might imagine their helper comforting them in difficult situations. These internal representations often help clients cope between sessions.

On the other hand, relationships in the external world can sometimes present obstacles to progress in therapy. Perhaps the clearest example is when a client's changes threaten the status quo of family life, causing family members to undermine the client's progress. For example, a severely overweight man's weight loss may threaten his marital relationship. The wife may fear that the husband is now attractive to other women and, enjoying their attention, might lose interest in her. She may begin to cook tasty, fattening desserts to tempt the man to regain the weight and thus stabilize the relationship. These behaviors are not necessarily done consciously but often are desperate attempts to maintain stability in relationships (see Watzlawick, Weakland, & Fisch, 1974).

Hence, events in the external world can both help and hinder the therapeutic work. Helpers cannot just attend to what goes on in session; rather, they need to be aware of how external events influence the helping process. They also need to encourage clients to work on issues outside of helping to enhance the helping process and encourage clients to take responsibility for making changes in their lives.

OUTCOME

All of the variables we have discussed to this point (helper and client background variables, context variables, moment-by-moment interactional sequences, and the external world) interact to determine the outcome of the helping process. Thus, the outcome is influenced by many factors, and individuals react idiosyncratically to different aspects of the process.

Generally, we can examine the outcome of helping in terms of three areas: intrapersonal, interpersonal, and social role performance (Lambert & Hill, 1994). *Intrapersonal changes* refer to outcomes that occur within the client (e.g., decreased symptoms, increased self-esteem, improved problem-solving abilities, new behavioral skills such as assertiveness, or increased subjective feelings of well-being). *Interpersonal changes* take place in the client's intimate relationships (e.g., improved communication, increased marital satisfaction, or more healthy relationships). *Social role performance* refers to the client's ability to carry out responsibilities in the community (e.g., improved job performance, increased participation in community activities, more involvement in school, or reduced antisocial behaviors). For example, a client may feel better about herself, have a clearer sense of who she is and the meaning of her life, have an improved relationship with her husband, and have fewer days of absence at work related to illness.

Helpers, clients, and significant others often have different perceptions of the outcome of the helping process (see Strupp & Hadley, 1977). For example, a helper might feel very pleased with her performance as a helper with Jack and believe that Jack benefited a great deal from the helping because he said he was going to change his major. In contrast, Jack might feel that he only participated in counseling to please his parents and that he listened politely and responded compliantly in the session to appease the helper but dismissed all the helper's advice as soon as he left. Jack's parents might feel sad because their son is not choosing the career that they want for him and resigned that even helping did not improve their relationship with their son. Thus, the outcomes of helping can be quite different depending on the individual's perspective.

EMPIRICAL RESEARCH ON THE THREE-STAGE MODEL OF HELPING

Because students need to understand the empirical basis of the model, we present the results of some studies on the process model throughout this chapter (note that the results of studies on individual helping skills are presented in the relevant chapters). The findings of this research can be summarized as follows (although the results need to be replicated before we can have confidence in them).

1. Helpers used intentions and response modes that fit their theoretical orientations (e.g., psychoanalytic vs. behavioral) and professional roles (e.g., career counseling vs. psychotherapy).

2. Helpers had different intentions for using the same helping skill (e.g., open questions can be used to get information, focus, clarify, promote catharsis, explore cognitions, explore feelings, and deal with the therapeutic relationship). Thus, a complete description of the helper's verbal intervention must include both the intention and the helping skill.

3. Helping skills had a significant but small impact on immediate outcome in helping sessions.

4. Interpretation and self-disclosure have generally been found to be helpful response modes, although both were used infrequently by helpers.

5. Client involvement (i.e., level of experiencing) in the helping process was related to the immediate outcome of helper interventions, such that specific helper

interventions made the most difference when clients were at lower levels of experiencing (i.e., were recounting or telling stories) but made less difference when clients were at moderate levels of experiencing (i.e., talking about their feelings or thoughts).

6. Helpers were better at detecting positive than negative client reactions.

7. Clients used fewer head nods when they were experiencing negative reactions.

8. Clients hid negative reactions, left things unsaid during sessions, and kept major life secrets from their helpers.

Research in helping skills is very difficult because the helping process is complex and because our research methods are crude for studying this helping process. We hope that others become excited about helping skills and find new methods for investigating the helping process. In particular, new measures need to be developed to assess other components of the process model (e.g., how helpers go about devising new intentions–skills on the basis of their evaluation of the client reactions). Research is also needed to determine how the components of the process model interact with one another and with the external world to lead to outcome. We present more ideas for research at the end of the sections on each stage.

CONCLUDING COMMENTS

The whole helping process undoubtedly seems incredibly complex, especially to the beginning trainee. Similarly, all the components of driving at first seem overwhelming to a person learning to drive, but later driving becomes so familiar that the driver often does not even think about the separate steps (e.g., turning the wheel to make a turn). We are presenting you with a broad overview of the model so that you can have a framework for understanding the individual skills. Then we focus on learning and practicing each skill individually; only then do we discuss how to integrate them in the helping process.

What Do You Think?

- We have described the helping process as being very complicated. Do you agree?
- What components have we left out of the helping process, and where have we included irrelevant components?
- What parts of the helping process do you think are unconscious (i.e., not open to awareness)?
- How might helpers and clients increase their awareness of their intentions and reactions?
- How do you explain that helpers and clients often experience the same interaction differently?
- How important do you think helping skills are in relation to the therapeutic relationship in terms of leading to client change?
- Can people can be trained in helping skills, or is helping an ability that cannot be taught?

LAB 1 Interactional Sequence

Goal: To familiarize students with thinking about intentions and reactions.

Students should be arranged in dyads, with one person acting as the helper and one as the client. Roles should be alternated after going through the exercise so that each person has the opportunity to perform each role. The session should be taped (preferably videotaped), so that the helper and client can review the session.

Helper's and Client's Tasks During the Helping Interchange

1. The helper should turn on the audio or video tape recorder.
2. The helper can start the interaction with an introductory statement such as, "Hi, my name is _____. The purpose of our meeting today is to give me a chance to practice helping behaviors. What would you like to talk about?"
3. The client should talk briefly about something nonthreatening, such as how she or he feels doing this exercise.
4. The helper should respond in as helpful a way as possible.
5. Continue for 5 min or until the helper has the opportunity to do about 10 interventions.

Reviewing the Helping Interchange

1. Immediately after the interchange, the helper should play back the helper's first statement.

   a. Helper's task: Using the helper intentions list (Appendix A), the helper should write down the numbers of up to three intentions for the intervention. Helpers should place themselves back in the session and recall what they were feeling at the time rather than how they feel at the time of the review. If the helper was not aware of his or her intentions, he or she should make an educated guess about what the intentions might have been.

   b. Client's task: Using the client reactions system (Appendix D), the client should write down the numbers of up to three reactions for the intervention. Clients should place themselves back in the session and recall what they were feeling at the time rather than how they feel at the time of the review. If the client was not aware of her or his intentions, she or he should make an educated guess about what the reactions might have been.

2. This process should be repeated for 10 interventions.

SWITCH ROLES

Personal Reflections

- Which were your most typical intentions and reactions?
- How difficult was it to reflect on the intentions and reactions?
- Were the intentions and reactions apparent to others? For example, was the client aware of the helper's intentions and was the helper aware of the client's reactions?

4 Ethical Issues in Helping

Intellectual integrity, courage, and kindness are still the virtues I admire most.

Gerti Cori

Imagine that you are ending a helping relationship with a client who has become very special to you. You have enjoyed the sessions with the client, and you feel that you have become a better helper as a result of working with this client. The client indicates that the sessions have been very helpful in resolving several longstanding problems and enhancing confidence at work and in relationships with others. The client asks if the two of you might get together for coffee and then presents you with a gift—a beautiful and very expensive Cartier watch! What do you do?

BEGINNING HELPERS may encounter ethical dilemmas similar to the one described above as they learn and practice helping skills. When they face an ethical quandary, beginning helpers are often uncertain about how to respond in a professional and ethical manner. This chapter is designed to help you work through ethical dilemmas and make responsible decisions about how to resolve ethical questions. We provide an overview of salient ethical issues related to helping behaviors, beginning with a description of ethical behavior. Six basic ethical principles are then introduced, and some of the ethical dilemmas that beginning helpers may encounter are discussed. Finally, a strategy for resolving ethical dilemmas is presented and an example of how to follow this strategy is provided. After reading this chapter, you should be able to apply a decision-making strategy to respond to the ethical dilemma presented above.

AN OVERVIEW OF ETHICS

What Does Being Ethical Mean?

Ethics are moral standards that ensure that professionals provide quality services and are respectful of the rights of the people with whom they work. Acting in an ethical manner also involves following the laws and rules governing one's profession. Although beginning helpers are not yet professionals, it bodes well for them to realize that their supervisors and the organizations they represent must adhere to the laws and rules of the profession and that they must follow standards of ethical behaviors, on which the justice system evaluates competency and responsibility in helping relationships. In the previous example of the client who asked the helper to go out for coffee, the helper might consider the ethical issues that impinge on this situation prior to formulating a response to the client.

She would contemplate whether meeting for coffee would be therapeutic for the client or whether this extension of the relationship could encourage dependency (and thus be harmful). In addition, although the helper might be tempted to accept the beautiful watch, she should ponder the impact on the therapeutic relationship of accepting a generous gift.

Ethical Codes of Conduct

Many professions (e.g., counseling, medicine, nursing, psychology, social work) have developed ethical codes that are intended to protect the consumers of the field. These codes provide professionals with assistance regarding the best action to take in challenging, confusing, or novel situations. Often, these codes begin with an aspirational statement that invites the members to act in a responsible manner, ensure quality client care, and contribute to society through their work. Many of the codes delineate basic ethical principles to which professionals aspire. Rather than providing "the right answer," ethical codes provide basic guidelines to assist helpers in behaving in a responsible manner and resolving ethical dilemmas. Exhibit 4.1 provides a list of references for the ethical codes of several professional organizations.

GENERAL ETHICAL PRINCIPLES

Many ethical codes stress the importance of the following six basic ethical principles: autonomy, beneficence, nonmaleficence, justice, fidelity, and veracity (Beauchamp & Childress, 1994; Kitchener, 1984; Meara, Schmidt, & Day, 1996). Following is a description and an applied example of each of these ethical principles.

Autonomy

Autonomy refers to the right (of both the consumer and the provider) to make choices and take actions, provided the results do not adversely affect others. This principle grants individuals the opportunity to determine their actions on the basis of their belief systems, which is a value of extreme importance in American society. For example, a helper may be working with a client to assist her in determining her future career direction, independent of her parents' hopes for her to pursue law school. Suddenly, the client announces that she is ending counseling and giving up her scholarship to pursue a

---

▨▨▨ **EXHIBIT 4.1. ETHICAL CODES**

American Association for Marriage and Family Therapy. (1991). *AAMFT code of ethics*. Washington, DC: Author.

American Counseling Association. (1995). *Code of ethics and standards of practice*. Alexandria, VA: Author.

American Psychological Association. (1992). Ethical principles and code of conduct. *American Psychologist, 47*, 1597–1611.

American School Counselor Association. (1992). *Ethical standards for school counselors*. Alexandria, VA: Author.

National Association of Social Workers. (1996). *NASW code of ethics*. Washington, DC: Author.

career as a country music singer. The helper might suggest that the client reevaluate this decision and consider the pros and cons of life as a country music singer. However, the principle of autonomy allows the client the right to make her own decisions, provided these decisions are not harmful to others. Hence, in this example, the helper supported the client's decision to attend college in Nashville and simultaneously pursue her dream to become a musician.

Beneficence

Beneficence refers to the intent "to do good" by helping and promoting growth in others. Many helpers enter professions that allow them to assist people and make a positive difference in the lives of others. This principle clearly states that helpers should be committed to the growth and development of their clients. A helper who sees clients solely to make money and does not demonstrate care about their welfare would be in violation of this important principle. However, helpers who strive to provide the most comprehensive up-to-date services to their clients are embodying the principle of beneficence.

Nonmaleficence

Nonmaleficence can be described using the phrase "above all, do no harm." Professionals are asked to ensure that their interventions and actions do not inadvertently harm their clients. Thus, neglect (even unintentional) on the part of the helper would be problematic. For example, a student in a helping class might be out drinking margaritas with friends and telling them about the practice helping session that he had in class that day. Later, he might notice that his practice client was in the booth next to him and had probably overheard him telling his friends about her issues. Although the helper may not have used the client's name or intended to harm her, he would be responsible for the unintentional harm that could result from having disclosed confidential information about his practice client.

Justice

Justice can be defined as fairness or ensuring equality of opportunities and resources for all people. Some people might interpret this to mean that they have an ethical responsibility to contribute part of their time to helping others without receiving benefits or payment for their service. Helpers can contribute to rectifying the unequal distribution of helping services by making their services more accessible to those who are unable to pay. For example, helpers might use a sliding fee scale for clients who have limited incomes. It seems important that our commitment to serving those who are less fortunate should extend beyond our training years (during which many helpers learn counseling skills by working with marginalized populations), to encompass our entire careers. An additional method to promote justice involves attempts to influence public policy or legislation to ensure that mental health services are available to those in need regardless of ability to pay, location, language preference, or disability status. Moreover, helpers can contribute to building a just society by using their helping skills (under supervision) at not-for-profit agencies. Several students who have completed a helping skills course at our university have gone on to volunteer in many settings, such as shelters for battered women and clinics for people with AIDS.

Fidelity

Fidelity refers to keeping promises and being trustworthy in relationships with others. Fidelity is a critical component of the relationship between helpers and clients. Without confidence in the helper's ability to be faithful to the agreements articulated in the helping session, minimal progress can be made. For example, the agreement between helpers and clients typically involves both parties meeting at a certain time for a specified number of sessions. If helpers are consistently 20 min late for each session, they would be breaking the promise to be available to clients at an arranged time. Violations like these can have a detrimental impact on the development of the helping relationship.

Veracity

Veracity, which refers to telling the truth, is a powerful and necessary principle in dilemmas encountered in both helping and research settings. Clients often rely on their helpers to provide honest feedback about their interactions in the helping sessions. One example involves a 21-year-old client who worked with a helper for many months. Takiesha had not made much progress in the last few sessions and asked the counselor for some direct feedback about her work in the helping sessions. The helper provided several positive remarks and also indicated that at times, Takiesha appeared to place responsibility for her problems on others instead of empowering herself. Although Takiesha was upset about hearing this feedback, she was grateful to the helper for being honest and was able to understand how her reluctance to take responsibility limited her from making necessary changes in her life.

To summarize, the six basic ethical principles outline general rights that individuals have in helping situations. These principles not only help to protect clients who seek assistance in resolving problems, but also provide helpers with guidelines for addressing ethical dilemmas. Some of the ethical issues that beginning helpers may encounter are presented in the next section.

ETHICAL GUIDELINES FOR BEGINNING HELPERS

Recognize Your Limits

It is critical that helpers recognize and practice only within the areas for which they have been trained and are competent. For example, as a beginning helper, you may be recognized as having expertise in performing basic helping skills (e.g., listening and reflecting feelings). A friend may discover that you are learning helping skills and may ask you to speak to her cousin who has been acting in a strange manner for several weeks. She may tell you that her cousin has been hearing voices that tell him to destroy the psychology building at school. Appropriate ethical behavior in this case would involve telling your friend that meeting with her cousin is outside of your area of competence. You might offer to speak to your professor to obtain a referral to a competent practitioner with training and expertise in working with people who hear voices.

In a related vein, we encourage helpers to be honest about their qualifications. In a helping situation, helpers who describe themselves as counselors or who advertise that they provide psychological interventions that they have not been trained to use would be violating ethical behaviors. For example, a practice client may refer to you as his "psychologist." Ethical behavior would involve telling the client that you are in training to learn helping skills and do not yet have a degree or license.

Furthermore, helpers must consult with supervisors to serve best the people with whom they work and are advised to promote ethical behavior among peers. In one helping class, a student met with a client who mentioned that she had considered suicide because of all of the stressors in her life. The student immediately contacted her lab leader and they consulted with the instructor, who then intervened with the client to provide the necessary assistance. In less dangerous helping situations, supervisors provide ongoing feedback to enable helpers to provide quality services to clients. For example, Johnny was struggling with his decision to marry his long-term girlfriend. The helper also was considering making a life-long commitment to his partner of 8 years. The helper realized the potential for harm in this situation and in his weekly meeting with his supervisor discussed how to ensure that his personal issues related to commitment would not have a negative impact on his helping sessions with Johnny.

Focus on the Needs of the Client

When helpers act in an ethical manner, they are concerned with the needs of the people with whom they work. First of all, clients have a right to understand the nature of the helping relationship. Many clients have never experienced a formal helping relationship and are uncertain about what to expect. Helpers have an ethical responsibility to educate clients about the process of helping. For example, helpers should provide information about fees, length of the helping relationship, techniques used, and the supervisor's name. As noted above, helpers must inform clients about the limits of their assistance and their status as helpers (e.g., that they are not professionals). For example, when beginning helpers engage in practice sessions with volunteer clients, they should introduce themselves and tell the client that they are in training to become helpers.

Furthermore, informed consent must occur in helpers' work with clients. Clients have the right to understand what procedures will be used and what outcome can be expected. If helpers plan on audiotaping or videotaping helping sessions, they must obtain permission from their clients prior to taping the interactions. Furthermore, when providing services to families or couples, helpers must clarify their roles and the relationships that occur during the time of service. For example, a helper was seeing an adolescent client whose parents were going through a divorce. The mother was struggling during this time and asked if she could talk privately with the helper to discuss some of her issues related to the divorce. The helper gently reminded her of the importance of having a special relationship with the client (the daughter) and indicated that this relationship might be jeopardized by even one helping session with the mother. The mother was provided with referrals to other qualified helpers.

As the helping relationship progresses, helpers are responsible for ensuring coverage of psychological services if they are out of town or unavailable (i.e., on vacation) and for ending helping when the client has met the treatment goals or is no longer benefiting from the helping sessions. When ending a helping relationship, counselors need to assist clients in terminating the relationship and in mobilizing internal and external resources to enable healthy functioning. Strategies for ending the helping relationship are outlined in chapter 22.

Behaving in an ethical manner also includes attending to the client's rights to privacy and confidentiality. Students enrolled in beginning helping classes may encounter issues related to confidentiality on a regular basis. For example, practice sessions require that students share real problems with practicing helpers. It is important that helpers respect a client's expectations of confidentiality by not divulging information shared in the helping session, except in limited circumstances (e.g., with their supervisor or as required by law). Sometimes, maintaining confidentiality can be challenging if students in the class interact outside of the sessions or if they have friends in common. However, the success of the helping relationship is due in part to the client's ability to trust, with rare exception, that the information shared with helpers in practice sessions will be held in confidence.

At times, the best interests of clients may conflict with the needs of the helpers. For example, a helper may enter a helping session with a client after a difficult interaction with her partner. The helper may prefer to think about the interaction with her partner or even hope to end the session early to attempt to resolve the conflict that occurred. However, it is critical that the helper focus on listening carefully to the concerns of the client and being as present as possible in the helping session.

An interesting situation results when the client's unresolved issues result in behaviors that benefit the helper. For example, Himee noticed that her helper often had a soft drink on his desk. Himee then began to give the helper a soft drink at the beginning of each helping session. Although it might be in the best interest of the helper to accept his favorite drink, ethical behavior requires that the helper try to understand the meaning of Himee's behavior and act in a manner that places her needs first. In this case, the helper might assist Himee in uncovering her desire to please the helper and her fear that the helper might abandon her if she does not bring gifts to the sessions. Perhaps the best interest of the client would be to assist her in viewing herself as valuable in relationships independent of the gifts she presents to others.

Understand the Role of Culture

Ethical behavior mandates that helpers are mindful of differences among individuals and use basic helping skills that reflect an understanding of the people with whom they are working. It is important that beginning helpers do not assume that the helping skills transfer across cultures and individuals. Perhaps the most commonly cited abuse of this kind occurs when helpers assume that maintaining eye contact is a sign of openness, interest, and willingness to participate in the session. In some cultures (e.g., Asian cultures), a lack of eye contact signifies respect for an authority figure and thus should not be interpreted using majority American society norms in helping sessions.

At times, helpers who are working with clients from a different culture either neglect (or attach too much significance to) the culture of their clients when providing interventions. It is important for helpers to realize that helping in the traditional manner may (or may not) be sufficient for these clients. For example, heterosexual helpers who are working with lesbian or gay clients should investigate the literature about working with these clients and be aware of the special challenges that may be present for these clients (while also understanding that lesbian and gay clients may share many similarities with heterosexual clients). For example, Shawn was depressed and hopeless when he sought counseling at the university counseling center. His helper assumed that because Shawn was a gay man, his depression ensued from the discrimination that gay men experience on campus. The helper told Shawn that he understood how painful it must be to be a gay man on a predominantly heterosexual college campus. Shawn was stunned and disappointed in the helper as he had sought assistance because his sister was killed in a car accident the previous week. Thus, it seems critical to consider but never assume that the client's cultural background and related experiences are the primary motivators for seeking assistance.

Furthermore, a helper who is working with a client from a different culture should not assume that the client's goals are to assimilate (or not assimilate) into the majority culture. For example, Bridget immigrated to the United States from another country and asked for assistance in selecting a career. She explained to her helper that her parents wanted her to go to medical school but that she was doing poorly in her science courses. The helper incorrectly assumed that Bridget did not want to pursue a medical career and began to direct her to select a different occupation on the basis of her interests, values, and abilities (because making career decisions in terms of individual needs and abilities is a cultural value for many people living in the United States). However, if the helper had listened carefully to Bridget, he would have discovered that her primary struggle was feeling devastated about her inability to meet her parents' expectations and dreams (in part because of her cultural background, which valued familial harmony and parental approval).

Demonstrating interest in clients' cultures is often appreciated, but reliance on clients to educate helpers about diverse cultures is inappropriate. Helpers should not expect clients to educate them about their cultures but should initiate learning through obtaining supervision, reading relevant materials, and seeking exposure to the culture. An African American client who worked in a battered women's shelter expressed frustration not only with being a member of a group of people who have less power in American society but also with being asked to train and educate European American people about her culture. She often encouraged helpers to take the initiative in learning about their clients' cultures by reading books, interacting with people from that culture, eating foods from different cultures, and traveling to different countries.

In addition, ethical behavior goes beyond having an awareness of individual and cultural differences to embracing a commitment to eliminate bias and discrimination in one's work. This commitment may involve actively examining our biases, confronting colleagues who act in a discriminatory manner, advocating for those with less power, and working for social change. For example, some helpers facilitate growth or empowerment groups for clients who have been marginalized in society. Another helper used her experience as a counselor, teacher, and researcher to write a book about empowering clients through the process of counseling (McWhirter, 1994).

Be Aware of Your Values

Helpers need to be aware of the influence of their values and beliefs in their interactions with clients. For example, a helper who believes that all women should work outside the home in high status, nontraditional occupations may inadvertently discourage a client from selecting a traditional career that seems to be a good fit for her interests and would enable her to focus on her family. Beginning helpers, like advanced clinicians, should work to understand their biases. Thus, we encourage helpers to increase their awareness of their values and to ascertain the influence of their values on the helping process.

The influence of values in helping can be subtle. Helpers can influence the direction of sessions and clients' selection of actions through nonverbal behavior that they are not aware of, such as smiling or nodding their heads at particular moments. Beginning helpers sometimes struggle with inadvertently encouraging clients to talk about situations that are comfortable for or interesting to the helper. For example, a helper might use nonverbal behaviors to indicate great interest when the client is talking about her romantic relationship but seem somewhat disinterested when the discussion moves to roommate concerns.

Avoid Harmful Dual Relationships

Helpers are encouraged to examine their dual relationships with clients to determine whether there is a likelihood that problems may arise. A potentially harmful dual relationship occurs when someone in power (e.g., a helper, professor, or supervisor) adds another role to his or her interaction with an individual who is less powerful (e.g., a client, student, or supervisee) and that interaction may lead to harm or exploitation of the less powerful person. For example, it would not be unusual or problematic for a supervisor also to be a student's professor and evaluator; but if the supervisor–professor also took on the role of therapist, the dual relationship would be considered harmful because confidential information disclosed in that capacity could potentially be used to the student's detriment. Helpers need to be aware of the power differential when working with others and ensure that clients are not harmed by their interactions. For example, a beginning helper also may be a teaching assistant in a psychology class. If the helper were assigned to provide a helping session to a student in the class, harm might occur if the student felt that she had to disclose more personal information than she initially intended to ensure that the helper would not be punitive when grading her exams.

Helpers also should not provide helping sessions to friends or family members. Although helping skills can be used to communicate more effectively in personal relationships, taking on the role of helper with friends can be detrimental for several reasons. First, it is difficult to be objective when listening to the problems of friends or family members. A lack of objectivity could have a negative impact on a helping session because the helper's own agenda could interfere with assisting the client to act in her or his best interests. Second, the role of helper is a powerful role and could disturb the power dynamics in the relationship. For example, Alfonso began to rely on his friend to play the role of helper while he was going through a divorce. In time, Alfonso became dependent on this friend for assistance when problems emerged at work or with his children. His relationship with his friend-turned-helper was harmed because their interactions were always focused on Alfonso's problems. Finally, the fastest road to burnout involves taking care of others without paying attention to relaxation and caring for one's own needs. Helpers who assist clients in their jobs and then, during their free time, also take care of the needs of friends and relatives should examine this potentially unhealthy pattern carefully.

Perhaps the most harmful example of dual relationships involves having a sexual relationship with a client. Research has shown that sexual involvement with clients (and former clients) results in negative outcomes (Pope, 1994). Thus, many professions have developed explicit rules prohibiting sexual intimacies between helpers and clients. In addition, providing counseling to people with whom one has been sexually involved in the past can be very destructive to the client. Helpers typically cannot be objective and provide quality services to clients with whom they have been intimately involved.

A related topic is that of sexual attraction to clients. Feeling attracted is not unethical, but acting on that attraction can harm clients and is considered unethical behavior. Research has demonstrated that approximately 87% of surveyed helpers reported that they have been sexually attracted to clients at some point in their careers (Pope, Keith-Spiegel, & Tabachnick, 1986). Although helpers should never have a sexual relationship with a client, helper sexual attraction toward clients is a common occurrence in helping relationships. Research has shown that discussing these feelings in supervision can assist helpers in working through these feelings in a healthy, rather than a destructive manner (Ladany et al., 1997; Pope, Sonne, & Holyroyd, 1993). As a beginning helper, you may find yourself sexually attracted to someone whom you are helping. Although discussing this topic with a supervisor could be uncomfortable (i.e., some people may feel ashamed or guilty for having these feelings), talking with a supervisor can assist you in working through the issues related to the attraction in a way that does not harm the client. For example, a helper found herself attracted to a client who communicated admiration, respect, even awe for the assistance that she provided to him. Although she had a good relationship with her partner, she enjoyed the positive feedback from the client and began thinking about the client in a romantic way. Fortunately, she talked with her supervisor, who assisted her in sorting out her feelings related to the attraction to the client and in understanding how sexual involvement might harm the client. The helper benefited from coming to understand how these feelings developed and how they could negatively influence the helping process. The supervisor also normalized the helper's feelings by letting her know that many helpers become attracted to clients during their careers.

Act in a Virtuous Manner

Professionals concerned with ethical behaviors have begun to move from a focus on behaving in an ethical manner (i.e., following the guidelines delineated in an ethical code) to behaving in a virtuous manner. Virtue differs from ethics in that one is not as concerned with laws and rules as much as striving to be a person of positive moral character (Meara et al., 1996). Part of this change results from the reality that ethical codes, in and of themselves, cannot provide exact specifications for behaviors. Helpers need to be trained to internalize the six basic ethical principles, practice a comprehensive ethical decision-making model, and monitor themselves and their behaviors to ensure respectful interactions with clients. For example, a helper had a very successful helping session with a client at the university counseling center. She used her basic helping skills to provide a safe and open environment. The client shared much personal information in the session and struggled with concerns of importance in his life. The following weekend, the helper ran into the client at a party. She was confused about how to deal with this situation because her training had not addressed guidelines for meeting clients in social situations. This was a case in which knowledge of the "right" behavior or rule for intervention was missing. However, the helper was a sensitive and respectful woman, and she responded to the client in a mature and caring way, waiting for him to acknowledge her first and returning his brief greeting as they passed. Her response was consistent with virtuous behavior and provides yet another reason to promote virtuous interactions with others. We cannot always provide helpers with answers to every ethical situation that they encounter. Encouraging helpers to respond in a caring and respectful manner is consistent with virtuous (and most likely) ethical behaviors.

Take Care of Yourself to Ensure That You Can Care for Others

One final dimension of ethical behavior that often gets ignored involves helpers taking care of themselves. Helping can be an exhausting enterprise that requires helpers to give much of themselves to others. It behooves helpers to monitor their health and energy to ensure the provision of quality services. Helpers might evaluate regularly the presence of added stressors, poor health, and exhaustion. We suggest that helpers strive to achieve balance in their lives by integrating rewarding work, supportive relationships, regular exercise, and healthy eating habits. Of course, we strongly encourage helpers to seek counseling if they need support or assistance with pressing concerns.

WORKING THROUGH AN ETHICAL DILEMMA

Although beginning helpers may not encounter many ethical dilemmas, learning how to work through these situations can be helpful so that helpers can be prepared when ethical dilemmas arise. Ethical dilemmas occur when there are competing ethical reasons to act in ways that are mutually exclusive (Kitchener, 1984). At times, the actions that helpers would take to uphold one ethical principle could violate another ethical principle. Kitchener described inherent contradictions that exist in ethical codes (e.g., individual autonomy vs. making decisions for clients; confidentiality vs. protecting others). For example, ethical codes often ensure a client's right to privacy and confidentiality. They also endorse the importance of working to minimize harm to others. These important standards can, at times, be in conflict with one another. For instance, one helper worked with an adolescent client who was threatening to kill herself and did not want the helper to discuss this with her parents. The adolescent felt that her parents would not take her seriously and might punish her for disclosing these thoughts to her helper. The helper was faced with an ethical dilemma that was not easily resolved by examination of her profession's ethical code. In this case, the helper talked with the adolescent about the importance of disclosing this information to her parents to ensure that she would be safe from harm, and then, in the presence of the client and with her permission, discussed the client's concerns with her parents.

The A–B–C–D–E strategy for ethical decision making (Sileo & Kopala, 1993) is a framework that can be followed when helpers are confronted with ethical dilemmas. To illustrate its application, we pose an example of an ethical dilemma in which a client discloses to a helper that she was raped the previous night by her boyfriend's best friend. The helper in this case is an experienced clinician who has a degree in counseling psychology and is working under the supervision of a licensed psychologist. The helper feels outraged by the crime that has been committed and wants to call the police immediately. The client, however, is concerned about her relationship with her boyfriend and definitely does not want the rape to be reported. The helper realizes that he is facing an ethical dilemma between reporting a crime against the client's wishes and maintaining confidentiality. The helper uses the A–B–C–D–E strategy for ethical decision making to work toward a decision about how to proceed in this challenging situation.

Step 1. Assessment

The helper identifies the situation, the client's status and resources, and the helper's values, feelings, and reactions to the situation. We advise the helper also to consider what laws or rules might apply. In this case, the helper notes that the client is a well-adjusted, bright, and competent young woman who is finishing her 4th year in college and majoring in business administration. She reports having a good relationship with her boyfriend and states that she has two close friends who have promised to support her through her recovery from the rape. She also has indicated an interest in attending a rape survivors' group.

The helper, in identifying his values, feelings, and reactions, determines that he feels very strongly that the rapist should be punished for what he did to the client. He acknowledges, to himself, that the strength of his emotions about this issue may result from remembering his feelings of helplessness when he learned that his younger sister had been raped during her 1st year in college.

Step 2. Benefit

The helper considers what benefits the client, the helping relationship, and significant others. In this case, the helper believes that disclosure of the rape to the police and subsequent prosecution of the rapist could benefit the client, her boyfriend, and possible future victims. However, he also acknowledges that the client believes that she would be helped most by discussing the rape with her helper, her two best friends, and a rape survivors' support group. As with many ethical dilemmas, different benefits are present for several possible solutions.

Step 3. Consequences and Consultation

The helper considers the ethical, legal, emotional, and therapeutic consequences that could occur from possible actions. The helper also consults with a supervisor who provides assistance in identifying and working through salient ethical issues. In this case, the helper is being supervised by a licensed psychologist who helps him identify that his disclosure of the rape to the police would undermine the trust he had worked to develop with the client. Moreover, he would be violating her confidentiality and right to privacy. His reporting of the rape might reinforce feelings of powerlessness that the client felt after being raped. It is important to note that beginning helpers confronting a situation in which their own issues might influence the helping sessions or the resolution of an ethical dilemma should immediately consult with their supervisors.

Step 4. Duty

The helper considers to whom a duty exists. In this case, the helper's primary duty or responsibility is to the client rather than to her boyfriend or other women that the rapist might harm. His job as a helper is to do no harm to his client and to provide services that enhance her growth and potential. The helper is beginning to realize how important it is to abide by the client's wishes for nondisclosure, despite his desire to prosecute the rapist.

Sometimes, the helper may have a duty to protect someone other than the client (i.e., an identifiable person whom the client is threatening to harm). In situations where a child is being abused, helpers are mandated by law to report the abuse or to assist the client in reporting the abuse. Furthermore, in cases where the client threatens to harm herself or others, the helper must ensure the safety of the individuals identified to be at risk for harm. For example, if this client told her helper that she planned to murder the rapist and had enlisted the assistance of an assassin to carry out the plan, the helper would have a responsibility to prevent harm to the rapist.

Step 5. Education

The helper reviews his education to determine what he has learned about appropriate actions to take in dealing with similar ethical dilemmas. The helper refers to his notes from his courses and determines that in this ethical dilemma, the best strategy is to maintain the client's confidence and assist her in her recovery from the rape. The helper also decides to pursue counseling to address his residual feelings about the rape of his younger sister.

CONCLUDING COMMENTS

Ethical dilemmas can be aptly described by the two symbols that the Chinese use to represent *crisis*: danger and opportunity. Ethical dilemmas can be dangerous in that the welfare of the client may be compromised. However, they also present an opportunity for helpers to reflect on what they have learned and what they value and then to act in a manner that is consistent with the mores of their profession and (one hopes) their personal values. Ethical dilemmas provide a unique challenge for helpers to confront and resolve important questions and to ensure, to the best of their abilities, that clients' needs are served.

▬▬▬   ## What Do You Think?

Identify the ethical issues in each situation and then apply each step of the A–B–C–D–E strategy for resolving ethical dilemmas to the case.

> Case 1: A beginning helper wants to practice his helping skills and notices someone (Sam) in his residence hall who seems to have a lot of problems and few friends. Outside of class (and without supervision), the beginning helper asks Sam if he could practice with him. Sam begins to share a lot about his life with the helper and wants to have additional "sessions" throughout the week. What should be the helper's response if he were acting in accordance with the ethical guidelines described in this chapter?

> Case 2: A beginning helper is interested in working with clients who have eating disorders because she went through counseling for this issue. Recently, she has been under a lot of stress and her eating has become erratic and uncontrollable. She is assigned a client who has an eating disorder. What should be the helper's response if she were acting in accordance with the ethical guidelines described in this chapter?

> Case 3: A beginning helper has been working with a client for three sessions. The client is a single, attractive male who has many qualities that the helper (also a single male) admires in a romantic partner. During the third and final session, the client indicates an interest in talking more over drinks. The helper is attracted to the client yet uncertain about what to do, given that the helping relationship is ending and that it may or may not have risen to the level of "real" counseling. What should be the helper's response if he were acting in accordance with the ethical guidelines described in this chapter?

> Case 4: Using the knowledge that you have gained from the material and exercises in this chapter, indicate the action that you would take with regard to the ethical dilemma presented at the beginning of this chapter. Describe the strategy that you used to make your decision.

EXPLORATION STAGE

5 Overview of the Exploration Stage

> When one pours out one's heart, one feels lighter.
>
> *(Yiddish proverb)*

Jihad was having difficulty making friends when he moved to this country. He recently had told his parents that he felt miserable, lonely, and worthless. He desperately wanted to have a close friend with whom he could talk about his deepest feelings. His parents were concerned about him and suggested that he talk with a helper. During his first session with the helper, Jihad indicated that he felt like he was going to "burst from loneliness." Since moving to this country, he had not talked to anyone other than his parents, and he was hesitant to tell them how bad he felt because he worried that they would get too concerned and could not really do anything to help him. The helper listened carefully and reflected his feelings of isolation, sadness, and rejection. Jihad began to cry and was able to talk about how he felt different from the other kids because he was from another culture. The helper let him talk and express all his feelings. She accepted him and listened nonjudgmentally, interested in understanding his experiences. At the end of the session, Jihad told the helper that he felt much better. He felt like he was different but okay; he had renewed energy to make friends. Just talking to a caring, understanding person helped lift the burden that had been bothering him and make him feel better about himself.

IN THIS chapter, we present the theoretical background for the exploration stage and then describe the major goals of this stage: establishing rapport and developing the therapeutic relationship, encouraging clients to tell their stories and explore feelings and thoughts, facilitating arousal of emotions, and enabling helpers to learn about their clients. We then discuss some common obstacles that trainees face in meeting these goals and suggest several strategies that helpers can use to overcome these obstacles and manage anxiety. Chapters 6 through 9 describe the major skills (attending and listening, restatement, open question, and reflection of feelings) used to reach the goals of the exploration stage. Chapter 10 presents several additional skills (approval and reassurance, closed question, self-disclosure for exploration, information about the process of helping) that are used infrequently but can sometimes be valuable. Chapter 11 presents an integration of the skills used in the exploration stage.

THEORETICAL BACKGROUND: ROGERS'S CLIENT-CENTERED THEORY

Much of what takes place in the exploration stage is influenced by Rogers's theory of personality development and psychological change (see Rogers, 1942, 1951, 1957, 1959,

63

1967; Rogers & Dymond, 1954). Carl Rogers had a profound influence on the field of psychology with his optimistic and hopeful assertion that all people have the potential for healthy and creative growth. His orientation was client-centered, and he was a phenomenologist, which means that he placed a strong emphasis on the experiences, feelings, and values of the client, or what is often called the *inner life* of the client. He believed that perceptions of reality vary from person to person and that subjective experience guides behavior. In other words, he believed that people are guided by their internal experience rather than by external reality. Similarly, he believed that the only way to understand individuals is to enter their private world and understand their internal frame of reference.

According to Rogers (1942, 1951, 1967), the only basic motivational force is the tendency toward self-actualization, which propels each person to become what she or he is meant to become. He believed that each person has an innate "blueprint" or set of potentialities that can be developed. Rogers likened the forces toward self-actualization in people as similar to the natural order. He noted that plants and animals grow without any conscious effort, provided that the conditions for growth are optimal. Similarly, he believed that people have an inherent ability to fulfil their potential. Furthermore, he believed that people are resilient and can bounce back from adversity given this innate growth potential.

Theory of Personality Development

According to Rogers (1942, 1951, 1967), infants evaluate each experience in terms of how it makes them feel, which he called the organismic valuing process (OVP). Rogers believed that because behavior is governed by OVP, infants can perceive experiences as they actually occur without disorting them. In OVP, no experiences are more or less worthy—they just are. In other words, every event is interesting and open for investigation without prior prejudice. Infants evaluate experiences as to whether they enhance or maintain the organism. For example, if an experience (e.g., being hugged) enhances the organism, the infant feels good and is satisfied and might smile or laugh. On the other hand, if experiences do not enhance the organism (e.g., being cold or having a dirty diaper), the infant does not feel good, is not satisfied, and so might cry. Infants evaluate events by how they actually feel, not by how someone else tells them they should feel. The OVP, then, is an internal guide that everyone has at birth. People freely seek those experiences that enhance them when they trust this internal guide. Rogers believed that infants could trust these inner feelings because they have positive strivings and a natural curiosity about life.

Rogers theorized that the infant does not initially have a self and, hence, can not distinguish between "me" and "not me." The self (or the self-concept) develops as the child begins to discriminate experiences as self-experiences (i.e., as ones that originate from within oneself) versus experiences that belong to other people or things in the environment. As awareness of her or his own being and functioning develops, the child acquires a sense of self. Rogers defined *self* as the organized, consistent perceptions that people have of themselves. The self is the organization of our experiences and is the origin of our feelings. The self allows us to express our unique reactions to life as we know it. The development of the self (or self-concept) is a dynamic process that changes on the basis of a person's perceptions of his or her experiences in the world.

Persons with a healthy sense of self accurately symbolize or internalize their experiences as self-experiences. They feel their feelings without undue anxiety and understand that their feelings come from them; they do not blame others for feeling the way that they do. This freedom to understand that one's feelings originate from within oneself is basic to being able to be involved in healthy relationships.

When governed by OVP, the self remains consistent and whole and the person lacks defensiveness. Burke (1989) suggested that persons with no conflicts in their sense of self can be described as open to their experiences, accepting of their feelings, capable of living in the present without preoccupation with the past or future, free to make choices that are best for them and to act spontaneously on those choices, trusting of self and human nature, capable of balanced and realistic expressions of both aggression and affection, and creative and nonconforming.

Rogers speculated that parents play a fundamental role in a child's formulation of a sense of self. He believed that children have a need for unconditional positive regard. In other words, they need acceptance, respect, warmth, and love without conditions of worth (i.e., they are loved just because they are themselves and not because they do anything). When they receive this from others, they can begin to experience self-acceptance and self-love. When a child feels prized, accepted, and understood by others, she or he develops a healthy sense of self with little or no conflict. The prized child is able to attend to his or her OVP and make good choices on the basis of inner experiencing.

Unfortunately, because parents themselves are not perfect, they place conditions of worth on their children, demanding that they fulfill certain requirements to be loved. For example, parents may give messages such as, "I will not love you unless you are a 'good girl,'" "I will not love you unless you keep your room clean," or "You must be beautiful to receive my love." Because parents communicate (not necessarily through words) that children are lovable and acceptable only when they behave in accordance with imposed standards, children come to believe that they must be and act in certain ways to earn their parents' love.

Consequently, the conditions of worth, rather than the OVP, guide a person's organization of their self-experiences. In other words, children sacrifice their OVP to receive love from their parents (e.g., children give up being spontaneous and playful to sit "properly" and be "good" to please their parents). When a child introjects or internalizes the parents' conditions of worth, these conditions of worth become a part of the child's self-concept and prevent the child from functioning freely.

Conditions of worth lead children to feel conflict between their self-concept and their inner experience. For example, a mother may communicate to a young girl that it is not acceptable for her to hate her brother. The girl may feel that to be loved, she must be a good girl, and so she may disown the hate as not being part of herself. Hence, rather than learning that she may feel hate but cannot hurt her brother, she learns that her feelings are not acceptable. Another example is parents who punish or ridicule a boy for crying when he is hurt or needs help with a difficult task. The boy might repress his feelings of pain and dependency and become extremely independent to maintain his parents' approval. These two examples illustrate how externally imposed values can substitute for the OVP. When feelings of hate or dependency get aroused in these children, they misidentify or repress them and, thus, are not in touch with their inner experiencing. Children experience positive self-regard only when their self-experiences are consistent with feedback that they get from others (e.g., if a girl feels talented in playing the violin and others tell her that she is talented). Hence, feelings of self-worth become dependent on the conditions of worth that were learned in interaction with significant others. A child with conditions of worth would not be open to experience, accepting of feelings, capable of living in the present, free to make choices, trusting, capable of feeling both aggression and affection, and creative. He or she would have a conflicted sense of self.

Obviously, children must become socialized so that they are able to live in their families and society. Children cannot act on all their innate desires or get all of their needs met immediately, because the world is not a perfect place and because other people also have needs. Parents, for example, cannot always immediately meet the infant's needs because they have other demands on their time. In addition, parents cannot allow a child to hurt a sibling or another child. However, the manner in which parents socialize their children is crucial. For example, a parent can empathize with a young girl but still place limits on her (e.g., "I know you are angry at your brother, but you cannot hurt him"). The girl may feel frustrated but not learn to deny her feelings. Instead, she learns to experience her feelings but channel them in a harmless direction. In contrast, when parents humiliate a child (e.g., "Real men don't cry") or deny that the child has feelings (e.g., "You don't hate your teacher"), children become confused about their feelings. The child may feel sad or feel hatred, but the parents say he or she does not have these feelings. Whom do children trust—their inner experience or what their parents tell them they feel? If they do not pay attention to their parents, they risk losing parental approval and love. If they do not pay attention to their inner feelings and instead try to please others who place conditions of worth on them, they lose their sense of self. One can easily see how children come not to trust their inner experiences. Children must survive, so they often choose parents' attention and "love" over inner experiencing.

When conditions of worth are pervasive and the OVP is disabled, the sense of self is weakened to the point where a person is unable to label feelings as belonging to the self. For example, a woman might not even be aware of feeling angry and hurt when being verbally and physically abused by her husband because she thinks she deserves the abuse. When people cannot allow themselves to have their feelings, they often feel a sense of emptiness, phoniness, or lack of genuineness. Rogers (1957) identified this lack of genuineness about one's feelings, which he called *incongruence* or the split between the real and ideal self, as the source of anxiety, depression, and defensiveness in relationships.

Defenses

Rogers suggested that when there is an incongruence between experience and sense of self, the person feels threatened. For example, a person who acts pleasant and happy, when in actuality he is feeling grumpy and depressed, is in danger of losing touch with his inner self. If he were to perceive his depression accurately, his self would be threatened because he has built an image of himself as always happy. When people feel such a threat, they respond with anxiety, which is a signal that the self is in danger. Feeling this anxiety, the person invokes defenses to reduce the incongruity between experience and sense of self, thereby reducing anxiety.

One major defense is perceptual distortion, which involves altering or misinterpreting one's experience to make it compatible with one's self-concept. By distorting their experiences, clients avoid having to deal with unpleasant feelings and issues and can maintain their perceptions of themselves. For example, a woman may perceive herself as being of average weight even though she is quite overweight and no longer fits into chairs. She might say to herself that she does not eat any more than other people. In another example, a person with a sense of worthlessness who is promoted at work might misinterpret the reason for the promotion to be congruent with his negative sense of self. He might say that the only reason he got the promotion was that "the boss had to do it" or "no one else wanted the job."

A second defense is denial, which involves ignoring or denouncing reality. In this situation, people might refuse to acknowledge their experiences because they are inconsistent with the images that they have of themselves. By denying their experiences, clients avoid anxiety. For example, a woman who is being treated unfairly at work might ignore her anger at her boss because she has internalized her parents' belief that anger is bad and that she will not be loved if she expresses anger. Rather than allow herself to experience her anger, she may say that she is not trying hard enough or that she is not smart enough for the job.

Defenses block incongruent experiences from full awareness to minimize the threats to one's sense of self and to allow the self to function and cope. However, defenses also can take a toll on the self in at least three ways. First, the subjective reality (what one allows oneself to experience) can become incongruent with the external reality (the world as it is). At some point, the person may no longer be able to distort or deny the experience, which could lead to overwhelming feelings of threat and anxiety and disintegration of the self. For example, a child might struggle to maintain the illusion that things are fine between his parents despite their nightly battles. However, when his mother leaves without warning, the boy may not be able to handle the loss and may stop attending school and talking to others. In another example, a person might partition off parts of self that are unacceptable and exclude them from awareness. Second, a person might develop a rigidity of perception in areas where she or he has had to defend against perceiving reality. For example, a woman might have such a strong need to believe in the curative effects of a quack medicine for cancer that she does not listen to any disconfirming evidence, thus resulting in her not seeking proven strategies for treating her cancer. Third, the real self can become incongruent with the ideal self, suggesting a discrepancy between who one is and who one wishes to be. A woman might be average in intelligence but feel a need to be smart (particularly if she has internalized parental conditions of worth being based on high intelligence). If the real–ideal discrepancy is large, the person may feel dissatisfied and be maladjusted (e.g., depressed or anxious).

Reintegration

To overcome disintegration, rigidity, or discrepancies between real and ideal selves, a person must become aware of the distorted or denied experience. In other words, a person must allow the experience to occur and perceive the event accurately. The woman described above must acknowledge to herself that she is of average intelligence and accept and value herself for that rather than distort or deny the feelings. Rogers theorized that for reintegration to occur, the person must (a) reduce the conditions of worth and (b) increase positive self-regard through obtaining unconditional positive regard from another person. Conditions of worth lose their significance and ability to direct behavior when another person accepts the person as he or she is. In effect, individuals return to the OVP and begin to trust their inner self, thus becoming more open to experience and feelings.

A person can reintegrate without unconditional positive regard from another person if there is minimal threat to the self and the incongruity between self and experience is minor, but this is a relatively rare occurrence. Typically, individuals respond to years of having conditions of worth imposed on them by becoming increasingly defensive. Once developed, defenses are difficult to let go because the person anticipates being vulnerable and hurt again. In effect, defenses are very adaptive to help children cope, but fear and habit make them difficult to shed when they are no longer needed.

A helping relationship, then, is often crucial to assist individuals in overcoming their defenses and returning to trusting their OVP. A therapeutic helping relationship allows the individual's self-actualizing tendency to overcome the restrictions that were internalized in the conditions of worth. In a helping relationship, the helper attempts to enter the client's subjective world and understand the client's internal frame of reference. The helper also tries to provide an experience in which the client is accepted and cared for without conditions of worth. This helping relationship does not necessarily need to be from a professional helper and, in fact, many people seek healing relationships from supportive people in their environment (e.g., a couple experiencing communication difficulties may speak to their rabbi, minister, or priest). A person who has received training in helping skills, however, is more likely than an untrained person to be able to provide the important conditions to facilitate change.

Rogers believed that the helping relationship, in and of itself, produces growth in the client. He said, "I launch myself into the therapeutic relationship having a hypothesis, or a faith, that my liking, my confidence, and my understanding of the other person's inner world, will lead to a significant process of becoming" (Rogers, 1951, p. 267). Rogerian helpers believe that most clients benefit greatly from being listened to, understood, and accepted. The power of this kind of relationship is highly therapeutic and constructive. In the Rogerian approach to helping, the helper enters the therapeutic relationship with the facilitative attitudes of congruence (genuineness), unconditional positive regard, and empathy. Rogers (1957) postulated six conditions that he considered to be necessary and sufficient for change to occur.

1. The client and helper must be in psychological contact. A therapeutic relationship or emotional connection between the helper and client is essential.

2. The client must be in a state of incongruence. There must be a discrepancy between self and experience that leads the client to feel vulnerable or anxious. If a client feels no anxiety, she or he is unlikely to be motivated enough to engage in the helping process.

3. The helper must be congruent (genuine) or integrated in the relationship. The helper must be open to her or his own experiences and be genuinely available to the client. The helper cannot be phony in the helping relationship.

4. The helper must feel unconditional positive regard for the client. The helper values all feelings (although not necessarily all behaviors) and places no judgment on the feelings. Essentially, a helper is trying to understand a client's feelings and experience but is not trying to judge whether the person "should" or "should not" have the feelings or whether the feelings are "right" or "wrong."

5. The helper must experience empathy for the client. The helper tries to immerse herself or himself in the client's feeling world and understand the client's inner experiences. The understanding comes out of the helper's experiencing of the client's feelings, using the helper's inner processes as a referent. Hence, the helper not only experiences the client's feelings but also experiences having his or her own reactions to the client's feelings and is thus able to go beyond the words to understanding the client's implicit feelings (Meador & Rogers, 1973). The helper tries to feel "as if" she or he were the client and temporarily living in the client's life, without ever losing the awareness that they are separate individuals. The helper tries to sense and uncover feelings of which the client is unaware because they are too threatening. Rogers emphasized that empathy is not

passive but requires thinking, sensitivity, and understanding; he described *empathy* as follows:

> It means entering the private perceptual world of the other and becoming thoroughly at home in it. It involves being sensitive, moment by moment, to the changing felt meanings which flow in this other person, to the fear or rage or tenderness or confusion or whatever that he or she is experiencing. It means temporarily living in the other's life, moving about in it delicately without making judgments. (1980, p. 142)

We can distinguish empathy from sympathy, in which the helper feels pity for the client and often acts from a one-up power position rather than as an equal. We can also distinguish empathy from emotional contagion, in which a helper feels the same feelings as the client (e.g., becomes just as depressed as the client) and cannot maintain objectivity. Empathy involves a deep understanding of the client's feelings.

6. The client must experience the helper's congruence, unconditional positive regard, and empathy. If the client does not experience the facilitative conditions, for all practical purposes they do not exist for the client and the sessions are not likely to be helpful.

In summary, Rogers speculated that if helpers can accept clients, clients can come to accept themselves. When clients accept themselves, they can allow themselves to experience their real feelings and accept that the feelings come from themselves. Hence, the OVP is unblocked, and the person becomes open to his or her experiences. The client can begin to experience love, lust, hatred, jealousy, competitiveness, anger, pride, and other feelings. Of course, they may need assistance in learning how to deal with these feelings and experiences, many of which may be new to them. It is important to note, however, that acceptance of feelings is distinct from decisions about what to do about the feelings. For Rogers, the most important thing is accepting the feelings and coming to accept one's self.

How Rogers's Theory Relates to the Three-Stage Helping Model

Rogers's theory forms the foundation for the exploration stage and informs the insight and action stages. We agree with Rogers that helpers should maintain an empathic client-centered stance of trying to understand the client's experience as completely as possible with as little judgment as possible and with as few prior assumptions as possible. Empathy and a therapeutic relationship can be very effective in helping clients begin to accept themselves and trust their experiences.

For some people, being understood and encouraged to express their feelings is curative in and of itself and leads to change. Others, however, need to be assisted in moving toward insight and action. Hence, in addition to maintaining the facilitative conditions, helpers also need to facilitate insight and action. Additional theories (psychoanalytic, cognitive–behavioral) provide the foundation needed to assist clients in moving beyond exploration of thoughts and feelings; these are described in later chapters.

Furthermore, we do not completely agree with Rogers that people are inherently good and striving for self-actualization. There seems to us to be minimal evidence for these postulates. As discussed in chapter 2, we believe that people are neither good nor bad at birth and develop depending on the environment and early experiences. However, this difference in beliefs about human nature is not relevant to our firm belief in the need and value of the facilitative conditions in establishing the therapeutic relationship and helping clients explore their concerns.

GOALS FOR THE EXPLORATION STAGE

The goals for the exploration stage are related to establishing a relationship of trust: helping clients tell their stories, facilitating the expression of emotion and emotional arousal, and learning about clients. The sections that follow define these goals in more detail.

Establishing Rapport and Developing a Therapeutic Relationship

Helpers establish rapport (i.e., an atmosphere of understanding and respect) with their clients so that clients feel safe to explore. Rapport sets the stage for the development of the therapeutic relationship, which is very important in helping. Clients are more likely to reveal themselves when they believe that they have a caring, therapeutic relationship with their helpers. Clients generally need to feel safe, supported, respected, cared for, valued, prized, accepted as individuals, listened to, and heard. People often do not fully listen to others, so it is a gift to clients for helpers to listen attentively to what they say without rushing to say something next (such as telling a competing story, as friends often do). If friends and relatives would listen as carefully as we hope helpers learn to do in the exploration stage, communication would be greatly improved and we would live in greater harmony in the world.

During this stage, helpers are trying to understand their clients from the client's frame of reference. Helpers attempt to "walk a mile in the client's shoes" and view the world through the client's eyes. They try to understand the client's thoughts and feelings without imposing their thoughts or values on clients. They attempt not to judge clients and figure out if they are "right" or "blameworthy" but instead try to understand how clients came to be the way they are and how it feels to be who they are. Helpers try to align or attune themselves (i.e., try to feel what it is like to be the client) with clients so that they can understand the client's feelings.

We believe that if we can move clients back to an awareness of their inner experiencing, they can begin to trust themselves and then to heal themselves. We agree with Rogers (1957) that clients typically need to feel accepted and prized by others before they can begin to accept and value themselves. To do this, helpers need to accept clients as they are as much as possible and provide them with the facilitative conditions of empathy, unconditional positive regard, and genuineness. As mentioned earlier, *empathy* refers to understanding another person and feeling "as if" you are the other person (i.e., trying to put yourself in their place even though you are not that person and cannot ever understand them completely). *Unconditional positive regard* refers to accepting and appreciating another person without judgment. *Genuineness* (or what has also been termed *congruence*) refers to the helpers being open to their own experiences and being genuinely available to clients rather than being phony or inauthentic.

Much of establishing a relationship is not a matter of doing something as much as it is an attitude of acceptance, empathy, and respect. Helpers need to want to listen and try to understand clients without judging them. Although we stress that skills are not the same as the therapeutic attitude in establishing a relationship, we believe that using the appropriate skills places helpers in the framework whereby they are more likely to have a therapeutic attitude.

Helpers should not think that they can simply establish a relationship at one point in time and then ignore the relationship thereafter. They need to be aware of the relationship throughout the helping process. There is never a time in helping when the relationship does not matter. At any time throughout the process, the relationship can, and often does, rupture and need repair (see Hill, Nutt-Williams, Heaton, Thompson, & Rhodes, 1996; Petersen, Friedman, Geshmay, & Hill, 1998; Rhodes, Hill, Thompson, & Elliott, 1994; and Safran & Muran, 1996). Hence, helpers must always be aware of the relationship.

Beginning helpers often worry about the consequences of not liking their clients or of not establishing a rapport with their clients. For example, many beginning helpers think that they could never work with rapists or child abusers because they would be repulsed and horrified. However, we need to remind readers that the goal of being a helper is not to make friends. Helpers do not need to "like" clients in the same way that you like or choose to spend time with close friends. Rather, helpers have a responsibility to understand and assist clients and to feel compassion and caring for the human beings underneath the exterior presentations. One helper we know said that one of her greatest challenges was working with women in prison. Initially, hearing about the crimes committed by the women made it difficult for her to empathize and respect the women. However, after getting to know the women and their life circumstances, it became clear that these women had similar feelings to hers. Although actions are not universal, feelings are. Even though helpers may not have experienced the same life events as their clients, they have surely experienced many of the same emotions and, thus, can empathize with their feelings even if they disagree with their behaviors.

Helping Clients Tell Their Stories

Clients need a chance to talk about their problems. It often helps to talk out loud about what is going on inside. All too often people just continue on with their ordinary routines without exploring their problems in any depth. Frank and Frank (1991) noted that a person once said so aptly, "How can I know what I think until I have heard what I have to say?" (p. 200). Hence, being given a forum to express one's thoughts allows one to hear and think about the content of what one is saying. Clients need to know what they are thinking and have a chance to express these thoughts out loud.

Tapping Into Emotions and Facilitating
Emotional Arousal

Earlier we discussed the importance of emotions in Rogers's theory and suggested that emotions reflect a core part of human experience. Emotions are a key element in the helping process because they represent fundamental experiencing and are connected integrally to cognitions and behavior. In fact, mental health could be defined as allowing oneself to have a whole range of feelings and expressing these feelings in an appropriate manner.

One major goal of the exploration stage is for helpers to assist clients in experiencing their feelings about their presenting problems. Many clients learned as children to suppress their feelings. They have had to distort or deny their actual feelings to survive in the world and to gain approval from parents or other significant persons. Hence, many clients simply are not aware of their feelings and are distant from their inner experiencing. For example, if clients cannot allow themselves to feel hurt, they limit their range of emotions and stifle their hurt feelings. They might feel hollow or empty inside. One client stated that she felt that her "inner core was rotten." Clients might not know who they are and, hence, might rely on other people to tell them how they feel. In significant relationships, they might ignore their feelings of hurt and instead feel distant without knowing why.

Because the goal of this stage is to facilitate exploration of the client's experience, the actual content of what the client says is often not as important as the person's feelings about the topic. Sometimes helpers need to listen to the "music" (i.e., the underlying message) rather than to the words. Hence, having clients disclose all the details about their experiences is not as important as facilitating the experiencing of their feelings.

In addition, we want clients to focus on what they are feeling immediately in the present moment rather than telling stories about the past with minimal emotional involvement. The goal of sessions is not for clients to entertain helpers but rather for clients to experience immediate feelings. Experiencing feelings often is not very comfortable, so clients may want to run away and avoid their feelings. Through support and encouragement by helpers, clients often are able to tolerate the anxiety and discomfort of exploring their immediate feelings. For example, one client spent much of the session "catching the helper up" on events that occurred during the week. The helper gently challenged the client and urged him to explore his feelings in the present regarding these past events (e.g., "How do you feel right now about the event?"). The client accepted this invitation and the sessions became more intense and productive than previously.

Helpers sometimes need to be assertive and ask about other aspects of issues that clients are not discussing. For example, clients might need to be invited to talk about difficult feelings such as shame or being depressed or suicidal. In friendships, we often do not probe beyond what our friends choose to reveal because we feel that would be overstepping implicit boundaries. However, in helping relationships, helpers need to encourage clients to explore painful feelings that are hard to express. Some clients assume that helpers ask about the important things and do not reveal certain feelings unless helpers inquire, so helpers need to ask about personal and sometimes uncomfortable issues. On the other hand, helpers need to respect the rights of clients not to answer any questions or to go deeper than they choose. Thus, helpers walk a fine line between inviting clients to disclose but not forcing them into unwanted disclosure.

In addition, emotional arousal seems to be necessary for change to occur (Frank & Frank, 1991). Without emotional arousal, clients typically are not involved in the helping process and are not motivated to change. Many times, people deny or defend against their feelings because they do not want to deal with the overwhelming or painful nature of their feelings. In contrast, when we have strong emotional arousal (e.g., fury, despair), we are most aware of our feelings and more likely to be open to changing. Because emotional arousal is important in terms of setting the stage for change to occur, helpers can assist clients in becoming aware of and able to experience their emotions.

Learning About Clients

The exploration stage also enables helpers to learn about their clients. When a client first comes to a session, the helper has no way of knowing how to help that particular person. Helpers cannot assume that they know anything about particular clients or their problems, even if (or perhaps especially if) helpers have similar problems. In fact, encouraging an individual client to explore often requires a substantial amount of time because most people and problems are quite complex. In addition, because our goal is to help clients come to their own conclusions and decisions, helpers need to listen carefully to what clients say and how they feel before constructing an action plan to help them solve their problems.

In learning about clients, helpers must follow the lead that clients provide. Helpers can be prepared in general by knowing the helping skills, but then they have to pay attention to needs of individual clients. A parallel example is having a baby. Expectant parents can read lots of books about babies and generally be prepared for having a child, but they really learn parenting skills by attending to their own infant. Similarly, helpers really learn how to help each individual client by attending to that person's unique style and needs.

When helpers encounter client resistance in this stage, it sometimes occurs because clients are not motivated to participate in a helping relationship. However, sometimes helpers have not done a good enough job of facilitating clients in exploring their concerns. Helpers may not be using the skills appropriately for particular clients and may not have assessed the needs adequately. When problems arise, helpers need to look both at themselves and at clients to determine the origin of the difficulties.

DIFFICULTIES HELPERS EXPERIENCE IN THE EXPLORATION STAGE

In our experience, beginning helpers typically face several obstacles in trying to implement the exploration stage. If helpers are aware of these obstacles ahead of time, they can be prepared to cope when difficulties inevitably arise.

Inadequate Attending and Listening

Several factors might interfere with helpers being able to attend and listen adequately to their clients. Many helpers get distracted from listening because they get involved in their own thoughts or they think about what they are going to say next. In addition, helpers sometimes judge the merits of what clients are saying rather than listening to understand them. One type of judgment that is particularly hard to avoid is evaluating clients using one's own cultural standards. For example, a European American, middle-class, female helper might have difficulty listening to and understanding an upper-class African American man or a very poor Asian woman. Sympathy can be another impediment to listening to clients because helpers sometimes become so involved and feel so badly for clients that they cannot maintain objectivity; they try to "rescue" clients instead of attending to feelings.

Asking Too Many Closed Questions

Beginning helpers often ask too many closed questions because they feel that they need to gather all the details of the problem. Many helpers think that the helping process is similar to a medical model in which they should collect a lot of information to diagnose the problem and provide a solution for the client. However, we believe that the helper's task is to aid clients in coming to their own solutions, so we have less need for knowing all the details of the problem. Instead, such skills as facilitating exploration of thoughts and feelings are the important ones for helping clients explore before they can arrive at solutions.

Some helpers ask too many questions simply because they do not have anything better to say. These helpers do not necessarily want to hear the answers to their questions; they just want to fill the time or satisfy their curiosity. When asking questions, it is important to clarify for whom the question is being asked (i.e., to assist the client or to fulfill the helper's need).

Talking Too Much

Some helpers talk too much in helping sessions. They might talk because they are anxious, because they want to impress clients, or because they like to talk in general. However, if helpers are talking, clients cannot talk and, hence, cannot explore their concerns. In our research, we have found that clients generally talk about 60–70% of the time (Hill, 1978; Hill et al., 1983). In contrast, in nonhelping situations both people in an interaction ideally talk about 50% of the time. It can be difficult for helpers to adjust to listening rather than talking.

Giving Too Much (or Premature) Advice

Beginning helpers often rush into giving advice. They feel pressured to provide answers, fix problems, rescue clients, or have perfect solutions. Many clients and beginning helpers are under the misguided notion that helpers have a responsibility of providing solutions after hearing the facts about the problem. However, giving clients answers or solutions is often detrimental, because clients have not come to the solutions on their own and, therefore, cannot own them. Furthermore, when given answers, clients do not learn how to solve their future problems without depending on other people. Clients most often need a sounding board or someone to listen to them think through their problem or to help them figure out how to solve their problems rather than someone telling them what to do. It is critical to realize that the need to provide answers often originates in the helper's insecurity and desire to help, which are normal feelings at the start of learning helping skills.

We should note, on the other hand, that some clients do want answers from helpers. However, we do not believe that it is typically beneficial for helpers to provide answers prior to helping clients explore and come to insight (except in major crises such as suicidal or homicidal threat or threat of psychological breakdown). Rather, helpers need to teach clients the benefits of coming to their own solutions on the basis of a thorough exploration of their problems, feelings, and situation. If clients still want someone to give them advice, helpers can discuss this as an issue or refer them to other types of helpers.

Being "Buddies"

Sometimes beginning helpers err by acting like "buddies" with clients instead of being helpers. The role of helper often necessitates providing a connected yet clearly defined relationship to maintain objectivity and offer maximum assistance. Being a buddy can be limiting because helpers might choose interventions that would make clients like them rather than help clients change. For example, Sam, a beginning helper, began every session by talking with his client, Tom, about recent sporting events. Tom responded enthusiastically to talking about sports but was reluctant to discuss more personal issues. Sam avoided changing the topic because he wanted to maintain a friendly connection with Tom. Unfortunately, because of his desire to be buddies, Sam was not able to help Tom explore his personal issues.

Not Allowing for Silence

One of the most daunting tasks for beginning helpers is to cope with silence. Trainees often rush to fill voids in sessions, fearing that clients are bored, anxious, critical, or stuck. Rushing to fill voids often results in saying things that are superficial and not very helpful.

Helpers should try to understand their fears about silence in sessions. Helpers can ask themselves what concerns they have (e.g., not appearing competent, not helping the client) and work on these fears outside of sessions rather than rushing to fill the silence in sessions. We discuss the therapeutic use of silence further in chapter 6.

Prematurely Self-Disclosing

One of the biggest problems that we have observed in beginning helpers is the urge to self-disclose. Because client issues are often similar to their own issues, beginning helpers want to share their experiences with their clients. It seems natural to disclose and tell one's stories, as one would with friends. Helpers also sometimes want help for themselves and are distracted by their own problems while listening to clients. It is sometimes difficult to listen to someone else's issues when one is going through the same thing. For example, beginning helpers in their early 20s often have difficulty listening to students their own age talk about identity issues, relationship difficulties, problems with parents, and plans for the future because these are issues with which the helpers are dealing. Beginning helpers who are older might have difficulty listening to problems about parenting and aging. Adopting the professional identity of a helper who listens but does not disclose much is often a major and challenging shift in perspective for beginning helpers. However, because inappropriate self-disclosure can be very detrimental and hinder the therapeutic relationship, helpers need to learn to restrain themselves.

Discouraging Intense Expression of Affect

Beginning helpers sometimes feel awkward when clients express intense affect, such as despair, intense sadness, or strong anger (especially if the anger is directed toward the helper). Sometimes helpers are uncomfortable with negative feelings because they do not allow themselves to feel their own negative feelings. They may deny or defend against their internal "demons." For these helpers, hearing a client's negative feelings can be very stressful. Sometimes helpers feel a need to make clients feel better immediately because they do not want their clients to suffer. They mistakenly think that if clients do not talk about the feelings, the feelings go away. They also might feel afraid to have clients get into the negative feelings because they feel inadequate to help them. Guilty feelings might emerge for helpers if their interventions result in clients crying. These helpers err on the side of keeping things "light" or minimizing feelings so that they do not have to face "tough" situations where they feel helpless. Recently, an attractive adolescent client told her helper that she felt totally fat and ugly. She expressed disgust with her body and astonishment that anyone would want to be around her. A helper who is uncomfortable with intense negative feelings might give the socially sanctioned response of reassuring this client that she is attractive and suggesting that her feelings are not accurate. Ironically, this response would negate the client's feelings and could make the client feel worse because she would feel misunderstood.

Now might be a good time to ask yourself how you feel about overt expressions of affect. What do you instinctively want to do when someone begins to sob uncontrollably? Most of us feel an urge to get the person to stop crying and to feel better. Helpers should be extra sensitive to their tendencies to reduce the expression of intense emotions. Often, the expression of emotion is extremely therapeutic, especially in the presence of a supportive helper. The skills that we discuss in the exploration stage can be particularly valuable for giving helpers tools for allowing clients to stay in moments of intense emotions.

Dealing Inadequately With Suicidal Feelings

As helpers who have provided crisis counseling know, dealing with someone who is contemplating suicide can be very challenging. Beginning helpers often fear that asking about suicidal feelings encourages clients to think about or commit suicide. In fact, the opposite is typically true—by talking about suicidal feelings, clients can bring their worst fears into the open. Clients often appreciate that helpers view their problems as serious. If helpers are not willing to discuss suicidal feelings, clients often feel even more alone, ashamed, strange, or "crazy." Perhaps the worst thing to do is to diminish or negate the feelings (e.g., "You'll feel better tomorrow"), point out positive aspects of their lives (e.g., "You have so much to live for"), or give false reassurance (e.g., "Everything will be okay"). These responses often result in clients not only feeling desperate because they cannot get help, but also feeling hopeless that they are beyond help, misunderstood, and thinking that their suicidal feelings are unacceptable. Dealing with suicidal feelings is discussed further in chapter 11.

Dissociating and Panicking

Sometimes beginning helpers become so anxious about their performance that they feel that they are outside their bodies observing themselves in the helping role instead of being fully present and interactive in the helping session. At the worst, these helpers become completely frozen and cannot say anything. These dissociative experiences can feel frightening to helpers, who then panic and tell themselves that they can never be good helpers. In fact, anxiety is often more of a problem than lack of skills. In the next section, we offer ways to manage anxiety.

STRATEGIES FOR OVERCOMING THE DIFFICULTIES AND MANAGING ANXIETY

To overcome a lack of skills, helpers can learn and practice the helping skills that we teach throughout this book. We like to compare the skills to tools in a toolbox; helpers learn about the different tools available for different tasks. Some tools work better than other tools for some helpers and some clients. It is important for helpers to have many tools (e.g., helping skills and methods for managing anxiety) in their toolboxes so that they have a lot of options to help clients and manage their own anxiety in sessions.

To manage anxiety, we offer several ideas in this section. We hope all helpers find some strategies that they can use.

Deep Breathing

One way that helpers can manage anxiety is to breathe deeply from the diaphragm rather than taking short breaths from high in the chest. To determine if your breathing is from the diaphragm, put your hand over your stomach. When you breathe, you should feel your hand move in and out. Deep breathing serves several functions. First, it allows helpers to relax. Before saying anything, helpers can take several deep breaths. When the diaphragm is relaxed, it is harder to be anxious physiologically. Second, taking a deep breath gives helpers a moment to think about what they want to say. Helpers can take time to focus their energy and think of responses instead of being distracted by thinking about what to say in the next intervention. Third, it gives clients a chance to think and consider whether they have anything else to say. Sometimes helpers interrupt too quickly when clients could keep exploring productively. Because the goal is exploration, helpers do not need to say anything if clients are working productively.

Focus on the Client

All too often, beginning helpers are so concerned with their own behavior that they cannot listen attentively to clients. By shifting focus and being more concerned with the client than with themselves, helpers can listen more to clients (Williams, Judge, Hill, & Hoffman, 1997). The goal is for helpers to facilitate clients in exploring feelings rather than for helpers to show off how much they understand clients. By focusing on the client and attempting to immerse onself in the client's world, many beginning helpers are able to lessen their anxiety.

Positive Self-Talk

We all talk to ourselves as we do things. We say things like, "I can do this" or "I think I am going to panic." Some people have called this the "inner game" because it occurs beneath the surface. Positive self-talk has a positive influence on performance in helping sessions, whereas negative self-talk has a negative influence on performance (see Nutt-Williams & Hill, 1996), so helpers need to be attentive to what they are saying to themselves. Helpers can practice using positive self-talk before sessions so that they have positive sentences ready to use to coach themselves in sessions. Alternatively, helpers can write down some positive self-statements (e.g., "I know the skills," "I am competent") on index cards and glance at them before or during practice sessions.

Viewing Models

Watching skilled helpers in helping sessions is an excellent way to observe the skills being done appropriately. The skills come alive when one can see them demonstrated by other people. Although reading about theories and skills is important, imagining how they come across is often hard unless models are available. Bandura (1969) has shown the effectiveness of watching a model as one step in the learning process. We recommend watching many different helpers to illustrate that there are many ways and styles of helping. Viewing several models also helps to reduce the tendency to copy one powerful style and, hence, not develop one's own style. Live sessions or videotapes are excellent media for observing helping sessions.

Imagery

In sports psychology, we know that when athletes have the requisite skills, practice through imagery can be a beneficial addition to actual practice (Suinn, 1988). Similarly, in helping situations, helpers can imagine themselves using appropriate attending behaviors and helping skills in different situations. For example, a beginning helper who feels uncomfortable with silence might close her eyes and visualize herself in a session with a quiet client. She might imagine herself sitting comfortably with the client and allowing the silence to occur. She might also visualize breaking the silence after a period of time by asking how the client is feeling.

Role-Play

Prior to sessions with clients, helpers can role-play using the specific helping skills. Helpers can also role-play the mechanics of sessions, such as starting and stopping the session, responding to silence, and dealing with anger directed toward the helper. By doing role-plays with supportive partners (e.g., classmates), helpers are more likely to learn the skills at a comfortable pace.

Practice

Perhaps the main method for managing anxiety is practice. The more that helpers practice and pay attention to what they do well and how they can improve, the better and more comfortable they are likely to become in helping sessions. Throughout the book, we provide exercises that helpers can use to gain practice in the helping skills. We encourage helpers to participate in many practice sessions with sympathetic and helpful volunteer clients.

Personal Psychotherapy

We very much encourage helpers to become involved in personal psychotherapy for themselves. Therapy can enable helpers to recognize personal issues that could interfere with their ability to help because they are preoccupied with themselves and their problems. Furthermore, therapy can also enable helpers to work on their own growth and self-understanding. An occupational hazard of being a helper is that the helping process stirs up personal issues that might otherwise lay dormant. For example, if a client talks about problems with alcoholism and the helper has not resolved similar problems, it might be difficult for the helper to be detached enough to attend to the client's pain instead of focusing on his or her own pain. Many helpers become interested in being helpers because of their interest in understanding themselves. Although helpers learn a great deal about themselves through the process of being helpers, having their own personal therapy gives them an outlet for working on themselves in an appropriate setting rather than taking time away from clients who have come for help and deserve full attention.

Being in therapy as a client can also teach helpers about the process of helping. Being a client enables helpers to learn what it is like to be on the receiving end of helping skills, to see what is and is not helpful, and to experience how difficult it is to open up and reveal painful material about oneself. Receiving help when one is in pain is the most powerful learning experience of the potential of the therapeutic process for helping others. Being in therapy also provides a model for helpers about how they would (or would not) want to be in sessions with clients. Thus, the firsthand experience of what it is like to be on the receiving end of helping is invaluable.

It is troublesome when helpers-in-need refuse to seek help themselves but are willing to be helpers for others. We worry about the motivations of such persons for wanting to be helpers. For example, some people want to be helpers to feel superior to other people who are worse off and who have problems (see Bugental, 1965). Helpers who have an attitude that helping is only for weak or defective people may inadvertently communicate that attitude and cause clients to feel ashamed for seeking help.

CONCLUDING COMMENTS

The exploration stage is important because it facilitates the development of the relationship, gives clients a chance to explore their concerns and immerse themselves in their immediate experiencing, and provides helpers with an opportunity to learn about the client's presenting issues and assess the client's appropriateness for what the helper can offer. For Rogerians, the exploration stage is all that is needed for helping. Rogerians believe that the facilitative attitudes of empathy, unconditional positive regard, and genuineness allow clients to begin to accept themselves, which releases the inner experiencing and unblocks the potential for self-actualization. Indeed, some clients need only a listening ear to solve their problems. Hence, we believe that helpers should spend a lot of time in the exploration stage because it can be helpful by itself. However, because many clients cannot make progress on their own with exploration alone, insight and action are usually necessary to help them change. In this case, exploration sets the stage for everything else that follows.

An important caveat throughout the exploration stage (and the rest of the helping process) is that there are no absolute "right" interventions to use. Although we can provide general guidelines, we cannot provide a cookbook to tell helpers exactly what to do in different circumstances. Individual clients require different things from helpers. It is up to helpers to determine which interventions are productive and which are not useful by paying attention to the individual client's reactions and responses.

In chapters 6 through 11, we discuss skills that helpers can use to facilitate client exploration (e.g., attending and listening, restatement, open question, reflection of feelings, closed question, approval and reassurance, self-disclosure for exploration, and information about the helping process).

▬▬▬ **What Do You Think?**

- How well do the tasks of the exploration stage fit your personal style?
- What techniques do you think are needed to establish a therapeutic relationship?

Comment on whether you think establishing a relationship is more a matter of attitudes or techniques.

- Describe the challenges that you would face in developing a relationship with someone you believe has done awful and despicable things (e.g., rape, murder).
- What is the optimal level of advice and self-disclosure in helping interactions?
- Check all of the obstacles that you are likely to face in your development as a helper:

  ____ inadequate attending and listening

  ____ asking too many closed questions

  ____ talking too much

  ____ giving too much or premature advice

  ____ being "buddies"

  ____ not allowing silence

  ____ prematurely self-disclosing

  ____ discouraging intense expression of affect

  ____ difficulty dealing with suicidal feelings

  ____ dissociating and panicking.

- Identify all of the strategies that could help you cope with obstacles that arise when you are a helper:

  ____ deep breathing

  ____ focus on the client

  ____ positive self-talk

  ____ viewing models

  ____ imagery

  ____ role-playing

  ____ practice

  ____ personal psychotherapy.

6 Attending and Listening

> The one who listens is the one who understands.
>
> *(African [Jabo] proverb)*

The students in one class prearranged to manipulate their professor's behavior through non-verbal responding. Whenever the professor moved to the right, they looked up, paid rapt attention, and smiled encouragingly. Whenever the professor moved to the left, they looked down, rustled their papers, coughed, and whispered. The professor soon had moved to the right so much, he fell off the stage! This example illustrates the power of attending skills.

ATTENDING AND listening are basic skills that helpers use throughout the entire helping process to enable clients to feel safe and to explore their thoughts and feelings. *Attending* refers to helpers orienting themselves physically toward clients. *Listening* refers specifically to capturing and understanding the messages that clients communicate, either verbally or nonverbally, clearly or vaguely (Egan, 1994). As we examine the individual helping skills in subsequent chapters, we discuss the product of our listening in terms of what we communicate to clients, but at this point we emphasize the general attitude of listening carefully to hear what clients are communicating.

The goal of attending in helping sessions is for helpers to communicate to clients that they are paying attention to them and to facilitate clients in talking openly and exploring their thoughts and feelings. In effect, attending lays the foundation for the implementation of all the other helping interventions. Clients feel that they are valued and worth being listened to when helpers attend to them. In addition, attending can encourage clients to verbalize ideas and feelings because they feel that helpers want to hear what they have to say. Furthermore, attending behaviors can reinforce appropriate client behavior.

Attending is communicated mostly through nonverbal behaviors, which we cover in the next section of this chapter. Through our nonverbal behaviors, we convey what we wish to express and also what we do not intend to express. For example, a helper may try hard to be empathic and look very concerned but may feel irritated and bored with the client. This boredom might leak out through excessive foot tapping or stifled yawns. Helpers need to be aware of how they use nonverbal behaviors in their helping interactions.

Although attending can orient helpers toward clients and position them so that they can listen, listening goes beyond just physically attending to clients. Listening involves trying to hear and understand what clients are communicating. Reik (1948) talked about listening with a third ear, by which he meant listening carefully not only to what clients say overtly but to what they really mean, that is, putting the verbal and nonverbal messages together and hearing what the client is feeling.

Listening provides the raw material from which helpers develop their verbal and nonverbal interventions, but listening should not be confused with the ability to deliver these interventions. Helpers could listen without being able to produce a reflection of feelings, but they could not produce a good reflection of feeling without first having listened. Likewise, the attending behaviors set the stage for allowing helpers to listen, but attending does not necessarily ensure listening. Helpers could attend physically but not be listening (e.g., they could be thinking about dinner that night and not hear what clients are saying). Thus, from watching sessions, you could not actually tell if helpers were listening, although you could infer that they were listening if they were able to produce statements that reflected that they heard the client. The components of attending and listening are presented in Exhibit 6.1.

CULTURAL RULES FOR ATTENDING AND LISTENING

Each culture develops rules for nonverbal communication. An example of such a cultural rule is the pattern of greeting that might take no more than a third of a second. This pattern involves looking at the other person, smiling, lifting the eyebrows, and nodding the head. These behaviors seem to act as a releasor in that they elicit the same response from another person. Rules for nonverbal behaviors are typically outside of conscious awareness. In other words, most people probably could not articulate the nonverbal rules in their own culture. We learn these rules as young children through social interactions and example rather than by explicit verbal instruction.

The rules for nonverbal behavior vary by culture. Hence, nonverbal behavior that is appropriate in one culture might not be appropriate in another culture. When interacting with someone from another culture, one might feel very uncomfortable because the person does not interact in the same way as oneself. A whole industry has arisen around teaching diplomats and travelers about the nonverbal rules of other cultures. For example, in Asia, it is important for people not to praise themselves and instead to appear humble. So if an American started to boast, this might not be received well.

If you are involved in interpersonal interactions in which your rules for nonverbal behaviors are not followed, you might feel intense discomfort. You might not be able to understand or articulate why you feel uncomfortable, but you know that something is not right. For example, if you are caught staring at someone, you might feel embarrassed because it is inappropriate in our culture to be caught staring at someone for too long. If someone stands too close to you and grabs your arm when you are talking, you might feel an urge to move away because the person has violated your personal space.

Helpers need to adapt their style to each client's nonverbal style rather than expect clients to adapt to them. Helpers can take their cues from the clients as to what makes them feel comfortable. For example, if a client acts nervous with too much eye contact, the helper might experiment with looking away and observe whether the client responds differently. In addition, helpers might ask clients for feedback about what feels comfortable or uncomfortable for them.

TYPES OF ATTENDING BEHAVIORS

Several areas of attending behaviors have been identified: eye contact, facial expressions, proxemics, paralanguage, and kinesics (bodily movement). We review these behaviors in general and then talk about their use in helping relationships.

Exhibit 6.1. Overview of Attending and Listening

Definition	*Attending* refers to orienting oneself physically toward the client. *Listening* refers to capturing and understanding the messages that clients communicate, either verbally or nonverbally, clearly or vaguely.

Types of attending behaviors	Eye contact
	Smiling
	Proxemics (distance)
	Paralanguage (the way things are said)
	    Nonlanguage sounds (e.g., sigh, laugh)
	    Nonwords (e.g., "er," "um," "ahem")
	    Pitch, intensity, and range of voice
	    Speech disturbances (e.g., incomplete sentences, slips of the tongue, stutters)
	    Acknowledgment (e.g., "mmhmm," "yeah")
	    Interruptions
	    Silence
	    Matching language style or using language that is similar in cultural and educational level
	Kinesics (communicating with body movements)
	    Arm movements
	    Leg movements
	    Head nods
	    Body posture (lean forward or backward)
	    Touching
	    Interactional synchrony or coordinated movement between people

Typical helper intentions	To support, to instill hope, to encourage catharsis, to reinforce change (see Appendix A)
Possible client reactions	Understood, hopeful, lacking direction (see Appendix D)
Desired client behaviors	Recounting, affective exploration, cognitive–behavioral exploration (see Appendix E)
Difficulties helpers experience in attending and listening	Being distracted by their internal thoughts and feelings (e.g., negative self-talk) Being insensitive to cultural differences in nonverbal behaviors Not noticing client reactions to verbal and nonverbal behaviors Using a formulaic attending stance rather than being natural and relaxed

Eye Contact

Eye contact is a key nonverbal behavior. Looking and gaze aversion are typically used to initiate and maintain communication. With a gaze, we can communicate intimacy, interest, submission, or dominance (Kleinke, 1986). Eyes are used to monitor speech, provide feedback, signal understanding, and regulate turn taking (Harper, Wiens, & Matarazzo, 1978). One could say that we meet people with our eyes or that "the eyes are the windows into the soul." In contrast, gaze avoidance or breaking eye contact often signals anxiety, discomfort, or a desire not to communicate with the other person.

The time spent in eye contact in interactions ranges from 28% to 70% (Kendon, 1967). Mutual gaze, however, is usually no more than 1 s. Dyads typically negotiate how much and when to look at each other, although this negotiation takes place at a nonverbal level and people are not usually consciously aware of the negotiation. Too little eye contact can make the recipient feel that the listener is not interested, whereas too much eye contact can make the recipient feel uncomfortable, intruded upon, dominated, controlled, and even devoured.

Norms for eye contact differ across cultures. In White middle-class North America, people tend to maintain eye contact while listening but look away when speaking; in African American culture, people typically look while speaking but look away when listening (LaFrance & Mayo, 1976). In some Native American groups, sustained eye contact is considered offensive and a sign of disrespect especially if done by the young to an older person (Brammer & MacDonald, 1996). Some cultural groups (certain American Indian, Inuit, or Aboriginal Australian groups) generally avoid eye contact, especially when talking about serious topics (Ivey, 1994).

Helpers need to observe clients for discomfort associated with eye contact. They also need to be aware of possible misinterpretations when someone from another culture uses eye contact differently than they do. Judgments should not be made automatically about the amount of eye contact. For example, if a European American helper greets an Asian client who does not make eye contact, the helper should not assume that the client suffers from guilt or low self-esteem, but should pay close attention to whether this nonverbal behavior has a different meaning in the client's culture.

Facial Expression

Darwin (1872) speculated that before prehistoric people had language, they communicated threats, greetings, and submission through facial expressions. He believed that this shared heritage explains why all humans express basic emotions through similar facial expressions. Darwin (1872) wrote

> the movements of expression in the face and body, whatever their origin may have been, are in themselves of much importance for our welfare. They serve as the first means of communication between the mother and her infant; she smiles approval, and thus encourages her child on the right path, or frowns disapproval .... The movements of expression give vividness and energy to our spoken words. They reveal the thoughts and intentions of others more truly than do words, which may be falsified .... These results follow partly from the intimate relation which exists between almost all the emotions and their outward manifestations. (p. 366)

The face is perhaps the most important body area for nonverbal communication because we communicate so much emotion and information through our facial expressions (Harper et al., 1978). Interestingly, more than 1,000 facial appearances have been identified (Ekman, Friesen, & Ellsworth, 1972). We pay a lot of attention to facial expressions because they give us clues about the meaning of the verbal message.

In Shakespeare's (1607/1980) *Macbeth*, Lady Macbeth says to her husband, "your face, my thane, is a book whereon men may read strange matters" (Act 1, Scene 5, p. 17).

Many of these facial expressions appear to have similar meanings to people all over the world. Ekman and Friesen (1984) showed photographs of facial expressions to people in different parts of the world and found that several facial expressions had the same meaning across cultures. Thus, around the world, people cry when they are distressed, shake their heads when defiant, and smile when happy. Even blind children who have never seen a face use the same facial expressions (Eibl-Eibesfeldt, 1971). In addition, research has supported that we read fear and anger mostly from the eyes and happiness mostly from the mouth (Kestenbaum, 1992).

Although different cultures share a universal facial language, they differ in how and how much they express emotion. For example, emotional displays are often intense and prolonged in Western cultures, whereas Asians display emotions of sympathy, respect, and shame but rarely display self-aggrandizing or negative emotions that might disrupt communal feelings (Markus & Kitayama, 1991; Matsumoto, Kudoh, Sherer, & Wallbott, 1988).

An important facial feature for helping is smiling. Although smiling makes a person look friendly in general and can encourage exploration, we caution helpers from smiling too much during helping sessions because smiling can be perceived as ingratiating or inappropriate when clients are talking about serious concerns. Helpers who smile excessively could be viewed as not being genuine or as mocking the depth of clients' problems.

Proxemics

Proxemics refer to how people use space in interactions. E. T. Hall (1968) described four distance zones for middle class Americans: intimate (0–18 inches), personal (1.5 to 4.0 ft), social (4–12 ft), and public (12 ft or more). If rules for prescribed distances are not followed, people can feel very uncomfortable, although they are not usually aware of what is making them feel uncomfortable. Hall noted that once these patterns for space are learned, they are maintained largely outside of conscious awareness. The personal to social distance typically is considered appropriate for seating arrangements in helping relationships, although individuals vary in the amount of distance that feels comfortable for them personally. Some helpers place the chairs close together, whereas others place the chairs far apart when they have control over the arrangements. We know of therapists who place a number of chairs in their offices and allow clients to choose where and how far away to sit from them.

Americans and British people generally prefer to be relatively distant from other people and rarely touch each other. In contrast, Hispanics and people from the Middle East generally prefer less distance. For example, Arabs and Israeli Jews often stand close, touch, talk loudly, and stare intently. Hence, helpers need to take cultural considerations into account rather than just reacting unconsciously to someone from another culture who uses different proxemic patterns. In addition, helpers need to be aware of within-culture differences. For example, a helper should not assume that all Hispanic clients want to be hugged at the beginning and end of each session just because Hispanic people often hug when greeting and leaving. Differences exist within cultures, and acculturation to the dominant culture may influence clients' comfort with physical closeness.

Paralanguage

Paralanguage refers to the way in which things are said that seems to reflect emotions. For example, a client who stutters, speaks softly, and has lots of hesitancies and silences while speaking is more likely to be anxious than another client who says the same verbal content without these nonverbal distractors. Paralanguage involves such behaviors as nonlanguage sounds (e.g., moans, yells, sighing, laughing, and crying), nonwords (e.g., "er," "ah," "ahem"), vocal style (i.e., pitch, intensity, and range of voice), and speech disturbances (e.g., incomplete sentences, slips of the tongue, stutters). For helping, the paralanguage behaviors that we focus on are minimal encouragers and acknowledgment, interruptions, silence, and matching language style.

Minimal Encouragers and Acknowledgment

Helpers encourage clients to keep talking through nonlanguage sounds, nonwords, and simple words such as "mmhmm," "yeah," and "wow." Helpers frequently use minimal encouragers and acknowledgment to communicate attentiveness, provide noninvasive support, monitor the flow of conversation, and encourage clients to keep talking. Minimal encouragers and acknowledgments are often used in conjunction with and serve the same purpose as head nods and other nonverbal attending behaviors. Helpers can use too few or too many minimal encouragers and acknowledgments. Too few can feel distancing, whereas too many can be distracting and annoying to the client. We suggest that helpers use minimal encouragers and acknowledgments occasionally at the ends of client sentences or speaking turns (i.e., everything a client says between two helper interventions). Interrupting a client to provide minimal encouragers can be distracting, so helpers should pay attention to the appropriate timing of this intervention.

Interruptions

In ordinary conversation, people often interrupt each other because they are impatient to speak. Another type of interruption is when people finish sentences for others. On the one hand, it can seem that the listener is so in tune with the speaker that he or she can intuit what the person is about to say and thus provide the right words. On the other hand, completing the sentence can indicate impatience with clients who speak slowly. If helpers say something other than what clients would have said when they complete sentences, clients can feel irritated because the helpers are not "in tune" enough to know what they were going to say. In general, it is probably best for helpers to "wait their turn" to speak and give clients plenty of opportunity to express themselves at their own pace. An exception to this general guideline is when clients talk nonstop about nontherapeutic topics and do not allow helpers a chance to speak. As we discuss further in chapter 11, helpers may need to interrupt in these instances to keep the focus of the helping situation on therapeutic issues. Clients also sometimes interrupt helpers in midsentence because they are so eager to speak, which can be good if the client is working productively but could also reflect a lack of attention on the part of the client to what the helper has to say (at what point the helper might need to examine whether she or he is talking too much).

Silence

A silence is a pause of at least 5 s that occurs after a client's statement, within a client's statement, or after a simple acceptance of the helper's statement. For example, after the client says something like, "I just feel so confused and angry and don't know what to say," the helper might pause to allow the client time to think more about the feelings. If the client pauses in the middle of saying something, the helper might let the client think without interrupting. If the client just responds minimally to something the helper has said, the helper might be silent to see if the client can think of something to say.

To say nothing is not the same as to do nothing. Helpers can be very attentive and supportive, and they can listen without saying anything. In fact, sometimes the most useful thing a helper can do is to say nothing. Silence can be useful to allow clients time to think through what they want to say without interruption. Some people pause for a long time between thoughts because they process things slowly and thoroughly. Helpers can give such clients a few seconds after speaking to see whether they have anything else to say, rather than interrupting them. Other clients may need time to cry before being able to talk again.

Silence can be useful when clients are in the middle of thinking through something and need some time to get in touch with their thoughts and feelings. At such times, silence is respectful because it allows clients space to think without feeling pressured to say anything. At other times silence is frightening for clients who feel isolated and out of touch with the helper or do not know how to express themselves. Hence, helpers have to assess what is going on for clients during the silence and determine at the moment whether it is better to continue the silence or break it (see also Ladany, Hill, Thompson, & O'Brien, 1999).

Silence is used by psychoanalytic therapists during long-term therapy to encourage free association (i.e., saying whatever comes to mind; see Basch, 1980). During free association, silence also can be helpful to raise the client's anxiety because clients do not receive feedback about what the helper wants or feels. Like a stimulus deprivation experiment, silence sometimes increases discomfort and forces clients to rely on their inner resources and to examine their thoughts, or as one therapist said, "to let clients stew in their juices." With silence, helpers do not rescue clients or take over for clients.

However, we do not advise using silence extensively until a therapeutic relationship has been firmly established, clients understand the process of helping, and clients have shown that they can benefit from increased anxiety (i.e., not until the middle stages of long-term therapy). When helpers use too much silence during initial sessions, clients often become anxious and worried about what the helper thinks. Silence is not typically helpful when clients are very anxious because they become even more anxious and uncomfortable. Clients can feel paralyzed when they do not know what helpers want from them, especially at the beginning of the helping experience.

Many beginning helpers are uncomfortable with silence. They do not know what to do and are often concerned about how clients might perceive them. We suggest that helpers breathe deeply, relax, and think about the client and what might be going on inside the client. In other words, helpers should try to establish an empathic connection with their clients during silence rather than focusing on themselves. If silences go on for a long time (i.e., more than a minute) or clients are obviously uncomfortable with them, however, helpers can break the silence and ask the client how she or he is feeling.

Matching Grammatical Style

Another way helpers communicate attending is through matching the grammatical style of their clients such as their language. Language must be appropriate to the cultural experience and educational level of clients. If a client says, "I ain't never gonna make it with chicks," the helper might say something like, "You're concerned about finding a girl-friend" rather than "Your inferiority complex prevents you from establishing relationships with appropriate love objects." We do not suggest that helpers compromise their integrity by using language that feels uncomfortable to them, but we do recommend that helpers modify their language styles to be closer to those of their clients. Each of us has a range of language within which we feel comfortable, and helpers need to find the place within that range to meet each client as much as possible. After all, the goal of helpers is to facilitate change rather than to add additional barriers to change.

Kinesics

Kinesics refers to the relationship of bodily movements, such as arm movements, leg movements, and head nods, to communication. Bodily movements can be catego-rized into several types, each of which has a different function (Ekman & Friesen, 1969). *Emblems* are a substitute for words (e.g., a wave is a universal greeting). *Illustrators* ac-company speech (e.g., we might show the size of a fish with our hands). *Regulators* (e.g., head nods, postural shifts) monitor the conversation flow. *Adaptors* are habitual acts that are often outside awareness and have no communicative purpose (e.g., head scratching, licking one's lips, playing with a pen). Emblems, illustrators, and regulators are impor-tant accompaniments to verbal messages, whereas adaptors can detract from the helper's effectiveness by turning the focus away from the client and onto the helper's inappropriate nonverbal behaviors. Too many adaptors or an inappropriate use of emblems, illustrators, or regulators is often a sign of "nonverbal leakage" (i.e., the person has a feeling that she or he does not want to communicate or is trying to hide but the feeling leaks out through nonverbal channels).

Bodily movements provide information that one often cannot obtain from either verbal content or facial expression. As Freud (1905/1953) so eloquently stated, "he that has eyes to see and ears to hear may convince himself that no mortal can keep a secret. If his lips are silent, he chatters with his fingertips, betrayal oozes out of him at every pore" (p. 94). Ekman and Friesen (1969) noted that leg and foot movements are the most likely sources of nonverbal leakage because they are less subject to conscious awareness and voluntary inhibition. The hands and face are the next best sources of clues for nonverbal leakage. Hence, if a helper sees that a client is repeatedly tapping his or her foot, the helper should consider what the client might be feeling.

Head Nods

The appropriate use of head nods can make clients feel that helpers are listening and following what they are saying. Indeed, verbal messages are sometimes not needed because helpers are communicating through head nods that they are "with" clients. As with other nonverbal behaviors, however, there is an optimal level of head nods. Too few head nods can make clients feel unattended too; too many can be distracting.

Body Posture

A body posture that is often recommended for helpers is to lean toward clients and maintain an open body posture with the arms and legs uncrossed (e.g., Egan, 1994). This leaning and open body posture often effectively conveys that the helper is paying attention, although helpers can sometimes appear rigid if they stay in this position too long.

Touching

Touching can be a natural inclination when helpers want to indicate support to their clients. Montagu (1971) has noted that touch is a natural physical need and that some people hunger for touch because they do not receive enough physical contact. In some nursing homes, pets are popular because they provide people who feel isolated from society with important physical touch and acceptance. Unfortunately, Highlen and Hill (1984) reported that the few studies that have been conducted on touching in therapy were inconclusive. Some studies have shown positive effects of touching, whereas others have found no effects. Touch can have positive effects on clients in making them feel understood and involved in a human relationship (Hunter & Struve, 1998), but it can have negative effects if clients feel invaded. We recommend that beginning helpers refrain from any type of touching because of the possible misunderstandings about the meanings of the touch and because of the ethical issues associated with touching clients (see chapter 4).

Interactional Synchrony

Another interesting finding in the nonverbal research involves interactional synchrony, which involves coordinated movement between people (Bernieri & Rosenthal, 1991; Cappella, 1981). Synchrony may be similarity of movements, such as both people crossing their legs at the same time, or it can involve both people talking at the same tempo. You might notice that when you are intensely engaged in a conversation, you shift arms and legs at the same time or have the same body position as the person with whom you are communicating. As Condon and Ogston (1966) noted, "the body of the listener dances in rhythm with that of the speaker" (p. 339). In fact, a good metaphor is of the helper and client dancing, with the helper following the client's lead. Research has shown that synchrony is related to rapport (e.g., Bernieri, 1988; Bernieri, Davis, Rosenthal, & Knee, 1994), such that there is more coordinated movement when people feel more of a bond. Helpers should not try to create synchrony with their clients because that would be artificial, but they might notice when synchrony happens spontaneously.

Notetaking

Another issue related to attending behaviors is taking notes during sessions. In general, we do not recommend that helpers take notes during sessions because it reduces their ability to attend to clients. While the helper is taking notes, the client is often unengaged and sitting passively waiting for the helper to finish writing, reducing the intensity of the immediate experience. Clients sometimes also feel suspicious about what helpers are writing and curious about why they write some things and not others. We recognize that helpers often want notes so that they can remember what occurred during sessions, but we recommend the less intrusive method of taping sessions and later listening to the tapes to recall the specific details of the session.

The one time we would suggest that taking notes is acceptable is when clients present something complicated that helpers need to be able to remember to help the clients. For example, when clients tell dreams, we recommend that helpers write down the key images so that they can recall them later when they ask the client to go back through the images to associate to them (see Hill, 1996).

EMPIRICAL EVIDENCE

Some researchers (e.g., Archer & Akert, 1977; Haase & Tepper, 1972) have shown that nonverbal behaviors play a more important role in the communication of emotions than do verbal behaviors. In other words, these researchers suggested that we communicate more about our true emotions through our nonverbals than through our verbal expressions. The results also suggest that if there is a discrepancy between verbal and nonverbal behaviors, the nonverbal behaviors are more reliable indicators of the true emotion. We do not believe that there is enough evidence to indicate the relative importance of verbal and nonverbal behaviors in communication, but the evidence does convince us that helpers should pay attention to both verbal and nonverbal behaviors.

Several nonverbal behaviors have been shown to be important in the helping setting. A review of this literature (see Highlen & Hill, 1984) indicates that smiling, a body orientation directly facing the client, a forward trunk lean, both vertical and horizontal arm movements, and a medium distance of about 55 in. between the helper and client are all generally helpful nonverbal behaviors.

HOW TO USE ATTENDING BEHAVIORS

The literature that we have reviewed suggests a number of attending behaviors that helpers can use to show clients that they are paying attention and are interested in them. We emphasize that there is no "right" or "wrong" way to attend, and we encourage helpers to develop their own natural helping style. It can be helpful, however, to use an acronym to remember the appropriate helping skills. Egan (1994) suggested the acronym SOLER (face the client *squarely*, adopt an *open* posture, *lean* toward the client, maintain moderately consistent *eye* contact, and try to be relatively *relaxed* or natural). Our acronym, which includes additional important attending behaviors, is ENCOURAGES:

E = maintain moderate levels of *eye contact* (avoid looking away frequently or staring).
N = use moderate amounts of head *nods*.
C = maintain a respect and awareness of *cultural differences* in attending.
O = maintain an *open stance* toward the client (don't keep arms closed tightly, lean toward and face the client squarely).
U = use acknowledgments such as *"umhmm."*
R = *relax* and be natural.
A = *avoid distracting behaviors* (e.g., too many adaptors, too much smiling, giggling, playing with hair or objects).
G = match the client's *grammatical style* (use the same language style as the client within the limits of one's own style).
E = listen with a third *ear* (listen attentively to verbal and nonverbal messages).
S = use *space* appropriately (e.g., do not sit either too close or too far).

We do not suggest that helpers take these prescriptions too literally. It is not terrible, for example, if helpers cross their arms once in a while as long as they maintain an attitude of listening and involvement with clients. The important thing is to be aware of the effects of the nonverbal behaviors on clients. Helpers can ask themselves, "How much does my present behavior communicate openness and availability to the client?"

We hope that each individual helper determines which attending behaviors feel comfortable to her or him. We suggest that helpers try our suggested stance and then modify these behaviors according to what makes them and their clients feel comfortable. We strongly encourage helpers to observe the reactions of clients to their attending behaviors. A helper's knitting during a session might feel relaxing for one client, whereas another client might feel wounded because she might believe that the helper could not possibly pay full attention to her while knitting. We suggest that helpers ask for feedback about their attending behaviors during training to become aware of how they affect others. In addition, as we noted earlier, many attending behaviors have different meanings in different cultures, so helpers also need to be sensitive to possible misunderstandings with clients from different cultures.

We want to emphasize the importance of not just appearing, but actually being relaxed. Many beginning trainees try so hard to maintain an attending stance that they appear artificial or posed. They perform all the "right" behaviors but end up being too attentive, which makes clients feel like they are being examined too closely. Trying to relax and be oneself is one of the most difficult tasks of helpers. However, when helpers integrate attending and listening behaviors into their way of being, clients often respond by exploring their concerns.

In addition, being aware of their nonverbal behaviors can enable helpers to get in touch with their underlying feelings at the moment. For example, if you feel your muscles tensing or note that you are withdrawing physically from clients, you might ask yourself if you are feeling anxious. Awareness is key to being able to handle situations. Once you know how you are feeling, you can make more informed decisions about how to act rather than having the reactions "leak out." Paying attention to bodily reactions also provides an incredible amount of information about clients. If you feel bored, anxious, attracted, or repulsed by a client, chances are other people feel this way toward the client. We discuss how to use these reactions therapeutically in the chapter on immediacy.

An effective way for helpers to obtain feedback is to videotape themselves in a helping situation (with the client's permission) and later observe their nonverbal behaviors and the client's reactions carefully. We also suggest that helpers experiment with nonverbal behaviors with friends or classmates. When friends are talking about something important, helpers might use attending behaviors appropriately and observe the friend's reaction. Then helpers might use attending behaviors inappropriately (or not at all) and see if friends react any differently. Helpers can later tell their friends what they were doing and solicit feedback about reactions to the different nonverbal manipulations. To illustrate attending behaviors within a helping setting, we provide a contrast between inappropriate and appropriate attending. A dialogue is included to provide context, but readers should focus on the attending behaviors (see Exhibit 6.2).

HOW TO LISTEN

Verbal Messages

Clients communicate with helpers in a variety of ways, the most obvious being the words they use to express their thoughts, feelings, and experiences. Helpers can listen carefully to the words. Focusing on the client by using attending skills and minimal encouragers (e.g., "mmhmm") and freeing their minds from distractions allows helpers to

---

Inappropriate

Helper: (leaning back with arms folded and looking at the ceiling) "So, how come you came today?"

Client: (very softly) "Well, I'm not sure. I just haven't been feeling very good lately about myself. But I don't know if you can help me."

Helper: (shifts forward in seat and looks intently at client) "Well, so what is happening?"

Client: (long pause) "I just don't know how to . . . ."

Helper: (interrupts) "Just tell me everything."

Client: (long pause) "I guess I really don't have anything to talk about. Sorry I wasted your time."

Appropriate

Helper: (using all the ENCOURAGES behaviors) "Hi. My name is Debbie. We have a few minutes to talk today so that I can practice my helping skills. What would you like to talk about?"

Client: (very softly) "Well, I'm not sure. I just haven't been feeling very good lately about myself. But I don't know if you can help me."

Helper: (matches the client's soft voice) "Yeah, you sound kind of scared. Tell me a little bit more about what's been going on lately."

Client: "I've been kind of down. I haven't been able to sleep or eat much. I'm behind on everything, and I don't have the energy to do any work on my schoolwork."

Helper: (pauses, softly) "It sounds like you feel overwhelmed."

Client: (sighs) "Yes, that's exactly how I feel. It just seems like there's a lot of pressure in my first year of college."

Helper: "Mmhmm." (head nod)

Client: (continues talking)

---

get into a listening stance. We also suggest that helpers try to imagine themselves in the client's position. Thus, helpers listen by seeking to understand what clients are experiencing from the client's perspective rather than from the helper's viewpoint. For example, an adolescent client, Kathleen, complained that she felt devastated and worthless because she had not been asked to the prom. From the perspective of the helper, a 35-year-old married woman, not being asked to the prom was not a catastrophic event. However, while listening to Kathleen, the helper could imagine what this experience might feel like for this young woman.

A key to listening is for helpers to pay attention to clients without formulating their next response. All too often, we are half listening to what someone is saying because we are thinking about what we want to say next. In helping, it is crucial to listen carefully to what clients are saying so that we can learn about how they are thinking and feeling. Clients who have different verbal styles than their helpers can cause confusion for their helpers. Helpers who are introverted might assume that talkative clients are comfortable, when in fact they could be talking too much out of anxiety. Hence, it is important for helpers not to project their feelings and their personal style onto their clients.

Nonverbal Messages

Not only is it important for helpers to listen to the client's words, but they also can learn a lot by listening to their nonverbal behaviors. Clients who are nervous often use a lot of adaptors, are very quiet, stutter, or cannot speak coherently. Clients who are defensive or closed often cross their arms and legs, almost as a barricade to the helper. Clients who are ashamed might look down as they speak. Clients who are scared might speak softly and look away and have a closed posture. In contrast, clients who are comfortable and in tune with the helper often lean forward and talk with animation and feeling in their voices.

We want to emphasize, however, that helpers should not interpret nonverbal behaviors as having fixed standard "meanings." Fidgeting can reveal anxiety, but it could also reveal boredom; folded arms can convey either irritation or relaxation. For example, if a client sits with legs and arms crossed, she is not necessarily withholding or defending herself. It could mean that she is cold or is in the habit of sitting with arms and legs crossed. Hence, we cannot "read" another's body language as a universal language, but we can use our observations as hints or clues about what clients might be feeling. If a client is sitting with arms and legs crossed and has scooted the chair back, the helper might hypothesize that the client is needing distance from the helper. However, the helper needs to investigate this hypothesis further by talking about it with the client. Thus, helpers can use nonverbal data to form hypotheses and then gather more data to determine the accuracy of the hypotheses.

Clients who have different nonverbal styles than their helpers can cause confusion for helpers. For example, a helper who does not like to make a lot of eye contact might assume that a client who makes eye contact feels very comfortable and in control of the situation. However, too much eye contact can be just as much of a defense or indication of anxiety as is too little eye contact; both styles make it difficult for people to get close to others. To summarize, awareness of client nonverbal behavior can aid listening and communication if helpers do not assume that certain behaviors have specific meanings, but rather explore to learn more about the meaning of the nonverbal behaviors.

A key to listening to nonverbal behaviors is the context in which they take place (Egan, 1994). Rather than becoming fixated on the details of the nonverbal behaviors, helpers need to pay attention to everything about the client: the verbals, the nonverbals, the setting, the culture, and the presenting problem. For example, Archie appeared angry and hostile, but his behavior made sense in that he had just been stopped and frisked by a police officer apparently because he was an African American man in a White neighborhood. Hence, context is important to take into account when thinking about behaviors.

Some people are more sensitive than others to nonverbal cues. When Rosenthal, Hall, DiMatteo, Rogers, and Archer (1979) showed clips of emotionally expressive faces and bodies, they found that some people were better at detecting emotion than others. In addition, they found that women were generally better at detecting emotion than men. Miller (1976) provided a social-learning explanation for why women, who have had traditionally less dominant roles, might be better at detecting emotion than men:

> Subordinates (women), then, know much more about the dominants than vice versa. They have to. They become highly attuned to the dominants, able to predict their reactions of

pleasure and displeasure. Here, I think, is where the long story of "feminine intuition" and "feminine wiles" begins. It seems clear that these "mysterious" gifts are in fact skills, developed through long practice, in reading many small signals, both verbal and nonverbal. (p. 10)

Helpers who are aware that they are not as natively sensitive to nonverbal cues can try harder to pay attention than they would naturally. Furthermore, practice helps people become somewhat more nonverbally sensitive. A few studies have suggested that trainees can be taught to increase their sensitivity to nonverbal communication (e.g., D. J. Delaney & Heimann, 1966; Grace, Kivlighan, & Kunce, 1995).

EFFECTS OF ATTENDING AND LISTENING

Helpers need to evaluate the effectiveness of their attending and listening behaviors. We suggest that helpers watch a videotape of their sessions and use a 3-point scale to assess the effectiveness of their attending and listening behaviors. This scale stresses the effects of attending and listening on clients' reactions:

1 = When attending and listening are unhelpful, a client might move away from the helper, get fidgety, appear uncomfortable, or become distracted. For example, if a helper sits back with his legs spread apart, some clients might interpret this as a sexual advance, look away, and become very uncomfortable. If helpers fiddle with their hair or play with pens, some clients might become distracted and feel irritated that they are not important enough to receive the helper's full attention.

2 = If the attending and listening behaviors are at least moderately adequate, clients are able to continue talking but may not feel completely comfortable.

3 = If the attending and listening behaviors are very good, clients feel comfortable in the setting and feel that helpers are listening and concerned. Clients probably feel safe to continue talking about personal concerns.

Of course, helpers must be aware that clients are not always responding to the helper's attending and listening behaviors. Sometimes clients are upset because of the content of their presenting concerns and are not responding at all to the helper's attending behaviors. Helpers need to try to determine what clients are reacting to.

DIFFICULTIES HELPERS EXPERIENCE
IN ATTENDING AND LISTENING

One of the problems that helpers have in attending and listening is being distracted by their internal thoughts and feelings. For example, helpers often engage in negative self-talk (e.g., "I'm not doing this right," "I'm not sure that the client likes me," "I wonder if I'm giving too much eye contact?"). Because they are so distracted by what they are thinking, helpers have a hard time focusing on clients and listening attentively.

Some helpers may not be sensitive to cultural differences in nonverbal behaviors. Hence, when someone from another culture does something nonverbally that is different from their custom (e.g., using eye contact differently), some helpers judge these clients according to their own cultural standards.

Another thing that causes problems for helpers is not paying attention to client reactions to their nonverbal behaviors. Clients rarely tell helpers directly that a nonverbal

EXHIBIT 6.3. HELPFUL HINTS FOR ATTENDING AND LISTENING

- Try out the attending behaviors suggested in the acronym ENCOURAGES and see how they fit for you.
- Discover for yourself how you feel comfortable in attending. Develop your own style.
- Be aware of how others react to your nonverbal behaviors. Solicit lots of feedback from friends and clients about the impact of your nonverbal behaviors.
- Do not interrupt clients unless absolutely necessary (e.g., client is talking nonstop about irrelevant things).

behavior is annoying or intrusive, but they often provide subtle cues when they feel uncomfortable (e.g., becoming more quiet, looking away). Helpers need to attend to the client's nonverbals to detect their reactions.

Beginning helpers frequently assume the "correct" nonverbal position rather than find a nonverbal position that feels natural and relaxed. Helpers need to try out different positions, watch themselves on videotape, and ask for feedback about their nonverbal stance (see Exhibit 6.3).

CONCLUDING COMMENTS

In conclusion, attending behaviors are important to set the stage for helpers to listen and to make clients feel like they are being heard. Helpers also need to listen carefully to clients' verbal and nonverbal behaviors to hear what clients are saying and to pick up clues about underlying feelings. Attending and listening set the foundation for all of the other skills that are taught in this book. Thus, helpers should be particularly attentive to learning these skills to ensure that they have the foundation from which to build the other helping skills.

▬▬▬ **What Do You Think?**

- What are the differences between attending and listening?
- What are some of the rules for nonverbal behavior in your culture?
- How do rules get established for nonverbal behaviors? Can these rules be changed?
- What happens when helpers do not follow the rules of the client's particular culture?
- What are your thoughts about manipulating your nonverbal behaviors to achieve desired goals with clients?
- Discuss the appropriateness of being manipulative with nonverbal behaviors if the goal is to help clients.
- Describe instances of interactional synchrony that you have experienced with friends.

LAB 2 Attending and Listening

Before beginning these exercises, we would like to caution you that the first few labs might feel somewhat artificial for students. We divide the helping process into individual skills, so that you can learn to implement each skill before moving to integrate the skills. We realize that in real helping sessions, you do not use just one skill at a time, but we believe that you cannot integrate the skills unless you can perform each of them individually. Our experiences have taught us that the best way to master the helping skills is to focus on each one intensely and separately. We ask that you bear with us for the first few exercises as you practice the individual skills, after which we give you the opportunity to integrate the skills.

We should also warn you that some students feel overwhelmed with these lab exercises because they worry that they will not remember everything that they are "supposed" to do. We assure you that you probably will not remember everything. It takes a lot of practice before you can begin to use everything you have learned. Our main piece of advice—try to relax. You do not have to be perfect; it is enough to try to do your best. Just get in there and try the exercises and see what happens. These exercises are designed to give you the opportunity to practice the skills in a relatively safe place.

Exercise 1

Goals

1. To enable helpers to become accustomed to being in the helper role.
2. To allow helpers an opportunity to determine which attending behaviors feel most comfortable and congruent.
3. To provide feedback to helpers about their attending behaviors.
4. To allow helpers an opportunity to observe and learn about the meanings of clients' nonverbal behaviors.
5. To give helpers an opportunity to practice skills of listening without interpreting, without making any judgments about what clients say, and without thinking of what they want to add or respond.

Students should be arranged in groups of three, with instructors or lab leaders monitoring the groups. Within groups, roles should be alternated after each turn so that each person participates at least once in each role (helper, client, and observer).

Helper's and Client's Tasks During the Helping Interchange

1. The helper should get into a relaxed position and use appropriate attending behaviors with the client.
2. The helper can introduce himself or herself and ask what the client would like to talk about. (See Lab 1 in chapter 3 for an example of an introduction.)
3. The client should talk for one or two brief sentences about an easy topic. (See Exhibit 1.1 in chapter 1 on safe topics for disclosure.)
4. The helper should first pause briefly and then repeat verbatim what the client said. Repeating verbatim probably will feel awkward to many helpers, but we

repeat that the goal of this exercise is to give helpers the opportunity to listen carefully and make sure they hear what clients are saying. This is the first step to developing other skills, although later helpers will not be asked to repeat what clients have said.

5. Continue for 8–10 client-speaking turns. Be sure to focus on this task and not talk about life in general. Although it is difficult (especially the first time), try to stay in the role of helper and client.

Observer's Task During the Helping Interchange

1. Take notes about your observations of the helper regarding

   a. helper's ability to repeat exactly what client said.
   b. one positive and one negative attending behavior.

2. Take notes about your observation of the client regarding

   a. what you noticed about client's nonverbal behaviors.
   b. what you infer about the meaning of the nonverbal behaviors.

3. Encourage the helper and client to stay on task.

After the Helping Interchange

1. The helper can discuss which attending behaviors felt comfortable and how it felt to repeat everything the client said.
2. The client can talk about how it felt to be the recipient of the helper's attending and listening skills.
3. The observer can give feedback (both positive and negative) to the helper.
4. The helper and observer should note and hypothesize about the meaning of the client's nonverbal behaviors, asking the client to confirm or deny the hypotheses.
5. Discuss differences in attending behaviors related to multicultural differences between the helper and client.

Exercise 2

Goals

1. To give helpers an opportunity to attend and listen to clients.
2. To encourage helpers to focus on the most important part of the client's statements.

Use the same format as in Exercise 1, except that the helper only repeats the single most important word or phrase that the client has said. Be sure to select the word that reflects the issue from the client's perspective. For example, if the client says, "I am having a terrible dilemma. I just found out that my best friend's boyfriend cheated on her. I don't know whether I should tell her because she would be so hurt." The helper should choose a word or phrase that reflects the client's concern, such as "dilemma," "unsure," or "having a terrible dilemma," rather than a word that focuses on the friend's problem, such as "hurt." Continue for 8–10 client-speaking turns.

(Continues)

Personal Reflections

- What was your experience in the role of helper, client, and observer? Which role did you prefer?
- What attending behaviors do you personally find most helpful as a helper and as a client?
- Although helpers often do not like having to repeat verbatim everything the client has said, many have reported later that they found this exercise helpful in teaching them to listen carefully. They commented that often they had been more concerned with what they were going to say than with actually listening to the client. Students also have indicated that this exercise helped them become more comfortable with being in the helper role because they were doing a relatively easy task. Some were bored, though, and found this exercise too easy. What was your experience?
- What multicultural issues (e.g., gender, race, ethnicity, age) arose in your helping dyads?

7 Restatement

The world is made of stories, not atoms.
Muriel Rukeyser

After Jason's parents were killed in a random drive-by shooting, he was filled with anger and rage and needed a chance to talk. His helper listened supportively, showed appropriate and encouraging nonverbals, and rephrased the content of what Jason was saying (e.g., "You're still trying to understand what happened," "You can't make sense of their deaths," and "You want to hurt their murderer"). These restatements helped Jason express his thoughts about the shooting.

When Jackie talked in great detail about her difficulties in dealing with her job because of the changes in technology, the helper restated Jackie's message, "So the new technology is changing the way you do things." This restatement helped Jackie focus on what she was saying and further explore her situation. Jackie replied that it was not the new technology as much as her resistance to learning new things that made it difficult.

RESTATEMENTS ARE a repeating or paraphrase of the content or meaning of what a client has said that typically contains fewer but similar words and usually is more concrete and clear than the client's statement. Restatements can be phrased either tentatively (e.g., "I wonder if maybe she said something like that you were kind of late?") or more directly (e.g., "She said that you were late"). Restatements can paraphrase material that the client just said or they can relate to material that the client said earlier in the session or treatment. The emphasis is on the substance or content of the dialogue rather than on the feelings or inner experience (see Exhibit 7.1). Restatements do not include feelings even if the client expressed feelings. (We discuss reflection of feelings in chapter 9.)

Summaries, which are often given at the end of sessions, are a kind of restatement. Summaries tie together several ideas or pick out the highlights and general themes of the content expressed by clients. Summaries do not go beyond what clients have said or delve into the reasons for feelings or behaviors; they simply consolidate what has been said. Summarizing also helps to clarify or focus a series of scattered ideas and to clear the way for new ideas. Helpers also can use summaries to reassure clients that they have been listening. Likewise, summaries allow helpers a chance to check on the accuracy of what they have been hearing. For example, a helper might say, "In sum, you are thinking a lot about your mother and the way she has treated you, and you are trying to decide how you want to behave with her in the future." Summaries are particularly useful when clients have finished talking about a particular issue or at the end of sessions as a way of helping clients reach a sense of closure regarding what has been explored. Summaries also can be

---

EXHIBIT 8.1. OVERVIEW OF OPEN QUESTIONS

Definition	*Restatement* is a repeating or rephrasing of the content or meaning of client's statement(s) that typically contains fewer but similar words and usually is more concrete and clear than the client's statement. The restatement can be phrased either tentatively or as a direct statement. Restatements can paraphrase either immediately preceding material or material from earlier in session or treatment.
Examples	**Client:** "It's important to learn helping skills so that I can help others."
	Helper: "You want to be an effective helper."
	Client: "I can't believe it. My mom called and said that they waited until I went to college but that now they are going to break up."
	Helper: "You just learned that your parents are going to get divorced."
	Helper: "Just to summarize, you seem more clear on what you would like to do about attending the wedding."
Typical helper intentions	To clarify, to focus, to support, to encourage catharsis (see Appendix A)
Possible client reactions	Supported, understood, clear, negative thoughts or behaviors, stuck, lacking direction (see Appendix D)
Desired client behavior	Cognitive–behavioral exploration (see Appendix E)
Difficulties helpers experience in using restatements	Parroting
	Restating only surface thoughts
	Feeling frustrated because of not "doing" enough for client
	Focusing on someone other than the client

---

helpful at the beginning of subsequent sessions to recap past sessions and provide a focus for the upcoming session.

INTENTIONS

The overall intention for using restatement is to help clients explore their concerns deeply. Specifically, restatements are used to help clients clarify when they are unclear and focus when they are rambling or vague. Restatements can also be used to support clients, to allow them to talk, and to encourage catharsis. In general, helpers want to enable clients to talk about how they think about themselves and their presenting problems.

WHY USE RESTATEMENTS?

When using restatements, helpers serve as sounding boards so that clients can hear what they are saying. The use of restatement goes back to Rogers (1942), who believed that helpers need to be mirrors, enabling clients to hear what they are saying without judgment. In fact, with healthy clients who are trying to understand major problems or make decisions, helpers might never need to go beyond this type of intervention because these clients only need an opportunity to hear what they are thinking. Thinking about problems on one's own is often difficult because people get blocked or stuck, do not have enough time or energy to examine their problems thoroughly by themselves, may rationalize their behaviors, or may give up and quit trying. Having another person listen and serve as a mirror of the content allows clients a golden opportunity to explore their thoughts.

Given that clients often feel confused, conflicted, or overwhelmed by their problems, receiving restatements allows them to hear how their concerns sound to another person. Hearing paraphrases of their issues, then, can help clients reevaluate their thinking. Restatements also can enable clients to clarify matters or explore certain aspects of the problem more thoroughly and to think about aspects that they had not considered before. Just taking the time to think through a problem carefully with the benefit of an interested listener can lead to new insights. For example, if a client presents a confused and jumbled statement of her concerns and a helper provides restatements that do not encapsulate the content accurately, the client can clarify what she means so that both of them understand the situation better. Restatements thus allow clients a chance to clarify mistaken impressions that the helper may have received.

An additional benefit of restatements is that they require that helpers put their listening into words and play an active role in the helping process. Rather than assuming that they have understood what clients have said, restatements allow helpers the opportunity to check out the accuracy of what they have heard. Having to listen to what clients say and summarize in fewer and more concise terms requires that helpers attend carefully and determine the key components of what clients have revealed. Saying "I understand how you feel" or asking questions can be easy but is often empty, whereas restating the client's statements is much harder and requires that helpers not only listen but struggle to understand enough of what clients have said that they can restate the essence of their messages. Although at first it may seem as if restatements are a passive mode of responding, helpers actually are engaged very actively in trying to capture the essence of the client's experience.

Restatements can be particularly appropriate with clients who are cognitively oriented rather than affectively oriented. Such cognitively oriented clients really like to analyze their thoughts about problems and might be threatened if asked to focus too much on feelings.

EMPIRICAL EVIDENCE

Restatement and reflection of feelings typically have been combined into a category called *paraphrase* in much of the research (except for one study reviewed in chapter 8). Hence, the research findings for restatement are considered together with those for reflection of feelings in chapter 9. We hope that future researchers will separate these skills and study their unique effects.

HOW TO USE RESTATEMENTS

Restatements are generally shorter and more concise than the client's statement, typically focusing on the most important material rather than repeating everything verbatim. For example, if the client has been talking at some length about the many things that have been getting in the way of studying, the helper might give a restatement such as, "so you have not been able to study lately" or "studying has been difficult for you lately."

Formulating a restatement can be difficult when the client has talked for a long period of time. Beginning trainees often think that they need to capture everything the client has said. Capturing everything would not only not be possible but would probably be counterproductive. The focus would shift from the client to the helper because the repeating would take too much time and would take the emphasis off the client. The momentum would be lost in the session. The client would be put in a position of trying to remember everything that he or she said to determine if the helper repeated everything accurately. In contrast, an effective restatement keeps the focus on the client and is almost unnoticeable in subtly guiding and encouraging the client to keep talking.

Rather than paraphrasing everything that clients say, helpers try to capture the essence of what clients have said. Specifically, they try to capture the "growing edge" of what clients have revealed—what clients are most uncertain about, what is still unexplored, or what is not completely understood. Helpers, then, should pick out the salient message or the issue that clients are still working on to facilitate further client exploration. Attention to nonverbal messages can also assist helpers in determining the salient content of the client's message.

Furthermore, the emphasis of restatements should be on the client's thoughts rather than on those of other people. This client focus enables clients to think about their role in problems rather than blame or focus on others. For example, a client was discussing her decision to change jobs and move to the East Coast. During the session, she continuously focused on her colleagues' and friends' reactions to her decision. The helper worked very hard to focus the restatements on the client ("You wonder how your friends will feel when you move") rather than on her friends and colleagues ("Your friend doesn't want you to move").

The goal of restatements is to enable clients to focus and to talk in more depth about an issue, as well as to assist clients in figuring out issues rather than just restating what the client already knows. Thus, focusing on one piece of an issue at a time is important to allow clients the opportunity to delve deeply into a concern. Helpers can return later to other important aspects of the problem after one part is explored thoroughly.

Helpers often worry that selecting the most important part of the client's statement requires a judgment call and removes them from a client-centered approach to helping. We would argue that helpers stay within a client-centered approach because they are trying to use their empathic skills to figure out the most important aspect for the client. Hence, helpers have to listen to clients at a deep level to understand what they are most concerned about. The attitude of being client-centered is very important for helpers when formulating restatements. The emphasis is on helping clients explore more deeply rather than on helpers having agendas for what content should emerge. Helpers should not be judgmental and should not assume that they know or understand what clients are experiencing. Helpers should not be invested in solving problems or disclosing their own problems; rather, they should be focused on hearing the client's story and facilitating exploration.

To reduce the tendency to become repetitive, helpers can vary the format of restatements. There are several ways to introduce restatements, such as, "I hear you saying . . . ," "It sounds as though . . . ," "I wonder whether . . . ," "You're saying that . . . ." Alternatively, helpers can just repeat and slightly draw out a key word that clients have said, such as *divorce, music,* or *headache.* If the key word is presented in a questioning or inviting tone, it encourages the client to tell the helper more about the topic. For example, if a client has been talking about her daughter having just been tested with an incredibly high IQ score, and the helper wants the client to explore more about IQs, she might simply say, "IQ . . . ?," thereby inviting the client to tell her more about what IQ means to her.

The following is an example of how a helper could use restatements (in italics) with a client:

Client: "I have to go on a pilgrimage to Mecca. I don't really want to go because it's the middle of my last semester in college and I'm worried that my grades will suffer if I leave for two weeks, but I don't have much choice. According to my religion, I have to go."

Helper: *"So you're going to take a pilgrimage."*

Client: "Yeah, for my religion, we have to take a pilgrimage. Everyone has to do a pilgrimage before they get married. It's just expected. And my father has to go with me because a man has to be on the pilgrimage, but I don't have a very good relationship with him and he's not very well, so I don't know if he can withstand the rigors of the trip."

Helper: *"You said you don't have a very good relationship with your father."*

Client: "Right. He wasn't around much when I was growing up. He was always too busy. And now to spend 2 weeks with him is a lot. I don't even know what we could talk about. I feel like I don't know him. I get anxious just thinking about spending a lot of time with him. But on the other hand, I wish I knew him better, so maybe this is an opportunity to get to know him."

Helper: *"Really know him."*

Client: "Yeah, really know him. I've always wanted to have a good relationship with him. People say that we're a lot alike. And he could teach me a lot about the religion and my culture that I don't know much about, given that I came to the United States when I was very young."

Helper: *"So you could learn something from your father."*

Client: "Oh yeah, I think I could learn a lot from him. He is a wise person. I just hope I can be myself with him. I've always felt like such a little kid, and I would rather feel like an adult with him the way I can with my mother." (Client continues to explore.)

EFFECTS OF RESTATEMENT

Helpers need to be aware of the impact of their restatements on clients. To become more aware, helpers can watch tapes of their sessions and rate the impact of each of their restatements, using the following 3-point scale:

1 = With very ineffective restatements, clients stop exploration. They do not know what else to say or do not feel encouraged to talk further. Clients may also respond with frustration and anger if they perceive that helpers are parroting what they have said (e.g., they might feel or say, "I just said that").

2 = With moderately ineffective or neutral restatements, clients keep talking but are likely to repeat themselves, going over the same territory, or doing what is called *circling*. They do not have a sense of what is important to talk about next or do not feel influenced by the intervention.

3 = With effective restatements that capture the cutting edge of what the client is concerned about, clients typically talk extensively and elaboratively about their thoughts. Rather than just repeating themselves, clients discuss additional facets of their problems. They explain more about their issues so that helpers can obtain a clearer picture of their concerns. Effective restatements help clients feel understood, especially when they are phrased to capture the essence of what clients are communicating rather than just repeating what the client said.

DIFFICULTIES HELPERS EXPERIENCE IN USING RESTATEMENTS

Helpers run the risk of sounding like parrots if they continually use the same format to introduce their restatements (e.g., "I hear you saying …") or if they repeat the client's message verbatim. Clients can become annoyed with this predictability and neglect focusing on their concerns because they are distracted by the helper. In a related vein, some helpers are afraid of making a mistake in choosing the key aspects of the client's message and so repeat everything, taking the focus off the client and halting the flow of the interchange. Not too surprising, clients quickly become bored and annoyed with such restatements, saying things like, "That's what I just said." Moreover, clients might feel stuck and aimless when restatements are mere repetitions of everything clients have said. By choosing the key components, focusing on the "growing edge" of what clients are concerned about, varying the format, and keeping the restatements short, helpers can often deal with these problems.

Some helpers feel frustrated when they use restatements because they feel that they are not "doing" anything or giving the client specific answers. Because restatements are used to help clients explore and tell their stories rather than come to insight or action, helpers rarely feel brilliant when using them. In fact, clients often are not able to remember restatements because the focus is on them rather than on the helper.

HELPFUL HINTS

- The cardinal rule: Do not assume that you understand anything about the client. Even if you are the same age, gender, race–ethnicity, and so on, you have not had the same experiences as the client. Sometimes working with someone you perceive as similar to you is more difficult, because it is easy to assume that their experiences and feelings are similar to yours. It is best to assume that you know nothing and then learn as much as you can from the client.

- Pick the most important part of client statements to restate. Do not try to paraphrase everything. Even though several points of information in a client's statement may be important, only one issue can be dealt with effectively at a time. Clues for determining what is most important for the client can be gathered by attending to their nonverbal messages, to what the client focuses on most, what they seem to have the most involvement in talking about, what they seem to have questions or conflict about, and what is left unresolved.

- Keep restatements short and concise. The goal is to turn the attention back to the client right away so that she or he continues exploring. Remember that in helping, helpers typically talk only 30–40% of the time.

- Give the restatement slowly and supportively (take a deep breath before responding) rather than just rushing to say something.

- Be tentative in the tone of restatements so that clients can reject restatements if they do not seem accurate.

- Focus on the client rather than on another person, even when the client's focus is on another person. Remember that you cannot often influence the other person, so your best bet is to focus on the client. For example, when a client talks about her husband's nagging, focus on what the client thinks about the nagging rather than on how terrible the husband is for nagging.

- Remember that, by definition, restatements do not include feelings even if clients have expressed feelings. The focus is on the content of the client's statements to help clients hear what they said. We are not suggesting that feelings are not important (in fact, we believe that reflection of feelings, covered in chapter 9, is a very helpful skill), but in restatements, the focus is on thoughts.

- Use restatements (as opposed to reflection of feelings) when you want to assist a client in clarifying or focusing or when you want to summarize what a client has said.

- Use the client's language style as much as possible, but avoid too much repetition.

- Do not rush to give a restatement when the client is talking productively. Allowing clients to talk and explore their thoughts and feelings is the most important task in the exploration stage. When the client stops talking completely, a restatement can be given.

- Pause before restating because it gives clients a chance to keep talking if they have something more to say. In addition, deep breathing before delivering restatements can help you relax when you feel anxious.

- Vary the manner in which you deliver restatements. Restate the content in a sentence (e.g., "You are having trouble with your mother"), restate the major theme in a key word or two (e.g., "mother," "trouble with mother"), or begin with lead-ins such as, "I hear you saying ... ," "It sounds as though ... ," "I wonder whether ... ," or "You're saying that ... ."

- If you truly do not understand what the client has said, asking clients to repeat themselves is better than pretending you understand. If you ask for clarification too many times, clients might feel that you are not listening or that they are bad communicators, but an occasional query is appropriate.

PRACTICE EXERCISES

Pretend that a client says the following statements to you. Read each of the following statements, write down what your intentions would be, and then write a restatement. (Recall that the typical intentions for using restatements are to clarify, focus, support, and encourage catharsis.) Compare your responses to the possible helper responses that we provide at the end of the section. The helper responses that we provide are not the "right" or "best" restatements but give you some idea of different possibilities.

Statements

1. **Client:** "I have a lot of work to do for my classes. But I don't know when I'm going to do it because I have to work 20 hours a week at my job. When I come home

from classes and working, I just don't have any energy for doing schoolwork. I feel like I need a chance to just 'veg' out and watch TV."
Helper intention(s): _____
Helper response: _____
_____

2. **Client:** "After I graduate, I am going to take a cross-country trip. At first I was just going to go by myself, but then my roommates heard about it and both of them said they wanted to go. I rearranged my schedule to accommodate them, and now one of them says he isn't going."
Helper intention(s): _____
Helper response: _____
_____

3. **Client:** "My mother is going through a divorce. She calls me every night to talk. She says she has no one else to talk to. The guy she married after my father left her is a real jerk. He beat her up and is an alcoholic."
Helper intention(s): _____
Helper response:_____
_____

Possible Helper Responses

1. "You don't have much energy right now for your schoolwork." (intent: to encourage catharsis)
   "When you get home from work, you don't really want to do schoolwork." (intent: to encourage catharsis)
   "I hear you saying that you're not getting your homework done." (intent: to focus)
2. "You've made a lot of adjustments in your plans for your friends." (intent: to encourage catharsis)
   "You just learned that your friend will not be accompanying you on your cross-country trip." (intent: to focus)
   "You are planning a trip with another person." (intent: to focus)
3. "You're thinking a lot about your mother lately." (intent: to encourage catharsis, to support)
   "You talk to your mother every night and are very involved in her problems." (intent: to encourage catharsis)
   "You think your mother needs you a lot right now." (intent: to support, to focus)
   "Lots of responsibility." (intent: to encourage catharsis)

What Do You Think?

- How do you decide what part of the client's statement to restate?
- Debate the efficacy of restatements compared to responses that are more typically used in friendships such as advice and self-disclosure.
- Have you experienced similar feelings to the client in the first example of the practice exercises? If so, was it difficult for you to focus on the client because of thinking about your own issues?

- Discuss what you think would happen if you focus on other people rather than the client (e.g., in the second practice example, you might have focused on the roommate or the client).

- In his early theorizing, Rogers (1942) promoted restatement as the most important helper skill. He thought restatements were useful to provide a mirror for clients. What do you think?

LAB 3 Restatement

Goal: For helpers to learn to restate the content of client's speech. Remember that the focus is on paraphrasing content rather than feelings.

Students should be arranged in groups of three, with lab leaders monitoring the groups. Within groups, roles should be switched so that each person gets a chance to participate at least one time as the helper, client, and observer.

Helper's and Client's Tasks During the Helping Interchange

1. The helper should introduce himself or herself (see Lab 1 for possible format).
2. The client should talk about a topic for a few sentences. (See Exhibit 1.1 in chapter 1 for suggestions for topics.)
3. The helper should listen attentively during the client statement without thinking of what she or he is going to say next. After the client statement, the helper should pause, take a deep breath, think of what to say, and then restate what the client has said using fewer words and focusing on the most essential part of the statement. For purposes of this exercise, the helper should only do a restatement, so there should be no focus on feelings. (Note: It is difficult to avoid feelings at first but we want you to focus on being able to rephrase content during this lab.) Helpers should remember to use appropriate attending behaviors throughout the exercise.
4. Continue for 5–10 turns.

Observer's Task During the Helping Interchange

Take notes about the helpers' restatements and attending behaviors.

After the Helping Interchange

1. The helper should talk about how it felt to do the restatements.
2. The client should talk about how it felt to be the recipient of the restatements and provide feedback about the helper's restatements.
3. The observer should give feedback to the helper about the restatements and attending skills.

SWITCH ROLES

Personal Reflections

- How did you handle any anxiety that you might have experienced giving restatements?
- What did you learn about yourself in practicing restatements? What were your strengths and weaknesses?
- In the past, some students have had difficulty formulating short concise restatements. Others have had trouble focusing on content rather than feelings. Additional difficulties have been figuring out what to focus on in the client's statements, talking too much, and taking the focus off the client. Which of these experiences did you have? How can you handle these challenges in the future?

8 Open Question

Questioning is the door of knowledge.
(Irish proverb)

Miya said that she was very nervous about taking a trip by herself to France for business. She had never been out of the country before and was concerned about traveling on her own and being able to communicate when she did not know the language. The helper asked, "What is it like for you to be alone?" Later, the helper asked "What are your fears about not being able to communicate with others in a foreign country?" and "What experiences have you had before when you didn't know the language?" These open questions helped Miya explore her reluctance to travel independently.

OPEN QUESTIONS ask clients to clarify or to explore thoughts and feelings. When helpers use open questions, they do not want a specific answer from clients but instead want to encourage clients to explore whatever comes to mind. In other words, helpers do not purposely limit the nature of clients' responses to a "yes," "no," or a one- or two-word response, even though clients may respond that way. Open questions can be phrased as queries ("How do you feel about that?") or they can be phrased as directives ("Tell me how you feel about that") as long as the intent is to help the client clarify or explore thoughts and feelings.

Our focus in this chapter is on using open questions for exploration. (Open questions also can be helpful to clients in the action stage for determining what actions have been tried before and for assessing client readiness to change; these questions are covered in chapters 18–21. We discuss closed questions—questions that ask for specific answers—in chapter 10.) In the next sections, we discuss different types of open questions: those that encourage exploration, those that explore expectations about helping, those that explore different parts of problems, those that request exploration, those that encourage clarification, those that encourage exploration of thoughts, those that encourage exploration of feelings, and those that request examples (see Exhibit 8.1). Note that open questions can be in the form of statements such as "tell me ..." when the intent is to encourage exploration. A variety of open questions are listed in Exhibit 8.2.

INTENTIONS

Helpers use open questions to assist clients in opening up and exploring their concerns. Specifically, helpers intend to encourage clients to clarify when they are unclear, focus clients when they are rambling or vague, encourage catharsis so that clients can tell

EXHIBIT 8.1. OVERVIEW OF OPEN QUESTIONS

Definition	*Open questions* are questions that ask clients to clarify or explore thoughts or feelings. Helpers do not request specific information and do not purposely limit the nature of the response to a "yes," "no," or a one- or two-word response, even though clients may respond that way. Open questions can be phrased as queries ("How do you feel about that?") or they can be phrased as directives ("Tell me how you feel about that"), as long as the intent is to clarify or explore.
Examples	"What issues would you like to explore further?"
	"Tell me more about that."
	"What do you mean by that?"
	"What happened the last time you tried to be assertive?"
	"Give me an example of what you do when you're angry."
	"How do you feel about that?"
	"What feelings do you have in your body right now?"
Typical helper intentions	To focus, to clarify, to encourage catharsis, to identify maladaptive cognitions, to identify and intensify feelings (see Appendix A)
Possible client reactions	Clear, feelings (see Appendix D)
Desired client behaviors	Recounting, cognitive–behavioral exploration, affective exploration (see Appendix E)
Difficulties helpers experience in delivering open questions	Using the same format of open question repeatedly
	Using only open questions instead of a variety of interventions in sessions
	Asking open questions to satisfy their curiosity instead of to help clients explore
	Asking multiple questions at one time
	Using closed instead of open questions
	Asking "why" questions
	Focusing on someone other than the client in the open question
	Focusing on past instead of present feelings

their stories, identify maladaptive cognitions as clients hear what they are saying, and identify and intensify clients' feelings. In general, helpers want to enable clients to talk about how they feel and think about themselves in relation to their presenting problems. Asking open questions is one of the most important and fundamental skills in a helper's repertoire for facilitating exploration.

▬▬▬   **EXHIBIT 8.2. TYPES OF OPEN QUESTIONS**

1. *Encourage Exploration*

Open questions can be particularly effective in encouraging clients to begin talking.
"What would you like to talk about today?"
"How have things been going for you lately?"

2. *Explore Expectations About Helping*

Open questions can be used to uncover the client's expectations and thoughts about the helping situation.
"What did you think would happen in this session?"
"What would you like to have happen in this session?"
"What feelings do you have about coming to helping sessions?"

3. *Explore Different Parts of Problems*

Helpers can also facilitate exploration by asking clients about different aspects of their problems.
"How is this similar to past experiences?"
"How is this situation dissimilar to other experiences that you have had?"
"How would you like this to be in the future?"
"How does this affect your relationships with others?"

4. *Request Exploration*

Open questions can sometimes be phrased in the form of requests; they are still considered to be open questions because they require exploration.
"Tell me more about that."
"Tell me how your behaviors contribute to your feeling so depressed."

5. *Encourage Clarification or Focus*

Helpers can also use open questions when clients are vague, rambling, terse, or unclear. In these instances, open questions help clients clarify, focus on one topic, or explore issues further.
"Explain that to me a bit more."
"What do you mean?"
"What is your role in those problems?"
For example, Chiga was struggling with her career choice. She indicated that she had made a decision to pursue graduate school but then contradicted herself and said that she was uncertain about what she wanted to do. At this point, the helper was confused because of the shifts and so asked Chiga, "What does graduate school mean to you?" Chiga responded that graduate school was an opportunity for her to have a different type of life than her parents had and that it would finally give her knowledge so that she could help others. Thus, open questioning allowed Chiga the opportunity to clarify and explain her assumptions about what graduate school meant to her.

(Continues)

6. *Encourage Exploration of Thoughts*

Open questions often are used to facilitate the exploration of reactions or thoughts. Clarifying thoughts, reactions, and expectations is often helpful because people do not always think about the complexity of the reactions that they have experienced.

"What was your reaction when she said that?"
"What did you think about that?"
"Tell me what thoughts you were having about the other person at the time."
"What were your fantasies?"
"What did you want to say?"
"What do you hope the other person was thinking about you?"
"Say more about what was going on in your mind."
"What is the most important question that you might ask yourself?"
"What would you have liked from him?"
"What were you expecting at that point?"
"What message did you want to give her?"
"Say more about what you wanted to tell her."
"What prevented you from telling him what you wanted to say?"
"Tell me what would have made it easier to tell her."

7. *Encourage Exploration of Feelings*

Open questions can be used to ask about feelings and to encourage clients to talk more deeply about their inner experiences. For clients who are not in touch with their feelings, an open question can suggest that they should talk about feelings. They let the client know exactly what it is that the helper wants them to explore.

"What else have you been feeling?"
"Say more about how you felt about that"
"How are you feeling right now?"
"How did that make you feel about her?"
"Tell me what feelings you were aware of."
"What do these feelings mean to you?"
"What did you do about the feelings that you had?"
"What bodily (or physical) sensations did you have?"

8. *Request Examples*

Helpers can also ask for examples, which provide concrete evidence to obtain a clear sense of the problem. Examples demonstrate what actually happened in at least one instance. Hence, when a client is talking vaguely about being unassertive and being taken advantage of, the client and helper can get a better picture of what the client is experiencing and how the client behaves by asking for details about a specific occurrence. These open questions encourage clients to be more concrete and specific about problems.

"What happened the last time that you were taken advantage of?"
"Tell me exactly what occurred, step by step, when your roommate asked to borrow your new outfit."
"Give me an example of the last time you felt this panic sensation."
"Tell me what you said to your husband the last time you had an argument."

WHY USE OPEN QUESTIONS?

Open questions enable clients to explore the many aspects of their problems. They can be particularly useful when clients keep saying the same things over and over again but have not really explored much about the problem. They also can be used to provide direction for clients who are not very verbal or articulate. Clients often get stuck in describing the bare details of the problem and need questions to help them think more about different aspects of the problem.

Open questions can be used most effectively when helpers focus on one part of the problem at a time. Clients cannot talk about everything at once, so helpers need to pick the most important or salient issue to focus on and return to others later. Typically, the issue that helpers want to focus on is one for which clients have the most energy or affect. For example, if Justin has been talking about receiving a bad grade and has explored his feelings and then the dialogue stops, the helper might ask Justin about what a bad grade means for the future and compare how this situation relates to past experiences with grades or how this grade affects his relationship with his parents. These questions could help Justin talk more completely about important aspects of the problem.

EMPIRICAL EVIDENCE

A number of researchers have found that open questions are used frequently in therapy, with proportions ranging from 9 to 13% of all responses (Barkham & Shapiro, 1986; Hill, Helms, Tichenor, et al., 1988). Open questions were generally rated as moderately helpful and led to exploration and experiencing (Elliott, 1985; Elliott et al., 1982; Hill, Helms, Tichenor, et al., 1988). Hill and Gormally (1977) compared open questions about feelings, restatements, and reflections of feelings in a single session in an experimental study. After an initial baseline period of responding only minimally to clients, helpers responded to clients with only one type of response—either open questions about their feelings, restatements, or reflections of feelings. Results indicate that open questions about feelings, in contrast to restatements or reflections of feelings, led to clients talking more about their feelings. Thus, clients were most likely to talk about their feelings when they were directly asked to talk about them. Note that client satisfaction with the interventions was not measured in this study and that the interventions were very artificial in that only one type of helping skill was used in any given session. However, this study suggests that open questions were an effective way of encouraging clients in talking about feelings.

A number of studies have been conducted in developmental psychology examining the effects of different types of questions with children. For example, two studies show that open-ended invitational questions lead to longer and more detailed responses than directive, leading, or suggestive questions when used in forensic interviews with children (Lamb et al., in press; Sternberg et al., 1996, 1997).

These studies suggest that open questions can be a useful intervention, encouraging clients to talk longer and more deeply about their concerns. When open questions are done in the manner suggested in this chapter, they can be particularly helpful.

HOW TO ASK OPEN QUESTIONS

In asking open questions, helpers should maintain the appropriate attending behaviors because the manner of presenting open questions is very important. The tone of voice should be kept low to convey concern and intimacy, the rate of speech should be slow, and the questions should be phrased tentatively to avoid sounding like you are interrogating the client. Helpers should be supportive, nonjudgmental, and encouraging of whatever clients say. There are no "right" or "wrong" topics to explore and no "right" or "wrong" answers to the questions.

To formulate possible open questions, helpers can think about the purpose, focus, tense, and object of the question. Hence, helpers can ask questions for different purposes: to help clients explore (e.g., "What would you like to talk about?"), to clarify ("What exactly do you mean by abuse?"), or to have clients give an example ("Tell me about the last time that happened."). Questions can also have different foci: thoughts ("What do you think about that?"), feelings ("How do you feel?"), or behaviors ("What did you do in that situation?"). In addition, tense can be varied, such that helpers can focus on what past events led to the present situation, what and who are involved in the present situation, and what the client expects to happen in the future. Finally, the object of the open question can be varied, such that helpers can ask about how the client thinks or feels about self ("What impact did that insult have on you?") or about others ("How do you feel about your mother after the fight?"). Responses to these types of open questions can lead to a greater understanding of the situation. To remember these different suggestions, helpers can think of purpose (explore, clarify, example), focus (thoughts, feelings, behaviors), tense (past, present, future), or object (self, other).

Several guidelines are useful in thinking about formulating open questions. First, open questions should be short and simple. Second, helpers should avoid asking several questions at once because this can be confusing for clients. Multiple questions ("What did you do next and how did you feel and what did you think she was feeling?") can have a dampening effect on the interaction because clients do not know which question to respond to first and often feel bombarded. Clients might ignore important questions because they cannot respond to all the questions. Third, helpers should keep the focus on the client. Rather than turning the attention to other people ("What did your mother do in that situation?"), the focus should remain on the client ("How did you feel about your mother's behavior?") to help the client explore what is going on inside. For example, if Jean often argues with her mother, the helper can ask about Jean's feelings and thoughts ("What makes you angry?") rather than asking Jean about her mother's feelings and thoughts ("Why do you think your mother gets so angry with you?"). Although it could be helpful to understand more about the mother, the mother is not in the room asking for help and the helper is likely to get a one-sided view of the mother. The person we are most likely to help is the client, so the focus should remain on the client. Fourth, the focus should generally be on the present instead of past, although the client may have intense feelings and reactions in the present moment to past experiences or events (e.g., "How do you feel now about how your mother treated you?" rather than "How did your mother treat you?").

In addition, helpers should avoid closed questions (questions that have a specific desired answer, such as "yes" or "no" or specific information) because these tend to limit exploration. One way to differentiate between closed and open questions is to see whether you can make the question more open; if you can, it is probably a closed question. For example, you can change the closed question, from "Did you get an *A*?" to "How did you do on the test?" In contrast, you cannot make "How did you do on the test?" much more open. One particularly egregious type of closed question occurs when the helper is condescending or tries to coerce the client into responding a particular way (e.g., "You really don't want to keep drinking, do you?"). Such questions take the focus away from the client and make the helper seem like the expert who knows how the client should behave.

We also suggest that helpers avoid "why" questions (e.g., "Why did you blow up at your boyfriend the other night?," "Why are you not able to study?"). As Nisbett and Wilson (1977) indicated, people rarely know why they do things. If they did know why they acted as they did, they probably would not be talking to helpers. Furthermore, "why" questions often make clients feel challenged and defensive. When someone asks you why you did something, you might feel like they are judging you and deriding you for not being able to handle the situation more effectively. Instead of asking "why" questions, we suggest that helpers rephrase the questions into "what" or "how" questions (e.g., instead of "Why didn't you study for your exam?" the helper could ask, "How did you feel about your performance on the exam?," "What was going through your mind when you were trying to study?," or "What is going on that makes it difficult for you to study?").

The following is a brief example to illustrate an interchange in which the helper uses open questions (in italics).

Client: "My younger sisters are fighting a lot with each other. They really get nasty and have been hurting each other. And my youngest sister was caught stealing from a store recently. My parents aren't doing anything about it, and my sisters are just going wild."

Helper: *"How do you feel about your sisters going wild?"*

Client: "I'm really upset. I wish there was more I could do to help them. If I were still at home, they would listen to me. I think they don't have anyone to turn to. My parents are divorcing so they're just not available to my sisters."

Helper: *"Tell me more about what it's like for you not to be there."*

Client: "Well, on one hand, I'm delighted to be away and out of the mess. On the other hand, I feel guilty, like I survived the Titanic crash and came out alive but they're sinking."

Helper: *"What is it like when you are with your family?"*

Client: "My parents are still living together, but they fight all the time. Things are pretty scary around the house because my parents get pretty violent with each other. I have to look out for my sisters. I am really more their parent than either of my parents are. I guess I got to be pretty strong by having to fend for myself so much."

Helper: *"How are you feeling right now as you think about your family?"*

Client: "I feel helpless, like there's nothing I can do. I guess I could go home, but actually I know that that wouldn't do any good. Maybe I'm selfish too because I want to be here at college. This is what I need to be doing at this stage of my life. But I still feel badly that they are there in that situation." (Client continues exploring.)

EFFECTS OF OPEN QUESTIONS

Helpers can watch tapes of their sessions and rate the effects of their open questions on clients using the following 3-point scale:

1 = If open questions are not very helpful, the client does not respond or responds in a very minimal way. A minimal response suggests that the open question was not very useful—it did not help the client explore or it stopped exploration. The client also might respond negatively or with hostility to ineffective open questions. An example of this is when clients get annoyed and frustrated with helpers who continually say the same question (e.g., "How do you feel about that?").

2 = If open questions are at least moderately helpful, clients continue talking but keep repeating or rephrasing the same things rather than exploring new things. Again, such a client response suggests that the open question did not facilitate the client in thinking about other aspects of the problem.

3 = If open questions are very helpful, the client delves deeper into the problem and explores other aspects of the problem more thoroughly. The client also might reveal feelings, thoughts, and pertinent information about various aspects of the presenting problem. This response suggests that the open question has facilitated the client's exploration.

DIFFICULTIES HELPERS EXPERIENCE
IN DELIVERING OPEN QUESTIONS

The most common problem we have noticed is that helpers tend to ask the same type of open questions repeatedly, most often "How do you feel about that?" Many clients become annoyed when they continually hear the same type of question and hence may have a hard time responding. We recommend that helpers vary the phrasing of their open questions and ask about different types of things (e.g., thoughts, feelings, examples, past experiences, future expectations, reactions of others, the client's role in maintaining the problem).

Similarly, some beginning helpers use only open questions rather than interspersing open questions with other types of interventions, such as restatement and reflection of feelings. The interaction can become one sided if helpers ask too many open questions. Helpers are not demonstrating to the clients that they are hearing what the clients are saying or struggling to understand the clients. The tone of the session becomes a stilted interview rather than a mutual struggle to explore and understand the client's concerns. Because open questions are relatively easy, helpers use them instead of other skills, especially when they are anxious. Open questions are useful, but they are best when interspersed with restatements and reflection in the exploration stage.

Helpers may inappropriately use questions to satisfy their curiosity. They might ask for information out of curiosity rather than for helping the clients explore. For example, Martha has been working on her feelings of jealousy and competitiveness with her older sister. Martha comes into the session and announces that her sister had a date with a "hot" movie star. The helper might exclaim, "Wow, how did she meet him?," "What was he like?" Although extreme, this example illustrates how helpers can get carried away with wanting specific information for their own curiosity rather than to help clients explore. It also illustrates how the focus can easily shift away from the client to others. Additional problems that we have already discussed involve asking multiple questions, using closed instead of open questions, asking "why" questions, focusing on someone other than the client, and focusing on past rather than present feelings.

▬▬▬ **HELPFUL HINTS**

- Make sure your questions are open (i.e., do not ask questions that purposely limit the client's response to a "yes" or "no" answer). Rephrase closed questions into open questions (e.g., ask "What could you do tonight?" rather than "Have you thought about calling a friend tonight?").

- Remember that the goal of asking open questions is to facilitate exploration. If the client is already exploring, there is no need to interrupt.

- Vary your questions so that you are not always asking the same thing. If you feel stuck because the client is going in circles or repeating everything, think about asking a different type of open question. To help the client explore, you can ask questions about purpose (explore, clarify, example), focus (thoughts, feelings, behaviors), tense (past, present, future), and object (self, other).

- Avoid asking multiple questions without giving the client a chance to respond between questions (e.g., "What did you do then, and how did you feel, and what happened after that?").

- Avoid asking too many questions in a session. Too many questions can make clients uncomfortable. Clients also often wait passively for the next question when a helper is in a questioning mode.

- Avoid *why* questions. They put people on the defensive and are difficult to answer candidly. Why questions ask for speculation about motives, but clients may be unaware of their motives. Why questions also can imply criticism. Rephrase the why questions to make them less blaming. Rather than "Why did you fight with your husband?," ask "How did you and your husband start fighting?"

- Keep the focus on the client rather than on other people. Rather than asking "What did your friend say?," helpers can ask, "What was your reaction to her statement?"

- Be aware of attending behaviors, specifically tone of voice: Keep tone low to convey concern and intimacy, keep the rate of speech slow, and make the questions tentative to avoid sounding as though you are interrogating the client.

- Have a therapeutic intention for every question that you ask. Be prepared for the possibility that the client may want to know why you are asking the question. The ultimate test of the appropriateness of the open question is "Will the question that I am about to ask be helpful to the client?"

- Never beg the client for more information. Do not extort information or feelings from the client.

- Avoid questions that already have an answer because they can convey condescension (e.g., "You don't really feel that it's right to act that way, do you?").

PRACTICE EXERCISES

Pretend that a client says the following statements to you. Read each of the following statements, write down what your intentions would be, and then write an open question. (Recall that the typical intentions for using open questions are to clarify, focus, encourage catharsis, identify maladaptive cognitions, and identify

~~and intensify feelings.~~) Compare your responses to the possible helper responses that we provide at the end of the section. The helper responses that we have given are not the "right" or "best" open questions, but they are provided to give you some idea of the different possibilities.

Statements

1. **Client:** "I got my exam grade yesterday."
   Helper intention(s): _____
   Helper response: _____
   _____

2. **Client:** "I saw on the news that a college student died because she drank too much."
   Helper intention(s): _____
   Helper response:_____
   _____

3. **Client:** "We talked in class about the concept of a "chilly climate" and how female students don't get called on in the classroom as much as male students."
   Helper intention(s):_____
   Helper response:_____
   _____

4. **Client:** "I don't want to be here. I wouldn't be here if I didn't have to be; but my parole officer told me I had to come."
   Helper intention(s):_____
   Helper response:_____
   _____

Possible Helper Responses

1. "How do you feel about your grade?" (intent: to identify and intensify feelings, to encourage catharsis)
   "How does your grade make you feel about yourself?" (intent: to identify and intensify feelings, to encourage catharsis)
   "Talk to me about your thoughts about your grade." (intent: to identify maladaptive cognitions)

2. "What was your reaction to hearing this news?" (intent: to identify and intensify feelings, to identify maladaptive cognitions, to encourage catharsis)
   "Tell me more about your reaction to that." (intent: to identify and intensify feelings, to identify maladaptive cognitions, to encourage catharsis)
   "How do you feel about your drinking behavior?" (intent: to identify and intensify feelings, to encourage catharsis)

3. "How do you feel about the climate here?" (intent: to identify and intensify feelings, to encourage catharsis)
   "How do you feel about the ways your teachers treat you?" (intent: to identify and intensify feelings, to encourage catharsis)
   "How does the climate here compare to what you've had in the past?" (intent: to encourage catharsis; to clarify)

4. "How does it feel to have someone make you come here?" (intent: to identify and intensify feelings, to encourage catharsis)

"What do you generally do when someone makes you do something?" (intent: to encourage catharsis)

"What would you like to do with our session today?" (intent: to focus)

What Do You Think?

- How do you respond when people use open questions in conversation with you?
- In this chapter, we suggest that it is difficult for clients to respond to "why" questions. Describe your position on the use of "why" questions.
- Provide several examples of when helpers might use open questions in the helping process.
- Compare restatements and open questions in terms of their ability to facilitate exploration.

LAB 4 Open Question

Goal: For helpers to practice using open questions to help clients explore their thoughts and feelings. The goal is not to solve problems.

For this exercise, students should be arranged in groups of three. Initially, one person should be the helper, one the client, and one the observer. Then, students can switch roles, so that each person has the opportunity to participate in each role.

Exercise 1

Helper's and Client's Tasks During the Helping Interchange

1. Helpers should introduce themselves.
2. Clients should talk about a topic for a few sentences. (See chapter 1 for suggestions for topics.)
3. After each client statement, the helper should ask an open question. For this exercise, helpers should use only open questions and no other interventions. Keep the open questions short and simple.
4. Continue for 5 to 10 turns. The helper should ask the client about many different aspects of the topic: purpose (explore, clarify, example), focus (thoughts, feelings, behaviors), tense (past, present, future), and object (self, other). Remember to focus on the client rather than on others.

Observer's Tasks During the Helping Interchange

Take notes about helper's questions. Note the number of closed versus open questions. Write down the specific questions so that they can be discussed in the feedback. Note which ones were effective (e.g., enabled client to explore deeper) compared to which ones were less effective (e.g., were confusing, distracted the client from the main topic). Note the manner of the delivery of the questions—was the helper gentle and supportive or intrusive like an interrogator?

After the Helping Interchange

1. Helpers should talk about how it felt to ask open questions.
2. Clients should talk about how it felt to be the recipient of questions.
3. Observers should give positive and negative feedback to helpers about the appropriateness of the open questions and the manner in which they were delivered. Discuss specific questions that were helpful and less helpful.

SWITCH ROLES

Exercise 2

The tasks in this exercise are exactly the same as in Exercise 1 for clients and observers; helpers can use both restatements and open questions.

Personal Reflections

- What difficulties did you have asking open questions?
- How did the client respond when you asked open questions?
- What did you learn about yourself in trying to use open questions?

9 Reflection of Feelings

> It seems to me that clients who have moved significantly in therapy live more intimately with their feelings of pain, but also more vividly with their feelings of ecstasy; that anger is more clearly felt, but so also is love; that fear is an experience they know more deeply, but so is courage.
>
> *Carl Rogers*

In a jubilant tone, Sarah told her helper that she had received a scholarship and would now be able to quit her job and go to school full-time. The helper responded, "You must feel very relieved that you don't have to worry anymore about financing your education." This reflection enabled Sarah to talk further about her anxieties about money and her relief that she would be able to continue her education.

Tyler, an aspiring actor, had been in an automobile accident that left him crippled and made it unlikely that he would ever be able to act again. Throughout the session, his helper used a number of reflections (e.g., "You feel angry because you can no longer do what you love to do," "I wonder if you feel afraid that people will laugh at you," "It sounds like you feel anxious about going out in public") to help Tyler talk about the many feelings he had so that he could identify and accept what was going on inside him.

A REFLECTION of feelings is a repeating or rephrasing of the client's statements with an emphasis on the client's feelings. The feelings may have been stated by the client (in either the same or similar words) or the helper may be able to infer the feelings from the client's nonverbal behavior or the content of the client's message (see Exhibit 9.1).

INTENTIONS

Helpers typically use reflections to help clients identify, clarify, and express feelings. In fact, reflection is one of the most important skills for facilitating client exploration. The expected response is for the client to explore feelings more deeply. Helpers thus hope that clients become immersed in their inner experiences. Rather than just articulating an intellectual label of a feeling, then, helpers want clients to experience feelings in the immediate moment. For example, a couple might recount an incident in which they became angry with one another. The helper would encourage them to express their current feelings of anger and talk to each other about how they are feeling right now about the incident. Another intention is to encourage emotional catharsis with reflections. By encouraging clients to experience their feelings, helpers hope to provide cathartic relief. Additional intentions are to promote self-control and instill hope through encouraging clients to express, accept,

EXHIBIT 9.1. OVERVIEW OF REFLECTION OF FEELINGS

Definition	A *reflection of feelings* is a repeating or rephrasing of client's statements, including an explicit identification of client's feelings. The feelings may have been stated by the client (in exactly the same or similar words), or the helper may infer feelings from the client's nonverbal behavior, the context, or the content of client's message. The reflection may be phrased either tentatively or as a statement.
Examples	"You feel angry at your husband for not taking care of the children."
	"You seem pleased that you told your boss that you didn't want to work late."
Typical intentions	To identify and intensify feelings, to encourage catharsis, to clarify, to instill hope, to promote self-control (see Appendix A)
Possible client reactions	Feelings, negative thoughts or behaviors, clear, responsibility, unstuck, scared, worse, misunderstood (see Appendix D)
Desired client behavior	Affective exploration (see Appendix E)
Difficulties helpers experience in delivering reflections	Dealing with intense feelings such as anger and sadness
	Capturing the essence (or most intense feeling) to reflect to the client
	Separating one's own feelings from the experiences of clients
	Stating feeling words too adamantly, such that clients have difficulty correcting you or expressing other feelings

and learn how to cope with their feelings. A final intention for using reflection is to help clients clarify and explain themselves.

WHY USE REFLECTION OF FEELINGS?

As Rogers noted, emotions are a key part of our experience. Often we ignore, deny, distort, or repress our feelings because we have been told that they are unacceptable. Hence, we grow apart from our inner experiencing and cannot accept ourselves. We need to return to our emotions and allow ourselves to feel them because only then can we decide what we want to do about them.

Importance of Emotions

Feelings are at least as important as content in client communication. Many beginning helpers are very concerned about learning all the details of events, as they might in a friendship or when they are asked to solve a problem, but they ignore the feelings.

Gathering details implies that helpers are going to do something to solve the problem, and it allows the client to move away from painful or confusing affect. We believe that clients are best able to solve their problems when their feelings are clear and experienced.

Clients' expression of emotions enables helpers to know and understand them. Because people respond differently to events, we need to know how experiences are interpreted by individual clients. For example, when Varda came to a helper's office because her father died, the helper assumed that Varda felt sad, depressed, and lonely because that is how the helper felt when her father died. In fact, Varda felt anger because she had been having memories of childhood sexual abuse since her father died. It was safe for Varda to remember the occurrences of abuse only when her father was no longer able to hurt her. In addition, Varda felt relief that her father died because she no longer had to deal with him. This example illustrates that helpers must listen carefully so that they do not impose their assumptions about feelings on clients.

If clients accept their emotions, they can become open to new feelings and experiences. Feelings are not static but rather change once they are experienced. When a person experiences one feeling fully and completely, new feelings emerge. For example, once Varda experienced her anger, she became aware of other feelings such as sadness, which then led to feelings of acceptance and peace. In contrast, unaccepted feelings are likely to "leak" out, sometimes in very destructive ways. For example, Robert might become subtly rude or hostile to his friend who was accepted into a prestigious law school after learning that his application was rejected. All of us know people who do not directly say when they are angry but still manage to communicate subtle, nasty messages that make it difficult to respond to them. At other times, if people cannot accept their feelings, they get stuck. Similar to the obstruction that occurs when a river gets dammed up, people also get blocked if they do not allow themselves to have and express their feelings.

Because feelings are rarely simple or straightforward, clients might have several conflicting feelings about a topic. For example, Diana might feel excited about taking a new job and pleased that she was selected over other candidates. However, she might also feel anxious about what is required of her, afraid of working too closely with the boss who reminds her of her father, insecure about how others may view her, and worried about whether she can make enough money to pay the rent. As helpers, it is important to try to allow clients to express as many of these feelings as possible without worrying about whether the feelings are contradictory. In fact, if clients present only a unidimensional picture of feelings, helpers might wonder if the opposite feelings are also present. Some Gestalt therapists believe that every feeling has two sides. Hence, if clients talk only about fear, helpers might wonder about wishes; if clients talk only about love, helpers might wonder about hate. Furthermore, Teyber (1997) noted that feelings often exist in constellations, such that underneath anger is sometimes sadness and shame, and underneath sadness is sometimes anger and guilt. By fostering deeper thought about the feelings, helpers enable clients to admit the multitude of feelings that they might not otherwise have been able to acknowledge.

We should also note that there are cultural differences in expressing emotion and revealing personal experiences. In the United States, people are generally encouraged to be open about their feelings and experiences. One only needs to tune in radio and television talk shows to see how many people share their innermost experiences freely. People from other cultures, however, might be more reserved about expressing feelings. In addition, people have different experiences attached to feeling words. For example, if one does not expect much, one might feel relieved if someone is nice, whereas if one demands a lot from others, one might feel insulted if someone is merely courteous. Hence, helpers have a responsibility to explore what feelings are like for particular clients.

Helpers also should remember that some people, especially men, have a hard time expressing feelings. Men are not socialized to be sensitive to feelings and often feel threatened if asked to indicate what they are feeling (Cournoyer & Mahalik, 1995; Good et al., 1995; O'Neil, 1981). Clients who can experience their feelings and come to accept and own them can then decide how to behave. One does not have to act on the feelings but can make a more informed decision about what to do when the feelings are out in the open. In other words, when one feels murderous, one does not have to murder but can figure out other avenues of expression. Being aware of one's feelings makes one less likely to act out on them unintentionally.

Benefits of Reflection of Feelings

Reflections of feelings are ideal interventions for enabling clients to enter into their internal experiences, especially if they are delivered with concern and empathy for the client's reluctance to experience the painful feelings. Clients often need such assistance to recognize and accept their feelings and themselves. Reflections also validate the feelings. Laing and Esterson (1970) suggested that people stop feeling "crazy" when their subjective experience is validated. Although it may sound easy, experiencing and expressing feelings can be difficult and often painful.

Clients often have difficulty identifying and accepting their feelings on their own, perhaps because they do not know how they feel or are ambivalent or negative about the feelings. Furthermore, feelings are difficult to articulate because they are often sensations rather than fully understood awarenesses that can be symbolized in words. So if clients have difficulty identifying their feelings, they might feel very anxious and unsure when helpers ask, "How are you feeling about that?" Such questions can confuse or concern clients because they are not sure what helpers want to hear and how they "should" feel. Sometimes asking how they feel stimulates defenses and makes clients shut down. With such questions, clients also sometimes feel annoyed that helpers are not really listening to what they are saying or trying to empathize with their feelings. In contrast, reflecting feelings ("You seem upset about that") might feel more facilitative and less threatening to clients.

Reflecting feelings can also model the expression of feelings, which could be useful for clients who are out of touch with their emotions. Many people have an experience of an emotion but do not have a label for the feeling. For example, saying "I wonder if you feel frustrated with your sister" suggests but does not explicitly state that frustration is a possible feeling that a client might have in this situation. By labeling feelings, helpers also imply that they are not afraid of feelings, that feelings are familiar, and that helpers continue to accept clients regardless of their feelings. Reflections of feelings might feel safer to clients than being asked about feelings because reflections provide an example of how the client might be feeling rather than being asked to reveal feelings of which they might not be aware. By suggesting a feeling, reflections might circumvent defenses or possible embarrassment about having the feelings. Helpers indicate through reflections that the feelings are normal and that they accept the person who has the feelings, which can be a relief to clients.

Hearing reflections enables clients to rethink and reexamine what they really feel. If a helper uses the term *disgusted*, this forces the client to think about whether *disgusted* fits his or her experience. This searching can lead to deeper exploration of the feelings in an attempt to clarify the feeling. It is often difficult for clients to verbalize their deepest, most private thoughts and feelings. In a safe and supportive relationship, they can begin to explore the feelings, which are often quite complex and contradictory. They can feel a combination of love, hatred, and guilt toward the same person in the same situation. Being allowed to admit these ambivalent feelings to another person and not be rejected can enable clients to accept feelings as their own.

Coming up with reflections requires that helpers work at least as hard as clients are working. Reflections demonstrate that the helper is actively engaged in trying to understand the client. It also forces helpers to communicate this understanding to investigate the accuracy of their perceptions. One could say, "I understand exactly how you feel," but this statement does not demonstrate to the client the content of the understanding. Reflections provide the opportunity for helpers to show evidence of their understanding. Beginning helpers quickly discover that accurately perceiving how another person feels is difficult. We can never truly understand another person, but we can struggle to get past our own perceptions and try to immerse ourselves in the client's experiences.

Hence, reflections of feelings are ideal interventions for encouraging client expression of feelings because helpers give examples of what feelings clients might be experiencing so that clients can begin to recognize and accept feelings, and helpers accept clients' feelings as natural and normal. In addition, clients can give helpers feedback about what they did and did not understand when helpers clearly articulate what they think clients are feeling. Finally, reflections build the relationship because helpers communicate their understanding to clients.

How Reflection of Feelings Relates to Empathy

Some authors have equated reflection of feeling with empathy (e.g., Carkhuff, 1969; Egan, 1994). We disagree with this stance; we believe that it is too narrow to define *empathy* as just a reflection of feeling (see also Duan & Hill, 1996). We would agree more with Rogers (1957), who believed that empathy is an attitude or way of being in tune with the experience of another person. We would expect that a reflection of feelings, delivered appropriately, could be a manifestation of empathy. However, we can also imagine that a technically correct reflection of feelings could be unempathic because it was delivered at the wrong time or in an inappropriate manner. For example, if a helper says, "you feel humiliated" in an all-knowing, firm voice, the client might feel put down or misunderstood. The client may feel that the helper understood her better than she understood herself, which could make her mistrust her own feelings and submit to the helper as the authority.

We can also imagine times when it would be more empathic to use a helping skill other than a reflection (e.g., a challenge). A helper responding to a client who feels stuck in an abusive relationship might challenge her to seek shelter in a battered women's program. This response might be very empathic given the dangerous situation in the home and the helper's valuing of the client as a person deserving of a healthy relationship.

Caveats

Sharing feelings has positive benefits in that clients can experience relief from tension, come to accept their feelings, and feel proud that they had the courage to express and face their feelings. However, sharing feelings can be problematic if clients feel so good after expressing their feelings that they are not motivated to make changes. It can also be problematic if clients just spew forth different feelings without really experiencing their feelings. In addition, problems occur when clients reveal more feelings than they can tolerate at the time. If client defenses are overwhelmed, clients can deteriorate under prolonged emotional catharsis. They may not be ready for the feelings and may not feel supported enough to risk deep exploration. Brammer and MacDonald (1996) suggested that helpers should be cautious about encouraging expression of too many feelings when

- a client has a severe emotional disorder, delusional thinking, or extreme anger, and helpers are not experienced in dealing with such clients
- a client is going through severe emotional crises, and discussing feelings would add more pressure than he or she could handle
- a client has had major difficulty in dealing with emotional crises in the past
- a client shows strong resistance to expressing feelings
- there is not enough time to work through the feelings.

An additional concern is that clients might accept the helper's reflection as accurate not because it necessarily is, but because the helper is in a position of authority. Clients might feel that their helpers know more about them than they actually do. Helpers thus need to be careful to observe whether clients comply too readily with what helpers say rather than generating their own feelings. As tempting as it might be, acting as an omniscient authority with regard to clients' feelings often leads to client dependency, misunderstandings, or difficult realizations of the limitations of the helper.

These cautions are included not to discourage helpers or make them fearful about dealing with client feelings, but to increase helper awareness of the possible hazards of expressing feelings. In general, reflection of feelings is appropriate and beneficial, but helpers need to be aware that reflections can sometimes lead to clients feeling overwhelmed by uncontrollable feelings.

EMPIRICAL EVIDENCE

Because judges in research studies have not been able to distinguish between restatements and reflections and because the two helping skills seem to have similar effects, they have been grouped together in much of the existing research under "paraphrase." In previous studies (Barkham & Shapiro, 1986; Hill, Helms, Tichenor, et al., 1988), paraphrase was used in 10–31% of the therapist interventions. In the Hill, Helms, Tichenor, et al. study of brief therapy, paraphrase was rated as moderately helpful and led to moderate levels of client experiencing (i.e., being able to talk openly about and experience their feelings). Restatements and reflections were generally more effective than open and closed questions—the other main helping skills used in the exploration stage. Initially, we were surprised that restatements and reflections of feelings were not rated as more helpful, given that we believe that they are the building blocks that form the foundation for insight and action. We propose that even though these interventions are typically rated as less helpful than those of other more powerful interventions (e.g., challenges, interpretations, self-disclosures, immediacy), they are absolutely crucial in establishing the relationship and helping clients explore. As we mentioned previously, clients often do not even notice when helpers are using good restatements and reflections because they are simply facilitated in their exploration. Perhaps other types of measures are needed to determine the effects of restatements and reflections.

HOW TO REFLECT FEELINGS

Clients need to feel safe enough in the therapeutic relationship to risk delving into their feelings. They must feel that they will not be disparaged, embarrassed, or shamed but rather accepted, valued, and respected when they reveal themselves. Hence, reflections must be done gently and with empathy.

Format of Reflection of Feelings

When learning to do reflections, helpers may begin by using the following format: You feel __ because __. In other words, they should make sure to say both the feeling and the reason for the feeling; for example, "You feel frustrated because you didn't get your way." The "because" clause paraphrases the content of what the client has been discussing to lend support to why the client would have the feeling. Although it is not always necessary to use the "because" clause (e.g., helpers often say, "You feel __"), it can be useful for providing supporting data for why the client might have the feeling.

As with restatements, helpers should pick only what they perceive to be the most salient feeling rather than try to reflect all of the feelings. Obviously, selecting the most salient feeling requires a judgment call, so helpers need to be attentive to clients' verbal and nonverbal behavior. For example, helpers can pay attention to where the most or least energy is in what the client is saying or how they are reacting nonverbally to detect the most powerful immediate feelings.

Given that our goal is to allow clients to immerse themselves in their feelings so that they can come to accept them, we suggest that helpers focus on present feelings rather than past feelings so that clients experience their immediate feelings rather than telling stories about past feelings (e.g., "You sound irritated right now as you talk about your mother" rather than "It sounds like you were upset with your mother").

We also suggest that helpers allow clients time to absorb and think about the reflections that are presented rather than rushing quickly to the next thing. If clients start crying or getting upset, helpers can encourage clients to experience and express these feelings rather than trying to "take away" the feelings or make them better.

Furthermore, because our goals are to reflect and to keep the focus on the client, helpers need to be very aware of staying in the background and facilitating exploration in their clients. Maintaining a supportive and listening stance can aid helpers in reaching this goal. In addition, helpers can vary the format of reflections so that clients do not become annoyed with repetitive formats (e.g., "It sounds like you're feeling __"). Good reflections (and restatements) should almost not be noticed by clients because these interventions help the clients continue exploring, thus paying more attention to themselves than to the helper.

Identifying Feeling Words

Many beginning helpers have difficulty coming up with a range of words to describe the emotions expressed in a given situation. In Exhibit 9.2, we present a checklist of emotion words broken down into 13 categories (developed for the Hill, Siegelman, Gronsky, Sturniolo, & Fretz, 1981, study). Six of the categories are of positive emotions, whereas seven are of negative emotions. Research has found that negative emotions generally outnumber positive emotions by about two to one (Izard, 1977). When clients talk about problems in helping, they are even more likely to discuss negative emotions than positive

EXHIBIT 9.2. EMOTION WORD CHECKLIST

Calm–relaxed

at ease	easy going	peaceful	safe	tame
calm	mellow	quiet	serene	
cool	mild	relaxed	soothed	

Happy–joyful

amused	enchanted	humorous	optimistic	terrific
carefree	fantastic	jolly	overjoyed	thrilled
cheerful	funny	joyful	pleasant	wonderful
comical	glad	lighthearted	pleased	
elated	good-humored	lucky	silly	
ecstatic	happy	marvelous	splendid	
excited	high	merry	superb	

Vigorous–active

active	daring	enthusiastic	spirited	vivacious
adventurous	energetic	lively	vigorous	wild
alive				

Competent–powerful

authoritative	courageous	forceful	masculine	strong
bold	delighted	heroic	mighty	successful
brave	dominant	important	powerful	sure
brilliant	effective	independent	proud	wise
capable	efficient	influential	responsible	
competent	firm	majestic	self-reliant	
confident	fearless	manly	steady	

Concerned–caring

brotherly	considerate	helpful	kindly	understanding
caring	forgiving	hospitable	neighborly	unselfish
charitable	generous	humane	nice	
comforting	gentle	interested	obliging	
concerned	giving	kind	sympathetic	

Respectful–loving

admired	lovable	loved	loving	respectable
respected				

Tense–anxious

alarmed	impatient	jumpy	panicky	uneasy
anxious	jittery	nervous	tense	worried
fidgety				

Sad–depressed

blue	gloomy	lonely	sad	tearful
dismal	glum	low	somber	unhappy
down	grim	miserable	sorrowful	unloved
depressed	heartsick	mournful	sullen	upset

Angry–hostile

agitated	bitter	furious	nasty	sadistic
aggravated	bloodthirsty	harsh	outraged	spiteful
angry	cold-blooded	hateful	peeved	stormy
annoyed	combative	heartless	perturbed	vengeful
antagonistic	cross	hellish	poisonous	vindictive
bad-tempered	cruel	hostile	resentful	violent
belligerent	disgusted	inconsiderate	rude	vicious
biting	enraged	inhuman	ruthless	

Tired–apathetic

apathetic	bushed	fatigued	sleepy	tired
bored	exhausted	run down	sluggish	weary

Confused–bewildered

baffled	doubtful	perplexed	shaken	stranded
bewildered	hesitant	puzzled	spaced out	uncertain
confused	lost	scattered	speechless	unsure

Criticized–shamed

abused	criticized	laughed at	put down	scorned
belittled	embarrassed	mocked	reprimanded	shamed
cheapened	humiliated	ostracized	ridiculed	slandered

Inadequate–weak

cowardly	inadequate	insignificant	small	unworthy
feeble	incapable	lame	trivial	useless
flimsy	incompetent	meek	unable	vulnerable
fragile	ineffective	powerless	unfit	weak
helpless	inefficient	puny	unimportant	worthless
impaired	inferior	sickly	unqualified	

Note. Data from Hill et al. (1981).

---

emotions. Perhaps it is human nature to "forget" the good things that happen to us and instead to dwell on the negative things, especially in a helping setting where the focus is most often on problems.

Sources of Reflections

Clues for what the client is feeling can be found in four sources: the client's portrayal of his or her feelings, the client's verbal content, the client's nonverbal behavior, and the helper's projection of his or her own feelings onto the client. Helpers need to be aware that the last three sources only provide clues and may not necessarily be accurate reflections of clients' feelings.

Client's Expression of Feeling

Sometimes clients are aware of their feelings and express them openly. For example, a client might say, "I was really upset with my teacher. I was so mad that she wouldn't even listen when I told her my feelings." In this case, the helper might use another word (e.g., "furious") to describe the feelings so that the client can begin to experience feelings at a deeper level and explore other aspects of the feelings. The client has signaled her or his readiness to talk about feelings, so the helper needs to be able to help the client move into deeper exploration. We recommend using synonyms rather than repeating the exact feeling word the client has used, so that the client can think about different parts of the feelings. In addition, helpers need to remember that feelings are multifaceted and change over time, so understanding and reflecting feelings at one point in time are just the beginning of entering into an experiential process. Hence, helpers need to be constantly attentive to looking for new feelings that fit in the immediate moment.

Client's Verbal Content

Another source for clues about feelings is verbal content. Although the client may not be mentioning feelings directly, it may be possible to infer what the feelings might be from the client's words. For example, clients often respond to a major loss with feelings of sadness; people often respond to success with feelings of pleasure; clients often respond to anger directed at them with fear. Hence, helpers can make some preliminary hypotheses about what clients might feel. For example, an adolescent client might mention that she received her report card and had improved her grades in almost every subject. The helper might say, "You must feel proud of yourself for raising your grades." However, helpers need to be cautious and ready to revise the reflections on the basis of further feedback. Helpers cannot know everything there is to know about clients, so they may need to amend their reflections as they gather more information and as the feelings emerge and change in sessions.

Nonverbal Behaviors

How the client appears to be feeling is a third source of clues for feelings. For example, if the client is smiling and looks pleased, the helper might say something like, "I wonder if you feel happy about that." Helpers should remember to look at all the nonverbal behaviors for clues. Remember that, as discussed in chapter 6, there is often nonverbal leakage in arm and leg movements because people do not monitor themselves as closely in these areas as in their facial expression. Hence, when a client is kicking his or her foot, a helper might wonder if the client is nervous or angry. The meaning of nonverbal behaviors is not always the same, however, so helpers must use nonverbals as clues to possible feelings rather than as indicators of feelings.

Projection of Helper's Feelings

A final source for detecting client feelings is ourselves: How would I feel if I were in that situation? For example, if a client is talking about an argument with a roommate over cleaning their apartment, helpers can recall how they have felt in arguments with roommates, siblings, or friends. Helpers are not judging how clients "should" feel but are attempting to understand the client's feelings by placing themselves in the client's shoes and thinking about how they have felt or would feel in that situation. Helpers can use these projections, as long as they always remember that the projections are possibilities rather than accurate representations of the client's reality. The helper's feelings might not apply to someone else. However, helpers can hypothesize about the client's feelings using their projections and then search for supporting evidence in the client's verbal content and nonverbal behaviors. Helpers must remember to keep the focus on the client's (rather than their own) experiences. When personal feelings become overwhelming for the helper, we recommend that the helper seek therapy.

Accuracy of Reflection

The feeling word provided by the helper does not have to be perfectly accurate to be helpful, although it does need to be "in the ballpark." If the feeling word is relatively close to what the client is feeling, it can enable the client to clarify the feeling. For example, if a client has been talking about feeling scared and the helper uses the word *tense*, the client can clarify and say that the feeling is more like *terror*. Hence, clarifying the feelings gives the helper a clearer understanding of the client and enables the client to clarify what he or she is experiencing internally. One could even argue that reflections that are too accurate could halt client exploration because there would be no reason to try to clarify or explore the feelings. On the other hand, feelings that are "out of the ballpark" can be damaging. If a helper uses the word *happy* after the client has said *tense*, the client might feel that the helper was not listening or could not understand.

Helpers are rarely accurate with every single reflection. More often, helpers struggle in every reflection to understand their clients more completely. Often it is the client's awareness of the helper's struggle that really conveys the empathy rather than the precise reflection. Understanding another person's feelings is something we strive for but remain humbly aware of how difficult it is to achieve. Hence, helpers should not be as concerned with assessing the accuracy of a particular intervention as with trying to understand the client.

Reflection Example

The following is a brief example of how a helper could use reflection of feelings (in italics) in a session:

> **Client:** "I had to miss classes last week because I got a call right before class that my father had been in a serious car accident. He was on the beltway and a truck driver fell asleep at the wheel and swerved right into him, causing a six-car pile-up. It was really awful."
>
> **Helper:** *"You sound very upset."*
>
> **Client:** "I am. All the way to the hospital, I kept worrying about whether he was okay. The worst thing is that he had already had several bad things happen to him. His third wife had recently left him, he lost money in the stock market, and his dog died."
>
> **Helper:** *"You're concerned about him because of all the things that have happened lately."*
>
> **Client:** "Yeah, he doesn't have much will to live, and I don't know what to do for him. I try to be there, but he doesn't really seem to care."
>
> **Helper:** *"It hurts that he doesn't notice you."*
>
> **Client:** "Yeah, I have always tried to please my father. I always felt like I couldn't do enough to make him happy. I think he preferred my brother. My

brother was a better athlete and liked to work in the shop with him. My father just never valued what I did. I don't know if he liked me very much."

Helper: *"Wow, that's really painful. I wonder if you're angry too?"*

Client: "Yeah, I am. What's wrong with me that my father wouldn't like me? I think I'm a pretty nice guy." (Client continues to explore the situation.)

EFFECTS OF REFLECTION

Helpers can determine whether their reflections are effective by attending to the client's response (see also Egan, 1994). A 3-point scale can be used to assess the impact of the reflection:

1 = When the reflection is not accurate or is very unhelpful, the client might not respond or might reject the helper's statement (e.g., "No, I don't feel that at all"). Alternatively, the client might say something like, "That's what I just said" and not explore further, or the client might ignore the helper's reflection and not respond with any feelings.

2 = When the reflection is at least moderately effective, clients continue talking but may not go deeper into their feelings. They might say something like, "you're right" or "yeah" but not go on to explore.

3 = When reflections are very helpful, clients might pause and say something like, "Wow, you're right, I never thought of it that way before, but that is what I have been feeling." They then go on to talk in greater depth about their feelings. Often new feelings emerge as clients immerse themselves in their immediate experiences.

DIFFICULTIES HELPERS EXPERIENCE IN DELIVERING REFLECTION

Beginning helpers are often nervous about dealing with expressions of intense negative affect, such as sadness or anger. They become anxious when clients cry because they feel uncomfortable with crying, uncertain about how to handle emotions, and ineffectual because thay cannot make everything better. Feelings of guilt might also emerge when clients cry because helpers might think that their interventions upset the client or caused the pain. Furthermore, helpers might be afraid that if they encourage clients to express their feelings, the clients will get stuck in the feelings and not be able to emerge from them. In addition, helpers might have difficulty accepting intense feelings both in themselves and in their clients. We stress that feelings are natural and that clients need to be able to express feelings so they can begin to accept them. When helpers accept clients' feelings, it conveys to the clients that their feelings are okay. Hence, helpers are encouraged to learn to accept and cope with their anxieties so that they can enable clients to express and accept their feelings. Many helpers learn that taking a deep breath and trying to focus on the client and understand the client's feelings helps them deal with the intense expression of affect in sessions.

At times, beginning helpers have difficulty capturing the most important feeling to reflect back to the client. They might hear several feelings and be confused about which one is the most important to reflect first. Helpers should pay attention to the feeling that seems to elicit the most intensity or depth of feelings. Practice helps tremendously. Helpers can practice by guessing the most salient emotions that are displayed in movies, reflecting strong feelings of friends when they are talking about problems, and role playing in practice exercises.

Some helpers also have difficulty separating their own feelings from the experience of the clients. They assume that clients must have the same feelings they do. Some helpers overidentify with clients and feel the client's feeling so much (i.e., feel sympathy or emotional contagion) that they cannot be objective and helpful. We urge helpers to become aware of their own feelings as much as possible so that they can differentiate what is coming from clients and what is coming from themselves. As we have mentioned before, personal therapy can be invaluable in this task.

Sometimes helpers state the client's feelings too definitely (e.g., "You obviously feel angry") rather than tentatively (e.g., "I wonder if you feel angry"). If clients are passive and have difficulty disagreeing with their helpers, direct statements of feelings by helpers can become a problem because clients are not thinking for themselves or examining their experiences. A more tentative statement about feelings can be more respectful and encourage the client to verify or dismiss the feeling word.

At about this point in the course, some students have told us that they felt like they were getting worse rather than better. They were focusing so much on each individual skill and watching everything they did that it became hard to perform at all. An analogy can be drawn to learning to drive. When you first learned to drive, you were probably conscious of every little thing you did. Like beginning drivers, beginning helpers focus on each thing they do in the helping encounter. Similarly, in learning helping skills we practice the individual ones (and often unlearn many habits that are not facilitative for helping) and then put all the skills together. Although difficult initially, it should begin feeling easier when you come to put them all together. Hence, if you are feeling badly about your skills as a helper right now, give yourself some time. Students often feel better after practicing for a few more weeks. (Of course, some students come to realize that they do not want to be helpers. For us, both outcomes are valuable because students learn more about themselves.)

HELPFUL HINTS

- Listen for the basic underlying feeling. Look for what the client says with the most intensity. Further clues for feelings include listening for feeling words, hearing the verbal content, watching the nonverbal expressions, and projecting your own feelings from similar situations. Remember, however, that these are clues and may not necessarily accurately reflect the client's feelings.

- When you are starting to learn how to do reflections, we recommend using the format, "You feel __ because __" to make sure you capture the feeling word and the possible reasons for the feeling. For example, you might say, "You feel upset because your mother won't talk to you." Do not interpret where the feelings came from beyond paraphrasing the feeling in what the client has said. Later, you can also use the format, "You feel __" without adding the reasons for the feeling.

- Reflect present feelings rather than past feelings. A focus on present feelings keeps the client from telling stories and not being immediately involved. Remember that a client could still be very upset about an event that occurred a long time ago—but these are present feelings about a past event. For example, rather than "You felt angry when he said that," you might try "You sound angry right now when you describe the situation."

- You do not have to say the perfect feeling word. You just have to get the approximate feeling word. If the feeling is close enough, the client can correct it and let you know more about how she or he feels. If it is too different than the client's intention, the client might feel misunderstood and communication might stop.

- Reflect what you think is the most important or intense feeling at the moment rather than trying to capture everything the client has stated. You have more opportunities in the session to reflect other important feelings as they emerge. Your goal is to enable the client to focus and experience feelings at a deeper level, and reflecting too many feelings at once could be distracting and diffusing.

- Keep the reflection short and concise. Trainees tend to talk too much, which takes the focus off the client.

- Use an empathic tone, convey concern, and show that you are trying to understand. Clients can tell whether you are parroting and using a pat phrase or whether you are genuinely interested. Don't judge clients (e.g., "You feel angry about *that?*"). Speaking softly and slowly can make your voice sound warmer.

- Use a tentative tone so that clients can reject or modify feeling words if they are not correct.

- Focus on the client rather than on other people, even if the client's focus is on the other person (e.g., "You feel angry at your mother" rather than "Your mother sounds like she is angry").

- Vary the format to avoid sounding like a machine. Clients often feel very irritated when helpers sound like parrots repeating the same phrases over and over. Variations that you could try include the following:

    "It sounds like you feel . . . ."

    "Perhaps you feel . . . ."

    "If I were you, I would feel . . . ."

    "I wonder if you feel . . . ."

    "You seem . . . ."

    "So you're feeling . . . ."

    "And that made you feel . . . ."

    "I hear you saying . . . ."

    "My hunch is that you feel . . . ."

    "So what you're saying is that you might feel . . . ."

    "I'm sensing that you feel . . . ."

    "You're . . . ."

    "Maybe you feel . . . ."

    "Upset" (or whatever word applies)

- Vary the feeling words that you use. Exhibit 9.2 offers a list of feeling words developed by Hill et al. (1981). We encourage you to add feeling words to this list to make it as "user friendly" as possible.

- Use feeling words that the client can understand. For example, a 9-year-old might respond better to "You are mad that you were treated badly" than to "You feel aggrieved that your rights were abridged."

- Take a deep breath before you give your reflection. The deep breath helps you relax and gives you a chance to think about what you want to say. There is no need to rush.

- When the client is stuck or cannot think of what to say, the helper can reflect immediate feelings (e.g., "You feel stuck right now," "You're not sure what to say next," or "You feel irritated that I didn't understand what you said").

- If a client responds with something like "that's it" but does not explore further, pause for a minute and give the client an opportunity to reflect on her or his experience and see if anything new emerges. After that, offer a new reflection that seems appropriate for the immediate moment (e.g., "Even though you are aware that you feel upset, you feel unsure what to do about that feeling" or "You feel stuck with where to go with your feeling"). By focusing on the immediate feelings, the client can explore more about the experience in the moment and might even give you feedback about how to be more helpful to her or him.

- Some students have expressed concerns about what to do if a client starts crying. If you reflect feelings and clients begin to experience their feelings, undoubtedly some of their feelings are of sadness and pain. We encourage you to stay with the client and not try to "take away" their sadness but to accept the client and the feelings. You might want to be quiet for a minute and allow the client to cry and then give a reflection in a soft tone of voice to help the client begin to verbalize the feelings.

- If you make an inaccurate reflection or if a client does not respond well to your reflection, our suggestion is not to apologize but to ask the client to explain more about how he or she feels and try again to understand the feelings. Try to avoid negative self-talk (e.g., "I'm a lousy helper because I didn't give a perfect reflection"). Try instead to view the "mistake" as an opportunity to learn more about how the client really feels.

PRACTICE EXERCISES

For each of the following examples, indicate your intention(s) and write a reflection. (Recall that typical intentions for reflections are to identify and intensify feelings, encourage catharsis, clarify, instill hope, and promote self-control.) Compare your responses to the possible helper responses provided at the end of the section.

Statements

1. **Client:** "I'm really having difficulty with my schoolwork right now. I have a hard time concentrating because there are so many other things going on. My mother is in the hospital and I wish I could be there to be with her because she may die soon. When I'm thinking about her, it's hard to get into my work. But I know that the thing that would upset her most is if I got bad grades and didn't finish school."

   Helper intention(s):_____

   Helper response:_____

2. **Client:** "They're building a new building next to my apartment complex. The noise is really loud. I have a hard time sleeping early in the morning. I complained to the landlord, but he said there's nothing he can do. What do you think I should do? Do you think I should talk to the landlord again or move out? What would you do?"
Helper intention(s):_____
Helper response:_____
_____

3. **Client:** "My roommate is really nice. I really like her. She is so much like the sister I wish I had when I was younger. It's really nice to have somebody to do things with. I was so lonely on campus last year, but having her as a roommate makes me feel like I belong. She's from a real poor family and she hardly has any money. Fortunately, my parents send me a lot of money, so I'm glad I can share some with her."
Helper intention(s):_____
Helper response:_____
_____

4. **Client:** "I just got in a fight with my mother. She was saying awful things to me, like I would never succeed in school because I'm lazy. I got so angry at her, I was shaking. I just don't know what to say to her when she does that. Why can't she be supportive like my friends' mothers? The worst thing is that I still have to live at home because I don't have enough money to move out."
Helper intention(s):_____
Helper response:_____
_____

Possible Helper Responses

1. "So you're feeling torn between your school work and worrying about your mother." (intent: to identify and intensify feelings, to encourage catharsis)
   "You're so worried about your mother that it's hard for you to concentrate on anything else." (intent: to identify and intensify feelings, to encourage catharsis)
   "You feel trusted because your mom counts on you to do well in school." (intent: to identify and intensify feelings, to encourage catharsis)

2. "You're feeling unsure about how you should handle the noise situation at your apartment." (intent: to identify and intensify feelings, to promote self-control)
   "I hear you saying that you feel upset about not being able to sleep." (intent: to identify and intensify feelings, to encourage catharsis)
   "You feel exhausted." (intent: to identify and intensify feelings, to encourage catharsis)
   "It sounds like you feel irritated because your landlord was so unresponsive." (intent: to identify and intensify feelings, to encourage catharsis, to clarify)

3. "I hear you saying that you feel very close to your roommate." (intent: to identify and intensify feelings, to encourage catharsis)
   "You're really pleased that you can help your roommate financially." (intent: to identify and intensify feelings, to encourage catharsis, to instill hope, to promote self-control)
   "You feel relieved that you finally feel like you belong." (intent: to identify and intensify feelings, to encourage catharsis)

4. "You are full of rage at your mother." (intent: to identify and intensify feelings, encourage catharsis)

"I can see how mad you are at your mother." (intent: to identify and intensify feelings, to encourage catharsis)

"You feel trapped because you have to live at home." (intent: to identify and intensify feelings, to encourage catharsis)

"You feel hurt that your mother doesn't believe in you." (intent: to identify and intensify feelings, to encourage catharsis)

What Do You Think?

- Compare and contrast restatements and reflections. When would you focus on cognitions (restatement) versus feelings (reflection)?

- Compare and contrast open questions about feelings and reflections of feelings. How well does each intervention facilitate discussion of feelings? How might clients react to open questions about feelings as compared to reflections of feelings?

- How do you choose which feeling to reflect if a client has a lot of different feelings?

- How can you tell if clients are agreeing with your reflections because you are in the "power position," because they want to please you, or because they really had the feeling?

- How much should you mirror feelings that the client is aware of versus encourage clients to experience feelings of which they might not be aware?

- How did you feel in the second practice example when the client asked you a direct question? How do you think you should respond?

- In the third practice example, what would you do if you had a strong reaction and wanted to tell the client not to give her roommate money because she could be hurt? How could you remain nonjudgmental in such a situation?

- In the fourth practice example, how would you handle wanting to disclose about your issues with your mother to the client but feeling that it would be inappropriate?

<u>**LAB 5**</u> **Reflection of Feelings**

Goal: For helpers to learn to reflect feelings. The focus is on paraphrasing the person's feelings, although content can be added to indicate why the client has the feelings.

There are three exercises in this lab. We begin with the easiest level of trying to identify feeling words. Then we move on to having everyone in a group generate reflections so that you hear a lot of different possibilities without feeling pressure to come up with the "right" reflection. Finally, we move to dyads where each person has an opportunity to practice reflections with a client. In addition, we urge you to practice reflections outside the lab so that you can have a firm grasp on how to use this important skill.

Exercise 1

In a large group, each student should say three feeling words that reflect how she or he is currently feeling. Students should practice using feeling words that they would not typically use so that they can broaden their feeling word vocabulary. See Exhibit 9.2 for ideas. Remember that this list is not exhaustive by any means; there are thousands of feeling words, and you can add words to personalize the list for yourself.

Exercise 2

Students should be arranged in groups of four. One person should be the client and the other three should be helpers. Each person should take a turn being the client. Note that getting into feelings can be threatening for some people. Focusing on feelings often leads clients into issues of which they were not aware and are not sure they want to reveal (especially in class). On one hand, this reaction illustrates the power of reflections as a tool for helping. On the other hand, we want to remind you that those playing the role of clients can stop at any time. No one should venture into territory that is uncomfortable. We also want to remind you that the focus in these exercises is on the helper learning the skills rather than the helper trying to fix the client.

Helper's and Client's Tasks During the Helping Interchange

1. The client should talk for a few sentences on a topic about which he or she has strong feelings (e.g., an instance in which the client felt put down or angry or a time when the client felt particularly proud).
2. Helpers should listen while the client is talking without trying to think of what to say. After the client finishes talking, helpers should pause for a moment and try to think of reflections of feelings. For purposes of this exercise on learning how to do this skill, helpers should give only reflections of feelings, even if other skills seem more appropriate. Each helper should take turns giving a single reflection using the format, "You feel___" or "You feel___because___."
3. Clients should respond briefly to each reflection so that helpers see the effects of their reflection.
4. After all helpers have delivered reflections, the client should discuss which reflections were most helpful and why.

5. The helpers who gave the most helpful reflections should describe how they thought of the reflections.

Exercise 3

Divide into groups of three people: one helper, one client, and one observer. Everyone should take turns doing each role.

Helper's and Client's Tasks During the Helping Interchange

1. The helper should introduce herself or himself.
2. The client should talk for a few sentences on a topic about which he or she has strong feelings.
3. After each client speaking turn, the helper should do a reflection using fewer words and focusing on the most salient feeling and reason for that feeling. For purposes of this exercise, the helper should do only a reflection and not other interventions. Use the format, "You feel___" or "You feel___because___." Helpers should take their time, pause before delivering reflections, and consider: "How is the client feeling?" "What might the nonverbal behavior be revealing about the feelings?" "How would I feel if I were the client?" Keep the reflection short and simple. A variety of feeling words should be used.
4. Continue for 5–10 turns.

Observer's Task During the Helping Interchange

Take notes about the helper's reflections and attending behaviors. Write down the helper's feeling words so that you can refer back to these notes during the feedback. Note the accuracy of the feeling words. Note the manner of the delivery of the reflections—did the helper use a variety of feeling words, did the helper keep the statement short and concise? Note the client's reactions to the reflections (e.g., did the reflections seem to facilitate further exploration of feelings?).

After the Helping Interchange

1. The helper should talk about how it felt to give reflections.
2. The client should talk about how it felt to be the recipient of the reflections. Discuss specific reflections that were more helpful and those that were less so.
3. The observer should give feedback to the helper about her or his reflection skills and attending behaviors.

SWITCH ROLES

Personal Reflections

- What did you learn about yourself when delivering reflections?
- What would you do if a client started to cry?
- What was your experience in picking out the feeling to reflect? In the past, some students have had a hard time selecting the most important feeling. Some became overwhelmed by lengthy descriptions and could not differentiate the forest (the feelings) from the trees (all the words). Some people were worried about hurting the client if they gave a "bad" reflection. Others had difficulty figuring out the feelings if the client did not explicitly state feelings. Others had

(Continues)

trouble when clients were very articulate about their feelings because they did not want to repeat the client's feeling words, particularly if clients used strong feeling words.

- Are there particular feelings that you have difficulty dealing with because of your own discomfort or problems?
- Talk about your confidence in becoming an effective helper. We have found that many students experience an initial decline in confidence after beginning to learn helping skills (Hill, Zack, et al., 1998), but that confidence increases over time with practice. What pattern do you see emerging with regard to your confidence as a helper?

10 Additional Skills for the Exploration Stage

I get by with a little help from my friends.
John Lennon

á Karina was a Ukrainian woman who traveled to the United States to obtain her Ph.D. She sought help because she was not able to complete her dissertation even though she soon had to go back to her country. She was not sure what the helper expected from her, and she knew very little about helping. The helper explained the process of helping to Karina and reassured her that he would help her identify and express her feelings. He also let her know that he appreciated her courage in coming to another country to gain an education and in pursuing helping so that she could resolve her anguish and achieve her goals. He revealed that he had experienced difficulty in finishing his dissertation. The helper asked Karina a few closed questions to identify exactly what her problems were in completing the dissertation and then asked her to explore her feelings about finishing her degree and returning to her country.

ALTHOUGH RESTATEMENT, open question, and reflection of feelings can be used for most of the situations that arise to help clients explore, there are some situations for which they are not the most appropriate interventions:

- when clients need specific information about what to expect in helping or about the helper's credentials
- when clients need reassurance, support, normalization, or reinforcement
- when helpers need specific information
- when helpers want to let clients know that they have had similar feelings

In this chapter, we present several skills (information about the process of helping, approval and reassurance, closed questions, and self-disclosures for exploration) that helpers can use in the exploration stage to intervene in these situations. These skills can be useful additions to a helper's repertoire; however, each has significant drawbacks of which helpers should be aware so that they can use them appropriately and with caution. We present an overview of these skills in Table 10.1.

Many of the skills are ones that beginning helpers have used with friends prior to training, so the skills seem more natural to helpers. In fact, helpers typically have to learn how to use these skills less often in helping sessions. We hope that an awareness of the possible consequences of these skills can aid helpers in making choices about when and when not to use these skills.

TABLE 10.1. Information about the Helping Process, Approval and Reassurance, Closed Question, and Self-Disclosure for Exploration

	Information about the helping process	Approval and reassurance	Closed question	Self-disclosure for exploration
Definition	Educates clients about what to expect during helping	Provides emotional support, reassurance, encouragement, and reinforcement	Requests a one- or two-word answer (a "yes," "no," or a confirmation) and is used to gather information or data	Reveals personal nonimmediate information about the helper's history or credentials or about feelings
Examples	"Our first task today is to complete some measures about how you are feeling."	"It's very hard to have a parent who is dying." "I'm pleased that you were able to try the homework."	"Where are you in the birth order among your siblings?" "Is that what you meant?" "What did you say?"	"This is my first class in helping skills." "When I don't get invited to parties, I feel very hurt."
Typical intentions	To give information, to set limits	To support, to instill hope, to encourage catharsis, to reinforce change, to relieve helper's needs	To get information, to clarify	To identify and intensify feelings, to encourage catharsis, to clarify, to instill hope, to promote self-control (see Appendix A)
Possible client reactions	Educated, hopeful, no reaction	Supported, hopeful, relief	No reaction	Feelings, negative thoughts and behaviors, clear, responsibility, unstuck, scared, worse, misunderstood (see Appendix D)
Desired client behavior	Agreement	Recounting, cognitive–behavioral exploration, affective exploration	Recounting	Affective exploration (see Appendix E)
Difficulties helpers experience in delivering intervention	Desire to be viewed as the expert who knows and directs what is going to happen in session	Being too giving Becoming too sympathetic and not being able to separate self from the client Minimizing or denying feelings	The helper might not be listening enough to the client The focus might turn onto the helper	Difficulty in dealing with intense feelings such as anger and sadness Projecting own feelings onto client

INFORMATION ABOUT THE PROCESS OF HELPING

Providing information about the process of helping can educate clients about what to expect. Clients need to know about the helping process so that they can determine whether they want to participate in the process and decide how to behave in the sessions. For example, they need to know the length of sessions, fees associated with sessions, rules of conduct in sessions, and the appropriateness of contacting the helper outside of sessions. Helpers often tell clients their rules or give a list of their rules at the beginning of the initial session (Nakayama, Thompson, Knox, & Hill, 1998). They inform clients about other rules as the need arises (e.g., when clients ask for information that is too personal, the helper might explain why he or she chooses not to divulge such information). Helpers might also deliver information about helping throughout the process to let clients know what they might encounter. For example, helpers might inform clients about what to expect as they move into the action stage. By informing clients about what to expect, helpers hope that clients become more involved and collaborative in the helping process. We discuss additional uses of information in the action stage in chapter 19.

The following is an example of using information (in italics) about the helping process:

> **Helper:** "Hi. *My name is Deborah. I wanted to let you know a few things first about the way we operate here. This is a training clinic, and I'm a beginning helper learning the skills. I have a supervisor who will be watching us through a one-way mirror, and, as you know, I'm taping the session so that I can listen to the tape and improve my skills. Our session today will be 30 minutes, and you can talk about whatever you like.* Do you have any questions?"
>
> **Client:** "Yes. Why is the supervisor there?"
>
> **Helper:** *"The supervisor is there to observe me and give me feedback about my skills."*
>
> **Client:** "What kind of program are you in?"
>
> **Helper:** *"I'm taking a class on helping skills.* What would you like to talk about today?"

Note that the helper provides a brief introduction and answers questions briefly, but then turns the focus back to the client so that the client can explore her concerns.

APPROVAL AND REASSURANCE

Approval and reassurance are sometimes helpful to provide emotional support and reassurance and foster exploration. It indicates that helpers empathize with or understand clients. It suggests that what clients are feeling is normal or to be expected. For many clients, reassurance that their problems are normal and that they are not alone in their feelings can be empowering:

"That's really hard to handle."

"That's a devastating situation."

"How awful!"

"Wow! That's an awesome opportunity!"

Approval and reassurance can also be used to provide reinforcement, indicating that helpers approve of something clients have done or said. Some clients like to have others acknowledge that they have done something well. In addition, some clients need reinforcement to persist in exploring and working on their goals and action plans. Helpers often want to reinforce clients to increase the probability that they perform certain behaviors again.

"Good try!"

"That was really terrific that you were able to fight back!"

Approval and reassurance used for support or reinforcement can sound false if done excessively, prematurely, or insincerely. Such interventions (e.g., "I think you're right to feel guilty about getting an abortion") may also run the risk of directing clients in ways that are consistent with helper's values or beliefs. They tend to stop client exploration or make clients feel compelled to agree or comply with helpers. In addition, certain approval and reassurance statements can negate the conflicting feelings that clients might be experiencing. Hence, we suggest that helpers use approval and reassurance cautiously and sparingly.

In addition, approval and reassurance are sometimes used inappropriately to alleviate anxiety or distress, to minimize feelings, or to deny feelings (e.g., "Don't worry about it," "Everyone feels that way"). When used in this manner, approval and reassurance are typically counterproductive to our work as helpers because the intervention does not facilitate clients in exploring and accepting feelings. Such statements can make clients feel that they have no right to their feelings. Helpers sometimes use these interventions as misguided attempts to reassure others that everything is okay. Unfortunately, problems typically do not go away just because they are minimized or denied. Most of us have heard the old sayings, "Give it time" or "Time cures all." In our experience, it is not "time" that makes feelings go away; in fact, feelings often fester when they are bottled up or denied. We believe that awareness, acceptance, and expression of feelings aid in resolution of painful affect. To reiterate, our goal is to help clients identify, intensify, and express feelings rather than minimize or deny them.

In general then, we recommend that approval and reassurance be used sparingly to support clients, especially with the goal of facilitating greater exploration of thoughts, feelings, and experiences. Approval and reassurance should not be used to diminish feelings, deny experiences, or stop exploration. When helpers find themselves using approval and reassurance in that way, they might want to think about what is going on inside them and perhaps speculate about what might be making them uncomfortable.

The following is an example of using approval and reassurance (in italics) in a positive way:

Client: "I just learned that my sister needs to have a kidney transplant. She's been sick a lot lately and hasn't been getting better."

Helper: *"That's too bad."*

Client: "Yeah, I feel terrible for her. She's only 21 and has always been real active, so this is a real shock for her. I feel guilty that she got this horrible disease and I'm healthy."

Helper: *"That's a pretty natural feeling to feel some guilt."*

Client: "Really? I'm glad to hear that. I have been trying to do more for her. I'm thinking of organizing a campaign to find a donor and raise money for her treatment. Because she has an unusual blood type, it will be difficult to find the right person, and it's going to cost a lot of money."

Helper: *"That's terrific that you would do that for her."*

CLOSED QUESTIONS

Closed questions request a one- or two-word answer (a "yes," "no," or a confirmation) and are used to gather information or data. Closed questions can ask for specific information:

"What was your test grade?"

"How old were you when your parents were divorced?"

"Did you call the counseling center?"

Helpers may ask closed questions because they could not hear or understand what clients said or they want to determine if their statements were accurate or if clients agree with them.

"What did you say?"

"Am I right?"

"Is that what happened?"

"Does that sound right to you?"

"Did I understand you correctly?"

The primary intention for using closed questions is to obtain information from clients. Helpers are usually looking for particular answers rather than encouraging clients to explore their thoughts or feelings. The typical client response is to provide information, but interestingly, the typical client reaction to a closed question is "no reaction." One client told us that she did not have many reactions to her therapist's closed questions: "I just told him what he wanted to know. They didn't help me open up or come to any new feelings."

Closed questions have a limited role in this helping model. Helpers occasionally need to obtain specific information from clients, and the most direct way to get this specific information is through closed questions. For example, when a client is vague about the family situation, the helper may need to ask for clarification (e.g., "Are you the oldest child?"). It can be useful to know if clients have a major in school, if they have contemplated suicide, or if they have friends. In such situations, asking for the needed information is better than making assumptions or being confused. Even when helpers need specific information, however, the task is not to "pin down the suspect" as one would in a court of law. Rather, helpers need to obtain information within the context of trying to understand the client and facilitate exploration.

Most often closed questions are associated with interviews of some sort, such as visits to a medical doctor, interrogations by lawyers during courtroom trials, or job interviews. The roles between the interviewer and interviewee are often quite distinct. The interviewer asks the question to get the desired information; the respondent answers the questions. The control of interviews usually stays with interviewers who direct the interaction.

Academic advisors often use closed questions. When a student goes to an advisor wanting to know about her or his chances of being accepted into graduate school, the advisor's goal is to gather enough information about the student's credentials (e.g., grade-point average, GRE scores, research and clinical experience, and career goals) to make an assessment. The best and most efficient way of gathering such information quickly is typically through closed questions (e.g., "What are your grade-point average and GRE score?," "What research experiences have you had?," "Where do you hope to be employed after graduate school?"). The advisor tries to ask the closed questions in a supportive, empathic, nonjudgmental fashion, without attempting to determine what students should do with their lives or pass judgment on their effectiveness as human beings. Once the advisor has the information, he or she can assess how likely it is that the student will be admitted to graduate school. If the advisor thinks that the student needs help in exploring values, feelings, options, and talents, he or she probably will refer the student to the campus counseling center because these tasks are not part of the advisor's role.

Helpers who are trying to assist clients in exploring whether they want to attend graduate school would be less likely to use closed questions. They do not need as much specific information because they want to facilitate exploration of values, feelings, options, and talents, with the eventual goal of having the client make a decision. They are more likely to help clients explore their feelings about graduate school and future plans so that they can make the best decisions possible. They would have no investment in clients' decisions.

Closed questions can be useful occasionally in helping sessions, when a client has difficulty talking. In these cases, however, helpers who use many closed questions may slip into an interviewer role and become responsible for directing the interaction. They become interviewers rather than helpers. Once trapped in the interviewer role and having to think about the next question, helpers often have difficulty changing the course of the session and focusing on clients. In these situations, clients often perceive the relationship as helper focused because they become dependent on helpers for the next question. Rather than speaking when they have something to say, they speak in response to questions.

Helpers often think they need to know a lot of information, but we suggest that helpers think first about what they are going to do with the information once it is provided. If helpers view themselves as the ones who must give answers or solutions, then they probably feel a need to gather a lot of information. For example, a medical doctor needs to gather a lot of information to make a diagnosis and prescribe medication. However, helpers who follow the helping model proposed in this book do not need as much specific information because their task is to assist clients in making their own decisions rather than making a diagnosis and providing solutions. Helpers can ask themselves, "Whose need is it for me to know the information that I gain from closed questions?" If it is to facilitate the process of exploring for the client, helpers should ask the question. If it is for voyeurism, curiosity, to fill the silence, or to make a diagnosis and fix the problem, helpers probably should not ask the question.

Our experience has been that beginners use far too many closed questions because this skill is a familiar way of interacting outside of the helping situation. The habit of using too many closed questions is hard to break. We do not suggest that helpers never use closed questions because closed questions can be helpful occasionally, but we encourage helpers to reduce the number of closed questions that they use and instead try to use open question, restatement, and reflection of feelings. When closed questions are used, helpers can follow up with open questions, restatements, and reflections of feelings so that clients can get back to exploration.

We especially caution helpers from using multiple closed questions. As with too many open questions asked at once, clients can feel bombarded and have a hard time knowing which questions to answer first.

Even more importantly, we encourage helpers to notice what happens when they use closed questions. Helpers should determine for themselves whether (as we claim) control of the interaction shifts back to them when they use too many closed questions. Do closed questions make you feel like a grand inquisitor? Helpers can also ask clients for their reactions to closed questions to determine the effects of these interventions.

Using closed questions is particularly useful in the assessment of suicide potential. In this situation, helpers need to ask very directly about suicidal thoughts. The following is an example of the appropriate use of closed questions (in italics) to assess a suicide risk:

> **Client:** "I get so depressed, I just feel like life isn't worth living sometimes. I want to crawl up into my bed and sleep all the time. I just don't want to face anyone."
>
> **Helper:** *"Have you had thoughts of killing yourself?"*
>
> **Client:** "Yes, quite often I wish I were dead. I would be better off."
>
> **Helper:** "Sounds like you're pretty depressed. *Do you have a plan for how you would kill yourself?"*
>
> **Client:** "I am not sure I would actually do it. I more fantasize that I would like to do it."
>
> **Helper:** *"Do you have any way to do it?"*
>
> **Client:** "No, I hate guns, I don't have any pills, I wouldn't like jumping. I think it's more of a fantasy of doing it and imagining how people would respond."

After assessing for suicidal risk, the helper would move on to other skills to help the client explore thoughts and feelings and underlying issues that make him feel helpless and hopeless. Further information about assessing suicidal risk is provided in chapter 11.

SELF-DISCLOSURES FOR EXPLORATION

Self-disclosures can be used in the exploration stage to reveal personal nonimmediate information about the helper's history and credentials. Disclosing such facts is sometimes appropriate to inform clients briefly about the helper and his or her professional background and training. Many helpers believe that it is beneficial to share information about their professional training or background:

"I am a beginning helper just learning helping skills."

"I am a psychologist with a Ph.D., have been practicing for 20 years, and have a humanistic orientation."

Clients from oppressed groups often want to know the helper's beliefs and values to determine whether it is safe to work with them or whether they will feel comfortable working with them. For example, a religious client might want to know if the helper is religious or tolerant of other religions. A gay client may need to know that the helper is not homophobic and will not try to alter his sexual orientation. A stay-at-home mother might be concerned about the helper's feelings about her lifestyle. A recovering alcoholic may want to know whether the helper is a recovering alcoholic. An African American man might be interested in learning whether the helper has had any experience working with African Americans.

Weijun Zhang in Ivey (1994) suggested that helper self-disclosure is particularly appropriate with clients from other cultures who often approach helping situations with considerable distrust. Some clients doubt that helpers from other cultures can understand them or help them and fear that the information they disclose might be used against them. Helpers might start an initial session by asking, "Do you have any questions you'd like to ask me?" and then honestly answer questions so that clients get to know them. He suggested that self-disclosure can be particularly important with Asian clients, who have a tradition against revealing personal and family matters to outsiders. By disclosing, helpers model that disclosure is acceptable and expected. However, he cautioned against too much helper self-disclosure with Asian clients because it could be considered unprofessional.

Although it is appropriate for clients to ask questions and for helpers to respond authentically with disclosures of facts, helpers might sometimes want to ask clients about what is motivating their questions (especially if the questions are excessive or personally intrusive). They might also want to ask how clients feel about the disclosures that are given. Holding a dialogue about the issues behind the questions is crucial for establishing a therapeutic relationship and for understanding salient client issues. We suggest that helpers typically not reveal much personal information unless it is for an identifiable reason; otherwise, the helper's problems rather than the client's may be what impels the helper to share such information.

Another type of disclosure that can be helpful in the exploration stage is disclosure of feelings. Helpers can also use self-disclosures to model for clients what they might be feeling (e.g., "When I was applying for my first job, I felt terrified about what I would say in the interview"). Helpers can say how they would feel if they were the client (e.g., "If I were you, I would feel mad at your father"), or they might state how they feel hearing the client talk ("I feel angry at your father"). After hearing a disclosure of feelings, clients might be able to recognize that they had similar (or very different) feelings. In other words, disclosures of feelings can stimulate clients to recognize and express their feelings. In effect, the disclosure of feelings is similar in intention and consequences to reflection of feelings. Disclosure of feelings can be helpful for clients who are afraid to experience their feelings, especially feelings of shame and embarrassment.

An additional goal of disclosure of feelings is to help clients feel more normal because they learn that other people have similar feelings. Many of us often feel that we are the only ones who ever feel lousy, inadequate, phony, or depressed. Hearing that others have felt the same way that we do can be tremendously relieving. In fact, Yalom (1995) posited that universality (i.e., a sense that others feel the same way) is a curative agent in therapy.

Disclosures of feelings also can be a good way for helpers not to impose feelings on clients. Rather than saying, "You do feel _____," the helper says, "I felt _____ in the past. I wonder if you might feel that way?" Hence, helpers are respectful by owning that they are the ones who have the feelings. They own their projections and investigate whether clients actually feel that way.

It is important, however, that beginners not use self-disclosures for their own needs. Beginning helpers often want to disclose feelings because they want to shift attention to their own problems or show clients how knowledgeable they are about certain issues. Hence, helpers have to be thoughtful about their intentions for disclosing feelings and must be careful to turn the focus back on the client after disclosing feelings.

In summary, disclosures can sometimes be helpful to inform clients and help them recognize their feelings, but helpers need to be very cautious so that the attention does not shift from the client to the helper. Disclosures used to promote insight are discussed in chapter 15. Disclosures for the action stage are discussed in chapter 20.

The following example demonstrates how self-disclosure (in italics) can be used appropriately to foster exploration:

Client: "How did you learn to be a therapist?"

Helper: *"I am just in the process of learning to be a helper. It will be many years and lots of training before I am qualified to consider myself a therapist.* Perhaps you're curious about my credentials?"

Client: "I just wonder if you're going to be able to help me."

Helper: "I can understand that fear. *I was nervous about going to see a therapist the first time too.*"

Client: "I am a bit nervous. This is the first time I've talked to anyone about my problems. I feel like I'm weak if I talk to anyone. My father always used to say that only crazy people go to therapists."

Helper: "*My father was pretty negative about therapy too, but I found it useful.*"

Client: "I can see that it could be helpful. I really want to have an opportunity to talk more about my feelings about my family—they are pretty messed up, and I guess I am too."

The helper would probably shift at this point to using other helping skills (such as reflections and restatements) to help the client explore more about her feelings about her family.

CONCLUDING COMMENTS

The additional helping skills described in this chapter should not be used extensively, but they can be very important at specific points in sessions. For example, sometimes clients need explicit reassurance to let them know that they are okay. At other times, helpers need specific information to be able to help clients. Furthermore, self-disclosure and providing information about the helping process can sometimes be beneficial, so that clients know what to expect in the helping process. Finally, by hearing helpers self-disclose feelings, clients can sometimes acknowledge having similar emotions and feel less judged for having feelings. With these skills, however, helpers need to be particularly attentive to keep the focus on clients because there could be a tendency to turn the focus onto the helper. In addition, helpers should observe client reactions and consider shifting to other skills if clients respond negatively.

11

Integrating the Skills of the Exploration Stage

It is a luxury to be understood.
Ralph Waldo Emerson

Dmitry, a new helper, was in his first session with a client. He asked several closed questions, which the client answered only briefly and then sat looking at him waiting for him to ask more questions. Dmitry panicked because he did not know what to do next. He felt himself sweating and wanted to run out of the room. Instead, he paused, took a deep breath, and thought of what he had learned about helping. His teacher's words echoed in his head, "Try restatements, open questions, and reflections of feelings." So he said, "How do you feel about school?" and was amazed when the client started talking about feeling scared and depressed because of doing poorly in his courses. Dmitry learned firsthand how to help clients explore.

AT THIS point, helpers should be able to identify (i.e., discriminate) and use (i.e., communicate) all of the separate exploration skills that have been discussed thus far. Now we want to integrate the skills so that helpers can begin to select whatever skills seem appropriate to use at different times in sessions to facilitate exploration. In this chapter, we also generate ideas for how to work with clients who have difficulty with exploration, and we offer suggestions for research to investigate components of this stage.

Helpers must remember that their goals for this stage are to establish rapport and help clients explore; it is important to accept clients unconditionally so that they can begin to accept themselves. Rather than make any assumptions, helpers must learn about clients from the clients themselves. In the process of productive exploration, clients might not even notice what helpers are doing because helpers are facilitating clients in the exploration process rather than coming up with new insights or suggesting actions. Jung (1984) phrased this well in talking about dream interpretation: "The greatest wisdom . . . [a dream analyst] can have is to disappear and let the dreamer think he [the dream analyst] is doing nothing" (p. 458). Our job as helpers is to have clients be so immersed in exploration that they do not notice our interventions—the interventions just facilitate rather than intrude on the process.

In addition, helpers are laying the foundation during the exploration stage to move on to insight and action. By keeping an awareness of the goals of the stage, helpers can be more grounded in trying to facilitate the process. Otherwise, it is easy to get lost and just let clients talk aimlessly or in circles.

CONDUCTING THE EXPLORATION STAGE

First Session

In the initial session, helpers might provide information about the helping process by explaining the structure of the process and talking about their expectations for what should happen. For example, "we are going to be spending 30 min together, and our goal is to help you explore whatever topic you would like to address." Helpers also can ask clients if they have any questions about what to expect from the process (e.g., "Is there anything you want to know about me or about the process?"). Helpers can also very briefly self-disclose about facts or credentials to educate clients about their background as helpers (e.g., "I am a beginning helper"). Then, rather than talking more, helpers can turn the focus over to clients by asking an open question, such as "What would you like to talk about?" or "What's on your mind?" In effect, helpers encourage clients to share their concerns.

Clients might start off the session saying "I don't have anything to talk about." Helpers can reflect feelings (e.g., discomfort, uncertainty) that clients might be experiencing at the beginning of the session to allow clients to focus on and accept their feelings. When helpers listen patiently and empathically, clients often begin talking within a few minutes. Some clients are anxious about whether what they have to say is important enough to be discussed in helping and need reassurance that the helper is listening and thinks that what they are talking about is important.

Markers Indicating Helper Skills to Use in the Exploration Stage

Table 11.1 summarizes our suggestions for which skills to use at different points in helping sessions. These suggestions are based on our clinical experiences rather than on empirical data because, unfortunately, minimal empirical data regarding the timing of interventions are available.

Throughout sessions, helpers should use appropriate attending behaviors. Using the acronym ENCOURAGES as a guide, helpers should maintain moderate levels of *eye* contact (avoid looking away frequently or staring), use moderate amounts of head *nods*, maintain a respect and awareness of *cultural* differences in attending, maintain an *open* stance toward clients (i.e., arms should not be closed tightly; helper should lean toward and face client squarely), use acknowledgments such as *"umhmm," relax* and act natural, *avoid* distracting behaviors (e.g., avoid too many adaptors, too much smiling, giggling, playing with hair or objects), match the client's *grammatical* style (i.e., use the same language style as client within the limits of one's own style), listen with a third *ear* (i.e., listen attentively to verbal and nonverbal messages), and use *space* appropriately (e.g., do not sit either too close or too far). These attending behaviors enable helpers to listen carefully to what clients are saying and encourage clients to explore. Helpers should also note client responses and modify their attending behaviors accordingly (e.g., if clients draw away from eye contact, helpers should not look at them intensely). In addition, helpers can offer approval and reassurance (e.g., "That's tough," "You're doing a good job talking about the problem") as long as they do not use it too frequently. When clients are talking productively about their concerns, helpers can just sit quietly and listen attentively.

The best exploration tool for most clients is reflection of feelings. When in doubt, helpers can rely on reflection of feelings because it demonstrates that helpers are listening and struggling to understand the client's experience. Reflections are particularly helpful

TABLE 11.1. A Guide for Which Helping Skills to Use During the Exploration Stage

Marker in session	When helper intends to	Helper might try
At all points	Support	Appropriate attending behaviors, listening attentively, and approval and reassurance
At beginning of session	Set limits Give information	Introduce self (disclose history or credentials) Explain structure and expectations (information about the helping process)
When client needs specific information about the process of helping	Give information Set limits	Information about the helping process
At the beginning of a session	Focus Get information	Open question
When a client is talking productively and exploring thoroughly	Promote catharsis	Silence Refrain from interruptions
When a client is talking and pauses When a client has a lot of feelings and is either expressing or not expressing them When helper wants to make sure she or he understands feelings When helper wants to model the expression of feelings	Identify and intensify feelings	Reflection of feelings Disclosure of feelings Open question about feelings
When a client is telling a story and is rambling When a client is confusing When a client has given information in response to the helper's question	Focus Clarify	Restatement Reflection of feelings Open question

(Continues)

TABLE 11.1. *(Continued)*

Marker in session	When helper intends to	Helper might try
When a client is talking about thoughts or behaviors and helper wants to encourage a client to continue	Identify maladaptive cognitions Identify maladaptive behaviors	Restatement Open question
When the helper wants to encourage a client to explore When a client is stuck or circling	Focus Clarify	Open question Restatement
When the helper has not heard what the client said When the helper needs specific information When the helper wants to know if the client has heard or understood what she or he said When the helper wants to make sure that the client has understood or agrees with what he or she said	Get information	Closed question
When the client is talking about someone else	Focus	Switch focus to the client using an open question or a reflection of feelings
When the client has a negative reaction	(Could be any of a number of intentions depending on the situation)	A different intervention, using one that fits with the intention

when clients pause and need encouragement to keep talking, when clients need to experience their feelings (whether or not clients are actively expressing the feelings), or when helpers want to show support or understanding. Reflection of feelings is also a useful way to identify possible feelings for clients who are out of touch with their feelings. Helpers can also self-disclose about their own feelings as a softer, more tentative way of proposing feelings that clients might have. Most clients respond to reflections of feelings or disclosure of feelings by talking about their feelings. However, some clients do not respond with their feelings, perhaps because reflections do not request that clients talk about their feelings. For these clients, we recommend that helpers alternate reflecting feelings with asking open questions about the feelings. In this way, helpers suggest possible feelings but then also encourage clients to identify and express their own feelings, thus assisting clients in becoming comfortable expressing their feelings.

If helpers want to focus the discussion or clarify what clients are talking about, they might use restatements (e.g., "so you flunked your exam" or just a repetition of the key word *exam*). When clients are confusing or rambling or just need to talk, restatements can serve as mirrors that allow clients to hear what they are saying. Thus, restatements help clients think more deeply about and clarify what they are saying.

Throughout the session, helpers can use open questions to keep the flow of the session going (e.g., "How are you feeling about that?" or "Tell me more about that"). If clients seem stuck or are repeating the same material over and over again, helpers can use open questions to ask about other aspects of problems that the client has not addressed. Helpers can ask open questions for different purposes: to help clients explore (e.g., "What's on your mind?"), to clarify (e.g., "What do you mean when you say anxious?"), or to solicit examples (e.g., "Go through the situation and tell me exactly what you said"). Helpers can also vary the focus of the open question, such that they might ask about thoughts (e.g., "What thoughts went through your head when you sat there listening to him?"), feelings (e.g., "What feelings do you have about graduation?"), or behaviors (e.g., "What do you generally do on your day off?"). The tense can be varied so that helpers focus on the past (e.g., "How does your present situation compare to what has happend in the past?"), present (e.g., "How are you feeling right now?"), and future (e.g., "What is your fantasy that you will be doing in 10 years?"). Finally, open questions can be about different objects, such as self (e.g., "How do you feel about yourself after you fight with your mother?") or other (e.g., "How do you feel about your mother after your fight?"). Using a variety of questions helps clients explore the complexity of situations and think about things they might not have thought about.

Once in a while, helpers can ask closed questions to gather specific important information from clients (e.g., "Is your mother alive?" or "When did you graduate from high school?"). We have heard a wonderful metaphor (but do not know whom to credit) that closed questions are the salt and pepper of communication and should be used sparingly and not as the main course (which are reflections of feelings, restatements, and open questions). We remind helpers, however, that the desire to get information is often (and inappropriately) for their own curiosity rather than out of a specific intention to benefit clients. Before using closed questions, then, helpers need to be clear about what they are going to do with the information and whose needs are being met (the helper's or the client's). Generally, we recommend that helpers try to rephrase closed questions into open questions or reflection of feelings.

We suggest that helpers follow the client's response to an open or closed question with a reflection or restatement to show that they understand what clients have said and to encourage clients to say more. Open questions are more demanding interventions that require clients to respond with an answer. In contrast, reflections of feelings seem to be gentler ways of suggesting feelings without the same level of demand. Alternating between open questions, restatements, and reflections can keep helpers from getting stuck in an interviewer mode. Restatements and reflections shift the responsibility of initiating the dialogue back to clients and show that helpers are listening to clients.

At all times, helpers need to remember to keep the focus on the client, even when clients talk primarily about others. For example, if a client says, "My mother is really awful," the helper can say, "You are really irritated with your mother," thus changing the focus from how terrible the mother is to the client's reaction to her or his mother. The guiding principle here is that it is easier and more efficient (and more ethical) to help clients change than to attempt to help the client change another person.

Helpers also need to maintain a focus on a specific concern (although of course each specific concern has a lot of parts). Many beginning helpers let clients jump from topic to topic so that by the end of a session clients have covered a lot of things superficially but have not explored anything in depth. Focusing on a specific issue is important, especially for brief treatments so that something concrete can be accomplished. Helpers can use a combination of skills to assist clients in focusing on one issue in depth. Specifically, they can observe clients to determine which issue has the most salience for them (e.g., where is the most intense affect?). After identifying the most important issue, helpers can reflect the feelings that clients are experiencing about that issue. Helpers can follow the clients' responses with restatements and open questions related to the salient issue. In other words, the exploration skills are used with the focus on the most salient issue.

At the end of the discussion about a particular topic or at the end of a session, summaries can be particularly helpful to integrate what has transpired. Summaries can also be beneficial at the beginning of a session to restate what has been discussed previously and to set a direction for the upcoming session. Ideally, summaries are a joint effort, with helpers and clients together trying to explicate what has been learned. Hence, helpers can either state a summary and check out with the client whether it is accurate (e.g., "Does that fit for you?") or ask the client to summarize what he or she learned (e.g., "What do you think you have learned about yourself today?").

Beginning helpers often have problems in the exploration stage because they are not able to facilitate deep exploration in their clients. Their clients seem to go around in circles, repeating themselves over and over rather than exploring problems deeply. Generally, this circling occurs when helpers use too many closed questions or use restatements or reflections that (a) are focused on someone other than the client, (b) are too global or vague, or (c) do not direct their open questions to ask about other aspects of the problem. Because beginning helpers sometimes worry about being too intrusive, they often skim the surface of issues rather than helping clients explore deeply with the skills suggested in this book. They might forget to attend and listen, or they might forget to be empathic and caring. It is not enough just to use the right skills, but helpers must use them in an empathic manner to fit what clients need at the time.

In summary, helpers can use a combination of reflection of feelings, restatements, and open question, with an occasional sprinkling of approval and reassurance, silence, closed question, self-disclosure of facts or credentials, self-disclosure of feelings, and information about the helping process, all within the context of appropriate attending behaviors and listening, to help clients explore. The helpers' primary intentions in this stage are to set limits, get information, support, focus, clarify, instill hope, encourage catharsis, identify maladaptive cognitions, identify maladaptive behaviors, encourage self-control, and identify and intensify feelings. The desired positive client reactions are feeling understood, supported, hopeful, relief, becoming aware of negative thoughts or behaviors, getting clarity, and experiencing feelings, although clients could have negative reactions such as feeling stuck, lack of direction, confused, misunderstood, and no reaction. The desired client behaviors are affective exploration and cognitive–behavioral exploration.

Helpers should pay attention to client reactions to their interventions. If clients are exploring and going deeper into problems, that is great. The helper is obviously on the right track. However, if the client becomes very quiet or passive or does not explore, the helper should assess what is not working. Perhaps the helper is not attending or listening, is asking too many closed questions, is focusing on someone other than the client, or is giving inaccurate restatements and reflections. In addition, the client might be bored, confused, or overwhelmed with negative feelings and thus retreat from further exploration. Using their assessment of the problem, helpers can change what they are doing and try different skills. Paying close attention to the client's reactions is crucial for enabling helpers to select appropriate interventions.

As one last caveat, there is no "right" way to implement this (or any other) stage in our helping model. Each helper has a somewhat different style, and each client needs somewhat different interventions and has unique reactions. So we cannot provide an exact road map or cookbook for helpers. We stress again that once helpers have learned how to deliver the specific skills, they need to develop their own intervention styles and integrate helping skills into their way of being. Helpers also need to apply the scientific method to each helping interaction (e.g., observe what does and does not work in each given situation and modify their behaviors accordingly). Being open to feedback from clients, teachers, and supervisors is an excellent way to improve one's skills.

HELPER TASKS

Develop Hypotheses About Clients

Thorough exploration should enable helpers to develop hypotheses about clients that lay the foundation for choosing interventions in the next stages of the helping process. Hence, we suggest that helpers spend time during the exploration stage thinking about their clients. They should pay close attention to the client's personality and verbal and nonverbal behaviors. How does the client respond to your interventions? How does the client's way of interacting influence the helping process?

Helpers can begin to make observations about clients and develop hypotheses about what factors led clients to come to where they are, although we do not suggest that you act on these hypotheses in this stage. Rather, these hypotheses can be stored away and continually revised as new information is obtained. These hypotheses and assessments of clients are useful during the insight stage of the helping model. After thinking about the client, helpers should be able to answer several questions.

- How serious is the problem?
- How is the client behaving?
- How much does the client disclose or withhold about the problem?
- Are there discrepancies in what the client is saying?
- What is the client's role in the creation and maintenance of the problem?

Be Aware of Your Feelings

We encourage helpers to use their inner experiences as tools for understanding what is happening in the helping process. By being aware of their reactions, helpers can make better decisions about how to intervene and are less likely to act out their reactions in helping situations. Moreover, helpers' reactions can provide valuable clues for how other people react to clients. For example, if the helper feels bored when a client talks in a monotone voice, chances are that other people in the client's life might also feel bored when the client talks that way. Hence, helpers have firsthand information about how the client comes across to other people, which is important data for the insight stage.

One clue that something is going wrong in a session is when the helper does not use the most appropriate skills with a client (assuming of course that the helper has the appropriate skills in her or his repertoire). Helpers can ask themselves, "What keeps me from doing what would be most helpful with this particular client at this particular moment?" It could be client resistance (discussed in the next section) or personal issues of the helper. Hence, prior to acting on any information gained from their own reactions, helpers need to think about whether their personal issues are involved. In other words, if a helper feels bored by a particular client, it is possible that the client reminds him of his father with whom he is angry. A helper who has no romantic involvements and is lonely might be attracted to a client; one who is insecure when dealing with male clients might be afraid of men. Helpers can ask themselves: How do I feel when I am with the client? More specifically,

- do I feel bored talking with the client?
- do I feel attracted to the client?
- do I feel irritated when the client does not agree with me?
- do I want to solve the client's problems for him or her?
- do I feel anxious or ill at ease with this client?
- am I trying to impress this client?
- am I acting differently with this client than I would like to act?
- what personal issues of mine might be stimulated by working with this client?
- how might I ensure that my personal issues do not have a negative impact on the helping sessions?

We recommend that helpers discuss their personal reactions with supervisors and therapists. In these settings, they can identify which feelings come from personal issues, which are stimulated by clients, and which are due to a combination of personal issues and client behavior.

Decide When Clients Have Explored Enough

Helpers know that clients have explored enough when helpers can answer the following questions:

- What is the client's problem?
- What is motivating the client to seek help now?
- How does the client feel about the problem?
- What does the client do to maintain the problem?

When helpers sense that clients have explored the situation thoroughly, they might use a restatement to summarize, to see whether the client has anything else to add, to provide closure, and to set the stage for insight. For example, a helper might say, "You've been talking a lot today about your feelings about your roommate. You seem concerned that the two of you are not as close as you have been in the past. You are not sure what you can do to fix the relationship. How does that fit for you?" Alternatively, helpers might ask clients to summarize (e.g., "How would you sum up what you have learned so far?") to get a sense of how much clients have absorbed. Sometimes, of course, summarizing is not necessary because clients naturally move directly to insight.

DEALING WITH PROBLEMATIC CLINICAL SITUATIONS

Many clients are eager and ready to work on their problems when they come to helping. Some clients, however, are not ready to work or are difficult to interact with. Sometimes the very reason they are clients is because they are hard to get along with. Rather than getting angry at them, helpers need to be aware of the issues causing them to be difficult, empathize with their underlying pain, and alter their strategies for working with them. In this section, we discuss three types of difficult clients that beginning helpers might face: reluctant and resistant clients, overly talkative clients, and suicidal clients. We remind beginning helpers that they should seek supervision and refer seriously disturbed clients and clients with serious problems because they need services that are beyond the helper's range of competency (see also chapters 1 and 4).

Reluctant and Resistant Clients

Some clients have difficulty exploring because of reluctance (they are not sure they want to pay the price of changing) or resistance (they feel coerced and want to fight back; Egan, 1994). Signs of reluctance are varied and often covert. Reluctant clients might talk only about safe subjects, seem unsure of what they want from helping, act overly cooperative, set unrealistic goals and then give up on them, not work very hard at changing, or blame others for their problems. Egan suggested that the roots of reluctance are fear of intensity, lack of trust, fear of falling apart, shame, and fear of change.

Whereas reluctance is typically passive, resistance is often active (Egan, 1994). Resistant clients often present themselves as not needing help and as feeling misused. They show minimal willingness to form a relationship and often try to manipulate the helper. They might be resentful, try to sabotage the helping process, terminate as quickly as possible, and act abusively or belligerently to the helper. Clients who come to helping because they are mandated to do so (e.g., are court ordered) are often resistant. For example, one male client who was ordered by a judge to participate in 12 helping sessions because he had urinated on public property was very resistant about being there and got very little out of the experience (he even asked the helper for a date!). Egan suggested that resistance can come from seeing no reason for helping, resenting being referred for help, feeling awkward about participating in helping, or having a history of rebelliousness. Other reasons for resistance are having values or expectations that are inconsistent with the help being offered, having negative attitudes about helping, feeling that going for helping is admitting weakness and inadequacy, feeling a lack of trust, or disliking the helper.

When faced with client reluctance or resistance, helpers often become confused, panicked, angry, guilty, or depressed (Egan, 1994). They might try to placate the client, become impatient or hostile to the client, become passive, or lower their expectations and do a halfhearted job. Alternatively, helpers might become warmer and more accepting to win over the client, engage in a power struggle with the client, allow themselves to be abused or bullied by the client, or try to terminate the helping process. The source of the stress is not only the client's behavior, but also the helper's self-defeating attitudes and assumptions. Helpers might be saying things to themselves like "All clients should be committed to change," "Every client must like and trust me," "Every client can be helped," "No unwilling client can be helped," "I am responsible for what happens to the client," or "I must succeed with every client." Once again, helpers need to become aware of their self-defeating attitudes and assumptions to reduce their influence on the helping process.

Helpers should not avoid dealing with reluctance and resistance, but they also should avoid reinforcing these processes in clients (Egan, 1994). Goldfried and Davison (1994) suggested that the role of the therapist is to make the client ready for change; hence, the challenge for helpers is to find creative ways to deal with reluctance and resistance. We have several suggestions for helpers in dealing with reluctance and resistance, some of which come from Egan (1994) and some from our own experiences.

- Helpers can learn to see reluctance and resistance as normal.
- Helpers can recognize that reluctance and resistance are sometimes a form of avoidance and are not necessarily due to ill will toward the helper.
- Helpers can explore their own reluctance and resistance to changing problematic aspects of their lives. Once helpers figure out how they cope with their own reluctance and resistance, they probably are more able to help clients with theirs. An awareness of their own foibles can make helpers more empathic and less impatient with clients.
- Helpers can examine the quality of their interventions. Helpers might be provoking resistance by being too directive or too passive, or by disliking the client.
- Helpers can try to be empathic, attempting to understand what it must be like to be the client.
- Helpers can work directly with the client's reluctance and resistance rather than ignoring it, being intimidated by it, or being angry at clients for their behaviors. Helpers should avoid moralizing but can point out the reluctance or resistance and help clients explore their feelings about the reluctance or resistance to helping.
- Helpers can be realistic about what they can accomplish with clients.
- Helpers can establish a relationship on the basis of mutual trust and shared planning rather than trying to assume all the power.
- Helpers can work with clients to search for incentives for changing.
- Helpers can switch roles with clients so that clients see the effects of reluctance and resistance. (We suggest that helpers wait until they have established a therapeutic alliance with the client before they use this strategy.)

Overly Talkative Clients

Some clients talk nonstop about things that are not related to therapeutic goals (although helpers have to be careful about making judgments about what is worth discussing in helping). In the client behavior system (see chapter 3 and Appendix E), we considered this type of talking to be recounting rather than affective or cognitive–behavioral exploration. Overtalkativeness is often a defense on the part of clients and an attempt to keep helpers at a distance so that clients do not have to examine themselves. Helpers obviously cannot do much helping unless they intervene and interrupt the talking. We suggest that after the first 5–10 min, the helper stop the client gently and say something like, "Sorry to interrupt, but I'm not going to be able to help you unless I can add a few things here and there. Let me see if I understand what you're saying right now ....." In subsequent times, helpers could even hold up a hand and say, "Excuse me again, but I want to make sure I am hearing you correctly." Thus, helpers let clients know that they are interrupting to assist in understanding the client. Moreover, rather than getting angry at clients for monopolizing the conversation, helpers can hypothesize about why clients use talking as a defense. Note that interruptions done in a hostile manner ("Whoa, hold on there, you're talking too much") could hinder the therapeutic relationship and make the client feel that she or he had done something bad. If done appropriately, gently, and respectfully, however, clients could feel relieved that their helpers had the nerve to interrupt them to help them overcome their defenses and learn how to interact more appropriately.

Suicidal Clients

All helpers should be knowledgeable about the steps to take to assist those who are considering hurting themselves. Although the choice about suicide is ultimately up to the client, we assume that clients talking to helpers about the possibility of suicide are asking for help. There are a series of steps that helpers can follow with suicidal clients. First, a general assessment of suicidal risk usually involves asking directly about suicidal potential. Helpers might ask the following questions.

"Are you thinking about suicide?"

"Do you have a plan for attempting suicide?"

"Do you have the means to carry out the plan?"

"Have you attempted suicide in the past?"

"Do you use (or plan on using) alcohol or drugs?"

"Have you been withdrawn and isolated lately?"

"Have you been focused on death (e.g., giving away prized possessions or planning your funeral)?"

"Are you feeling helpless or worthless?"

"Do you have plans for the future?"

If a client indicates a clear intent to commit suicide and has a clear viable plan and the means to do it (e.g., a client plans on killing himself tonight and has purchased the pills and alcohol necessary to accomplish this plan), the helper needs to ensure the client's safety. The helper should first consult with a colleague or supervisor, but the client should not be left alone during the consultation because he or she might leave and carry out the plan or implement the plan in the helper's office.

In some cases, helpers (in consultation with supervisors) might decide that suicidal clients should be hospitalized to protect themselves from self-injury. Helpers may have to admit clients to the hospital against their will. In many cases, however, clients realize the danger and agree to be hospitalized to receive intensive psychological treatment. In other cases, helpers may ascertain that hospitalization is not necessary and instead develop a contract with clients that involves clients agreeing not to hurt themselves and promising to contact the helper or a crisis line for assistance if thoughts of suicide occur. In these cases, it may be useful for helpers to notify the client's family, close friends, or significant others about the client's suicidal ideation. Note that when clients threaten to harm themselves, confidentiality no longer applies. Hence, helpers can perform the necessary steps to ensure the safety of suicidal clients. For legal purposes, helpers should document in writing the procedures that they followed to assist suicidal clients, including the questions that were asked, consultations that occurred, and interventions that were made.

In some cases, a helper may decide that although a client is not actively suicidal, a contract would he helpful to ensure that the client has access to assistance if needed. Helpers can provide the number of a 24-hr crisis line and assist the client in identifying a support system. Additional sessions can be suggested or the helper can offer to call the client between sessions to provide extra support.

One of the most difficult issues any mental health professional can face is dealing with the aftermath of a client committing suicide. Many helpers agonize, feel guilty, and spend a lot of time second-guessing whether there was something else they could have done to prevent the suicide. A certain amount of introspection is important and may enable helpers to handle similar situations better in the future, but helpers should not unnecessarily take on too much responsibility. It is often wise for helpers to seek supervision and therapy after such a difficult situation to help them cope and understand their feelings.

AN EXAMPLE OF AN EXTENDED INTERACTION

The following is a sample of an interchange where the helper facilitates client exploration through an integration of the exploration skills. This example is not meant to be "perfect," but rather a realistic example of what might occur with a beginning helper. After each helper response, we provide the helper's intentions and skills in parentheses. As you go through the example, you might want to cover the helper's responses before you read them and see what you would say if you were the helper. You can then see how similar the helper's response is to what you did and determine which you think is most effective and which you would be most comfortable trying.

> Helper: "Hi! My name is Sandra. We have 30 minutes today to explore whatever you would like to talk about." (The helper intends to set limits by providing information about what the client can expect from the session.)
>
> Client: "Okay."
>
> Helper: "So, where would you like to begin?" (Helper asks an open question to focus the session.)
>
> Client: "I'm feeling anxious about a paper I have to write. I always end up waiting until the last minute to begin, and then I panic because I don't have enough time to write it. I know I do this, but I can't seem to stop myself."
>
> Helper: "You're really upset with yourself." (Helper gives a reflection to help the client experience feelings.)
>
> Client: "Yeah, I'm worried that I'm going to ruin my chances of getting into graduate school because I'm not doing as well in my courses as I should be."
>
> Helper: "You feel scared because your current behaviors might limit your future goals." (Helper gives another reflection because she wants to stay with the feelings and help the client explore more.)

Client: "Exactly, I really think that I could succeed in graduate school and I know I need a graduate degree to do what will make me happy. I'm so worried that I'll stay stuck and ruin everything I've worked for."

Helper: "Tell me about the last time that you had a paper to write. Take me through what went on inside your head." (Helper wants more information about exactly what goes on and wants to get the client to talk more concretely about the problem, so asks open questions.)

Client: "Well, actually, I have a paper due tomorrow, and I haven't begun to do it yet. I've gathered all the material that I need, and I've taken notes on the books, but I haven't written anything yet. And I've been up late several nights already this week, so I'm short on sleep."

Helper: "I can hear the panic in your voice." (Helper reflects nonverbal behavior to help the client recognize feelings.)

Client: "Yeah, I'm scared that I won't be able to pull it off this time. Usually I can just pull an all nighter and get it done, but it seems too big this time. The paper's supposed to be 20 pages."

Helper: "What are your plans for this evening?" (Helper again wants the client to get more specific about the situation to provide a clearer picture and again focuses by asking an open question.)

Client: "Well, I just want to go home and sleep. I just don't want to do it."

Helper: "Is anything else going on in your life that makes it difficult for you to work on the paper right now?" (Helper notes that client seems stuck and thinks that perhaps the situation is more complicated than the client has expressed. Hence, the helper asks an open question about other issues.)

Client: "It's funny you should ask about that. I just had a big fight with my boyfriend, and I feel very upset. He wants to get married and have kids right away, but I really want to go to graduate school. But if I go to graduate school, I will have to move away at least for awhile."

Helper: "So you feel conflicted between being with your boyfriend and going on to school." (Helper feels pleased that the client has opened up about other parts of the situation. Because helper wants to get the client to talk about her feelings about this conflict, helper uses a reflection that focuses on both parts of the problem.)

Client: "That's really true. It just feels like everything has to go his way. Just because he's already finished his school and is working, he wants me to be done too."

Helper: "I wonder if you're somewhat confused." (Helper's intent is to identify feelings through a reflection, but helper has inappropriately projected her confusion onto the client because she is in a similar situation.)

Client: "No, not really. As I think about it, I feel angry. I shouldn't have to give up my career for his. My mother did that, and she is very unhappy. She never even learned how to drive. She did everything for her kids, and now that we have all left home, she's depressed and lonesome. I think I want to have a career, but I don't know. I don't know if it's fair, and I don't want to risk losing my relationship with my boyfriend."

Helper: (in a softer voice) "It sounds like you are really torn up inside." (Helper realizes that last intervention was inaccurate and shifts focus back to the client's feelings by using a reflection.)

Client: (cries softly) "Maybe I can't write the paper because I'm so confused about this fight with my boyfriend and what's going on with my mother."

Helper: (Helper is silent for 30 s to give the client a chance to experience her feelings of sadness.)

Client: (cries and then blows her nose)

Helper: (softly) "I'm sure this is very difficult for you to talk about." (Helper wants to support the client, so gives her a supportive statement.)

Client: "Yeah, it sure is. What do you think I should do?"

Helper: "Well, I think you should go talk with your instructor and see if you can get out of writing the paper tomorrow. Then I think you need to talk to your boyfriend and try to work things out. Perhaps you should encourage your mom to get counseling." (Helper inappropriately gets caught up in the client's request for help and gives direct guidance about what client should do.)

Client: "Oh." (silence) "Well, I don't know." (The client stops exploring and becomes passive.)

Helper: "Sorry, I got carried away with too much advice. How do you feel about a career?" (Helper realizes that the client has stopped exploring and so apologizes briefly. She then tries to go back to the exploration by returning to the last major issue they were discussing before the client got stuck.)

Client: (Client continues to explore.)

What Do You Think?

- How would you as a helper have handled the situation in the extended example? Would you have used different interventions at any point?

- How would you have felt about the helper's interventions if you were the client in the extended example?

- What is your explanation for how the client was able to come to insight (i.e., "Maybe I can't write the paper because of my fight with my boyfriend and what's going on with my mother") in the extended example given that the helper did not provide an interpretation?

- Discuss whether you think helpers need to go on to the insight stage or whether the exploration stage is necessary and sufficient for client change.

- How do you balance using the skills with listening empathically to a client's needs and reactions?

- Identify what steps you might take if you were a helper dealing with the following suicidal clients.
  A. Ilya is a 23-year-old man who mentions that he feels really depressed because his girlfriend broke up with him last week. He states that he does not think he can live without her. He does not have a plan and has never attempted suicide before. He drinks occasionally and recently has been drinking more.

B. Jackie is a 45-year-old woman who recently lost her job as a manager for a well-respected public relations firm. She was divorced 5 years ago, and her husband has custody of their two children. At the time of the divorce, she attempted suicide by ingesting 50 aspirins. She was hospitalized at that time. She recently returned to counseling because of a general dissatisfaction with her life. She plans on taking 100 aspirins and has a bottle in her purse. She has written notes to both of her children.

C. Omar is a 17-year-old boy who was suspended from school for fighting with another student. His parents are angry with him and have insisted that he attend counseling. He states that maybe he should try to hurt himself because then they would really think he had a problem. He does not have a plan and has never attempted suicide before. He says, "I'd never really hurt myself. I want to go to college and get away from my parents and have fun."

IDEAS FOR RESEARCH

Much research is needed to understand more about the exploration stage. Here are some ideas to stimulate thoughts about investigations that could be conducted to determine which of the exploration skills are effective for what types of clients.

- We proposed markers in sessions for when different skills should be used (see Table 11.1). As stated in the beginning of this chapter, however, these markers are based on our clinical intuition and need to be tested.

- We need to know more about sequences of helper skills. What happens, for example, when helpers follow open questions with restatements or reflections versus additional open questions? How do clients respond when presented with a series of closed questions?

- What are the effects of exploration skills (e.g., restatements, reflections, open questions) for different types of clients (e.g., dependent, angry, passive, introspective)?

- What is the best method for teaching beginners to use exploration skills? For example, what combination of didactic information, modeling, and practice is most effective in teaching helping skills?

- Is knowledge of theories of counseling beneficial in learning helping skills?

- What issues arise for trainees in trying to learn exploration skills?

- What are the most common "mistakes" made by beginning trainees? What can teachers do about these errors?

- Why are beginning helpers reluctant to use exploration skills?

- Are certain types of trainees more amenable to learning the helping model presented in this book?

- We maintained throughout this section of the book that reflection of feelings is the most valuable helping skill in the exploration stage. Is this true? What are the advantages and disadvantages of using reflections? When would it not be advisable to use reflections?

- How do skilled helpers use silence to assist clients? What factors do experienced helpers attend to when making decisions about whether to allow silence to continue in sessions?

- How much exploration is needed before helpers assist clients in moving to the insight stage?
- With what types of clients would you be most likely to use approval and reassurance?
- How do skilled helpers determine which feelings to explore or which feelings to reinforce?
- Can everyone learn the exploration skills? If not, what factors predict what types of people are the most effective helpers?
- How do cultural differences between helpers and clients influence sessions?

For further information on research methods, see Heppner, Kivlighan, and Wampold (1999); Hill (1990, 1991); Hill, Thompson, and Williams (1997); and Lambert and Hill (1994).

LAB 6 Integration of Exploration Skills

You are ready to integrate the skills that you have learned so far. In this lab, you will meet with a client and use the skills that you have learned to facilitate client exploration.

Goal: For helpers to participate in a 20-min helping session using the basic helping skills (open question, restatement, reflection of feelings) as well as the minor skills (approval and reassurance, silence, closed question, self-disclosures for exploration, and information about the helping process).

Helper's and Client's Tasks During the Helping Interchange

1. Each helper should pair up with another student in the class.
2. Helpers should photocopy the necessary forms and bring them to the session: the session review form (Exhibit 11.1), the helper intentions list (Appendix A), and client reactions system (Appendix D).
3. Helpers should bring an audio- (or video-) tape recorder (tested ahead of time to ensure that it works) and a tape. They should turn the recorder on at the beginning of the session.
4. Helpers should introduce themselves and remind clients that everything they say remains confidential. Helpers should indicate exactly who will listen to the session (e.g., peer, supervisor).
5. Each helper should conduct a 20-min session with his or her client. Be as helpful to your client as possible. Use all of the different skills that you have learned so far. Watch for the client's reactions to each of your interventions and modify subsequent interventions when appropriate.
6. Watch your time carefully. About 2 min before you need to stop, let the client know that your time will soon end. Let your client know when the time is up by saying something like, "We need to stop now. Thank you for helping me practice my helping skills."

Supervisor's Tasks During Session

Supervisors should monitor sessions so that they can provide feedback to helpers about basic helping skills. Supervisors can use the supervisor rating form shown in Exhibit 11.2 to record their observations and evaluations.

Helper's and Client's Tasks During the Postsession
Review of the Tape

1. After the session, each helper should go over the tape with the client (review of a 20-min session takes about 40–60 min). Helpers should stop the tape after each helper intervention (except minimal acknowledgments such as "mmhmm" and "yeah"). Helpers should write down the key words on the session review form (see Exhibit 11.1), so that the exact spot on the tape can be located later for transcribing the session.
2. Helpers should rate the helpfulness of the intervention and write down the numbers of up to three intentions that they had for the intervention. Helpers should respond according to how they felt during the session rather than when listening to the tape of the session. Use the whole range of the Helpfulness Scale and as many categories as possible on the Intentions List. Do not complete these ratings collaboratively with clients.

(Continues)

3. Clients should rate the helpfulness of each intervention and write down the numbers of up to three reactions, circling any reactions that they hid from helpers during the session. Clients should respond according to how they felt during the session rather than how they feel listening to the tape of the session. Clients should use the whole range of the Helpfulness Scale and as many categories as possible on the reactions system (helpers learn more from honest feedback than from "nice" statements that are not genuine). Do not collaborate with helpers in doing the ratings.

4. Helpers and clients should write down the most helpful and least helpful event in the session.

5. Helpers should type a transcript of their 20-min session (see the sample transcript in Exhibit 11.3). You can skip minimal utterances such as "okay," "you know," "er," and "uh."

6. Divide the helper speech into response units (essentially grammatical sentences), using the directions provided in Appendix C.

7. Using the helping skills system (see Appendix B), determine which skill was used for each response unit (i.e., grammatical sentence) in your transcript.

8. Indicate on the transcript what you would say differently for each intervention if you could do it again. Use the helping skills system (Appendix B) to indicate which skill fits for each response unit of what you would say differently.

9. Erase the tape. Make sure that no identifying information is on the transcript.

Personal Reflections

- What did you learn about yourself as a helper from this experience?
- Which skills did you use most and least frequently?
- Which skills are you most and least comfortable using? How might you increase your comfort with skills that you were uncomfortable using?
- Which skills did you and the client find to be most helpful, and what made these skills effective with this client?
- Did your intentions match your skills?
- Some helpers have a hard time exploring because they want to rush to problem solving. If this was true for you, speculate on what makes it difficult for you to explore an issue deeply without feeling an urgency to problem solve.
- Compare the skills in what you did with what you would do differently. What does this tell you about what you need to work on?

▬ EXHIBIT 11.1. SESSION REVIEW FORM

Instructions: Stop the tape after each helper speaking turn (everything in between two client statements). DO NOT STOP for minimal interventions (e.g., "mmhmm," "okay," silence, head nods). Write down the key words. Helpers should indicate up to three intentions for their intervention; clients should indicate up to three reactions and circle any reactions that were hidden. Both should rate the helpfulness of the intervention using the Helpfulness Scale shown below (use the whole range of the scale). RESPOND ACCORDING TO HOW YOU FELT AT THE TIME IN THE SESSION. DO NOT COLLABORATE.

Helper code: _____   Client code: _____   Date: _____

		Hindering				Neutral			Helpful	
Helpfulness Scale		1	2	3	4	5	6	7	8	9

		Intentions/reactions			Helpfulness
Turn	Key words	1	2	3	rating
1	_____	____	____	____	_____
2	_____	____	____	____	_____
3	_____	____	____	____	_____
4	_____	____	____	____	_____
5	_____	____	____	____	_____
6	_____	____	____	____	_____
7	_____	____	____	____	_____
8	_____	____	____	____	_____
9	_____	____	____	____	_____
10	_____	____	____	____	_____
11	_____	____	____	____	_____
12	_____	____	____	____	_____
13	_____	____	____	____	_____
14	_____	____	____	____	_____
15	_____	____	____	____	_____
16	_____	____	____	____	_____
17	_____	____	____	____	_____
18	_____	____	____	____	_____
19	_____	____	____	____	_____
20	_____	____	____	____	_____
21	_____	____	____	____	_____
22	_____	____	____	____	_____
23	_____	____	____	____	_____
24	_____	____	____	____	_____
25	_____	____	____	____	_____

What was the most helpful event that occurred during this session? How was it helpful?
_____
_____

What was the least helpful event during this session? How was it unhelpful?
_____
_____

▬▬▬   **EXHIBIT 11.2. SUPERVISOR OR PEER RATING FORM OF HELPER EXPLORATION SKILLS**

Date: _____

Name of helper: _____   Name of observer: _____

Instructions: A supervisor or peer should complete this measure after watching the helper do a helping session. Please note that probably not all of the skills listed will be used at this point.

	Used skill?		If used, was it used inappropriately/appropriately					Example
Attending	Y	N	1	2	3	4	5	_____
Listening	Y	N	1	2	3	4	5	_____
Restatement	Y	N	1	2	3	4	5	_____
Open question	Y	N	1	2	3	4	5	_____
Reflection of feelings	Y	N	1	2	3	4	5	_____
Approval and reassurance	Y	N	1	2	3	4	5	_____
Closed question	Y	N	1	2	3	4	5	_____
Silence	Y	N	1	2	3	4	5	_____
Challenge	Y	N	1	2	3	4	5	_____
Interpretation	Y	N	1	2	3	4	5	_____
Self-disclosure	Y	N	1	2	3	4	5	_____
Immediacy	Y	N	1	2	3	4	5	_____
Information	Y	N	1	2	3	4	5	_____
Direct guidance	Y	N	1	2	3	4	5	_____

Strengths of helper (list at least two):

1. _____

2. _____

3. _____

Areas needing improvement (list at least two):

1. _____

2. _____

3. _____

Comments:

▬▬▬▬   EXHIBIT 11.3. SAMPLE TRANSCRIPT

Instructions: Type everything except minimal utterances (e.g., "okay," "you know," "er," "uh"). Use slashes (/) to divide helper statements into response units (i.e., grammatical sentences—every sentence must include a subject and verb).

> **Helper:** "Hello./ Thank you for coming in./Our session will hopefully last about 20 minutes./ You can talk about whatever you'd like to talk about if you have anything to talk about./ Do you have anything to talk about today?"/

Helper intentions	Verbal helping skills	Helper helpfulness rating	Client helpfulness rating	Client reactions	What would have been a better intervention?
4, 2	12, 12, 11, 11, 3	5	6	21	What would you like to talk about today?/(3)

> **Client:** "I'm having a problem with my roommate. We don't seem to be getting along. She's a real slob and never cleans up her part of the room. She leaves dirty dishes all over."/
>
> **Helper:** "I wonder, you sound like maybe you're a little bit maybe angry at her?"/

Helper intentions	Verbal helping skills	Helper helpfulness rating	Client helpfulness rating	Client reactions	What would have been a better intervention?
12	5	7	7	8	You sound angry at her./(5)

> **Client:** "I am angry at her. In fact, I'm furious. I don't see why I got stuck with such a slob. I indicated on my preference form that I am very neat. We're just totally different people. And I feel like I don't know how to handle the situation when she gets nasty about me not wanting to clean the room."/
>
> **Helper:** "Tell me more about how you feel./ Tell me about the last time she got nasty./ What would you like to do about all this?"/

(Continues)

Helper intentions	Verbal helping skills	Helper helpfulness rating	Client helpfulness rating	Client reactions	What would have been a better intervention?
2, 5	3, 3, 3	5	4	19	Tell me more about what went on in the recent conflict between the two of you./(3)

Intentions: During the session review, helper lists up to three intentions for each helper speaking turn. 1 = set limits, 2 = get information, 3 = give information, 4 = support, 5 = focus, 6 = clarify, 7 = hope, 8 = catharsis, 9 = cognitions, 10 = behaviors, 11 = self-control, 12 = feelings, 13 = insight, 14 = change, 15 = reinforce change, 16 = resistance, 17 = challenge, 18 = relationship, 19 = helper needs.

Helping skills: Using the session transcript, the helper or a judge indicates one verbal helping skill that best describes each helper response unit (i.e., a grammatical sentence which must contain a subject and a verb). 1 = approval and reassurance, 2 = closed question, 3 = open question, 4 = restatement, 5 = reflection of feelings, 6 = challenge, 7 = interpretation, 8 = self-disclosure, 9 = immediacy, 10 = information, 11 = direct guidance, 12 = other.

Helpfulness ratings: During the session review, helper and client rate each helper speaking turn. 1 = hindering, 5 = neutral, 9 = helpful.

Reactions: During the session review, client lists up to three reactions for each helper speaking turn. Circle any hidden reactions. 1 = understood, 2 = supported, 3 = hopeful, 4 = relief, 5 = negative thoughts or behaviors, 6 = better self-understanding, 7 = clear, 8 = feelings, 9 = responsibility, 10 = unstuck, 11 = new perspective, 12 = educated, 13 = new ways to behave, 14 = challenged, 15 = scared, 16 = worse, 17 = stuck, 18 = lack of direction, 19 = confused, 20 = misunderstood, 21 = no reaction.

III INSIGHT STAGE

12 Overview of the Insight Stage

Daring as it is to investigate the unknown, even more so it is to question the known.

Kaspar

Juan had been to a behavioral helper who taught him relaxation, assertiveness skills, and time management skills. He was now more organized, relaxed, and better able to carry on a conversation, but he still felt empty inside. He could not understand why he felt that life had no meaning. He went to a helper who believed in insight, and they began exploring his feelings about himself and his childhood. Through this experience, he came to the awareness that perhaps his anxiety and loneliness had roots in the fact that his mother died when he was 2 months old and his father sent him to live with his grandparents. Although his grandparents were very loving, he always felt that he was interfering with their retirement plans and that he was out of place. He realized that in social situations, he always placed himself on the outside so that others would not have the chance to reject him. He had lived his life as a defense against being abandoned again. He also came to realize that by removing himself from social situations, he had no opportunity to have close, satisfying relationships. In session, he found himself constantly worrying that the helper was bored and would rather be with other clients, which through discussion, he came to understand was a transference onto the helper of his feelings about his parents abandoning him because he was not lovable. Once he understood more about himself and could begin to see that the helper indeed cared about him, Juan began to rethink the idea that he was not lovable. He was able to reframe his perceptions of his grandparents to see that in fact they did love him for himself and had chosen to raise him. Juan felt better because he now had some understanding of himself.

DURING THE exploration stage, we wanted to establish a therapeutic relationship and help clients explore their thoughts, experience their feelings at a deep level, and examine the many facets of their problems. The exploration stage was client-centered in that we encouraged helpers to suspend judgment to try to understand the client's perspective. For some clients, this supportive, nonjudgmental listening is all that is needed to motivate them to make important changes in their lives. The helper's acceptance enables clients to experience their feelings and accept what is going on inside them. They become unblocked and able to think of how they want to be and what they want to do about their problems. Their actualization potential is released, and they can become creative and active problem-solvers. They no longer need outside intervention, although they might enjoy having someone with whom to share thoughts and feelings.

Unfortunately, not all clients can progress on their own after exploring their thoughts and feelings. Some clients have a hard time understanding the origins and consequences of their feelings and behaviors. Other clients get stuck and need someone to help them get past obstacles. People often cannot give up defenses that they learned early in childhood that protect them against internal pain and external harm. To give up these protective defenses is difficult because there is no assurance that the world is a safe place. In addition, when painful events occur, people often segregate experiences in their minds so that they do not have to think about them, making it difficult to integrate these experiences into their lives. Some people have done things a certain way for so long that they never question their actions or think about the reasons for what they do. Other clients simply are eager to learn more about themselves and their motivations; they want an objective perspective to provide feedback about how others perceive them. Hence, helpers need to promote insight to help clients improve their current level of functioning.

Going beyond exploration to insight and an understanding of inner dynamics requires a deep sense of empathy and belief in clients. Helpers have to see beyond defenses and inappropriate behaviors to the inner self. Being able to suspend judgment allows helpers to look deeper to try to understand clients, help them accept themselves, and help them understand more about themselves.

THEORETICAL BACKGROUND: PSYCHOANALYTIC THEORY

The primary theoretical foundation for the insight stage is psychoanalytic theory, which began with Freud and has evolved through many subsequent theorists (e.g., Jung, Adler, Erikson, Mahler, Klein, Horney, Sullivan, Bowlby, Greenson, Basch, Fairbairn, Winnicott, and Kohut). Psychoanalytic theorists typically believe that early childhood experiences are central to later functioning in life, although they differ in which aspects of development they consider important. They also believe that unconscious processes influence the behaviors of individuals and that defense mechanisms are used to reduce anxiety and conflict within an individual. Therapeutic goals include bringing unconscious processes to awareness and developing insight about one's feelings and behaviors. The processes used to obtain these goals include analyzing transference and countertransference, working through unresolved issues, and interpreting the material presented by clients so that the unconscious becomes conscious.

Development of Personality

Many different psychoanalytic theories of the development of personality have been developed. We discuss Freud's groundbreaking theory as well as three theories (by Erikson, Mahler, and Bowlby) that were developed to advance psychoanalytic theory. Although it is beyond the scope of this book to cover the full range of theories, we encourage interested readers to explore other sources to learn more about current psychoanalytic theory (e.g., Gelso & Hayes, 1998; Greenson, 1967; Kohut, 1971, 1977, 1984; Patton & Meara, 1992).

Freudian Psychosexual Development

Freud's (1940/1949) biological theory identified psychosexual development through universal stages as the key feature of personality development. He believed that children innately seek pleasure and initially are governed completely by id impulses. The id is the center of all biological urges and represents the libidinal drives of the individual.

He called children *polymorphously perverse* because their sexual pleasure could be gratified through a number of different bodily channels depending on the age. Initially, this sexual energy is focused on oral gratification because children derive their pleasure first from sucking and then from biting (birth–18 months). The task of the oral stage is to develop trust in oneself, in others, and in the environment. The erogenous zone moves to the anal region as toilet training becomes a primary focus between parents and children (18 months–3 years). The tasks of the anal stage are to move toward independence and autonomy, to deal with frustration, and to begin to incorporate a sense of self. The ego, which serves as the mediator between the id and the outside world, develops during the oral and anal stages as the child is forced to deal with reality.

In the phallic stage, the child's energy next shifts to the genital area. Children become attracted to the opposite sex parent and want to destroy the same-sex parent (called the Oedipal complex for boys and the Electra complex for girls). The Oedipal–Electra complex is resolved when individuals develop an identification with the same-sex parent (3–6 years old). Because of the tumultuousness of the Oedipal–Electra conflict, the child develops a superego upon resolution. The superego serves as the critical voice representing the mores of society and the standards of the parents. The superego acts to interrupt the impulses of the id, whereas the ego moderates between the id, superego, and the outside world. Tasks of the phallic stage are to accept sexual feelings and to have respect for one's body.

Children then move into a latency stage (6–12 years old), where their attention shifts away from sexuality. During this stage, individuals become socialized to interact with others and become interested in occurrences outside of themselves. They are challenged to develop skills that enable them to perform successfully at home, at school, and in the community. In the final stage, the genital stage, energy again shifts to the genital area and to more mature expressions of libidinal energy (age 12–adulthood). The tasks are learning how to be successful in love and work.

Healthy development is achieved by those who have advanced through all of the stages. However, children can easily become fixated at any of the stages, either from not having their needs met or from having their needs overindulged. At times of stress, individuals often regress to earlier and happier stages of development. For example, when his parents get divorced, a 10-year-old boy might regress to sucking his thumb and wetting the bed. People rarely advance through all of the stages without some fixations and regressions.

Erikson's Theory of Psychosocial Development

Because he disagreed with Freud's emphasis on sexuality, Erikson (1963) focused on the social and interpersonal aspects of human development. Specifically, he developed an eight-stage model that stressed the importance of the ego and the role of society in psychosocial functioning. He also extended Freud's model of development to reflect continued growth and change throughout adolescence and adulthood and old age.

Erikson suggested that the first task for infants is to develop trust in themselves and their caretakers (trust vs. mistrust) so that they come to believe that they are worthy of care. Infants whose needs are met are likely to develop the perception that other people can be trusted to provide assistance when needed. In the second stage, the young child is challenged to resolve the conflict between autonomy versus shame and doubt. This conflict is most clearly illustrated through the process of becoming toilet trained. The child has to learn to control his or her bladder and bowels without feeling humiliated. Moving to the preschool years, the third stage is the initiative versus guilt conflict, which involves beginning to plan actions and cooperate with others and results in the development of moral responsibility and the initiation of social activities. When children begin school, conflict occurs between industry versus inferiority. Unlike the relative calm of Freud's latency period, Erikson believed that children face many challenges during this stage, such as negotiating social interactions and academic tasks.

Adolescents entering puberty face the fifth stage (identity vs. role conflict) in which they struggle to define themselves, often through the selection of a career direction. Individuals who have difficulty with this stage may exhibit career indecision or the tendency to overidentify with peers or famous individuals. During early adulthood, people face the intimacy versus isolation crisis. In this stage, many people obtain a job and develop a serious relationship with a life partner. Middle adulthood is the longest stage, lasting from the mid-20s until about age 65. The conflict in middle adulthood is between generativity (caring for and contributing to others through relationships and work) versus stagnation. The final stage is integrity versus despair, in which the mature person reflects about his or her life, relationships, and accomplishments.

Erikson believed that people need to resolve one crisis before being able to go on to the next stage. When crises are not successfully resolved, a person has less energy to move on to the next crisis. For example, if a person does not successfully resolve the identity crisis, it is difficult for that person to become intimate with a partner.

Mahler's Individuation Theory

Mahler (1968) also focused on relationships between children and others. Right after birth, she hypothesized, infants make little or no differentiation between self and caregiver. They are concerned solely with the satisfaction of their own needs and tension reduction. Around the second month of life, infants begin to develop an awareness of their caretaker as an external being who meets some of their needs. Infants at about 4–5 months begin to *hatch*, which means they start to develop motor skills, engage in play, and direct attention to others besides the caregiver. They begin to explore their environment, often checking back for emotional refueling from a stable base. Children then begin to struggle with intense neediness versus powerful desires for separateness. The caregiver's response of allowing the child to move away and yet still providing the safe base is crucial to the successful resolution of this struggle. Mahler, Pine, and Bergman (1975) believed that humans reexperience components of the cycle between separation and neediness throughout their lives.

Bowlby's Attachment Theory

Bowlby (1969, 1988) developed attachment theory to explain the behavioral and emotional responses that keep young children in close proximity to their caregivers. In optimal attachment, caregivers provide a comfortable presence for the child that reduces anxiety and promotes a feeling of security. From this secure base, infants are able to explore their environment. Through an observational study of young children, Ainsworth, Blehar, Waters, and Wall (1978) found three patterns of attachment (secure, anxious–ambivalent, anxious–avoidant). Infants who were securely attached explored freely in their mother's presence, showed some anxiety upon separation, and were easily comforted when reunited. Infants with an anxious–ambivalent pattern were excessively anxious and angry, and they tended to cling to an extent that interfered with their exploration. They were also distressed during separation and were difficult to comfort upon reunion with mothers. Anxious–avoidant infants showed minimal interest in their mothers and displayed minimal affect throughout the observation. These observations have been replicated with other children and the results have been extended to adulthood, suggesting that attachment patterns in childhood carry over to relationships in adulthood (Ainsworth, 1989). Recently, Mallinckrodt, Gantt, and Coble (1995) used attachment theory to develop a measure of client attachment to therapists in therapy.

Defense Mechanisms

Not everything goes smoothly in the development of personality. Children do not always receive all the things they need to develop psychologically. One of the ways that people cope with adversity is through developing defense mechanisms. Freud (1933) and other more recent psychoanalysts have theorized that defense mechanisms are unconscious methods for dealing with anxiety through the denial or distortion of reality. Everyone has defense mechanisms because everyone has to cope with anxiety. Defense mechanisms can be healthy if used appropriately and in moderation, but repeated and frequent use of defense mechanisms can become problematic. Examples of defense mechanisms include

- repression (not allowing painful material into one's conscious thought)
- intellectualization (avoiding painful feelings by focusing on ideas)
- denial (actively rejecting painful affect)
- regression (engaging in behaviors from an earlier stage of development at times when one is anxious)
- displacement (shifting uncomfortable feelings toward someone who is often less powerful and less threatening than the individual from whom the feelings originated)
- identification (emulating characteristics in others)
- projection (perceiving that others have the characteristics that are unconsciously disliked in one's self)
- undoing (behaving in a ritualistic manner to take away or make amends for unacceptable behaviors)
- reaction formation (acting in a manner that is opposite to what one is feeling)
- sublimation (changing unacceptable impulses into socially appropriate actions)
- rationalization (making excuses for an anxiety-producing thought or behavior).

For example, Antonio has problems in his marriage because he projects onto his wife that she is dominating like his mother. He is not able to see that her questions are motivated by concern rather than by a desire to control. He is afraid of telling his wife about his anger at her for being dominating, and so he displaces his feelings by kicking the dog. If asked about his anger, he denies it and regresses to acting like a whiny 7-year-old who expects to be punished. These defense mechanisms protect Antonio from being aware of his anger at his mother and from learning how to deal with his feelings more appropriately.

Psychoanalytic Treatment

Freud (1923/1963) believed that examination and insight into troubling issues could assist in the resolution of problems. The helper listens patiently, empathically, uncritically, and receptively (Arlow, 1995). To facilitate insight, the analyst encourages the patient to *free associate*—to say whatever thoughts come to mind without censure as a means to make the unconscious conscious, which is a primary focus of psychoanalytic treatment.

The movement toward emotional and intellectual insight is thought to result in change (Ferenczi & Rank, 1925/1956). For example, a client who understands on an intellectual level that she screams at her boyfriend because she is very angry with her father does not achieve the same kind of growth and change that both intellectual and emotional insight engenders. If this client were to experience the feelings associated with this intellectual understanding (e.g., how bad she feels about transferring negative feelings toward her mostly innocent boyfriend, and how deeply frustrated she is that her father continues to have a negative influence on her life), she might develop the motivation to change her behaviors toward her boyfriend.

Furthermore, Freud (1933) believed that psychoanalysis could assist clients in gaining insight about the origins of behaviors and the influence of early childhood experiences on current behaviors. The goal of psychoanalytic treatment is to make the unconscious conscious or "where id is, there ego shall be." Although the majority of our mind is unconscious, according to Freud, we can strive to make ourselves as aware as possible of these primitive influences. Because of the difficulty of dealing with unconscious material, Freud proposed that we analyze things such as dreams or slips of the tongue, where the ego does not have as strong a control. In addition, psychoanalysts often believe that therapy assists clients in developing an awareness of frequently used defense mechanisms and in gaining more control over the use of these unconscious strategies to reduce anxiety.

Freud believed that manifestations of unresolved problems from early in childhood are repeated throughout the client's life. Often, the repetition is uncovered through analysis of the way in which the client relates to the therapist. For example, a client whose mother was unable to fulfill her needs as an infant may demonstrate neediness in her relationship with the therapist. The client might call the therapist at home, ask for extra sessions, and do her best to extend the limits of each session. The client might also ascribe to her therapist characteristics of coldness and an inability to meet her needs. Placing on the therapist characteristics that belong to other people with whom one has unresolved issues is termed *transference* (Freud, 1920/1943). Freud indicated that the analysis and interpretation of transference can be a powerful therapeutic tool to facilitate a greater understanding of the client's relationships with others and of significant unresolved issues for the client.

The helper's unresolved issues can also influence the process and outcome of helping. This process has been called *countertransference* and is defined as the helper's reactions to the client that originate in the unresolved issues of the helper. In the previous example, the therapist may have had unresolved needs to take care of others (perhaps related to having an alcoholic mother who relied on the helper to care for the younger siblings) and so might respond to the client's neediness by allowing the client to call her at home, stop by the office at any time, and delay payment until the client earns more money. If unrecognized, countertransference behaviors can influence the process of therapy in a negative way. However, awareness of countertransference feelings can assist helpers in ensuring that the helping process is not harmed by the helper's unresolved issues.

Therapists who follow strict Freudian principles are considered to be psychoanalytic. Therapists who modify the principles or who use them more liberally or in conjunction with other principles are considered to be psychodynamic.

How Psychoanalytic and Psychodynamic Theories Relate to the Three-Stage Model

The psychoanalytic emphasis on insight, dealing with the therapeutic relationship and the importance of early childhood experience, is consistent with our thinking about the insight stage. Psychanalysts talk about the importance for doing an "archeological dig" to determine the reasons for behaviors and for using the immediate therapeutic relationship as an example of how the client relates to others. We believe strongly that insight is helpful in enabling clients to make lasting changes and to solve new problems as they arise. Dealing with problems as they occur in the therapeutic relationship is also crucial because it provides clients with skills to handle relationships outside of therapy more effectively. In addition, the emphasis on the importance of early childhood experiences, from whichever perspective one thinks about it (that espoused by Freud, Erikson, Mahler, or Bowlby) is in concert with our thinking about the importance of early experiences, particularly with significant others.

Several theoretical assertions advanced by Freud are antithetical to our approach to helping. Specifically, Freud (1933) believed that people are motivated by libidinal (sexual) and aggressive drives, whereas we believe that people are not necessarily motivated by these drives unless early experiences influence them in that direction. In addition, Freud's theories about women (e.g., having penis envy; being masochistic, dependent, and passive) are offensive and outdated. Freud also ignored concerns about social injustice for clients of color (Leong, Wagner, & Tata, 1995).

Furthermore, psychoanalytic and psychodynamic approaches typically do not provide direct guidance or advice (Crits-Christoph, Barber, & Kurcias, 1991). Thus, these approaches often do not provide techniques for moving the clients to action—the last stage in our model. We believe that information and direct guidance can be useful when used at the appropriate time. Helpers using the three-stage model tend to be more active agents in helping, and the length of treatment tends to be shorter than in classical psychoanalytic therapy. Despite differences in some theoretical assertions, then, many therapeutic techniques advanced by the psychoanalytic or psychodynamic traditions can assist helpers in guiding clients toward increased insight and self-understanding.

GOALS FOR THE INSIGHT STAGE

The helper's major goal during the insight stage is to foster insight. Specifically, helpers work with clients to construct new understandings, to determine their role in creating and maintaining their problems, and to address issues in the therapeutic relationship. One of the hallmarks of our existence as human beings is wanting to have an explanation for our feelings, thoughts, and behaviors. Having an explanation, however right or wrong, helps most people feel more in control of their world. In the insight stage, we search for clues regarding what motivates people and what hinders them from achieving their potential.

What Is Insight?

Elliott et al. (1994) described four typical aspects of insight:

- seeing oneself in a new light
- making connections or understanding patterns, links, reasons, causes, categorizations, or parallels

- having a sense of suddenness, feeling of surprise, or "aha" experience where everything comes together all at once
- experiencing a sense of newness, or a feeling of making a new discovery rather than just thinking in the same ways.

When clients come to insights, they suddenly see things in a new way or from a new perspective, are able to make connections between things, or have an understanding of why things happen as they do. For example, Jihad might suddenly realize that his violent reaction to his girlfriend when she said she would not go to a party stems from his never having gotten his own way as a child; his anger is due to perceived past injustices and a belief that his girlfriend is doing the same thing to him that his parents did.

Several theorists have recognized the importance of insight in the therapeutic process. Freud (1923/1963) believed that psychological problems are developmental and that resolution can only be reached by obtaining insight into the problems. Symptoms generally make sense when considered in the context of past and present life experiences. For example, Jenna's fear of public speaking makes sense in light of her reluctance to achieve and possibly outdo her passive and depressed mother. Frank and Frank (1991) viewed insight as a reworking of the past that leads to the discovery of new facts, as well as a recognition of new relationships between previously known facts and a reevaluation of their significance. Hence, Jenna's insight that she has been trying to limit herself to placate her mother could lead her to understanding more about why she made the choices that she did throughout her life. This understanding can also give her a sense that she can make different choices in the future.

Insight must be emotional as well as intellectual to lead to action (Reid & Finesinger, 1952; Singer, 1970). If insight is only intellectual (e.g., "I am anxious because of my Oedipal conflict"), it has a barren, sterile quality that keeps clients stuck in understandings that lead nowhere. Many of us know people who can give a comprehensive history of their psychological problems and the sources of their difficulty but who cannot allow themselves to experience their feelings fully. If the insight involves an emotional component, the client typically has a sense of personal involvement and responsibility. For example, when Joan suddenly realizes that her conflict with her husband for having interests of his own is really due to the hurt that she felt because her father did not spend time with her, the insight is something that Joan can feel at a very deep level. She may feel the relief of a burden lifted from her. This insight might help Joan decide that it is okay for her husband to have some separate activities. Joan also might start thinking that she needs to develop some interests of her own and begin to question why she allows her identity to be based on her husband. The deep, emotional insight that Joan achieved would not have been possible if she had been provided with an interpretation that sounded right "on paper" but was not something that she could acknowledge as her own and feel at a deep level.

Why Is Insight Necessary?

Frank and Frank (1991) asserted that the need to make sense out of events is as fundamental to humans as the need for food or water. They suggested that people evaluate internal and external stimuli in view of their assumptions about what is dangerous, safe, important, good, bad, and so on. These assumptions become organized into sets of highly structured, complex, interacting values, expectations, and images of self that are closely related to emotional states and feelings. These psychological structures shape, and in turn are shaped by, a person's perceptions and behaviors.

Clients' interpretations of events determine subsequent behaviors and feelings, as well as their willingness to work on certain topics in a helping setting. For example, John, an 18-year-old male client, is reluctant to learn to drive. If John believes that his reluctance to drive is due to fears about having a major accident, he might present fear as the problem. If John believes that the fear is due to a reluctance to grow up and become independent, he might want to work on separation issues. One goal of helping is to discover what clients' beliefs are and then assist them in developing more adaptive beliefs. Helpers need to learn how clients currently construe events (both consciously and unconsciously) so that they can help them develop more adaptive constructs.

We also believe that insight must precede action. Action without insight is often meaningless. If clients just did whatever helpers told them to do, with no understanding or explanation for why these actions were important, they would not have a framework to guide their behavior when new problems inevitably develop. Clients would be dependent on others to tell them what to do as each problem arose. In contrast, if we teach clients how to work with their problems, in the future they are more likely to be able to explore their problems, achieve understanding, and decide what they would like to do differently on their own. In effect, we are teaching clients a problem-solving approach. In our example of the reluctant driver, if John comes to understand that his reluctance is due to his anxiety and guilt about leaving his sick mother, he can make an informed decision that fits his values about what he wants to do about his mother. Hence, we believe that insight is especially important in the helping process.

Use of the Helper's Perspective

In comparison to the exploration stage, helpers in the insight stage rely somewhat more on their perspectives and reactions to clients to try to understand where clients are getting stuck and what might be motivating them. Thus, helpers move somewhat away from being immersed in client experiences to a more impartial stance of trying to understand the issues that prevent clients from full functioning. The impartial stance is what clients often need to help them get unstuck. Of course, helpers still need to maintain empathy and collaboration with clients rather than being judgmental. Thus, helpers challenge and interpret while remaining caring throughout the process.

We emphasize that helpers do not have "the" insight or right perspective and should not force clients to accept their perspectives. Rather, helpers use their perspectives to help clients come to new awarenesses. There remains a sense of working together, with helpers aiding clients in discovering things about themselves. Our goal is for clients to have a sense of discovery of the new understandings. Even when helpers suggest insights, clients need to try them on and discover if they fit rather than accepting them blindly. Understanding what is going on inside oneself is an "aha" experience that is invaluable, but it must be discovered and experienced by the client to be truly beneficial.

Helpers have to be careful when using their own perspective to make sure that they are motivated by the best interests of the clients. When helpers are motivated by countertransference, in which they have reactions to clients or to the material that clients discuss, their interventions tend to be less helpful. Hence, helpers need to be aware of their countertransference reactions so that they do not act on them in sessions.

SKILLS USED IN THE INSIGHT STAGE

The most frequently used helper interventions in the insight stage are those that were basic to the exploration stage: attending and listening, restatement, open question, and reflection of feelings. Helpers at this stage continue to facilitate exploration but take the exploration to a deeper level using several additional skills that are discussed extensively in the next several chapters: challenge, interpretation, self-disclosure, and immediacy.

The skills in the insight stage are harder to learn and use than the skills in the exploration stage. We do not expect students to master this stage in their initial exposure to the model. In fact, it takes most students many years and lots of practice to learn the skills and be able to apply them in the appropriate situations in a helping setting.

DIFFICULTIES HELPERS EXPERIENCE IN THE INSIGHT STAGE

Moving Prematurely Into the Insight Stage

Helpers sometimes move into the insight stage before the therapeutic relationship has been firmly established, before the client has adequately explored the problems, or before the helper has a deep understanding of the problems. It is crucial that challenge, interpretation, self-disclosure, and immediacy be used within the context of a strong therapeutic relationship and with a strong foundation of understanding. Otherwise, these techniques have the potential for damaging clients. For example, if a helper challenges before the client trusts the helper, the client will probably doubt the helper's motives and might even terminate the helping relationship.

Taking Too Much Responsibility for Developing Insights

Some helpers feel that they have to be the ones to "put it all together" and connect all the client's past experiences with their present behaviors in a new way. Perhaps a helper has learned an interesting theory and is excited to discover that it applies to the client's difficulty (e.g., the theory that the client's current dependency and alcoholism are related to being pampered and dominated as a child and being granted no opportunity to express herself). The helper may be impatient because the client cannot see what is so blatantly obvious to the helper. To this helper, figuring out clients is more important than helping clients figure out themselves. From our perspective, the more important task is for helpers to empathize with clients, to determine what contributes to clients having difficulty putting it all together, and to work collaboratively with clients to construct insights.

Getting Stuck on One Theoretical Perspective

One of the dangers in the insight stage is that helpers may try to apply psychoanalytic theory too much even though the theory might not fit for an individual client. The psychoanalytic theories are incredibly cogent and thoughtful, and beginning helpers can easily become entranced by them, believing every word that Freud, Kohut, or someone else wrote. For example, a helper could be convinced that every client was suffering from an Oedipal–Electra complex because Freud said so rather than attending to the data that the client presents. In fact, psychoanalytic theories are clinical theories developed by clinicians and have not for the most part been proven, so one must be judicious in applying them.

Forgetting to Be Empathic

Some helpers get so excited about figuring out the puzzle of the client's problems that they forget to be empathic with clients. They do not remember the importance of keeping clients involved in the therapeutic experience. It is crucial to be constantly aware of how clients are feeling and reacting and to work at maintaining the collaborative relationship. The most typical interventions in the insight stage should be reflection of feelings, open question, and restatements, with only an occasional use of the specific insight skills (challenge, interpretation, self-disclosure, and immediacy).

Clients Not Needing or Wanting Insight

No matter how much we as helpers personally value insight, not all of our clients are equally enamored. Some clients (and even some helpers) do not want or need insight. They prefer support without challenge and insight, or they want immediate behavioral change without insight. They often strive to feel better and do not necessarily care to understand why they felt badly. Because our approach is essentially client-centered and we value empathy above all, it is important not to impose our value for insight on such clients but to respect their choice not to understand themselves. For such clients, we recommend making an assessment about whether they primarily need support, behavioral change, or something that we cannot offer. If clients need support for behavioral change, helpers can provide that and reduce the emphasis on the insight stage. If clients need other things (e.g., medication, support groups, welfare), helpers can refer them to other sources.

STRATEGIES FOR OVERCOMING THE DIFFICULTIES

Rely on the Exploration Skills

When in doubt or having problems, we recommend that helpers use the basic skills of attending and listening, open question, restatement, and reflection of feelings. In effect, helpers need to backtrack and rebuild trust and make sure they hear the client's real problems. Helpers can stay in the exploration stage until an idea for a challenge or interpretation emerges naturally and clients are ready to hear it.

Deal With the Relationship

In one study (Rhodes et al., 1994), satisfied clients were asked what their helpers had done to resolve major misunderstandings that arose in relationships. The clients reported that their helpers asked them how they were feeling about what was going on in the therapeutic relationship. They listened nondefensively for feedback and were willing to hear what they might have been doing wrong with clients. They apologized if they had made a mistake or hurt the client's feelings. We suggest that helpers acknowledge their part in the problems in the helping relationship, not only to serve as a model for clients of how to deal with mistakes but also to respond in a human way to another person. In addition, helpers can talk about their feelings about the relationship to let clients know how their behaviors influence others. Providing a place where clients can discuss both positive and negative feelings toward the helper and the sessions is both challenging and critically important. Finally, helpers can thank clients for sharing their feelings. It is often painful and difficult to process the therapeutic relationship, so clients need to be assured that they can bring up both positive and negative feelings.

CONCLUDING COMMENTS

Frankl (1959) emphasized the importance of having a life philosophy to enable one to transcend suffering and find meaning in existence. He argued that our greatest human need is to find a core of meaning and a purpose in life. Frankl's experience in a German concentration camp bears out his theory: Although he could not change his life situation, he was able to change the meaning he attached to this experience. By drawing on the strengths of his Jewish tradition, he was able to survive and help others survive.

The insight stage is important to assist clients in coming to new understandings of themselves and their problems. We believe that people strive to find meaning in their lives and often need to restructure their maladaptive thinking patterns to actualize their potential. We reiterate that the insight stage builds on the foundation of the exploration stage and in turn provides the foundation for the action stage.

What Do You Think?

- What is the role of insight for you in your life? Describe several situations in which you naturally sought out (or avoided) insight.
- Describe your thoughts about whether insight is necessary for helping. Provide a rationale for your thoughts.
- How accurate must insight be for clients to be helped (i.e., do you think insight must be accurate or could people feel better with any plausible explanation?)
- Check which of the following obstacles you are most likely to face in your development of insight skills:

  _____ moving prematurely into the insight stage
  _____ taking too much responsibility for developing insight
  _____ applying psychoanalytic theory too rigidly
  _____ forgetting to be empathic
  _____ clients not wanting or needing insight from helper

- Which of the following strategies might help you cope with the potential obstacles that you could face in the insight stage?

  _____ rely on the exploration skills
  _____ deal with the relationship

13 Challenge

And the trouble is, if you don't risk anything, you risk even more.

Erica Jong

- Ethan says he wants to go to graduate school, but then he doesn't study and so ends up with bad grades.
- Yun constantly tells everyone that she is unhappy in her job but when questioned about what she has done about it, she says it is not worth it to rock the boat to change anything.
- Eugene complains that his current boss treats him badly and suggests that the reason he has not advanced in his career is because the last several bosses have not liked him.
- Erica says that she can't lose weight because there is too much stress in her life.
- Frieda talks incessantly about how wonderful she is and then wonders why she doesn't have any friends.

These clients are expressing discrepancies, contradictions, confusion, and irrational ideas, perhaps stemming from defenses and inner conflicts, that keep them from functioning as well as would they like. Challenges could be used to help these clients gain awareness.

CHALLENGES ARE invitations to clients to become more aware of themselves, their issues, feelings, and behaviors. These interventions point out discrepancies or contradictions, defenses, or irrational beliefs of which the client is unaware or is unwilling and unable to change. Challenges can be stated either tentatively or using a confrontational tone. For example, in the above vignette the helper might challenge Ethan by saying, "You say you want to go to graduate school, but then you don't study. I wonder what's going on for you?" This challenge, especially when said in a gentle nonthreatening manner and followed by an open question, could raise Ethan's awareness about his behaviors and encourage him to think more about his commitment to graduate school.

TYPES OF CHALLENGES

Challenges may focus on discrepancies or contradictions, defenses, irrational ideas or involve humor; examples are provided in Exhibit 13.1.

Challenges of Discrepancies or Contradictions

Discrepancies and contradictions in clients are often signs of unresolved issues, ambivalence, suppressed feelings, or repressed feelings. Often these discrepancies occur

EXHIBIT 13.1. OVERVIEW OF CHALLENGE

Definition	A *challenge* points out discrepancies or contradictions, defenses, or irrational beliefs of which the client is unaware or is unwilling or unable to change.
Examples	Client: "I can't believe how devastated I have been since my husband died. It all happened so quickly. I'm so lonely. I just have so many feelings, I don't know where to begin."
	Helper: "You're feeling sad that your husband died, but I wonder if you're also angry at him for leaving you."
	Client: "I stay away from people as much as I can."
	Helper: "Do you really need to stay away from all people and protect yourself at all times?"
	Client: "My advisor said that my dissertation is ready, but I don't want to turn it in yet because it just doesn't feel quite right to me. I think I can make it better."
	Helper: "It sounds like you want it to be perfect. What would be the worst thing that could happen if you were not perfect?"
Typical helper intentions	To challenge, to identify maladaptive behaviors, to identify maladaptive cognitions, to identify and intensify feelings, to deal with resistance, to promote insight (see Appendix A)
Possible client reactions	Challenged, unstuck, negative thoughts and feelings, clear, feelings, responsibility, new perspective, scared, worse, stuck, confused, misunderstood (see Appendix D)
Desired client behaviors	Cognitive–behavioral exploration, affective exploration, insight (see Appendix E)
Difficulties helpers experience in using challenges	Fear of offending clients
	Fear of being intrusive
	Being too invested in challenging
	Unconsciously using challenges as an excuse to be mean or hurtful
	Minimizing painful feelings
	Using challenges in a culture-inappropriate manner.

because clients have not been able to deal effectively with feelings as they arise. With challenges, helpers juxtapose two things to make the client aware of the contradiction between them. The helper can focus on several types of discrepancies:

- between two verbal statements (e.g., "You say there's no problem, but you also say that he's angry at you")

- between words and actions (e.g., "You say you want to get good grades, but you spend most of your time partying and sleeping")
- between two behaviors (e.g., "You're smiling, but your teeth are clenched")
- between two feelings (e.g., "You feel angry at your sister, but you also feel pleased that now everyone will see what kind of person she really is")
- between values and behaviors (e.g., "You say that you're religious, but then you make fun of your friends")
- between one's self and experience (e.g., "You say that no one likes you, but earlier you described an instance where someone invited you to have lunch")
- between one's ideal and real self (e.g., "You say you want to achieve, but you also say you can't")
- between the helper's and client's opinions (e.g., "You say that you are not working hard, but I think you are doing a great job").

Challenges of Defenses

Many children develop defenses as protections against unreliable, punitive, or abusive parents or others, and they rigidly use these defenses later in life even when they are no longer needed. We believe that defenses are necessary for all people, but our goal is to have clients learn to discriminate when defenses are necessary. Thus, helpers need to challenge clients gently to help them become aware of defenses and then to make choices about whether they need to keep the defenses. For example, a helper might challenge a client by saying, "You say that you keep up a wall to protect yourself against everyone, but I wonder if you really need to keep it so high with people you can trust." By providing a safe place to examine defenses, helpers can work with clients to distinguish situations in which defenses are needed to protect the client and when it is safe to let go of unnecessary defenses. For a review of different types of defenses, see chapters 5 and 12.

Challenging Irrational Ideas

Ellis (1962, 1973, 1995) and Beck (1976; Beck & Weishaar, 1995) encouraged helpers to challenge clients' irrational beliefs and dysfunctional assumptions. According to cognitive theory, people feel badly not because of situations or events but because of their beliefs. Thus, how a person feels about an event that occurs (e.g., a breakup of a relationship) depends on what the person says to herself or himself about the event. If the person says something irrational (e.g., "It's awful that my boyfriend broke up with me because I loved him so much. I'll never find another person who I love so much. I must be a terrible person who no one could love. I mess up everything that I do, and I'll never be able to do anything right"), the person will probably be extremely upset. On the other hand, if the person says something rational (e.g., "It's too bad that he broke up with me. I feel sad and will need some time to grieve the loss, but I know I'm okay"), the person might be sad but not terribly upset and can decide what to do to cope with the situation. Note that the rational response does not deny feelings but accepts them ("I feel sad"). Helpers can thus challenge clients to become aware of their irrational thoughts (e.g., "You say you're nothing without him, but I wonder if that's really true?" "What makes you think it's awful?" "What's your evidence that you can't function without him?" "Let's examine whether no one will ever love you again"). Two of the most common irrational ideas are "Everyone must love me" and "I must be perfect." Hence, a helper might ask, "You act like you want everyone to love you, but I wonder if you love everyone?" or "Do you have to turn in a perfect paper?"

Challenges Using Humor

Sometimes challenges can be softened by using humor, as long as the client feels that the helper is "laughing with" rather than "laughing at" him or her. Helping clients to laugh at themselves can sometimes help them think about their problems in a different way. An example from Falk and Hill's (1992) study of the effects of therapist humor on client laughter involved a case in which the client had just described how her daughter, an honor student at a prestigious college, had belittled her A average at a community college. The therapist said, "It's not quite so often that I've run into a daughter's being so overtly competitive with her mother. Not that competition between mothers and daughters isn't a hallmark of our society for heaven's sake, but it's usually masked or disguised or, you know, somewhat less overt." The client responded to this statement with laughter and it helped relieve some of the tension that she was feeling.

In another example, a helper and client were dealing with issues related to control and perfectionism in the client's life, particularly in regard to eating and schoolwork. The client excitedly described her weekend in which she contacted several friends, coordinated their activities, and eagerly took on the role of the designated driver. She exclaimed, "I had so much fun." The helper commented, ". . . and so much control." They both laughed and the client began to talk about how her need for control pervaded many aspects of her life.

If clients can start laughing with helpers, they can begin to see things in a different light. Of course, as with other types of challenges, helpers need to have established a relationship with clients and use the humor to raise awareness rather than to make fun of the client.

Of the types of humor that Falk and Hill (1992) studied, the types that seem most appropriate for challenges involve revelation of truth (where the helper uses humor to challenge some assumption that the client has about self, others, or nature) and exaggeration or simplification (where the helper describes the client's situation with an overstatement or understatement of fact, thoughts, or feelings). A type of humor that is inappropriate for the helping situation is disparagement (where helpers ridicule clients or others, putting them down by condescension; mocking; criticizing appearance, behavior, or speech patterns; or using humor at the client's expense).

INTENTIONS

Helpers use challenge to assist clients in altering their ways of thinking, to help them see discrepancies in their thoughts and behaviors, and to increase awareness of defenses and irrational ideas. A second and related set of intentions is to identify maladaptive behaviors, cognitions, and feelings. By helping clients become more aware of thoughts, feelings, and behaviors, helpers can begin to help clients overcome problems in these areas. A third intention is to deal with resistance. Clients often think they want to change but are scared by it, so helpers help them work through their resistances to change. Finally, a challenge followed by an interpretation is an excellent way to promote insight and help clients achieve increased self-understanding. We stress that the intent of challenges is to raise awareness, not to figure out reasons for why the issues exist (this is done through interpretation).

WHY USE CHALLENGES?

During the exploration stage, helpers not only listen and help clients explore, but they also carefully observe what clients say and how they communicate. When the therapeutic relationship is established and clients have explored thoroughly, the time comes to challenge clients to become aware of things that might impede their growth and development. Bringing issues into awareness in a safe setting sets the stage for helping clients understand their issues and make changes.

Carkhuff and Berenson (1967) stated that the purpose of pointing out discrepancies is to help reduce ambiguities and incongruities in the client's experiencing and communication. They suggested that challenges encourage clients to accept themselves and become fully functioning. Confronting clients with the discrepant facets of their behaviors challenges them to understand themselves more fully. "At the point of confrontation the client is pressed to consider the possibility of changing and, in order to do so, utilizing resources that he has not yet employed" (Carkhuff, 1969, p. 93). "The confrontation . . . creates a crisis in the client's life. The crisis poses the client with the choice between continuing in his present mode of functioning or making a commitment to attempt to achieve a higher-level, more fulfilling way of life" (Carkhuff, 1969, p. 92).

Greenson (1967) defined *confrontation* (his term for *challenge*) as a demonstration to the client of his or her resistance (i.e., "all the forces within the patient that oppose the procedures and processes of psychoanalytic work"; p. 35). He suggested that confrontations should be delivered prior to interpretations because defenses need to be confronted first and brought into awareness before they can be understood. Confrontation, according to Greenson, serves to make the issue to be analyzed "explicit to the patient's unconscious ego" (p. 38). For example, he noted that before he could interpret why a client was avoiding a certain subject, he would first have to get the client to face that she or he was avoiding something. The confrontation goes only so far as to point out that the client is resisting; the questions of how and what the client is resisting remain to be addressed subsequently through clarification and interpretation. Greenson believed that clients could only profit from insight into why they used defenses after the defenses were brought into awareness. According to Greenson, confrontation paves the way to the heart of analysis, which is interpretation and working through issues. Greenson emphasized, however, that confrontation would be counterproductive if delivered before the client was ready to hear it. He suggested that if the client was not ready for confrontation, the helper should remain silent and allow the resistance to develop more fully so that the helper has plenty of clinical evidence of the behavior that indicates resistance.

Challenges can be useful to help clients become aware of feelings, motives, and desires that they do not like to acknowledge to themselves. If clients are angry at others but not able to admit it, they might make a lot of sarcastic comments and inadvertently wound others. In other words, their anger "leaks" out. Furthermore, clients might be invested in not being aware of their inappropriate behaviors. They may even blame other people rather than taking responsibility for their actions. For example, a middle-age person might continue to blame his parents for all of his problems rather than taking responsibility, because that would mean he would have to give up his rage at his parents and change his unhealthy behaviors. Often, challenges are needed to nudge clients out of denial, to help them see their problems in a different light, and to encourage them to take appropriate responsibility for their problems.

Challenges can cause a disruption because helpers no longer accept everything clients say at face value. If done properly, the challenge sets up a minicrisis that can motivate clients to change. For example, if a helper challenges a client by saying that she looks sad even though she says she is happy, the client is forced to examine the discrepancy. If the client does not face her unhappiness and make some changes in her life, she will probably remain unhappy. Of course, challenges must be done carefully and respectfully so that they are not too threatening for clients, or else clients quit listening, discredit the helper, or flee from the helping situation.

Although helpers are not interpreting or providing reasons when they challenge, sometimes simply hearing a challenge leads clients to insight. For example, a helper may confront a client by telling him that he says he wants help, but he does not disclose anything about his situation. This challenge might lead the client to realize that he is reluctant to reveal anything because he is afraid of being rejected. Without the challenge, the client might have been unaware of his reluctance.

Challenges can also help clients become aware of ambivalent feelings. Most of us have ambivalent feelings but cannot allow ourselves to feel both sides of issues because of beliefs about how we "ought" to be (e.g., "Nice girls don't get angry"). Challenges can be used to unearth feelings and thoughts so that clients begin to experience and take responsibility for their feelings and thoughts.

Challenges also sometimes enable clients to admit to having different or deeper feelings than they were previously able to acknowledge. For example, Angela said over and over that everything was going well until the helper challenged her about her poor grades. This challenge encouraged Angela to think about what might be going on at a deeper level and made her realize that she was trying too hard to ignore problems. Another example involves Gianni, who indicated that his relationship with his wife was great. The helper pointed out that Gianni's wife was never home and that they had not had sex for 3 years. This challenge invited Gianni to examine closely what was happening in his relationship with his wife.

Challenges must be done gently, however, to be effective. Our goal as helpers is not to break down or remove all of the defenses but rather to give clients the option of choosing when and how often to use defenses. Defenses exist for a reason—they help clients cope. All of us need some defenses to survive in the world. However, we need to look carefully at our reasons for maintaining defenses and determine whether they are still valid. For example, in the face of a hostile attacker, a defense of withdrawal might be appropriate, whereas withdrawal might be counterproductive in an intimate relationship. Hence, helpers work with clients to figure out how to use their defenses in a more judicious manner.

A few years ago, encounter groups were quite popular. Unfortunately, group members often were extremely confrontive and tried to break down defenses without being supportive, understanding, or spending an adequate time putting clients back together again. Research showed that charismatic group leaders who were authoritarian and impatient and insisted on immediate self-disclosure, emotional expression, and attitude change had negative outcomes and casualties (Yalom & Lieberman, 1971). We are reminded of the children's nursery rhyme: Humpty Dumpty sat on a wall. Humpty Dumpty had a great fall. All the king's horses and all the king's men couldn't put Humpty together again. Once a person's defenses are broken completely, it is often very difficult, if not impossible, to put that person together again. However, rather than never using challenges because of possible damaging effects, we need to remind ourselves of their potential power when used appropriately and respectfully in the context of a strong and supportive therapeutic relationship.

EMPIRICAL EVIDENCE

In the literature, researchers have studied confrontation (i.e., challenges of discrepancies) rather than challenge as we define it in this book. We use the broader term *challenge* because we want to be more inclusive of the varied things helpers can do to challenge clients (e.g., challenging defenses and irrational ideas and using humor). In addition, the term *confrontation* seems to imply a conflict, whereas the term *challenge* conveys less of a confrontational or aggressive manner. Hence, although the research on confrontation can give us valuable understanding, readers need to remember that challenges are broader than confrontations.

A number of studies show that confrontations are used infrequently, accounting for something like 1% to 5% of all therapist statements (Barkham & Shapiro, 1986; Hill, Helms, Tichenor, et al., 1988). Furthermore, Hill, Helms, Tichenor, et al. found that clients and therapists rated confrontations as moderately helpful but that clients had negative reactions to confrontations (i.e., felt scared, worse, stuck, confused, or misunderstood; lacked direction). They also found that clients did not explore their feelings after hearing confrontations and that therapists viewed sessions in which they did a lot of confrontations as not very smooth or satisfactory.

Using a sample of people who had problems with procrastination, Olson and Claiborn (1990) tested a hypothesis based on dissonance theory (e.g., Festinger, 1957; L. H. Levy, 1963): Arousal (e.g., being confronted by discrepancies) should lead to greater acceptance of "interpretations." Essentially, the theory postulates that clients would accept interpretations as a way of reducing the arousal or dissonance. Olson and Claiborn first determined that confrontations indeed led to greater arousal (as determined by galvanic skin response) than did reflections of feelings. Then, they set up three conditions: Counselors gave a confrontation followed by an interpretation, counselors gave a reflection followed by an interpretation, or clients did not receive an interview. The confrontations described a discrepancy between the client's statement in the interview and their behavior outside the interview (e.g., "You've been telling me that you plan to do something about your procrastination, but your repeated procrastination at school shows that you're resisting change"); they tended to increase arousal. The reflections were listening responses that did not describe any discrepancy (e.g., "That sounds really frustrating"). The subsequent interpretations presented clients with a view of procrastination that was discrepant from their own and included a guidance component to link understanding to action. One scripted interpretation was "You make a personal choice to procrastinate or not. Taking full resposibility for your own procrastination may be the key to actually doing something about it." The second scripted interpretation was "Change will come to you through hard work and effort. Choosing to take full responsibility for your procrastination may be one answer to your problem." Note that according to the definitions used in this book, we would consider these interventions to be information and direct guidance rather than interpretations. After interpretation, participants had lower arousal (i.e., lowered galvanic skin response) and greater acceptance of the interpretation in the high arousal (i.e., confrontation) condition than in the low arousal (i.e., reflection) or no interview conditions.

In the Salerno, Farber, McCullough, Winston, and Trujillo (1992) study, clients responded defensively to therapist confrontation and therapists confronted when clients were defensive, resulting in a downward spiral. Similarly, Miller, Benefield, and Tonigan (1993) found that a confrontational style led to client resistance, which in turn led to poor outcome for clients who were problem drinkers.

In summary, the results across several studies indicate that confrontations are indeed powerful, arousing interventions that can lead to defensiveness and resistance. Perhaps not surprisingly, results also indicate that confrontations are used infrequently and can result in negative reactions from clients. These findings argue for using challenge carefully and with empathy.

HOW TO CHALLENGE

The major task for helpers in using challenges is doing them in such a way that clients can hear them and feel supported rather than feel attacked. Quite unlike the supportive interventions that imply acceptance, challenge can imply criticism. With challenge, helpers indicate that some aspect of the client's life is incongruent or problematic and imply that clients should feel, think, or act differently. We suggest that helpers use challenges carefully because they have the potential for upsetting clients. Although it is sometimes important to confront clients' current ways of thinking, challenges should be done carefully, respectfully, thoughtfully, and with empathy.

Challenges must be delivered gently, tentatively, and with the goal of coming to understand the client and facilitate movement toward growth. Challenging someone's inconsistencies can be threatening and should be undertaken with caution. One might think of the metaphor of the client building a wall around himself or herself. Rather than attacking the wall directly with major weapons or armaments, the helper might do better to point out the wall. When the client is aware of the wall, the helper and client can together try to understand the purpose for the wall and decide whether the wall is needed. Hence, rather than battering down the wall, the helper might encourage the client to build a door in the wall and learn when to open and close that door. We propose that helpers use the following steps to provide challenges to clients.

Step 1: Observe the Client

Helpers formulate challenges of discrepancies or contradictions from their observations of inconsistencies in clients, so they must be alert for inconsistencies and trust their observations. Helpers can observe and listen to clients carefully for defenses, irrational ideas, or "sour notes." *Sour notes* are things that do not sound right, do not make sense, do not fit or go together, are done out of "shoulds," cause ambivalences, or result in struggles. These sour notes can point the way to issues about which clients feel contradictions and uncertainties.

Helpers ought to collect an adequate amount of evidence prior to making a challenge. Collecting several instances of discrepancies can allow helpers to clarify in their minds what is going on rather than jumping hastily to conclusions.

Step 2: Determine Appropriateness of Challenges on the Basis of Client Type or Client Readiness

Helpers need to think about whether challenges are appropriate for the particular client. Direct blunt challenges are likely to be less appropriate with Asian, Latina–Latino, and indigenous American clients (Ivey, 1994). Ivey presented the example of Weijun Zhang's first efforts to counsel in China after training in the United States. He confronted an older Chinese man using the standard format for challenges: "On the one hand you do X, but on the other hand you do Y; how do you put these two together?" The older man politely said his farewell and never came back. Zhang had forgotten that when Chinese people see the need to express disagreement, they generally take great care not to hurt the other person's feelings or cause the other person to "lose face." His direct confrontive technique was considered ill mannered and insensitive, especially coming from a younger person to an older person. Zhang suggested that it is not impossible to confront a Chinese person but that one needs to be sensitive and gentle. In fact, few people like to lose face, so it is important when challenging to be careful not to tear down client defenses and instead to use empathy.

On the other hand, Ivey (1994) noted that direct confrontation may be especially appropriate with acting-out male clients. These clients often find the soft and gentle approach meaningless and may even denigrate the helper for using it. Ivey stressed the need for flexibility and being responsive to each person. We also note that clients who are at precontemplation and contemplation stages of change (see the earlier discussion in chapter 3) are more likely to need challenges to jolt them out of their complacency and encourage them to change (Prochaska, DiClemente, & Norcross, 1992). Clients in the later stages of the helping process (e.g., action, termination, and maintenance) are less likely to require challenges to get them beyond defenses and past barriers to changing.

Helpers can look for specific markers that indicate client readiness for receiving challenges. These markers include expressions of ambivalence, contradictions, discrepancies, or confusion or feeling stuck or unable to make a decision. These markers suggest that the client may be motivated to allow the problem to "come into awareness." We recommend that helpers spend some time thinking about why the client might feel confused or stuck. Rather than blaming or condemning the client, the helper thus tries to understand the client's dynamics. The empathy generated through this process can assist the helper to become curious about checking out the hypotheses rather than becoming invested in pointing out a discrepancy or trying to make the client change.

Most important for any client, helpers need to assess whether the therapeutic relationship is strong enough to withstand challenges. Does the client feel safe? Does the client trust the helper? Has there been enough exploration? Has rapport been established adequately? Challenges are most effective in the context of a caring and respectful therapeutic relationship.

Step 3: Determine Intentions

Helpers need to think carefully about why they would challenge. What do they want to accomplish? Are the goals to raise awareness; identify maladaptive feelings, thoughts, and behaviors; deal with resistance; or promote insight? These are appropriate goals. However, helpers need to make sure they are not challenging simply to meet their own needs. They need to evaluate whether any of their issues might be influencing their desire to challenge the client (e.g., a helper who is irritated by passivity in a partner might be especially challenging of a client who becomes passive).

We suggest that helpers first look within themselves to determine whether the need for a challenge is coming from the client's material or the helper's issues. For example, a helper who has just gotten divorced might view all relationships as destructive, so he or she may challenge all clients about why they are staying married. In this case, however, the problem might really belong to the helper rather than to the client. Hence, helpers must determine whether their desire to challenge is for the client's benefit or their own.

Step 4: Present the Challenge

It is important that helpers not make judgments when they challenge. A challenge should not be a criticism but an encouragement to examine oneself more deeply. The goal is to challenge and work collaboratively with clients. If helpers are judgmental, clients may feel shamed and embarrassed and hence be more resistant to recognizing and changing the problems. Helpers need to remember that all of us have discrepancies and irrationalities and that we are not "better than" our clients. We need to be humble and empathize with how difficult it is to understand ourselves and make necessary changes. It is always easier to see someone else's inconsistencies than our own.

We suggest that helpers challenge clients gently and respectfully. The helper's manner should be one of understanding and puzzlement rather than hostility, of trying to help the client figure out a puzzle and make sense of discrepant pieces. Peter Falk's approach in playing the detective Columbo on television is a particularly disarming manner of challenging. Columbo has a bumbling, nonassuming way of getting at contradictory information. He makes comments such as, "Pardon me ma'am, but I'm just trying to understand. You said this, but then you said this. Can you explain that to me?" His tone is nonthreatening and disarming, but he is persistent in trying to clarify discrepancies. Rather than berating clients, then, helpers can empathically point out discrepancies, defenses, or irrational ideas and then follow these challenges with reflections of feelings and open questions about how it felt to be challenged.

In addition, helpers may need to repeat challenges several times and in different ways, so that clients can hear them. It is often difficult for clients to hear a challenge the first time because it is threatening, no matter how gently it is done. Hence, helpers might have to persist in gently presenting the challenge several times.

Challenges should be done soon after the client's inconsistent behaviors. If a helper waits too long, the client might not remember what the helper is talking about. For instance, if the helper says "Last session when you spoke about your mother, you smiled in a strange way," the client is not likely to remember the incident. Thus, helpers should act fairly quickly (if they have enough data) while the behaviors and feelings are still recent.

When learning to challenge discrepancies, we recommend that helpers use the following formats to make sure that they include both parts of the intervention:

On the one hand _____ , but on the other hand _____ .
You say _____ , but you also say _____ .
You say _____ , but nonverbally you seem _____ .
I'm hearing _____ , but I'm also hearing _____ .

Sometimes the first part of the discrepancy is implied, and the helper states only the "but" clause. For example, the client might say that there are no problems, and the helper might respond, "But you said he was angry at you" (implying "You just said there were no problems, but . . ."). Or the helper might challenge by simply saying, "really?,". "oh yeah?," or "hmmm?," which questions the client in a challenging manner and indicates that the helper does not completely believe the client.

Step 5: Observe the Client's Reactions

Because challenges can have such a strong impact on clients, helpers need to be very attentive in observing client reactions. Helpers need to remember the research we cited earlier in chapter 3 that suggested that clients often hide negative reactions. Thus, helpers should not expect that they necessarily know when clients feel badly after a challenge. Clients could withdraw, and helpers would not know that they were upset. Hence, helpers have to ask how clients reacted to challenges and probe beneath the surface to understand the complete reaction.

If clients respond to challenges with denial, helpers need to rethink how they are presenting the challenges, whether clients are ready to hear them, or whether a challenge is the right intervention. If clients respond with partial examination or acceptance and recognition but no change, helpers can continue to confront gently to help clients move further. Helpers also can reflect how scary it is to change and help clients in exploring their fears. If clients respond with new awareness and acceptance, helpers can move on to interpretation. Helpers should not be surprised when clients react strongly to challenges. Instead, they should help clients express and work through their emotions. If clients do not show any reactions, helpers might ask the clients about their reactions to being challenged.

The following example shows how challenges can be done within a helping session (challenges are shown in italics).

Client: "My husband wants his parents to come and live with us. His father has Alzheimer's and his mother takes care of his father, but she can't drive and is not feeling too well herself. They are both pretty old and need more help."

Helper: "How do you feel about them moving in with you?"

Client: "Well, I think they need to do something. The situation is not improving and they are getting old. My husband really wants to take care of them. He feels some obligation since he's the oldest child."

Helper: (gently) *"I hear that your husband wants to take care of them, but I am not hearing how you feel about it."*

Client: "I have been brought up to believe that family takes care of family when they need help. I didn't take care of my parents, so I feel like we should do what we can to help them if they want it. They may not even want to move in. They might rather do something else."

Helper: *"I'm struck by how hard it is for you to talk about your feelings."*

Client: "That's interesting. You're really right. I feel like I don't have a right to my feelings. I feel like it's something I 'should' do. I don't have any choice, so I'm trying not to have any feelings. If I'm really honest with myself, I'm terrified of what it will be like if they move in."

Helper: "You sound upset."

Client: "Yeah, but it makes me feel guilty. I just don't know what to do. I guess I've always had a hard time standing up to his parents. Actually, I have a hard time standing up to most people, so this is just another example. I think it stems from my childhood." (Client continues to talk.)

EFFECTS OF CHALLENGE

Helpers can observe their sessions and use the following 3-point scale to evaluate the effects of their challenges on clients (see also a scale by Heesacker & Prichard, described in Ivey, 1994):

1 = If challenges are very ineffective, clients might deny them (e.g., "I'm not angry about the divorce"), get upset with the helper (e.g., yell at the helper), or stop attending sessions.

2 = If challenges are at least neutral, clients might accept and recognize the issue but not make any changes (e.g., "I guess I have mixed feelings about getting a divorce"). Alternatively, clients might partially examine what the helper has said but not consider the challenge fully or experience it emotionally (e.g., "Yes, I'm hurt and perhaps I should be angry, but I don't feel it").

3 = If challenges are very effective, clients accept them and develop new, larger, and more inclusive constructs, patterns, or behaviors (e.g., "You've helped me see that mixed feelings and thoughts are part of every relationship. I need to express my feelings. Maybe if I had expressed them before, I wouldn't be facing divorce now. I'm going to call my wife and see if we can develop a new way of thinking about the relationship").

DIFFICULTIES HELPERS EXPERIENCE IN USING CHALLENGES

Challenge is a difficult intervention for many beginning helpers. Most beginning helpers use too few challenges because they do not want to intrude on clients or sound accusatory. They just want to listen uncritically. However, if clients are being contradictory, confusing, or are stuck, they often cannot clarify their thinking without being challenged. Beginning helpers often become victims of the *mum effect*, a tendency to withhold bad news even if it is in the best interest of others to hear (Egan, 1994). In ancient times, bearers of bad news were killed, which not too surprisingly led to some reluctance to be the one to bear bad news or give negative feedback.

Helpers who want everyone to like them and fear offending others often have difficulty using challenges. Challenges can feel intrusive and clients may feel like helpers are forcing them to examine their "dirty laundry." Helpers also may worry that using challenges destroys the work they have done on building the therapeutic relationship and makes clients feel unsupported. Furthermore, confronting people is not considered polite in some cultures, and so helpers from such cultures may feel reluctant to use challenges.

In addition, some helpers who feel scared of negative feelings might use challenges to deny or minimize the negative feelings. For example, if a client talks about suicidal feelings, a helper might use a challenge that indicates that the client has a lot for which to live. A statement that a client has a lot to live for sounds like the helper is pointing out strengths. In fact, the helper might be anxious about being able to handle suicidal feelings and want to minimize them so that the client does not talk about the feelings.

Some helpers become too invested in having clients recognize their discrepancies. They become like detectives who present the evidence and want to force clients to admit their problems and confess that they are not being consistent. These helpers are also like lawyers in a cross-examination of witnesses in the courtroom in that they seem eager to "catch" clients in their discrepancies. Some helpers use challenge as an opportunity to get back at clients whom they do not like or who upset them in some way. Needless to say, such challenges can make clients feel unsupported and challenged. We agree with Egan (1994) that reluctance to challenge is better than being too eager to challenge.

Another problem for helpers is knowing how to respond when clients disagree with challenges and in effect challenge the helper in return. For example, the helper might say that it seems like the client is coming across hostilely with his friends, and the client might deny it saying that all his friends like him a lot and what does he (the helper) know about his interactions with his friends. Some helpers do not know whether to keep trying to get clients to see the evidence or whether to give up and try again later after they have more data to support the challenge. Helpers may even begin to distrust their perceptions when clients challenge them. At times, helpers might be wrong because they misperceived the situation in light of their issues or insufficient data. At other times, however, clients might be defensive, unwilling to examine themselves, or have a hard time acknowledging their behaviors. Having supervisors listen to tapes of sessions and provide feedback is helpful so that helpers can determine whether they were accurately perceiving the client's issues.

HELPFUL HINTS

- Be warm and empathic in challenging rather than being aggressive and blaming. Remember that you are offering your perception rather than providing the "truth." You should not be playing a game of "Gotcha" or trying to score points with how much you can point out the client's inconsistencies, defenses, or irrational beliefs. Be careful not to come across as a trial lawyer trying to pin something on the client.

- Use nonabrasive words and state the challenge as a hunch rather than an accusation.

- Check out the challenge with the client by saying, "You do this, but say that; I wonder what's going on?"

- Consider culture when giving challenges. If someone is from a different culture, be sensitive that the person might have different reactions than you to being challenged. Do not necessarily decide not to challenge, but be alert to client reactions to the challenge and talk about them.

- Don't make judgments or interpretations when you challenge. Try instead to be curious and collaborative in working with clients to become aware of the issues.

- Use specific examples as evidence for the challenge (e.g., "When you said that you were happy, you frowned") rather than being general or global in your statement (e.g., "You always seem so cheerful"). A specific behavioral example is easier to respond to than a global characterization.

- It is better to give an example of something that just happened than to give a distant example that clients are not likely to remember.

- Make sure the challenge is not for your needs (e.g., to appear insightful, to retaliate for the client being late or missing a session, or to elevate yourself in comparison to the client).

- Do not apologize prior to delivering the challenge or minimize its value (e.g., "I'm sorry to do this, but . . .," "I'm not sure I'm doing this right, but . . .," "Please don't get angry at me for saying this, but . . ."). Too often helpers couch what they say or apologize, which makes the client doubt its value and dismiss it. A better way to be gentle is to use a soft, nonjudgmental tone and have an attitude of genuine caring about the client.

- Watch carefully for the client's reactions to the challenge. Ask how he or she feels about the challenge. Keep the lines of communication open.

- If the client is upset by the challenge or you feel you have blundered badly, apologize and ask how the client is feeling. Avoid apologizing too much or too often, however, because it gives an unprofessional appearance and takes the focus off the client.

- Leave enough time after a challenge to talk about it and to help the client learn from it. It takes time to process the challenge and to teach clients how to use defenses more judiciously.

- Do not give up on positions that you think are true, but allow your thoughts to be modified by input from clients. Sometimes you may need to back off until clients can handle challenges or until you have more evidence for your observations. For example, you may experience a client as being extremely hostile and pushy with you although he perceives himself as being friendly and accommodating. Your first challenge could include, "You say you're easygoing, but you sound like you act somewhat aggressively with your friends," which might be negated by the client ("Nah, they all love me"). You might want to obtain more examples about friends from the client. However, you can trust your impression that this client is in fact aggressive with you. In time, you might present a reformulated challenge ("You say everyone finds you friendly, but you have criticized me with a hostile tone several times").

- Do not use too many challenges in any one session because they can create a negative, abrasive tone.

- Follow challenges with reflections of feelings and open questions about feelings. When clients have come to a new awareness about their thoughts, behaviors, or feelings, you might go on to interpretation to investigate the reason for them.

PRACTICE EXERCISES

Read each of the following examples, indicate your intention(s), and then write a challenge that you might use if you were a helper with the client. (Recall that the typical intentions for using challenges are to challenge, to identify maladaptive behaviors, to identify maladaptive cognitions, to identify and intensify feelings, to deal with resistance, and to promote insight.)

Statements

1. **Client:** "My family is really important to me. They mean more to me than anyone else in the world. I think about them a lot. I go home about once a year and I call them every month or so when I'm running out of money."
   Helper intention(s): _____
   Helper response: You say _____,
   but you _____.

2. **Client:** "I really want to go to graduate school, but I have lots of things going on right now and I just want time for myself to travel and play. I don't think I want to study as much as I know I would have to in graduate school, but I do want to be able to get a good job as a psychologist so that I can do therapy with kids."
   Helper intention(s): _____
   Helper response: You say _____,
   but you _____.

3. **Client:** "My parents are very religious. They tell me I have to go to church every Sunday as long as I'm living at home. I know I have to do it to please them, but I feel so confused about the whole topic. I don't know what I believe and nothing makes sense. I feel like I'm going through the motions. I feel guilty even

talking about this though, because they would be so upset that I don't agree with everything they say."
Helper intention(s): _____
Helper response: You say _____,
but you _____.

4. Client: "The guy I was going with said that he wants us to just be friends. He asked me to go to California with him on a big trip but just as friends. I don't know if I should go. I still like him a lot. Maybe if I went, he would start liking me again. I don't know what I did that made him quit liking me."
Helper intention(s): _____
Helper response: You say _____,
but you _____.

Possible Helper Responses

1. "You say your family is important to you, but you don't have much contact with them." (intent: to challenge, to identify maladaptive behaviors)
   "You told me your family is important to you, but you seem to talk to them only when you want money." (intent: to challenge, to identify maladaptive behaviors, to promote insight)

2. "You want the things that come from having a graduate degree, but you aren't so sure you want to do what it takes to get the graduate degree." (intent: to challenge, to identify maladaptive thoughts, to promote insight)
   "You say you want to get a graduate degree, but your voice doesn't sound very enthusiastic as you talk." (intent: to challenge, to identify maladaptive feelings, to promote insight)

3. "You want to please your parents, but you want to figure out for yourself what you believe." (intent: to challenge, to identify maladaptive feelings, to promote insight)
   "You feel guilty that you might believe something that your parents don't, but perhaps you also feel angry that they don't allow you to have your own feelings." (intent: to challenge, to identify maladaptive feelings, to promote insight)

4. "You want to go, but you're not sure if you should." (intent: to challenge, to identify maladaptive thoughts, to promote insight)
   "You are really upset that this guy doesn't want to be romantically involved anymore, but you think you can get him to change his mind." (intent: to challenge, to identify maladaptive feelings, to promote insight)

What Do You Think?

- Describe the circumstances in which you think challenges are necessary and helpful.

- Provide several examples of situations in which helpers should not use challenges.

- Compare and contrast the effects of challenges versus reflections of feelings.

- How can helpers maintain an attitude of curiosity and compassion for clients with their challenges rather than attacking them and getting invested in confronting them?

- What types of helpers might be likely to use challenges inappropriately?
- Discuss cultural differences in using and reacting to challenges. Describe how you could modify challenges to be more acceptable in various cultures.
- What does it mean to be respectful when you challenge?

LAB 7 Challenge

Goals: For helpers to practice using the basic helping skills (reflection, restate-ment, and open question) and then to learn to challenge once they have estab-lished a supportive relationship and identified discrepancies.

In groups of four to six people, one person should be the client, one person should be the initial helper, and the rest should be ready to take over as helper or give backup to the helper. Everyone should take turns being the client. Each group should have a designated lab leader (other than the helper) to organize and coordinate the session.

Helper's and Client's Tasks During the Helping Interchange

1. The client should talk about something that he or she feels conflicted or con-fused about (e.g., future career choices, lifestyle issues). The client should plan on being at least moderately disclosing, although we want to remind you that clients always have the right to say that they do not want to disclose further.
2. The initially designated helper should do basic helping skills (open question, restatement, and reflection of feelings) allowing the client to explore. If one helper gets stuck, another helper can take over to facilitate a thorough explo-ration.
3. The group leader should stop the helper after a few minutes of exploration, preferably when a discrepancy is clear to him or her.
4. Everyone except the client should come up with a challenge. Helpers should pause and take their time to think about what the client has said. Helpers should ask themselves, "Is there a discrepancy between two verbal statements, between words and actions, between verbal and nonverbal behaviors, between two nonverbal behaviors, between two feelings, between values and behav-iors, or between strengths and weaknesses?," "Is this a defense?," "Is this an irrational belief?" Once helpers have identified a discrepancy, defense, or ir-rational thought, they should consider carefully what their intentions are for challenging at this particular moment. They should also think about whether the client is ready to hear a challenge. They should then think about how to phrase the challenge so that the client can hear the intervention. Helpers should remember not to be judgmental but to be curious and collaborative.
5. Each helper in turn should deliver his or her challenge and give the client a chance to respond.

Observers' Tasks During the Helping Interchange

Everyone should observe how the helpers deliver the challenges. Were the helpers' challenges gentle yet firm or abrasive and hostile? Everyone should also observe how the client responds to each of the challenges. Does the client get interested and try to understand what might be causing the discrepancy, or does the client seem defensive, shut down, and unwilling to process the issue?

Processing the Helping Interchange

After everyone has had a turn and the client has responded, the client can talk about which challenges were most helpful and why. Clients should be

(Continues)

as open and honest as possible so that helpers can learn what they did well and what they did not do so well.

SWITCH ROLES

Personal Reflections

- Challenges are difficult for many helpers. It is worthwhile to examine your feelings about them both as a helper and as a client. How do you personally feel when you give or receive a challenge? What issues do challenges raise for you? (Note that we encourage you to talk about these feelings in your own therapy.)
- What are your strengths and areas needing improvement in terms of challenge? What things might get in the way of your providing clients with helpful challenges?
- How can you deliver challenges that clients can hear and absorb without being too aggressive or too passive?
- Describe what your intentions were for challenging and whether your clients reacted as you hoped.

14 Interpretation

Men go abroad to wonder at the heights of mountains, at the huge waves of the sea, at the long courses of the rivers, at the vast compass of the ocean, at the circular motions of the stars; and they pass by themselves without wondering.

St. Augustine

Jim told his helper that he was feeling depressed and aimless. He felt that nothing made sense and that he had no purpose in life. He also talked extensively about how his parents were anxious about him taking risks since his older brother had died in a motorcycle accident. With this and other information that the helper had learned about Jim through several sessions, the helper said, "I wonder whether your lack of purpose in life is because you are still grieving the loss of your brother and you haven't been able to make your own decisions and figure out who you are as a person." This interpretation helped Jim make sense of his depression and aimlessness. After continuing to talk with the helper and trying to understand what was going on inside him, Jim was able to see his life in a new perspective and to think about how he wanted to be.

INTERPRETATIONS ARE interventions made by helpers that go beyond what a client has overtly stated or recognized and present a new meaning, reason, or explanation for behaviors, thoughts, or feelings so that clients can see problems in a new way. Interpretations make connections between seemingly isolated statements or events; point out themes or patterns in a client's behaviors, thoughts, or feelings; explicate defenses, resistance, or transference; or offer a new framework to understand behaviors, thoughts, feelings, or problems.

Interpretations can be delivered through direct statements (e.g., "You are worried about whether you should get married, so you are diverting your anxiety about getting married into trying to make the wedding perfect"), done tentatively (e.g., "I wonder if your fear of failure could possibly be related to feeling that you are not sure you can please your mother"), or through questions (e.g., "Do you think you distrust men because of your bad relationship with your father?"). Although the last intervention is phrased as a question, it is clearly an interpretation because the content of the question assumes a relationship that the client had not articulated and provides an explanation for the behavior. Other examples are presented in Exhibit 14.1.

INTENTIONS

The typical intention for using interpretation is to promote insight. Helpers want to enable clients to understand more about themselves and their motivations. They want

EXHIBIT 14.1. OVERVIEW OF INTERPRETATION

Definition	An *interpretation* is a statement that goes beyond what the client has overtly stated or recognized and gives a new meaning, reason, or explanation for behaviors, thoughts, or feelings so that the client can see problems in a new way. It makes connections between seemingly isolated statements or events; points out themes or patterns in a client's behaviors, thoughts, or feelings; explicates defenses, resistances, or transferences; or offers a new framework to understand behaviors, thoughts, feelings, or problems.
Examples	**Client:** "My mother keeps nagging me about keeping my room clean and doing my school work. I don't know why, but I just don't feel like doing either."
	Helper: "Maybe you don't want to clean your room or do your work because you're angry with your mother."
	Client: "Suzie killed herself a few days ago, but I haven't been thinking about it much. I have been really angry at my boss for making me work overtime. Plus my roommate is driving me crazy. And my parents keep calling to find out how I'm doing. I feel so angry I could scream."
	Helper: "Ever since your friend committed suicide, you have been on edge and having a hard time coping. I wonder if you feel responsible for her death?"
	Client: "You act like you think you know everything about me, but you don't know anything."
	Helper: "I wonder if I remind you of your father. You said he acts like he knows everything."
	Client: "I just can't stand it anymore. My mother will never let up. She just doesn't trust me."
	Helper: "Perhaps you're trying to get her to distrust you so that you can get angry and leave. Otherwise it might be too hard to leave since she's alone."
Typical helper intentions	To promote insight, to identify and intensify feelings, to promote self-control (see Appendix A)
Possible client reactions	Better self-understanding, new perspective, clear, relief, negative thoughts or feelings, responsibility, unstuck, scared, worse, stuck, lack of direction, confused, misunderstood (see Appendix D)
Desired client behaviors	Insight, cognitive–behavioral exploration, affective exploration (see Appendix E)

Difficulties helpers experience in using interpretations	Not giving enough interpretations for fear of being wrong, premature, intruding on the client, or offending the client
	Need to appear insightful
	Thinking they know more than clients about the clients
	Not carefully observing client reactions
	Not working collaboratively with clients to construct the interpretations
	Delivering interpretations before clients are ready to hear them
	Providing interpretations that are too lengthy
	Providing too many different interpretations in a single session

to help clients learn about the reasons behind their thoughts, feelings, and behaviors. Helpers also want to model the interpretation process so that they can teach and encourage clients to introspect and come to new understandings on their own.

A second intention for using interpretation is to identify and intensify feelings. Sometimes by being provided with reasons for why they might feel a certain way, clients are freed up to have their feelings, which are now more understandable and less foreign.

An additional intention for using interpretation is to promote self-control so that clients begin to take responsibility for their actions rather than blaming others. For example, Suzanne continually blamed everyone else for her problems. She was angry at one daughter for moving out, at another daughter for going to boarding school, at her husband for divorcing her, and at her friends for abandoning her. She did not reflect on her responsibility for anything that was happening to her. A successful interpretation could lead Suzanne to recognize and own her role in causing and maintaining problems.

WHY GIVE INTERPRETATIONS?

Interpretations are often effective because they provide clients with a conceptual framework that explains their problems and offers them a rationale for overcoming their concerns. Frank and Frank (1991) noted that interpretations increase clients' sense of security, mastery, and self-efficacy by providing names for experiences that seemed confusing, haphazard, or inexplicable. The need for an explanation or label has been called the principle of Rumpelstiltskin, after the fairy tale in which the queen is able to break the wicked dwarf's power over her by "guessing" his name (Torrey, 1986). Frank and Frank (1991) asserted that interpretations relieve distress in part by relabelling client emotions to make them more understandable. They noted that the inexplicable loses much of its power to terrify when it is put in words. For example, if a helper interprets that Pablo's vague uneasiness at work as anger at the boss, who is a stand-in for the client's father, Pablo's uneasiness loses its power.

From a psychoanalytic perspective (e.g., Bibring, 1954; Blanck, 1966; Freud, 1914/ 1953; Fromm-Reichmann, 1950), interpretations are the "pure gold" of therapy, the central technique for producing self-knowledge and change in clients. Interpretation is created from client material that has been repressed and exists in the client's unconscious. Psychoanalytic theorists postulate that interpretations are effective because they stimulate insight, which can lead to more reality-oriented feelings and behavior (although the exact mechanism by which insight leads to action is not specified). Interpretations are thought to work by replacing unconscious processes with conscious ones, thus enabling clients to resolve these unconscious conflicts.

In psychoanalytic theory, the role of early childhood is very important and hence is often a focus of interpretive behavior, although which childhood events are focused on varies for different theorists. The early childhood event that is most often thought to be problematic, according to Freudian theory (Freud, 1940/1949), is the Electra–Oedipal conflict, in which the child seeks to have a romantic alliance with the parent of the opposite gender and depose the parent of the same gender. For Erikson (1963), the important early childhood events are interpersonal relationships. For Mahler (1968), the important early childhood event involves the symbiosis with the primary caregivers in very early years and the subsequent movement toward separation and individuation. For Bowlby (1969, 1988), attachment to the caregiver is the crucial event in childhood.

Because psychoanalytic helpers believe that early childhood relationships form the foundation for all ensuing relationships, interpreting the transference (i.e., a distortion by the client of the helper based on early childhood relationships) is one of the most significant types of interpretation. The assumption is that the client re-creates the problematic early relationship patterns with the helper either as a way to confirm or reject that the helper will act in the same way as the early caregiver. The client might act as he or she did as a child (e.g., the passive victim) and expect the helper to play the complementary role (e.g., the dominant or oppressive dictator). Conversely, the client might take on the role that the parent played in the relationship (the dominant one) and expect the helper to act like the child (e.g., the passive victim). The helper's reaction to the client's behavior is crucial in terms of confirming or disconfirming the client's expectations. For example, the helper might say to Amanda, "I wonder if you get so furious at me for seeing other clients because you always felt that your mother preferred your brother to you, and you don't like to have to share me with other clients."

Although psychoanalytic theory is the basis for our thinking about using interpretations, other theoretical orientations also use interpretations but postulate different mechanisms by which they work. From an information-processing perspective, L. H. Levy (1963) suggested that interpretations reveal discrepancies between the views of the therapist and client. In other words, an interpretation makes it clear that the helper has a different perspective than the client. The helper does not "buy" the client's view about the issue and postulates a different explanation. For example, a client might explain his depression by a chemical imbalance, whereas the helper claims that the depression is due to unresolved feelings about his mother's suicide and subsequent abandonment by his father. Once there is a discrepancy in views, the client either has to change in the direction of the helper's viewpoint, try to change the helper's mind, or leave the helping setting and discredit the helper. If the client resolves the discrepancy in the direction of the helper's interpretation, the client is able to relabel and reconstrue how she or he views the issue. From the perspective of information-processing theory, the accuracy of the interpretation is not important. What is important is that there is a discrepancy and that the client has to reduce the discrepancy. We believe, however, that damage could occur if a helper is not concerned about the client's best interest and tries to persuade the client in a negative direction.

Cognitive psychologists (e.g., Glass & Holyoak, 1986; Medin & Ross, 1992) also construe the effectiveness of interpretations in different terms than do psychoanalytic theorists. Cognitive theorists believe that all thoughts, feelings, sensations, memories, and actions are stored in *schemas* (defined in chapter 3 as clusters of related thoughts, feelings, actions, and images). With interpretations, helpers attempt to change the way that schemas are structured. They bring back the memories and try to come to new understandings about them on the basis of more current and complete information. In effect, the schemas are changed and restructured. The client has a new way of thinking, which must be reinforced or else it erodes. Hence, repeated interpretations with expansions to different areas of the client's life may be necessary for the connections to be made and retained. In addition, action and behavior change may be necessary to consolidate the changes in thinking. For example, Katerina may come to realize that she is lacking in self-esteem because she felt neglected as a child. However, she needs further interpretive work to understand the influences of the childhood experiences on her current life. In addition, making changes in her behaviors (e.g., getting a new job and leaving an abusive relationship) may help her begin to think more highly of herself and may also lead her to understand why she stayed in such a bad situation for so long.

Although several theories have been advanced for how interpretations work, there is not enough evidence to support any one of these theories. In fact, interpretations could work for all three reasons. They could work because people need an explanation for their behavior, they could work because revealing a discrepancy between perspectives propels clients to change in the direction of resolving the discrepancy, and they could work because interpretations cause changes in schematic connections.

EMPIRICAL EVIDENCE

A number of studies show that therapists use interpretations moderately often compared with other skills (ranging from 6% to 8% of all therapist statements; Barkham & Shapiro, 1986; Hill, Helms, Tichenor, et al., 1988) and, not surprisingly, that analytically oriented therapists use interpretations more often than behavioral therapists do (Stiles & Shapiro, 1995). Furthermore, Hill, Helms, Tichenor, et al. found that clients and helpers rated interpretations as very helpful, that clients had positive reactions to interpretation (i.e., clients indicated that interpretations helped them engage in therapeutic work), and that interpretations enabled clients to experience their feelings. Clients viewed sessions in which therapists gave a lot of interpretations as very satisfactory. Two other studies indicate that clients were more able to free associate (i.e., say whatever comes to mind without censoring thoughts, one of the major client tasks in psychoanalytic therapy) in response to interpretations than to other interventions (Colby, 1961; Spence, Dahl, & Jones, 1993). In fact, interpretation is the only intervention that has consistently been found to be helpful in a number of studies (see review in Hill, 1992).

Research also shows that interpretations of moderate depth are better than those that are either too superficial or too deep (Claiborn & Dowd, 1985; Claiborn, Ward, & Strong, 1981; Forsyth & Forsyth, 1982; Speisman, 1959). In other words, helpers interpret just beyond what the client is currently aware of to push the client gently to think about things. These findings about the importance of staying at a moderate depth support the psychoanalytic principle of interpreting just beyond the limits of client awareness (Fenichel, 1941). For example, a 31-year-old client who has difficulty being touched and who has thus far never been in a sexual relationship might have difficulty hearing a "deep" interpretation of possible sexual abuse. With this client, the helper might begin with a more moderate interpretation that the client has difficulty being touched and being in sexual relationships because of problems in her relationship with her parents.

Some research also has been conducted on the effects of transference interpretations (i.e., interpretations that relate client's behavior or feelings toward the helper to experiences toward significant others), which have been thought by psychoanalytic theorists to produce fundamental change (Freud, 1914/1953; Strachey, 1934). Early research by Malan (1963, 1976a, 1976b) supported the effectiveness of transference interpretations. However, more recent research shows that transference interpretations are not particularly effective (Hoglend, 1996; Marziali, 1984; Marziali & Sullivan, 1980; Piper, Azim, Joyce, & McCallum, 1991; Piper, Debbane, Bienvenu, de-Carufel, & Garant, 1986). However, McCullough et al. (1991) demonstrated that affective response of the client to the transference interpretations predicted improvement at outcome. So if clients respond affectively to transference interpretations, they are more likely to benefit from them. Furthermore, some more recent research comparing transference interpretations with interpretations that fit the psychoanalytic conceptualization of the client's problem shows the more effective interpretations to be those that are tailored specifically to the beliefs and needs of individual clients (Crits-Christoph, Cooper, & Luborsky, 1988; Messer, Tishby, & Spillman, 1992; Silberschatz, Fretter, & Curtis, 1986). In other words, rather than just automatically interpreting all conflicts as being due to transference, helpers need to craft interpretations as being related to specific client dynamics.

Hill, Thompson, and Mahalik (1989) examined the use of interpretations in a single case of successful brief psychotherapy. The client in this case was the middle of 16 children. Her mother had married at a very young age; when the father died, the mother abandoned the children. The client was currently divorced with three children and was depressed, blaming herself for being "spoiled." At the end of helping, the client and helper both indicated that the most important interpretation was that the client's current difficulties were due to a difficult childhood and inadequate parenting. The researchers went back and identified all the interpretations that related to this theme. They discovered that the helper did interpretations masterfully. She presented interpretations in a context of approval and support and interwove interpretations with questions, restatements, and reflections directed at catharsis. The interpretations were of moderate depth, were presented only in the second half of treatment, were repeated many times, and seemed to be accurate. The helper repeated the interpretation often and applied it to different situations, which she referred to in postsession interviews as "chipping away" at the client's defenses. The client not only accepted the interpretation but slowly began to incorporate it into her thinking, believe it, and expand on it (e.g., she changed from seeing herself as spoiled to seeing herself as neglected). The interpretations enabled the client to disclose important secrets (i.e., her father's attempted suicide and subsequent hospitalization in a mental hospital). Finally, the helper began to pair the interpretation with a directive that the client was a good parent to her children and hence could parent herself. The interpretation helped the client come to a greater self-understanding and, together with the direct guidance, enabled her to change in some fundamental ways (e.g., become a better parent, obtain a job, and begin an intimate relationship). These results illustrate that interpretations were not delivered randomly and that the consequences depended on the relationship, readiness of the client, timing within the treatment, repetition, and pairing with other helping skills (approval, restatement, reflection, question, and later direct guidance).

A study by Gelso et al. (in press) asked psychoanalytic helpers what strategies they used to deal with transference in long-term therapy. As expected, they responded that they used interpretation. However, they also reported using immediacy, open questions, information, direct guidance, and self-disclosure. These results suggest that interpretation of transference is important but that other interventions are also useful.

In summary, the research suggests that interpretations are powerful interventions. Moreover, we have learned that interpretations need to be delivered with care, to be of moderate depth, to be specific to the client, to be repeated often, to be applied to a number of situations, to be provided in a context of empathy, and to be interwoven with other interventions. However, additional research is needed to refine our knowledge about these important interventions. Spiegel and Hill (1989) presented important guidelines for researchers who investigate interpretations.

HOW TO INTERPRET

Step 1. Setting the Stage for Interpretation

Helpers pave the way for interpretation through empathy, reflections of feelings, and challenges. Then they watch for signals that clients are ready and eager for an interpretation. Hence, the client might say something like, "I just don't understand why I get so angry at my boyfriend. He usually does nothing wrong. I just all of a sudden get furious and I can't control my rage. I really wish I understood it because it is making me miserable and is about to destroy the best relationship I have ever had." On the other hand, if clients are doing things like telling a story, asking for advice, or blaming others for problems, they are probably not ready for an interpretation.

We note that some clients are psychologically minded and really enjoy probing into their dynamics and motives. Others, however, are not very interested in examining their motives. They are more concerned about behavior change and feeling better. Helpers probably are more successful using interpretations with the former than with the latter, although we stress that helpers should not assume from stereotypes that certain groups of clients (e.g., lower socioeconomic class clients) are not suited for interpretations. Furthermore, some clients can be taught to be more introspective.

Step 2. Determine Intentions

Helpers need to think about their intentions for providing an interpretation at a particular moment in the helping process. The most appropriate intentions are to promote insight, to identify and intensify feelings, and to promote self-control. Inappropriate intentions would be for helpers' needs (to make oneself look good at the expense of the client, to show off, to punish clients for being frustrating). If helpers realize that they want to give an interpretation to meet their needs, they can pause and think about themselves and the client and try to figure out what is going on in the relationship.

Step 3. Provide the Interpretation

Helpers should go into the interpretation process with an attitude of curiosity, of wondering what it is that makes the client act a certain way. They should also go into the process with a desire to help the client come to insight because insights that are discovered are typically better than those that are imposed. Another way of thinking about this is that helpers are encouraging clients to embark on an interpretive quest so that they are able to come to insights on their own without the aid of the helper after helping is completed.

An excellent idea is to begin by asking clients for their interpretation. Asking clients for their interpretations before providing them with the helper's thinking allows helpers to assess the client's current level of insight, stimulates clients to think about themselves, and gets helpers out of the position of being the ones who have to provide all the interpretations.

Helpers can also begin with a trial interpretation to see how clients respond. If clients are curious and engaged about gaining self-understanding, helpers might continue using interpretation (although judiciously). A single interpretation does not automatically trigger new behavior. Some clients require many reiterations of an interpretation before they begin to understand and use the insight. They need to hear the interpretation in relation to different contexts and settings and may need to hear it phrased in different ways. At first, interpretations may seem strange and foreign, but as clients hear them numerous times in different ways, they begin to understand them.

Psychoanalytic theorists suggest that it is important to provide interpretations that are not too far beyond what clients already have recognized (e.g., Speisman, 1959). If interpretations are too deep, clients cannot understand what the helper is talking about, whereas interpretations that are slightly beyond the client's awareness make more sense to the client. In the first session with a client who procrastinates, for example, the helper might not want to interpret the cause of the procrastination back to early childhood events because the client may not be ready to hear that interpretation. Instead, the helper might go just beyond what the client is aware of to push the client to slightly new levels of awareness (e.g., "Perhaps it's hard for you to study because you're afraid of succeeding"). Later, when the client is comfortable thinking psychologically, the helper might push for deeper interpretations such as the client's reluctance to supersede his or her parents. Helpers often develop mild interpretations by paying attention to what the client is half saying, saying in a confused way, or saying implicitly. The client has almost put it all together and just needs encouragement from the helper to begin to integrate all the pieces.

The phrasing of interpretations is crucial in terms of how likely they are to be accepted by clients. Phrasing the interpretation tentatively and without a lot of jargon makes it easier for clients to understand them. For example, saying, "I wonder if you might be afraid of what I could say because I remind you of your mother who was so mean to you" is easier for a client to hear than "You are afraid of me because you think I am just like your mean mother." The latter interpretation is difficult for clients to disagree with because it is stated so definitely.

It is not typically helpful for the interpretation process to be unilateral from the helper to the client. Natterson (1993) stressed that when a helper who wants to exert power over a client offers a shocking interpretation of a dream, it usually has an antitherapeutic effect because it discourages the client from sharing the dream. Instead, we believe that the process of providing interpretations should be collaborative, with both helpers and clients working together to understand new reasons for the present situation. Both helper and client work together to try to come to insights that the client can hear and assimilate. The process is a creative working together to understand, which should result in something that both helper and client are surprised about. Reik (1935) similarly emphasized the deep, collaborative nature of the therapeutic encounter. Reik also suggested that insights that come to clients as a result of interpretations should come as a surprise to both the helper and the client rather than the helper forcing a predetermined interpretation on the client. Similarly, Basch (1980) noted that any facile connections are usually trivial or wrong, whereas the important insights are those that come as a surprise to both client and helper.

For psychoanalytic theorists, the accuracy of the helper's interpretation is important. The helper is on an "archeological dig" and is trying to uncover what actually happened in the client's early childhood and understand how these events affected the client's current behavior. Of course, psychoanalytic therapists emphasize that what they hear in therapy is the client's perceptions about the early childhood events rather than actual events; thus, determining accuracy is very difficult.

In contrast, Reid and Finesinger (1952) suggested that insight must merely be believed or make sense to have a therapeutic effect. They thought that the psychological relevance of the interpretation to the client's problems was more important than the truth per se (i.e., does the interpretation help the client understand more about his or her problems). Similarly, Frank and Frank (1991) noted that interpretations do not have to be correct, only plausible. As an example, they cited a study by Mendel (1964) in which four clients responded with a drop in anxiety when they were offered the same series of six "all-purpose" interpretations (e.g., "You seem to live your life as though you are apologizing all the time"). We present these alternate hypotheses about the effectiveness of interpretations to make you think, but we do not suggest that you act on them. We do not believe that helpers should ignore the "truth" and just have a set of standard interpretations to give clients. Quite the opposite: We believe that helpers should try as much as possible to develop interpretations that fit all of the data that clients present. Helpers should remain humble, however, about how difficult it is to ever know whether an interpretation is accurate.

Basch (1980), a psychoanalytic therapist, indicated that whether clients agree or disagree with interpretations is not a good indication of accuracy. Rather, he suggested, the criterion of accuracy should be whether clients bring up material in the next session that indicates that they have gained insight into the problem. For example, if a helper interprets that Lao's fear of intimacy is based on feeling rejected by his father, the helper could conclude that the interpretation was accurate if Lao brings in additional memories of his father being distant and rejecting. We would disagree somewhat with Basch, however, because there is potential for clients to bring in (and even make up) memories to please helpers. We can never really determine the accuracy of interpretations because we cannot observe what actually happened in the past. In addition, we know that events are not just facts, but also involve people's recall of them. People perceive events idiosyncratically and then distort memories of events over time (Glass & Holyoak, 1986; Loftus, 1988). Research even shows that people can "remember" events that never happened (Brainerd & Reyna, in press). Thus, helpers need to be careful not to try to persuade clients to have certain memories (e.g., repressed memories about childhood sexual abuse).

Frank and Frank (1991) noted that the client is the ultimate judge of the truth of the interpretation. They suggested that the helper's power to present an interpretation that is accepted by the client as valid depends on several factors:

- whether the interpretation makes sense out of all the material the client has offered
- the manner in which the interpretation is offered; they must be presented in ways that catch and hold the client's attention, such as vivid imagery and metaphor, because clients need to be in a state of emotional arousal to be able to make use of interpretations
- the client's confidence in the helper
- the beneficial consequences for the client's ability to function and for the client's sense of well-being.

We suggest that helpfulness is a more important criterion for evaluating interpretations than is accuracy. We suggest the following criteria for determining whether interpretations are helpful for clients. When an interpretation is helpful, the client typically feels a sense of "aha," of learning something that "clicks," and has a feeling that things make sense in a new way. Clients also typically have a feeling of energy and excitement about their new discoveries. We stress that it is important this feeling come from the client rather than from the helper. In short, the client has arrived at some personally relevant insight and can use it to talk more deeply about problems.

Step 4. Follow Up on the Interpretation

Helpers should watch for the client's reactions. They should remember that clients do not always reveal their reactions, though, and hence should be ready to ask. Sometimes helpers move too quickly or slowly, so they need to hear from the clients what is helpful for them.

After effective interpretations, clients may add new information or suggest alternate interpretations of their own. Helpers respond by reflecting feelings or asking open questions. After hearing more information, helpers might restate a reformulated interpretation. The new interpretation might lead the client to new material that confirms or denies the validity of the interpretation. Thus, rather than helpers being the ones who have and deliver the "correct" interpretations to clients, the helper and client work together to create or construct interpretations. This collaborative process requires that helpers be invested in the interpretive process rather than in specific interpretations, so that they can revise interpretations when clients offer new information, explanations, or ideas.

If clients reject interpretations, helpers need to evaluate whether they think the interpretation is right and the client is not yet ready to hear it, or whether in fact the helper is wrong. If client readiness is a problem, helpers can return to the interpretation at a later stage when they think the client is more able to tolerate insight (because interpretations sometimes are painful to hear). If helpers are wrong, they probably need to return to the exploration stage to obtain more understanding of the client before attempting to interpret, or they should ask clients to provide an alternative interpretation that fits for them.

Helpers also need to extend the interpretations to a variety of situations to help clients reach more understanding. For example, if the interpretation involves the client being unorganized and sloppy as a reaction to an overly neat and compulsive mother, the helper can extend this insight to how the client is messy in her apartment, unorganized in terms of her studying behavior, and late for appointments. By talking about all of these different areas, the client is more likely to begin to understand herself.

SOURCES OF DATA FOR DEVELOPING
INTERPRETATIONS

A rich source of data for developing interpretations is in the content of what clients talk about. The simplest way is to make connections between things the client says. For example, if a client says that she is having a hard time performing on her job and then goes on to talk about a seemingly unrelated topic of anxiety over her parents' health, the helper might connect the two: "Perhaps you're having a hard time concentrating because of your anxiety about your parents."

Helpers can speculate about how a client's behaviors might be related to how the client has interacted with significant others in the past or present. When the client's responses to the helper are distorted because of experiences with others in the past or present, helpers have material for making a transference interpretation. For example, Keisha responded with silence and tears every time her helper provided positive feedback. The helper knew about Keisha's history with her father and so interpreted that Keisha was afraid of what might follow the positive feedback given that her father often told her something good and then yelled at her for her mistakes. (More discussion of transference interpretations is available in several excellent texts: Basch, 1980; Freud, 1923/1961; Gelso & Carter, 1985, 1994; Greenson, 1967; Malan, 1976a, 1976b; Strupp & Binder, 1984.)

A related way of examining transference is to look more generally at the client's typical style of interacting and conceptualize what the client is trying to accomplish in interactions. Luborsky and Crits-Christoph (1990) described how helpers can look at these core conflictual ways of responding to others (including the helper) in terms of the wishes or needs (what the client wants from others), expected responses from others, and the consequent response from the self. For example, Keisha might wish for affection and love but also wish to be in control. She might expect others to hurt and control her as her father did, and hence feel anxious and disliked. Interpretations can thus be formulated about the development of a client's characteristic way of responding to others.

An additional source of material for interpretations is to think about the client's life stage. Are clients on course or off course for mastering developmental tasks (developing friendships, separating from parents, completing schooling, making decisions about life partners and children, developing a satisfying career, developing satisfying adult relationships with others, letting go of children and careers, adjusting to illnesses and dying)? Interpretations can be developed linking clients' current emotions and functioning to what they might be expected to be feeling or not feeling at this stage of life.

Helpers can also examine existential concerns that the client alludes to but may not be fully expressing. Yalom (1980) provided an excellent description of four universal existential concerns. First, he postulated that all people struggle with death anxiety. Because we die at some point, we have to come to terms with the reality that we are not immortal. Particularly at times when a significant person is very ill or has recently died, clients are attuned to issues of loss and of their own future deaths. A second existential issue is freedom, which refers to the lack of external structure and the need to take responsibility for one's destiny. The third issue is isolation from both others and the world. Because each of us enters and exits existence alone, we must come to terms with our isolation in contrast to our wish to be part of a larger whole, to be taken care of and protected. The fourth existential concern is the meaning of life. We must all construct our own life meanings given that there is no predetermined path. By listening carefully to what clients say, helpers can often hear underlying existential concerns and then assist clients, via interpretation, to understand these critical existential issues.

Other sources for developing interpretations are through thinking about defenses, dreams, and slips of the tongue. Psychoanalytic theorists have long postulated that important unconscious material can be detected by looking at these manifestations.

The following is a brief example of how interpretation (in italics) might be used in a session.

Client: "When I'm in church, I have been getting very anxious lately. I have been starting to panic when we have to hold hands to say a prayer. My palms get very sweaty and I feel very embarassed. I start worrying about it so much ahead of time that I cannot concentrate on the church service. I just don't understand why I should get so nervous. I wish I could understand it, though, because it is making my experience of going to church very unpleasant."

Helper: "It sounds like you feel upset about it."

Client: "I do. I feel foolish. I mean, who cares about my sweaty palms? I'm sure the other people are just interested in going to church and don't really care about me. I don't know the people because I just started going to this church this fall when I moved here."

Helper: "Tell me a little bit about the role of the church in your life."

Client: "I was hoping to get to have a community like we had in my hometown. I need something apart from just the people I know at work. But it hasn't worked out. I haven't really met anyone there yet."

Helper: "So you just moved here and have been hoping to make friends through the church."

Client: "Church was always important in my family. I don't know how much I believe in the religion, but I do feel a need for the connection that you get in church."

Helper: "So you want to make friends and find a community, but you also feel some ambivalence and you're not sure what you believe."

Client: "Wow, that is really true. I do feel like I'm supposed to go to church, but I'm not sure I really want to. I feel like my parents expect me to go. But I don't quite know what I believe. I haven't taken the time to figure out what I believe separate from what my parents told me to believe."

Helper: *"I wonder if worrying about your sweaty palms takes your mind off of thinking about what you believe."*

Client: "Yeah, that's a good point. I sure cannot listen to much of the sermon if I'm worried about the person next to me and what they will think of me."

Helper: *"I wonder if going to the church is difficult because it reminds you so much of your family and what you were supposed to do as a child."*

Client: "You're right. I feel like I've been trying to establish myself as an independent person. I moved across country so that I could be on my own and make my own decisions, but I miss my family and my community. I don't know how much I want to be here. I feel like I'm struggling with trying to figure out who I am and what I want out of life." (Client continues exploring.)

EFFECTS OF INTERPRETATION

Helpers can watch tapes of their sessions and use the following 3-point scale to determine the effects of their interpretations on clients:

1 = If an interpretation is inaccurate or too deep, or if the client is not ready to hear it, he or she might deny or ignore it. The client might feel confused, blamed, or misunderstood. Signs that indicate that clients are not involved in the interpretive

process are passive acceptance without deeper exploration ("yeah, you're right"), passive aggressiveness ("yes, but ..."), or anger ("no, you're wrong").

2 = If interpretations are not awful but are not very good or are neutral, clients might agree compliantly but not really absorb, hear, or understand the interpretations. Clients might be able to repeat the interpretations but do not really grasp their significance intellectually or emotionally. If interpretations are at least moderately accurate and well-timed, clients might agree with them and think about them superficially.

3 = If interpretations are correct and well timed, clients might have an "aha" reaction and become very excited about the new understanding, believing that it provides them with a way to make sense of their world. Clients might engage in the interpretive process and add to or contradict the helper's insight; they also come up with new insights stimulated by the interpretive process. In subsequent interactions, clients might bring up additional thoughts and feelings that confirm the accuracy of the interpretation.

DIFFICULTIES HELPERS EXPERIENCE IN USING INTERPRETATION

Some helpers are hesitant to interpret because it feels intrusive to "poke around in clients' heads." They fear that they will be wrong, they will be giving interpretations prematurely, that the client might get upset or angry, or that they might destroy the therapeutic relationship. So they err on the side of passivity.

Other helpers are too eager to give interpretations and err on the side of aggressiveness. The interpretation process brings out the worst in some helpers. They become invested in the intellectual challenge of figuring out clients and are eager to use their powers of insight. They lose sight of the need for empathy and a strong therapeutic relationship and charge into putting all the pieces of the puzzle together. We agree that people are infinitely intriguing, interesting, and fun to figure out, but helpers must temper such sentiments with a strong compassion for clients and a desire to help clients understand themselves.

We caution helpers in the use and potential abuse of interpretations because they can be powerful interventions. We have the responsibility to use our power as helpers appropriately. We also caution helpers that clients may agree with interpretations because they want to please helpers, but they may not actually "buy" the interpretations. We need to be careful to encourage clients to become actively involved in collaborating on constructing interpretations. Helpers also need to be careful about the timing of interpretations, making sure that clients are ready to hear the interpretations and can build on them in constructing their own understandings.

Another problem that helpers have is giving too many interpretations in one session. Clients often need time to absorb and think about each interpretation, so helpers should gauge their pace on the basis of clients' reactions.

▓ HELPFUL HINTS

- Wait until the problem has been explored thoroughly. Provide an interpretation only when you have an idea of what is going on for the client and you think the client is ready to hear an interpretation.

- Pave the way for interpretations with empathy, reflection of feelings, and challenges.

- Base interpretations on an understanding of client motives, defenses, needs, styles, and childhood experiences.

- Wait until you hear a marker that indicates that the client is ready for an interpretation. Possible markers of readiness are (a) a clear statement of a problem (b) a statement of a lack of understanding, (c) an eagerness or willingness to understand, and (d) a high level of affective distress associated with the problem that is experienced as a pressure for resolution.

- Collaborate with the client in trying to figure out the origins of the problem, their role in the problem, and why the problem continues. As with a puzzle, you want to work with clients to try to put the puzzle together—each of you picks up a piece of the puzzle and tries to see where it fits. If the interpretation fits, try to understand more about how it fits current aspects of the client's life. If the interpretation does not fit for any reason (client lack of readiness, inaccuracy), recycle back to the exploration stage and try to understand the client's feelings.

- Refrain from showing off in terms of understanding what is going on for the client. Work with the client to construct insights collaboratively.

- Deliver interpretations tentatively and with empathy. Pose possible interpretations and ask clients for their perspectives.

- Interpretations should be at moderate depth and not far beyond what clients can readily understand and assimilate.

- Follow up on interpretations with open questions (e.g., "How did that feel?") and reflections of feelings ("I wonder if you feel scared right now"). Remember to return to the basic listening skills because clients are at a new level of understanding and need time to explore feelings.

- Do not make judgments in interpretations. You are trying to understand rather than evaluate clients.

- Keep interpretations short. Going on and on takes the focus away from clients.

- Do not provide too many interpretations in any one session.

- Watch for the client's reactions after interpretations.

- Leave enough time in sessions to discuss interpretations thoroughly.

- Ask for the client's interpretations and encourage introspection.

- If clients do not respond well to interpretations, reflect feelings and reconsider the usefulness of the interpretation and the readiness of the client. If you feel certain that the interpretation is accurate, rephrase the interpretation or use an example. Interpretations often have to be repeated several times over a number of sessions before clients are able to hear them.

PRACTICE EXERCISES

For each of the following examples, indicate your intentions and then write an interpretation. (Recall that the typical intentions for using interpretations are to promote insight, to identify and intensify feelings, and to encourage self-control.)

Statements

1. **Client:** "I'm not doing very well in school right now. I'm sure that it's my study skills. I just don't seem to be able to concentrate—I keep gazing out the window instead of getting my work done. So I try to make myself stay at my desk more and more, but I seem to be getting less done. I broke up with my boyfriend so that I could have more time to study, but it just doesn't seem to be working."
Helper intention(s):_____
Helper response:_____
_____

2. **Client:** "I'm about ready to graduate and I need to decide what I'm going to do next with my life. I'm getting a lot of pressure from my parents, but I can't quite figure out what I want to do. I keep having this recurrent dream where I flunk out of a math class. I can never seem to get to class, and when I do get there, I don't understand any of the work. I never quite get to the tests on time, and I know I'm going to flunk out. I don't know why I keep having this dream. Math has always been difficult for me, but I got an A in my last math class."
Helper intention(s):_____
Helper response:_____
_____

3. **Client:** "I really love my boyfriend and I want to get married, I really do. But you know recently I have not wanted to see him much. Every time we're together, I find myself criticizing him. You know he does stupid things sometimes that just irritate me. I can just imagine him drinking beer and belching in front of my father. You know my parents still haven't met him. I don't know quite why, but I haven't wanted to take him home."
Helper intention(s):_____
Helper response:_____
_____

Possible Helper Responses

1. "Perhaps you're not getting much work done because you regret breaking up with your boyfriend." (intent: to promote insight, to identify and intensify feelings)
"Perhaps your sadness at breaking up with your boyfriend is getting in the way of your schoolwork." (intent: to promote insight)
"Maybe a fear of commitment keeps you from committing yourself to your school-work or a relationship." (intent: to promote insight)

2. "I wonder if your anxiety about your future is related to a fear of failing." (intent: to promote insight, to identify and intensify feelings)
"Could it be that you fear that you will disappoint your parents if you don't succeed?" (intent: to promote insight, to identify and intensify feelings)

3. "Perhaps you're worried that your parents won't like your boyfriend." (intent: to promote insight, to identify and intensify feelings)
"I wonder if you might have chosen your boyfriend because he's so different from your father." (intent: to promote insight)
"Maybe your fear about taking your boyfriend to meet your parents is because

you're unsure about your feelings about him." (intent: to promote insight, to identify and intensify feelings, to encourage self-control)

What Do You Think?

- Provide several examples of situations in which you think it is appropriate to offer interpretations.
- Describe what helpers need to do to develop a collaborative process of constructing interpretations with clients.
- Debate both sides of the idea that interpretations are a necessary prerequisite for change to occur (i.e., argue for and against the idea that interpretations are the "pure gold" of helping).
- Discuss whether you think that helpers and clients can be taught to be more introspective.
- What do you think about the idea that interpretations should only be given after challenges?
- What are the dangers that helpers face in giving interpretations to clients?

LAB 8 Interpretation

Goals: For helpers to practice using the basic helping skills (reflection, restatement, and open question) and then learn to interpret once they have established a supportive relationship and perceive discrepancies.

In groups of four to six people, one person should be the client, one person should be the initial helper, and the rest can wait to take over as helper or to give ideas to the helper. Each person should take a turn being the client. Each group should have a designated lab leader (other than the helper) to organize and coordinate the session.

Helper's and Client's Tasks During the Helping Interchange

1. The client should talk about a problematic reaction that he or she had to a specific situation that he or she would like to understand. In other words, the client should talk about an event in which he or she had a strong reaction but did not understand why and the reaction seemed out of proportion to the situation. For example, perhaps the client was driving along and someone swore at him and he got instantly rageful. Or perhaps the client was sitting in a classroom discussion and suddenly, for no obvious reason, felt like crying. The client should plan on being at least moderately disclosing, although of course clients always have the right to say that they do not want to disclose further.
2. The designated helper should use the basic helping skills (open question, restatement, and reflection of feelings) for several minutes, encouraging the client to explore. If one helper gets stuck, switch helpers to ensure a thorough exploration of the problem.
3. The group leader should stop the helper after several minutes of exploration, preferably when an interpretation is clear to him or her.
4. Everyone except the client should come up with an interpretation. Helpers should pause and take their time to think about what the client has presented. Helpers can ask themselves, "What do I hear the person saying underneath the words?" "Are there themes in what the client is saying?" "What might be some of the reasons for how the client is feeling?" "What things might be connected to this problem?" Once helpers have an idea of a possible interpretation, they should think carefully about their intentions and what they can accomplish in a single interpretation. They can then phrase their interpretation so that the client can hear it.
5. Each group member in turn should deliver his or her interpretation and allow time for the client to respond.

Observers' Tasks During the Helping Interchange

Everyone should observe how the client responds to each interpretation. Does the client accept the interpretation and provide additional evidence, or does the client passively agree or disagree with what the helper has said?

After the Helping Interchange

After everyone has had a turn and the client has responded, the client can talk about which interpretations were most helpful and why.

(Continues)

SWITCH ROLES

Personal Reflections

- How do you personally feel when you give an interpretation? What issues does it raise for you personally? For example, did you feel like you had to be the expert who had the accurate interpretation, or did you feel like you were working collaboratively with the client to discover the roots of the problem? (Note: We encourage you to talk about these feelings in your own therapy.)
- What were your intentions for using interpretations? Were you able to phrase the interpretations so that the client could hear them? Describe any discrepancies between the reactions you expected from the client and the actual reactions that the client had.
- What are your strengths in giving interpretations? In which areas do you need to develop your skills?
- What theoretical approach do you prefer as a basis for developing interpretations?
- How do you feel about receiving an interpretation as a client? What factors about the delivery of an interpretation make it most likely that you will accept it?

15 Self-Disclosure

To know one's self is to know others, for heart can understand heart.
(Chinese proverb)

Olga was very emotional and upset when she revealed that her husband had left her for a younger woman. She felt abandoned and humiliated and did not want any of her friends to know that he had left. She talked in her helping session about how she had been feeling very depressed, isolated, alone, and hopeless, and she said that she was too old to start over. The helper said, "You know, I got divorced several years ago, and I never thought I would recover. I came to realize that I had believed that my worth was dependent on whether I had a man rather than who I was. I wonder if that's true for you?" This disclosure helped Olga understand why she was so upset about her husband leaving her. She did not really miss him given that they had not been getting along well for many years. Instead, she missed the sense of security that being married gave her. Once she understood that about herself, she could begin to adjust to the divorce.

SELF-DISCLOSURES reveal something personal about helpers. Self-disclosures are used in the insight stage to facilitate clients' understanding of their thoughts, feelings, behaviors, and issues. Instead of using challenges or interpretations, helpers share insights that they have learned about themselves in the hope of encouraging clients to think about themselves at a deeper level. Note that several types of self-disclosures are presented throughout the book. Disclosures of history and credentials and disclosures of feelings are presented in chapter 10, disclosures of immediate experiences in the therapeutic relationship are presented in chapter 16, and disclosures of strategies are presented in chapter 20. In this chapter, we focus only on self-disclosures used to stimulate insight (see Exhibit 15.1).

INTENTIONS

The primary intention for using self-disclosure in the insight stage is to promote insight. Helpers want to assist clients in attaining deeper levels of understanding and hope that by presenting a personal experience, clients might gain more awareness of themselves. It is sometimes easier for clients to learn by example than to be told directly. In addition, self-disclosures are sometimes used to challenge clients and to deal with resistance so that helpers can assist clients in thinking in new ways and in breaking out of old patterns. Finally, helpers sometimes inappropriately use self-disclosures to satisfy their own needs— to relieve anxiety, to be liked, to solve clients' problems—although they typically are not aware of this intention at the time. Sometimes helpers disclose because their own problems are so overwhelming that they cannot attend to the client.

■ **EXHIBIT 15.1. OVERVIEW OF SELF-DISCLOSURE FOR INSIGHT**

Definition	*Self-disclosure* refers to the helper's presentation of a personal experience (not in the immediate relationship) in which he or she gained some insight.
Examples	Client: "My roommate keeps wanting to know my grades. I feel awkward when she asks, so I just try to ignore her and change the topic."
	Helper: "In the past, I often did not want others to feel upset by my successes, so I would underplay anything I did well. I wonder if that happens for you?"
	Client: "I should quit procrastinating. I have not gotten anything done lately. I should get out more and meet people and volunteer so that I feel more productive. I'm just wasting time."
	Helper: "I indulge in some bad habits just like you. I know they're bad habits, just like you do, but I don't want to change them anymore. I've finally learned to accept these things about myself. Would that fit for you?"
Typical helper intentions	To promote insight, to deal with resistance, to challenge, to relieve the therapist's needs[a] (see Appendix A)
Possible client reactions	Understood, supported, hopeful, relief, negative thoughts or behaviors, better self-understanding, clear, feelings, unstuck, new perspective, educated, new ways to behave, scared, worse, confused, misunderstood (see Appendix D)
Desired client behaviors	Insight, affective exploration, cognitive–behavioral exploration (see Appendix E)
Difficulties helpers experience in using self-disclosures	Disclosing to gratify own needs Projecting own issues onto client Not returning focus to client after self-disclosure Providing lengthy self-disclosures Disclosing more than the client is comfortable being aware of

Note. Self-disclosures are also discussed in the exploration stage (e.g., disclosing history or credentials or disclosing feelings) and the action stage (e.g., disclosing strategies). Self-disclosures that are related to the immediate relationship are discussed in chapter 16 on immediacy.
[a]This intention is typically not therapeutic.

WHY USE SELF-DISCLOSURES?

Helpers disclose their experiences to help clients attain realizations of which they had not been aware previously. This type of self-disclosure gives a client the opportunity to hear how another person has understood him or her and to think about whether the insight fits him or her. This type of self-disclosure is useful when clients are stuck or are having a hard time achieving deep levels of self-understanding on their own. For example, if a client is talking about everything being just fine after leaving her abusive husband, but the helper suspects that the client has discrepant underlying feelings, the helper might say, "I remember feeling like I wasn't sure if I made the right decision after I left my partner. Change was real scary for me." The helper hopes the client will understand more about the feelings that she is experiencing by hearing about the helper's experience.

One goal of self-disclosure is to enable clients to see things in a less threatening way than they were able to see on their own. Sometimes hearing a disclosure such as "I also feel like a child when I go to visit my parents because I lose my identity and don't know who I am" or "I also have a hard time going to movies by myself because I feel like nobody loves me" provides an opportunity for clients to think about whether they have similar reasons for their behaviors. Rather than asserting a specific reason for the client's behavior, helpers are respectfully disclosing their personal insights and suggesting that these might also be true for the client, thus facilitating new and deeper insight. In effect, helpers are hoping that clients feel more free to look for underlying reasons after they have heard helpers disclosing their insights. Thus, self-disclosures have a modeling effect.

In addition, self-disclosures can alter the power balance of the helping relationship and lead to greater participation by the client in developing insight. Rather than helpers being the experts with the answers and clients relying on helpers to solve their problems, helper self-disclosures make clear that both are individuals who grapple with important human concerns. As we have said before, helpers are "wounded healers" who are engaged in a lifelong struggle to understand themselves; this struggle enables them to relate to client struggles and to participate collaboratively in uncovering underlying issues that affect client functioning.

We believe that self-disclosures can be very effective in enabling clients to gain insight when used properly. In this way, we are closer theoretically to the humanistic therapists than to the psychoanalytic therapists. Because humanistic theorists (e.g., Bugental, 1965; Jourard, 1971; Robitschek & McCarthy, 1991; Rogers, 1957; Truax & Carkhuff, 1967) believe that helpers should be transparent, real, and genuine in the therapeutic relationship, they believe that helper self-disclosure can have a positive effect on treatment. In fact, humanists believe that a more personal and transparent style of intervention benefits both the process and outcome of therapy because it allows clients to see helpers as real people who also have problems. In addition, humanists believe that when helpers disclose there is more of a balance of control in the relationship in that clients are not the only ones who are vulnerable. Humanists also contend that disclosure by helpers enhances rapport because clients feel more friendly toward and trusting of helpers who disclose. Interestingly, humanists also think that self-disclosure can help to correct transference misconceptions as they occur because helpers are direct and honest with self-disclosures and, hence, challenge distortions as they arise. Additional benefits claimed by humanists for self-disclosures are that helpers are able to be more spontaneous and authentic and can model appropriate disclosure. Moreover, helper disclosures can facilitate client self-disclosure and work on the therapeutic relationship. In effect, humanists believe that therapist self-disclosure encourages an atmosphere of honesty and understanding between therapists and clients that fosters stronger and more effective therapeutic relationships.

In contrast, psychoanalytic theorists (e.g., Basescu, 1990; Greenson, 1967; Simon, 1988) view psychotherapy as focused on working through patients' projections and transferences. They believe that helpers should be neutral or blank screens so that clients can project onto them their feelings and reactions toward significant others. For example, a client's childhood experiences might prompt the client to transfer onto the helper a fear that the helper is going to be punitive. An analytic helper might sit behind the client to enable the client to focus inwardly rather than watching the helper's face for cues about his or her reactions. If helpers are in fact being neutral, they can assist clients in seeing that the belief that the helper will be punitive is a projection. If helpers deviate from a stance of neutrality, it is difficult to distinguish client projections from realistic reactions to what the helper is actually doing. For example, if a helper is consistently late, it would be difficult to determine if the client's anger was a distortion based on previous experiences or legitimate anger at the helper's tardiness. Readers should not confuse neutrality with a lack of empathy, however, because competent analytic helpers are appropriately warm and empathic. Not too surprisingly then, given this emphasis on neutrality, psychoanalytic helpers typically do not self-disclose. In fact, psychoanalysts propose an inverse relationship between the client's knowledge of the helper's personal life, thoughts, and feelings and the client's capacity to develop a transference to the helper (Freud, 1912/1959). They believe that helper revelations contaminate the transference process and deleteriously demystify the therapy, thereby reducing the helper's status (Andersen & Anderson, 1985). In addition, Cornett (1991) suggested that helper self-disclosure might represent unresolved counter-transference difficulties on the part of the helper, which would seriously compromise the client's ability to profit from treatment. Furthermore, psychoanalysts argue that helper self-disclosure can expose helper weaknesses and vulnerabilities, thereby undermining client trust in the helper and adversely influencing outcome (Curtis, 1981, 1982).

We assert that both the humanistic and psychoanalytic theorists make good points but have been looking at different aspects of the same issue. We believe that helpers can self-disclose beneficially for clients if they do it for the appropriate intentions at the right moment. Disclosure for their own needs rather than for the clients can be damaging to the relationship. However, if helpers disclose in a manner in which they maintain an objective stance, focus on the client, and observe client reactions, we believe that disclosures can be helpful. In fact, we think that sometimes they can be more helpful than other insight skills because the helper is not "putting something on" the client but is respectfully offering different possibilities for what could be going on for the client to help the client gain insight.

EMPIRICAL EVIDENCE

The literature on helper self-disclosure (see Watkins, 1990) is inconclusive, perhaps primarily because different definitions of self-disclosure have been used, making it difficult to compare results across studies. For this book, we distinguished several different types of disclosures: disclosing history and credentials and disclosing feelings (both of which belong in the exploration stage), self-disclosure and immediacy (both of which belong in the insight stage), and disclosing strategies (which belongs in the action stage). Unfortunately, all five types have been combined in the research reported in this section. Hence, in this section *self-disclosure* refers to any statement in which a helper reveals something personal to a client.

A number of studies show that helpers use self-disclosure infrequently, ranging from 1% to 4% of all helper statements (Barkham & Shapiro, 1986; Hill, Helms, Tichenor, et al., 1988; Hill, Mahalik, & Thompson, 1989). Hill, Helms, Tichenor, et al. found that clients rated helper self-disclosure as very helpful and that self-disclosure enabled clients to experience their feelings, but therapists rated the self-disclosures as not very helpful. They speculated that therapists rated self-disclosures as unhelpful because they felt vulnerable after exposing their experiences.

Edwards and Murdock (1994) found that most helpers said they disclosed at least somewhat to increase feelings of similarity between themselves and clients. They most often disclosed professional qualifications and experiences. Geller and Farber (1997) found that helpers most commonly acknowledged or apologized for their mistakes and disclosed their reactions to a client's self-presentation (note that we would classify both of these interventions as immediacy). Helpers also often disclosed their beliefs regarding the efficacy of helping, personal information (e.g., whether or not they have children, location of their vacation, marital status, age, ethnicity, whether they have been in therapy). Helper disclosures were done most often in response to questions asked by clients. Helpers indicated that they disclosed to validate the clients' experience of reality, to normalize or universalize the clients' experience, to strengthen the therapeutic alliance, and to offer alternative ways of thinking and acting. Helpers indicated that they would not disclose if they sensed that it would remove the focus of attention from the client or would interfere with the flow of the client's exploration.

In a qualitative study, Knox, Hess, Petersen, and Hill (1997) asked clients currently in long-term helping to describe their experiences of disclosures. Clients reported that the disclosures were very useful and had a positive impact on the helping. Clients perceived that helpers gave disclosures to normalize clients' feelings and to reassure them. The disclosures typically consisted of personal nonimmediate information about the helpers (e.g., spending time at the shore during childhood, difficulty arranging transportation because of a disability). Clients indicated that disclosures led to new insight or perspective, made helpers seem more real and human, improved the therapeutic relationship, and resulted in clients feeling more normal or reassured. For example, in one case, a client who struggled with drug addiction had difficulty trusting her helper and opening up to him. She thought that he could not understand her struggle with drugs and asked him if he had ever tried street drugs. The helper disclosed that he had, in fact, tried street drugs. The client reported that this disclosure shocked her and "stopped the argument cold." It made her rethink her assumptions and stereotypes, allowed her to see the benefits of healthy disagreement, and enabled her to use the therapeutic relationship as a learning ground for other relationships. She thus became more assertive in expressing her needs and opinions rationally. The disclosure also changed her perspective of the helper, making him seem more human and similar to her, allowing her to feel closer to him, increasing her respect for him, and providing more of a balance in the relationship.

Barrett and Berman (in press) used a unique research strategy. Within the context of four sessions of helping, helpers increased the number of self-disclosures they made in response to client self-disclosures with one client and refrained from making self-disclosures with another client. When helpers gave increased self-disclosure, clients reported lower levels of symptom distress and greater liking of their helpers. (Of course, even under conditions of increased disclosure, helpers used an average of only five disclosures per session.)

In summary, helper self-disclosure is often effective, resulting in high ratings of helpfulness, high levels of client experiencing, and new insight or perspective. Furthermore, self-disclosure makes helpers seem real and human, improves the therapeutic relationship, makes clients feel more normal or reassured, leads to symptom relief, and results in a greater liking of helpers. Across studies, self-disclosures were used infrequently, which perhaps made them stand out more and seem like gifts to the clients. Hence, when self-disclosures are used infrequently and judiciously by helpers to normalize and reassure clients, they can be helpful.

HOW TO SELF-DISCLOSE

Helpers need to think honestly about their intentions for disclosing. If they have had an experience that could be helpful to clients in understanding more about themselves, this is an appropriate time to disclose it. If helpers are disclosing for their own needs, however, they should refrain from disclosing. To develop an appropriate self-disclosure, helpers can think about what contributed to their behaviors when they were in similar situations as their clients are in. By focusing on what insights they gained about themselves, helpers can be more open to trying to help clients attain insight.

If helpers decide that self-disclosures are appropriate for the client at a particular moment, they should keep the focus of the disclosure on the insight that they have insights from their experience rather than on recounting a lot of details of their experience. Helpers should be honest about their experience and should not make up experiences and learning just to have a disclosure. If they have not had a similar experience that led them to a new understanding, they should use a different intervention. It is important that when helpers disclose, they choose something that has occurred in the past, has been resolved, has resulted in a new perspective, can be helpful to the client, and does not make them feel too vulnerable. In addition, disclosures that are short and keep the focus on the client tend to be most effective.

Self-disclosures should not be used to discuss or solve the helper's problems (e.g., "You think you've got it bad, let me tell you how bad it was for me."). Harm can result if helpers use self-disclosure because they have unresolved problems and are needy. In this case, the focus shifts from the client to the helper, perhaps resulting in the client taking care of the helper. Because self-disclosure should be used to help clients gain insight, helpers need to keep the focus on the clients. Thus, once helpers have disclosed, they should return the focus to the client. Helpers can follow disclosures with open questions about whether the insight fits for the client (e.g., "I wonder how that fits for you?" or "I wonder if anything like that happens for you?").

If the self-disclosure does not work (e.g., the client denies or disavows having similar experiences or feels uncomfortable knowing information about the helper), it is best for helpers to refrain from making further self-disclosures. Several things could have happened. Helpers could be right, but clients might not be ready to gain insight. Or, helpers could be projecting insight about themselves onto the client. In addition, clients could become upset about learning anything personal about helpers because it alters the distance between them. In such instances, helpers can collect more evidence to determine whether helper projection, client lack of readiness, or the client needing distance is at issue. If lack of readiness is the problem, helpers can try other skills (e.g., reflection of feelings or challenge). If projection is the problem, helpers can seek supervision or therapy to address these problems. If the client prefers not to know anything about the helper, the helper can change strategies and limit self-disclosures. Of course, any extreme reaction should be investigated further to assist in understanding and gaining insight into the client's underlying issues.

The following is an example of how self-disclosure (in italics) could be used. Note that the helper returns the focus to the client immediately after providing the disclosure.

> **Client:** "I've been thinking a lot about death lately. I'm not thinking of suicide, but more about the inevitability of death. There are so many senseless murders lately—the news is full of them. But I cannot quite grasp the idea of death—it doesn't make sense to me. It doesn't seem fair to be killed in the prime of life."
>
> **Helper:** "You sound scared about the idea of dying."

Client: "Oh yeah, I really am. I really don't know what happens after death. Of course, my parents' religion talks about heaven and hell, but I can't quite buy all that. But if I don't believe what their religion says, I don't quite know what happens at death. And what is the meaning of life—I mean why are we here and why does everyone rush around—what difference does it all make? I'm sure this all sounds very confusing, but I've been thinking about it a lot lately."

Helper: "No, it makes a lot of sense. I think all of us need to grapple with the meaning of life and the fact that we are going to die. You know, though, let me make a guess about something. *When I have been most concerned about death and meaning in life is when I have been in moments of transition and trying to figure out what I want out of life.* I wonder if that's true for you now?"

Client: "Hmmm. That's interesting. I am about to turn 30, and it feels like a big turning point for me. I'm in a job I don't really like, and I haven't found the relationship that I always hoped I would find at this point." (Client continues talking productively about his personal concerns.)

EFFECTS OF SELF-DISCLOSURE

Helpers can listen to tapes of their session and use the following 3-point scale to evaluate the effects of their self-disclosures on clients.

1 = After an inappropriate or unhelpful self-disclosure, the attention might shift from the client to the helper, with the client trying to soothe or attend to the helper. Other possible reactions include clients becoming silent, talking about irrelevant material, or feeling contemptuous of helpers for self-disclosing.

2 = After neutral or somewhat helpful self-disclosures, clients might acknowledge and even like the disclosure but not use it to gain insight.

3 = After very helpful self-disclosures, clients might recognize the similarity between themselves and their helpers, feel a sense of relief that someone else has felt or done the same thing, and gain new insight about themselves. Clients might say something like, "yeah, I've felt that" and reveal more of their inner experiences at greater depths. Clients might admit to awareness and insights that they had not previously recognized. Some clients might feel a commonality with another human being and, thus, feel less alone and less isolated. Alternatively, clients might gain insight and clearly articulate how their feelings are different from the helper's perspective.

DIFFICULTIES HELPERS EXPERIENCE
IN USING SELF-DISCLOSURES

One danger in using self-disclosure is that helpers might project their feelings and reactions onto clients. For example, if a client has been talking about getting bad grades and a helper states, "I feel panicked when I get bad grades because I am still afraid of my parents' anger," the helper might have projected his or her own insight onto the client. The client might confirm that this is a projection by responding, "No, I feel more like I deserved the bad grade because I didn't study." Helpers need to remember that they are separate from their clients and have different experiences and that their personal insights might not apply to their clients.

When providing self-disclosure, some helpers also satisfy their urge to reveal themselves rather than using it intentionally to help clients gain insight. Similarly, some helpers mistake the notion of being open as an opportunity to say whatever is on their minds. Greenberg et al. (1993) called such impulsive helper openness "promiscuous" self-disclosure. This type of self-disclosure may result in clients feeling uncomfortable and losing respect for the helper. For example, a client sought help to address her concerns about death and dying. Unfortunately, her helper talked more about her own fears about death than the client did. The client terminated and found a different helper who used self-disclosures more judiciously. Greenberg et al. suggested that self-disclosures need to be done with disciplined spontaneity on the basis of the helpers' accurate self-awareness of inner experience shared in a facilitative manner at a therapeutically appropriate moment. In other words, helpers need to be aware of themselves and of their intentions and deliver self-disclosures when they are most likely to help clients.

Helpers often feel uncomfortable when clients ask them for personal information. For example, a client might ask where the helper went for vacation or whether the helper is married or has children. Our general rule would be to provide information to the degree that it feels comfortable but also to be curious about what motivates the client's desire for this personal information. Helpers might ask clients about their thoughts, fantasies, and concerns about them before answering the questions to provide an opportunity for clients to reveal their thoughts and fantasies. In other words, in addition to providing the personal information, helpers can investigate why clients want the information. Processing these issues can provide insights about the client and strengthen the relationship.

Beginning helpers tend to use too many self-disclosures. As with medical students seeing themselves in all the syndromes described in their medical texts, beginning helpers connect with many of their clients' struggles. They have a hard time setting aside their personal issues to focus on the client's problems. It is indeed difficult to shift from the mutual sharing that ideally occurs in friendships to the reduced amount of sharing that occurs in helping relationships.

Finally, some beginning helpers worry about making their self-disclosures perfect. They believe that disclosures could have negative effects if not done exactly right. They also worry about sounding patronizing, as if they have figured out everything for themselves whereas clients are still learning. They worry that they would feel too vulnerable and would lose any credibility they have as helpers if they disclose issues that they are currently involved in and do not understand completely. Other helpers are concerned that they might not have an appropriate disclosure because they have not faced a similar situation or have not gained any insight into the situation—perhaps they are really in the same boat as the client. We recommend that helpers use other interventions if they feel uncomfortable or vulnerable using disclosures. We would also note that practice under close supervision helps greatly in terms of teaching beginning helpers the bounds of appropriate disclosures.

HELPFUL HINTS

- Think carefully about your intentions for providing a self-disclosure. Are you doing it for your benefit or to help the client? If, on reflection, you realize that you want to give the self-disclosure for your own needs, do not disclose. If, on the other hand, you believe that the disclosure will help the client to increase insight, formulate the disclosure with the needs of the client in mind.

- Keep disclosures short. Long disclosures take the focus off the client.

- After you give a self-disclosure, turn the focus back to the client. For example, "When I was in your situation, I reacted with hostility because of my anxiety about being humiliated. I wonder what was going on for you." Remember that you are using disclosures to enable clients to become more insightful than they otherwise might be, so keep the focus on the client.

- Follow self-disclosures with open questions (e.g., "What was your reaction to my disclosure?") and reflections of feelings ("You seem surprised that I had a similar experience."). Remember to return to the basic listening skills; after attaining insight, clients may need time to explore their feelings about their new discoveries.

- Watch the client's reaction after disclosures. If the client reacts negatively to the self-disclosure, try a different intervention and talk about their reactions.

- Use self-disclosures infrequently. Remember that experienced therapists use self-disclosures only rarely. Disclosures may be effective and memorable because they are used infrequently.

PRACTICE EXERCISES

Recall that the typical appropriate intentions for using self-disclosure in the insight stage are to promote insight, deal with resistance, and challenge. Read each of the following examples, indicate your intention(s), and write a self-disclosure that you might use if you were the helper. Please remember that we recommend following the self-disclosure with an open question or reflection to shift the focus back to the client.

Statements

1. **Client:** "I felt so weird when I had to get up and speak in front of the class last week. Everyone else seemed to feel so confident when they gave their speeches. I just felt like a total jerk, not knowing what to say. I feel so embarrassed that I can't speak as well as everyone else."
   Helper intention(s):_____
   Helper response:_____

2. **Client:** "Every time I go home, I feel like I'm 10 years old again. My parents treat me like a little child, and I actually get back into the same role I played as a little child. Even though I'm a grown-up, responsible person and never act like a little child any place else, somehow I always revert to acting like a child when I visit my parents. I get so upset with myself."
   Helper intention(s):_____
   Helper response:_____

3. **Client:** "I just feel like women can't do much careerwise. It really is true that men run the world. Look how much more money they make than women, and they have all the good jobs. Plus if you have a career, you can't do a very good job of

raising children. It's probably not possible to have a family and a decent career."
Helper intention(s):_____

Helper response:_____

_____

Possible Helper Responses

1. "I felt terrified when I gave speeches in class because I was always afraid people were going to laugh at me. Could that be true for you?" (intent: to promote insight)

   "I feel embarrassed sometimes because my accent is different from other people and I fear that they will think I'm not adequate. I wonder if you feel that way?" (intent: to promote insight)

   "Even though I've been giving speeches for over 20 years, I still feel nervous. I feel like I'm an imposter and have nothing to say that anyone would want to hear. For me, it's related to never being listened to in my family. I wonder if you can identify where your nervousness comes from?" (intent: to promote insight)

2. "Yes, I do that too. I notice that I have a tendency to regress to being dependent unless I am careful. I wonder if that's true for you?" (intent: to promote insight, to challenge)

   "I feel upset with regressing too when I visit my parents, but there's also a part of me that loves to sink back and be taken care of. My fear is that I'll never want to leave. I wonder if you have that fear?" (intent: to promote insight, to challenge)

   "I can relate to that with my parents because they really don't want me to grow up and be different from them. What issues do you think get raised for you when you visit your parents?" (intent: to promote insight, to challenge)

3. "I've also had lots of struggles with thinking about my role as a professional woman and possibly having children. For me it's related to not being sure that I want both. I wonder if you experience any ambivalence about wanting both a career and a family?" (intent: to promote insight, to challenge, to deal with resistance)

   "I wonder if you're aware that I have a career and a family? I've had to figure out who I am and what I want out of life. I wonder if you've done that?" (intent: to promote insight, to challenge, to deal with resistance)

What Do You Think?

- Describe how self-disclosures are used in friendships as compared to helping relationships.

- Discuss the conditions under which you as a helper would not want to use self-disclosure.

- Discuss the notion that self-disclosure reduces the power imbalance between helpers and clients. What are the advantages and disadvantages of having a power imbalance in a helping relationship?

- Discuss the effects of self-disclosure on neutrality in the helping relationship.

- Discuss how much of self-disclosure is verbal as opposed to nonverbal. In other words, how much do people reveal about themselves through nonverbal mannerisms, clothing, and office decor?

LAB 9 Self-Disclosure

Goals: For helpers to practice using the basic helping skills (reflection, restatement, and open question) and then to learn to self-disclose once they have established a supportive relationship.

Exercise 1

In groups of four to six people, one person should be the leader, one person the client, one person the initial helper, and the rest should be waiting to serve as helper. Each person should take a turn being the client. Each group should have a designated lab leader (other than the helper) to organize and coordinate the session.

Helper's and Client's Tasks During the Helping Interchange

1. The client should talk about a common problematic experience (e.g., schoolwork, adjustment to college, or problems with friends).
2. The designated helper should use basic helping skills (open question, restatement, and reflection of feelings) for 5–10 min, allowing the client to explore. If one helper gets stuck, another helper can take over to ensure a thorough exploration.
3. The group leader should stop the helper after a few minutes of exploration, preferably when it is clear that a self-disclosure could enable the client to come to some insight.
4. It is very helpful to hear how other people disclose. Hence, everyone except the client should deliver a self-disclosure. Helpers should pause and take time to think about what the client has said. Helpers can ask themselves, "When I was in a similar situation, what contributed to what I was doing? What have I learned about myself and my motivations that might be helpful to this client?" Helpers should also pause to think about their motivation—are they self-disclosing for their own benefit or because the client could profit from the disclosure? When helpers have an idea of a possible self-disclosure, they should think carefully about how to phrase their intervention.
5. Each helper in turn should deliver his or her self-disclosure and give the client a chance to respond.

Observers' Tasks During the Helping Interchange

Everyone should observe how the client responds to each self-disclosure. Identify disclosures that led to further client exploration as compared to disclosures that shifted the focus to the helper.

After the Helping Interchange

After everyone has had a turn and the client has responded, the client can talk about which self-disclosures were most helpful and why. Helpers can talk about their intentions and their perceptions of the client reactions.

(Continues)

SWITCH ROLES

Exercise 2

Students should pair up, with one person as the helper and one as the client.

Helper's and Client's Tasks During the Helping Interchange

1. The client should talk about a common problematic experience (e.g., school-work, adjustment to college, or problems with friends).
2. The helper should use basic helping skills (open question, restatement, and reflection of feelings) for 5–10 min, allowing the client to explore, and then give a self-disclosure.

After the Helping Interchange

The client can talk about his or her reactions to the self-disclosure. The helper can talk about his or her intentions and perceptions of the client reactions.

SWITCH ROLES

Personal Reflections

- Describe your reactions and feelings to giving or receiving self-disclosures.
- Describe your strengths in giving self-disclosures. In which areas do you need improvement?
- Describe the types of information that you would feel comfortable knowing about a person who was your helper.
- Discuss whether certain types of people feel more comfortable disclosing.

16 Immediacy

There are, in fact, no more important communications between one human being and another than those expressed emotionally, and no information more vital for constructing and reconstructing working models of the self and other than information about how each feels towards the other ... it is the emotional communications between a patient and his therapist that play the crucial part.

John Bowlby (1988, pp. 156–157)

Evita constantly got angry at her helper, Angela. She criticized Angela for everything she did. Angela began to feel inadequate and angry at Evita and did not look forward to sessions. Angela consulted with her supervisor, who reassured Angela that she was using the helping skills appropriately and suggested that perhaps Evita's personal issues caused her to denigrate Angela. The supervisor suggested that Angela use immediacy in the next session to let Evita know how she was feeling. After being criticized for not saying the right feeling word, Angela said, "You know, right now I'm feeling badly because it feels like I cannot do anything right. I feel frustrated because I don't know how to help you. I wonder how you feel about our relationship?" Evita responded by breaking into tears and saying that she seemed to push everyone away. Angela was able to listen and eventually they came to realize that Evita pushed people away because she feared rejection. Thus, using immediacy allowed Angela to help Evita understand more about how she acted with others and strengthened the therapeutic relationship.

IMMEDIACY OCCURS when helpers disclose how they are feeling about themselves in relation to the client, about the client, or about the therapeutic relationship. Ivey (1994) called *immediacy* being "in the moment" with the client. In this vein, he pointed out that most clients talk in the past tense about events but might profit from talking in the present tense about what is going on in the helping relationship. As Egan (1994) suggested, immediacy can focus on the overall relationship (e.g., "It feels to me that we are getting along well now that we have worked through our initial discomfort"), a specific event in the session (e.g., "I was surprised when you said that you appreciated the sessions because I wasn't sure how you felt about our work"), or present-tense personal reactions to the client (e.g., "I am feeling frustrated right now because you get angry at everything I say"). Further examples are provided in Exhibit 16.1.

Immediacy can be thought of as a type of self-disclosure because helpers are disclosing personal feelings, reactions, or experiences (e.g., "I feel angry when you try to push me around"). Immediacy also can be considered a type of challenge because it can be used to confront clients about issues in the relationship (e.g., "I feel annoyed that you avoid my questions"). In addition, immediacy can sometimes be a type of information if it is used to point out patterns in a client's behavior (e.g., "Whenever I go on vacation, you cancel the

EXHIBIT 16.1. OVERVIEW OF IMMEDIACY	
Definition	*Immediacy* refers to the helper disclosing immediate feelings about self in relation to the client, the client, or the therapeutic relationship
Examples	**Client:** "I don't know why you keep telling me to do things that I don't want to do." **Helper:** "Right now I'm feeling very tense because you seem to be angry at me."
	Client: "I feel scared right now telling you all this stuff." **Helper:** "I feel nervous too, but I'm pleased that you're sharing some very deep and personal feelings with me."
Typical helper intentions	To promote insight, to deal with the relationship, to challenge, to identify maladaptive behaviors, to identify and intensify feelings, to relieve therapist's needs[a] (see Appendix A)
Possible client reactions	Relief, negative thoughts or feelings, better self-understanding, clear, feelings, responsibility, unstuck, new perspective, challenged, scared, worse, stuck, confused, misunderstood (see Appendix D)
Desired client behaviors	Affective exploration, cognitive exploration, insight (see Appendix E)
Difficulties helpers experience in using immediacy	Fears about intruding Uncertainty about feelings and perceptions of clients Anxiety about dealing with interpersonal conflicts Removing the focus from the client due to lengthy or inappropriate use of immediacy

[a]This intention is typically not therapeutic.

first two sessions after I return. I wonder if we could talk about this pattern?"). However, immediacy differs from feedback about the client (a type of information) because both people in the relationship are involved in immediacy interventions, whereas in information only the helper talks about the client (e.g., "You did a really good job when you spoke up to your mother"). Although immediacy overlaps with other skills, we highlight this intervention as a separate skill because it can provide clients with powerful feedback about how they are perceived in interpersonal relationships.

INTENTIONS

A primary intention for using immediacy is to promote insight. Helpers want clients to increase their understanding of why they behave as they do with other people. A related intention is for clients to identify maladaptive behaviors or things that they do that make other people react negatively to them (e.g., acting hostilely, being argumentative, seeming distant and withdrawn, acting overly nice or idealizing).

Another intention for using immediacy is to address issues in the therapeutic relationship that interfere with the helping process. Using immediacy in this way also often involves the intention of challenge. In any human relationship, problems and misunderstandings arise and need to be addressed. With immediacy, helpers deal with these problems in an open and genuine manner, revealing honest feelings in the service of helping clients by providing feedback about the effects of clients' behaviors. Helpers thus exhibit appropriate communication skills by demonstrating that they are able to deal openly with problems as they arise. When misunderstandings or mistakes arise in the therapeutic relationship, it is usually best to deal with them openly and directly.

An additional intention is to identify and intensify feelings. Talking directly about feelings in the immediate moment is intense and likely to arouse emotions, hence opening the door for change. Clients often can understand what is going on in the relationship because they have emotional reactions to the immediacy intervention. For example, a helper told her client that she felt discouraged because he always agreed with what she had to say but never seemed to think much about what they talked about or do much work outside of sessions. Because the client really liked and respected the helper and felt badly that the helper felt discouraged, the immediacy helped him think about why he was so reluctant to change.

Finally, helpers sometimes inappropriately (and often unconsciously) use immediacy to deal with their own needs. For example, a helper who had recently been divorced was feeling particularly vulnerable and needed affirmation that he was attractive and so encouraged his client to talk about her attraction to him. Usually helpers are not aware that they are using immediacy to deal with their own needs. They might become aware that they are doing so, however, if their behaviors have negative consequences for their clients (e.g., a client quits after the helper gets angry at her for being too quiet). Hence, it is crucial for helpers to be mindful of their needs, so that these needs do not intrude on the helping process.

WHY USE IMMEDIACY?

Kiesler's (1988) term for *immediacy* is metacommunication or impact disclosure. He stated that metacommunication occurs when helpers disclose to clients their perceptions of and reactions to a client's actions. He distinguished impact disclosures from other disclosures of personal factual or historical information about life experiences because they relate specifically to the helper's experience of the client. Kiesler, whose theory of metacommunication is based on both communications theory and interpersonal therapy, indicated that metacommunication is one of the most powerful responses in the helper's repertoire because the helper responds to the client in a different manner than that to which the client is accustomed. Rather than ignoring obnoxious behavior as is often the case in social interactions, the helper confronts the client directly and describes the impact of the client's behavior on the helper.

Because many clients have trouble with interpersonal relationships, including the therapeutic relationship, discussing problems in the immediate therapy relationship often results in clients coming to a deeper understanding of how they behave in relationships. The therapy relationship thus provides a microcosm of how clients relate in the real world. If clients are compliant with others, for example, they are often compliant in the helping process. If clients are arrogant and show off for the helper, chances are that they have acted similarly with other people. Therefore the client's general interpersonal style can be examined, at least in part, by an investigation of the relationship with the helper. Whereas helpers have to rely on clients' reports of how they act with other people, they have a firsthand experience of how clients behave with them.

Resolving problems between the helper and client can provide clients with a model of how to resolve interpersonal problems in relationships. Clients learn that it is possible to talk about feelings and come to some resolution and perhaps develop closer relationships as a result of the discussion. Being able to resolve interpersonal problems can be a powerful experience, in that it can teach clients that it is possible, although not always easy, to deal openly with issues. Greenberg et al. (1993) suggested that encountering another real human being who both cares and is authentic helps clients grow.

Another reason for using immediacy is to challenge clients to change maladaptive behaviors. When helpers are honest about their reactions, clients learn how they come across to other people and thus might change their problematic behaviors. Some examples of interpersonal behaviors that can cause problems for clients include being so talkative that the helper cannot speak at all, acting overbearing and arrogant and assuming that they are better than the helper, remaining passive and not saying anything without being asked, droning on in a monotone voice without maintaining eye contact, disagreeing with everything the helper says, or constantly bringing gifts to the helper. In the real world outside of helping, people might ignore these behaviors and spend as little time with the individual as possible but not tell the person what the problem is. People often do not give honest feedback about how they perceive others because it is too difficult, may hurt feelings, or could take too much time or effort. Because they do not receive feedback, clients often are not aware of how they come across to others. If individuals are oblivious to their own behaviors (which they often are because they are so used to them), they cannot change them. The helping relationship, then, provides an opportunity for clients to come to an awareness of how their behaviors affect another person.

Immediacy can also be used to make covert communication more direct. In some cases, clients talk covertly about the helping relationship because they are not sure of how helpers will react if they say something directly. For example, a client might say that no one can help him. Because the helper is trying to help him, it is not a huge leap to guess that at least part of the communication is directed toward the helper. In any communication, helpers can ask themselves what clients are trying to communicate to them about the therapy relationship, although whether they use an immediacy statement should be tempered by the clinical situation and client needs at the time.

In addition to addressing problems in relationships, immediacy can be used to discuss issues of importance to the helping relationship. For example, a helper might want to process feelings with a client about their encounter at a party, or a helper could discuss with a client what has worked well and what has not worked well in the helping process so that adjustments can be made. Given that many issues present themselves in a helping relationship, immediacy is a critical tool for enhancing understanding and reaching insight.

Helpers who gently provide honest feedback may be giving their clients a special gift. Letting clients know how you perceive them in a caring way requires deep levels of empathy. In addition, helpers take a huge risk in sharing these feelings. We emphasize that helpers must be providing feedback to help clients (rather than to punish them) and must be empathic about how clients feel when they receive the feedback. In effect, immediacy communicates to clients that helpers are willing to take the time to let clients know about the effect of their behaviors so that they can have an opportunity to increase awareness and change inappropriate behaviors.

Finally, immediacy can be used to highlight clients' strengths as well as their maladaptive behaviors. Clients sometimes put themselves down and do not recognize what they do well. Although helpers would not want to minimize and ignore problems, the acknowledgment of strengths by an authority figure can build self-esteem. All too often, helpers focus only on problems, which can be very discouraging if clients begin to think that they are not doing anything right.

EMPIRICAL EVIDENCE

To our knowledge, there is not much empirical evidence about the use of immediacy because it has not been included in most helping skills systems. Some indirect evidence for the effectiveness of immediacy, however, comes from a study on the resolution of misunderstandings (Rhodes et al., 1994). Clients were asked to describe what happened in specific events when they felt misunderstood in therapy. In cases where the misunderstanding was resolved, clients indicated that they told their helpers that they felt misunderstood. Sometimes this disclosure came after a delay of some time (often a few sessions) when the client had enough nerve to discuss the misunderstanding with the helper. When the client raised the topic, the helper and client engaged in a mutual repair process in which they tried to understand and resolve the event. This mutual repair process typically involved both people talking honestly about their feelings in the immediate moment. In some cases, the helpers apologized or accepted responsibility for their inappropriate behavior. In one case, for example, the helper had interrupted the client. The client in this case told the helper that she felt angry for having been interrupted because she felt that she "had not been given a chance" and that she was being dismissed. The helper acknowledged that she had been too abrupt and admitted that something personal was going on with her that caused her to approach the client in such a way (note that the helper in this case did not burden the client by disclosing the personal event because it was not relevant to the immediate situation). The client said that the event was important because it helped her address the issue of how she defended against her feelings in therapy and because she and her therapist were able to process the feelings in the relationship. Hence, by talking openly about what had transpired, the client was able to deal with an immediate problem and contribute to the development and maintenance of a positive therapeutic relationship. In contrast, we found evidence in another study (Petersen et al., 1998) that impasses can result when therapists and clients do not talk openly about problems in the therapeutic relationship.

HOW TO USE IMMEDIACY

Immediacy is a difficult and demanding skill. Helpers need to be aware of what is happening in the therapeutic relationship and have enough self-confidence and self-understanding not to react defensively to clients' open expression of feelings. Because they do not always face difficult interpersonal situations in nonhelping situations, helpers often feel frightened about doing so in helping. It takes courage, as well as skill, to be immediate with clients. With Kiesler's (1988), Cashdan's (1988), Teyber's (1997), and our own experience in mind, we propose several steps that helpers can use to formulate and provide immediacy responses to clients.

Step 1. Become Hooked

Helpers first need to experience personally the impact of a client's behavior, which Kiesler (1988) and Cashdan (1988) called becoming "hooked." They noted that helpers are pushed into a constricted, narrow range of responses by the client's maladaptive behaviors. Helpers respond to clients unconsciously according to client demands (e.g., dominant clients elicit submissive behavior from helpers; hostile clients elicit hostile behavior from helpers). Thus, helpers experience firsthand how clients interact with other people, so they need to attend carefully to these experiences to understand the problems that clients have in interpersonal relationships.

Step 2. Become Aware of and Pull Out of Being Hooked

Helpers must become aware of and stop their automatic reactions by looking inward and determining their inner feelings about clients. Sometimes this self-examination is difficult for helpers. Helpers typically like to think of themselves as being accepting and nurturing, but they might instead find themselves feeling bored, sexually attracted, angry, entertained, incompetent, annoyed, adored, overidentified, sympathetic, or pitying and hence may act in a nontherapeutic manner. Helpers can ask themselves, "What am I feeling when I am with this client?," "What do I want to do or not do when I am with this client?," "What keeps me from using the skills that I know I should be using with this client?"

Helpers need to cultivate a sense of curiosity about what contributes to clients acting as they do rather than blaming clients for their behaviors. Often, clients have developed these behaviors as defenses. For example, if a client is very talkative and does not let anyone else contribute to the discussion, the client could be defending against letting anyone get close for fear of becoming engulfed. Thus, the constant talking may serve a defensive function of keeping others at a safe distance. Helpers can aid clients in gaining insight about the reasons for their behaviors.

Helpers need to allow themselves to have their feelings without judging themselves as "bad" or incompetent. Rather, helpers can view themselves as instruments and use their feelings to determine how they resonate with or react to clients. Helpers often struggle with allowing themselves to have some negative feelings toward clients. Supervision can be very useful for normalizing such feelings. For example, the supervisor might say, "If I were in this situation, I would feel sexually attracted to this client. She is so beautiful that I might feel distracted in sessions." When supervisors are able to admit to having "politically incorrect" feelings, helpers often are then able to acknowledge their feelings. Thus, supervision is invaluable for enabling helpers to become aware of their feelings and also for ensuring that helpers do not act impulsively on their feelings.

By coming to an understanding of what clients are "pulling" from them, helpers regain some objectivity that permits them to distance themselves from their reactions and begin to help the client. For example, by becoming aware that a client's whining pulls for the helper to be sadistic, the helper can stop trying to silence the client and shift to wondering what causes the client to whine. The helper can then think about how to provide the client with feedback about the effects of her or his whining.

Step 3. Determine Intentions

Helpers need to determine their intentions for intervening with clients. (Recall that the typical intentions are to promote insight, deal with the therapeutic relationship, identify maladaptive behaviors, identify and intensify feelings, and relieve the helper's needs.) In doing so, helpers need to make sure that they are not projecting their own issues onto clients or serving their own needs. Thus, helpers need to evaluate whether any of their own issues could be implicated in the feelings that they have when they are with the client. Helpers also need to determine whether they have enough information about the client's behaviors before they intervene. Furthermore, helpers should assess whether the therapeutic relationship is strong enough to withstand direct communication between helper and client.

Helpers must also be careful not to let countertransference reactions interfere with their reactions to clients. For example, a helper might be very sensitive to clients being talkative and aggressive because the helper's mother is very dominant and talks incessantly.

Step 4. Use Immediacy to Talk About the Relationship

When using immediacy, helpers talk directly to clients about their interactions. In other words, helpers and clients metacommunicate about their communication. Kiesler (1988) stressed that the success of the metacommunication depends on the extent to which helpers balance the challenge of the metacommunication with being supportive and protective of the client's self-esteem. Helpers need to present the metacommunication as a gentle examination of the process in which helpers communicate that they are committed to working with clients to understand their actions and the effects of their behaviors on relationships with other people.

Helpers should take appropriate responsibility for their feelings when using immediacy (e.g., "I feel uncomfortable that you keep praising me" or "I feel bad that I interrupted you"). "I" statements have a very different impact than "you" statements ("you shouldn't praise me" or "you talk too much"). Clients often have an easier time owning their responsibility (e.g., "I was probably talking too much") when helpers have candidly admitted their contribution to the interaction. Furthermore, it is only fair for helpers to admit their responsibility if they demand that clients acknowledge their part. When helpers acknowledge their role in relationship problems, an open exchange can occur about how both people feel. Problems can be resolved, the therapeutic relationship can be enhanced, and clients can be encouraged to become actively involved in problem solving. For example, at midsemester, a helper discovered that her client (Maria) was in the same practicum class as the helper's partner. The helper repeatedly asked Maria to process this situation even though Maria indicated that she had worked through her feelings on her own at the beginning of the semester. The helper later apologized and indicated that she realized that she had many feelings about the situation and had inadvertently projected them onto the client.

It is crucial that helpers not prescribe how clients should change, because "should" statements imply that the helper is more knowledgeable about the client than the client, which goes against the client-centered nature of this model. Instead, helpers merely point out how they react when clients act in a particular way and wonder why they act that way. It is also important for helpers to be aware that their feedback about the client is based on their perceptions and reactions and that others might react differently to the client. Helpers might even suggest that clients gather feedback about how others react to the behaviors. An awareness of how they are perceived by others can enable clients to make choices about how to behave and decide whether they want to make changes.

Step 5. Process the Interaction

After being immediate with clients, helpers need to make sure to ask clients about their reactions to the immediacy so that the communication is two sided. Hence, after the helper says something like "I find myself pitying you when you talk," the helper can ask the client, "How do you feel about what I said" or "You became awfully quiet when I said I felt pity for you. What was going on inside you?" Thus, the helper tries to engage the client in a discussion of his or her interaction.

Because helpers have indicated that it is permissible to process the relationship, they need to be aware that clients may give them feedback about what they do not like about the helper's behaviors. After all, helping is a two-way interaction, and helpers may be doing things that are not optimal for clients. Some of this information may be accurate and valuable—clients are often wonderful sources of feedback because they are the recipients of what helpers do and know exactly how the interventions feel (in fact, we strongly urge helpers to obtain client feedback and reactions). However, helpers also must be aware that sometimes feedback is colored by distortions (i.e., transference). For example, Yutta may say that the helper is mean not because of what the helper has done but because of unresolved feelings she has about her critical mother that she projects onto the helper. Helpers have to determine what feedback is genuinely related to their behavior and what is related to transference issues. Typically, we would suggest that there is at least a grain of truth in most client feedback, and helpers should investigate both their own behaviors and the client's contribution because both may be implicated.

The following is a brief example of a helper using immediacy (in italics) in a session. We present only Steps 4 and 5 in this example.

Client: "I would really like to sleep with you. I think sex is very important and a natural way of relating to someone that you're close to. It's just a matter of time until you agree to sleep with me. I know you're attracted to me—I can see it in your eyes."

Helper: *"It makes me uncomfortable when you talk about having sex with me. I wonder what your intentions are in talking with me about it?"*

Client: "Well, that's how men and women are supposed to relate. You say you're trying to help me. What I really need is for you to go to bed with me. That would give me some security that I am attractive."

Helper: "So you have a hard time relating to me on a nonsexual basis."

Client: "Yeah, I guess I do.

Helper: *"I wonder if you have any ideas of what leads you to relate to me in a sexual way when it is not appropriate for what we are trying to do here?"*

Client: "Hmm, that's interesting. My mother was always very seductive. I've always reacted to women on a sexual basis. Women are usually pretty eager to sleep with me."

Helper: *"I wonder how it feels to talk about our relationship?"*

Client: "Well, I'm not used to it. I still can't see why you won't sleep with me."

Helper: *"I can understand more now that when you get anxious about talking with me, you change the topic to talking about sex. Do you notice that?"*

Client: "Yeah, I guess I can see that. I am uncomfortable talking. I'm more of an action-type person."

EFFECTS OF IMMEDIACY

Helpers can watch tapes of their sessions and use the following 3-point scale to determine the effects of their immediacy statements on clients.

1 = If the immediacy is not helpful or is poorly timed, clients could feel wounded, hurt, or abused. Some clients could become silent or wary. In addition, some clients might blame their helpers for making them feel bad or might not return for sessions because they felt so misunderstood.

2 = If the immediacy is moderately helpful, clients might listen to the feedback but not respond. They might be able to hear the feedback but be unwilling to share their thoughts or feelings.

3 = If the immediacy is very helpful, clients might engage in dialogue with the helper about the feedback. Clients might admit to their contribution to the interaction. Clients might become interested in what might have led to them acting this way and thus gain insight into their behavior.

DIFFICULTIES HELPERS EXPERIENCE IN USING IMMEDIACY

Beginners often have fears about intruding and making clients angry if they use immediacy. Indeed, clients sometimes become angry when helpers point out their maladaptive behaviors. For example, a helper suggested that Olivia was acting helpless when she expected her helper to take responsibility for her behavior and failures. Olivia became very angry and adamantly denied that her behaviors were similar to those of victims. Several sessions later, Olivia acknowledged that the immediacy intervention was accurate and helped her become motivated to take more control of her life. If the helper had withheld the immediacy intervention for fear of hurting Olivia's feelings, Olivia would not have learned a valuable lesson about herself. Although it is sometimes painful to hear, such feedback can be motivational and subsequently life-changing.

Another problem is that some helpers do not trust their feelings (e.g., "Maybe it is all my fault that I'm bored—if I were a better helper, I wouldn't feel bored"). They might feel unsure about their reactions and hesitant about communicating their feelings to clients appropriately and empathically. Some helpers simply avoid immediacy because it is frightening to talk directly and honestly about the immediate relationship. They are not used to such open communication in their relationships, and they feel vulnerable when sharing immediate feelings. They might feel anxious about dealing openly with interpersonal conflicts because their families had strong rules against addressing conflicts openly. In fact, most helpers have an easier time being empathic with clients but are less skilled when it comes to expressing negative feelings and working through problems. Once again, personal therapy can be useful for providing an opportunity for helpers to come to understand their own issues.

It is often hard for beginning helpers to imagine using immediacy because most of their interactions with clients are very brief and require that helpers stay primarily in the exploration stage. However, beginning helpers can still practice this skill in role plays and be aware of how it could be used in actual sessions with clients with whom they work for longer periods of time.

■ HELPFUL HINTS

- Use your inner reactions to the client as a guide. Allow yourself to be "hooked" but then step back and examine your reactions, become curious about what causes the client's behavior, think about your intentions and your contribution to the interaction, and assess the client readiness before intervening.
- Be gentle and tentative (but not apologetic) in using immediacy. Remember that you are giving your opinion or perspective, not the "truth."
- Keep the immediacy statement short and keep the focus on the relationship.
- Be specific about a recent behavior rather than vague and general about behavior that occurred in the past.
- Be ready to talk and process the feelings that arise after the immediacy intervention. Ask clients for their reactions to immediacy interventions.
- Take responsibility for your contribution to problems in the relationship. "Own" your feelings rather than blaming clients for "causing" you to feel a certain way.
- Use this intervention only when you are at an advanced level of training and can implement it first under supervision. Because of the potential benefit and damage of this skill, it needs to be executed carefully. Supervisors can work with you to ensure that your intentions are appropriate and to help you select the appropriate timing for intervening.
- We highly recommend that helpers read *Love's Executioner* by Yalom (1990). Yalom has written articulately and openly about his personal reactions to working with a variety of clients. He is refreshingly honest about his reactions and provides a model for how helpers can use their reactions to enhance the therapeutic process.

PRACTICE EXERCISES

For each of the following examples, indicate your intention(s) and write an immediacy statement. (Recall that the typical intentions are to promote insight, to deal with the therapeutic relationship, to challenge, to identify maladaptive behaviors, and to relieve helper's needs.) Compare your responses to the possible helper responses provided at the end of the section.

Statements

1. **Client:** "You know I thought about what you said last time, and I got really angry. I don't think you know what you're talking about when you suggest that I go to see my old boyfriend when I go into town to give a talk. He hasn't even tried to contact me for 10 years, and I'm supposed to be focused on my professional work and giving a talk. I couldn't possibly concentrate if I knew I had to spend time going to see him and worrying about what he would say."
   Helper intention(s):_____

Helper response:_____

_____

2. Client: "You sure haven't been very helpful today. You don't give me any good advice. I don't know why I bother coming here. It's a waste of time."
Helper intention(s):_____
Helper response:_____

_____

3. Client: (silent for 5 min)
Helper intention(s):_____
Helper response:_____

_____

4. (Client talks on and on without pausing for 15 min.)
Helper intention(s):_____
Helper response:_____

_____

Possible Helper Responses

1. "I'm sorry that I suggested that you contact your old boyfriend. It obviously was hurtful to you. Maybe we could spend some time talking about what was going on between us given that I don't usually tell you what to do." (intent: to deal with the relationship, to promote insight)
"I feel concerned that you are blaming me when my memory is that you were the one to suggest that you go to see him." (intent: to identify maladaptive behaviors, to deal with the relationship)

2. "I also am feeling frustrated that we don't seem to be getting anywhere." (intent: to deal with the relationship, to challenge)
"I feel upset right now because I have put a lot of time and energy into our relationtionship and yet it doesn't seem to be enough for you." (intent: to deal with the relationship, to promote insight, to challenge)

3. "I'm feeling that you're angry with me. Can we talk about what's going on inside you?" (intent: to deal with the relationship, to identify and intensify feelings, to challenge)
"I am worried about you right now because you seem so distant." (intent: to promote insight, to identify maladaptive behaviors)

4. "I'm feeling bored right now. I wonder if you're aware that you've been talking nonstop for 15 minutes? What do you suppose is going on inside you?" (intent: to identify maladaptive behaviors, to deal with the relationship, to promote insight, to challenge)
"I'm feeling a little irritated that we're not getting anywhere. You seem like you're more interested in telling stories than working today. How do you feel?" (intent: to identify and intensify feelings, to deal with the relationship, to challenge)

What Do You Think?

● How can helpers balance being direct with feedback and accepting clients for who they are?

- How might helpers respond when clients are angry at them?
- Discuss the idea that immediacy can be an enactment of a deep level of empathy.
- Discuss the advantages and disadvantages of using immediacy as compared to self-disclosure.

<u>LAB 10</u> **Immediacy**

Exercise 1

Goal: For helpers to practice immediacy in the context of the other helping skills.

This lab is meant for advanced students who are seeing "real" clients. In this lab, we recommend forming groups of four to six people. We suggest that a helper who is currently seeing a client present a case. The helper plays the part of the client so that the helper can portray how the client behaves (and also gain more empathy for the client by playing the client). A second group member plays the role of the helper. Other group members can provide ideas to the helper about other possible ways of intervening or take over the role of helper if the helper gets stuck. Each group should have a designated lab leader (other than the helper) to organize and coordinate the session.

Helper's and Client's Tasks During the Helping Interchange

1. The client (played by the actual helper) role-plays how the actual client presents himself or herself, trying to portray the client's behavior that makes it particularly difficult for the actual helper to respond appropriately. Note that the client (the actual helper) should not provide any introductory material or talk about the actual client or the history of the helping interaction at all prior to the role-play because we want group members to respond naturally without receiving potentially biasing information.
2. The helper should respond for several speaking turns using the basic helping skills (open question, restatement, reflection) until she or he has formed some rapport and has experienced an inner reaction to the client.
3. The lab leader should ask the helper to pause for a moment. The helper should take some time to think about and clarify feelings and intentions to make sure that the immediacy intervention is for the client's benefit.
4. The helper should render an immediacy statement, making sure to state her or his feelings (e.g., "I'm feeling stuck right now. I feel frustrated because you disagree with everything I say") rather than blaming the client or telling the client how to behave (e.g., "You are really hard to work with," or "You shouldn't disagree with me so much"). Remember to be tentative, gentle, empathic, respectful, concise, and curious about the client's behavior.
5. The client should respond naturally and the interaction should continue.

Observers' Tasks During the Helping Interchange

Everyone should note to themselves how both the helper and client handle the situation. How does the helper present the immediacy statement? Does the helper take responsibility for her or his feelings? How does the client respond to the immediacy statement? How does the relationship between the helper and client appear? How would you feel in each role?

After the Helping Interchange

1. The clients can talk about reactions to hearing the immediacy intervention.

(Continues)

2. The helper can talk about how it felt to use immediacy. The helper can describe his or her intentions and perceptions of the client's reactions.
3. Everyone can provide feedback about their observations and perceptions of the interaction.

SWITCH ROLES

Exercise 2

Goal: To practice all the exploration and insight skills.

Students should pair up, with one person as the helper and one person as the client.

Helper's and Client's Tasks During the Helping Interchange

1. Clients should talk about something that they do but do not understand why they do it or something that confuses or puzzles them.
2. Helpers should use basic helping skills (open question, restatement, and reflection of feelings) for 5–10 min, allowing the client to explore.
3. Once they have established some rapport, helpers should begin using insight skills (challenge, interpretation, self-disclosure, and immediacy) when appropriate, interspersed with continuing to use exploration skills.

After the Helping Interchange

Clients can talk about their reactions. Helpers can talk about their intentions and their perceptions of the client reactions.

SWITCH ROLES

Personal Reflections

- How do you feel about dealing with interpersonal conflict?
- What personal issues arose for you as a helper or client engaging in immediacy? Describe how these issues might interfere with your being able to give feedback to clients.
- For the helpers who played the roles of their clients, what did you learn about your clients? How did your feelings change toward the clients? Describe any new ideas you learned for dealing with your clients.
- How would you respond to a client who wanted to give you feedback?

17 Integrating the Skills of the Insight Stage

> He who has a *why* to live can bear with almost any *how*.
>
> *Nietzsche*

Benjamin, who has been unable to choose a career, comes to realize that he is afraid to compete with his father, who is an extremely successful but distant businessman. Yvonne comes to understand that her feelings of inadequacy are based on other children making fun of her for having a slight speech impediment. Nigel gains the insight that he avoids all risks because of his fear of dying at a young age as his father did. These are examples of new understandings that clients come to in the insight stage with the aid of helpers.

AT THE end of the insight stage, clients have a new understanding of themselves at a deep, emotional level. Clients see things in new ways or from different perspectives, are able to identify patterns or make connections, and have a deeper understanding of their inner dynamics. These insights usually have an "aha" quality to them, and clients feel relieved that they have an explanation for their behaviors and thoughts. Clients "own" their new understandings because they have been instrumental in helping to construct them.

HOW TO INTEGRATE SKILLS IN THE INSIGHT STAGE

In the insight stage, helpers assist clients in developing new perspectives about themselves, their feelings, and their behaviors. They retain their empathic connection with clients and continue using the exploration skills, but they do not necessarily accept everything clients say at face value.

As Table 17.1 illustrates, helpers use challenge, interpretation, self-disclosure, or immediacy depending on what clients are presenting at the moment, what clients can tolerate, their intentions, and their overall plan for the session. They challenge clients' discrepancies, irrational ideas, or defenses, sometimes using humor and always using empathy. They use interpretations to understand the underlying reasons or motivations for thoughts and behaviors. They self-disclose to urge clients to arrive at new insights. They use immediacy to help clients attain insight about inappropriate behaviors or to deal with tensions or misunderstandings in the therapeutic relationship. These interventions help clients achieve greater depths of self-understanding and insight about who they are, how they got to be the way they are, and how they are perceived by others. Clients may thus begin to reframe their present behaviors in light of past experiences. Armed with insights, clients can make better choices about how they want to live their lives.

TABLE 17.1. A Guide for Which Helping Skills to Use During the Insight Stage

Marker in session	When helper intends to	Helper might try
At all points	Support	Appropriate attending behaviors Listening attentively Approval and reassurance
When the client seems ready to come to some insights with a little encouragement	Promote insight	Open question
After the relationship is established and the client is contradicting herself or himself, indicating a lot of ambivalence, unable to make a decision, or is stuck	Challenge, encourage self-control, deal with resistance	Challenge Open question
After the relationship is established and the client seems receptive and (a) the client indicates a lack of understanding about behaviors, thoughts, or feelings; (b) the client seems to be acting from unconscious influences; or (c) the helper is aware of connections, themes, defenses, resistances, or transference	Promote insight, encourage self-control	Interpretation
After the relationship is established and the client has a hard time seeing things, feels blamed or isolated, or has difficulty revealing something that is not socially desirable	Challenge, promote insight, encourage self-control	Self-disclosure Reflection of feelings
If there is a problem in the relationship such that therapeutic progress is impeded or if the client's behavior has negative effects on the helper (and probably on others) and feedback would be helpful	Deal with relationship, encourage self-control, deal with resistance	Immediacy Challenge

Marker in session	When helper intends to	Helper might try
If the client does not completely understand or express disagreement with challenge, interpretation, self-disclosure, or immediacy	Deal with relationship, encourage self-control, deal with resistance	Assess the problem. If the problem is a lack of understanding, the helper can repeat the intervention in a different way; if the problem is a lack of readiness, the helper can wait until the client seems ready; if the problem is in the relationship, the helper can use immediacy, open questions about feeling, and reflections of feelings
After a challenge, interpretation, self-disclosure, or immediacy has been used and the client is trying to understand it	Focus, clarify, encourage catharsis, identify maladaptive cognitions or behaviors, identify and intensify feelings	Open question about feelings Reflection of feelings Restatement
If the helper has countertransference feelings that are interfering with the helping process	Not harm the client	Seek supervision or personal therapy

When to Use Exploration Skills

In the insight stage, helpers use exploration skills frequently. For example, when clients seem ready to gain some insight on their own with a little encouragement from the helper, the helper might need only to ask something like, "I wonder if you've thought of what might be going on to cause you to act in such an atypical manner?" Thus, rather than helpers giving insight, helpers can encourage clients to challenge themselves and think about what is going on inside. One advantage of encouraging clients to construct insights is that helpers are not always around to provide insights, so clients need to be able to think deeply about their inner dynamics and to be curious about their motives.

Exploration skills also are useful after helpers have challenged, interpreted, self-disclosed, or given an immediacy statement. Because clients are now at a new point and need time to process (or "work through") the new information, using the exploration skills can help clients talk about their thoughts and feelings. For example, a statement such as "You sound surprised and pleased to realize that you might be reacting negatively to your boss because he is similar to your uncle, not because he is a bad guy" could help the client think further about the new insight.

When to Use Challenge

Challenges are useful when clients are feeling ambivalent, contradictory, stuck, or unable to make a decision. Challenge can make clients more aware of what is going on inside them. For nonresistant clients, challenges are typically most helpful when done gently and tentatively, although they may need to be done more forcefully with resistant clients. Helpers are identifying blind spots, problems, defenses, irrational ideas, or incongruencies of which the client might not have been aware or was trying to avoid, and so they must be sensitive to delivering challenges in ways that clients can hear them. Using humor can sometimes be an effective way to help clients see themselves in new ways.

When to Use Interpretation

Interpretation can be useful when clients do not understand what motivates them to behave in maladaptive ways, are confused or curious about why they have certain thoughts or feelings, or seem to be acting from unconscious influences. Interpretations can be particularly useful to clarify the underlying reasons for current thoughts, behaviors, and feelings. The source of interpretations is often in childhood, the time when clients learned many of their maladaptive thoughts and behaviors. In a related vein helpers can also develop interpretations on the basis of transference (distorted expectations about the helper based on early experiences) and defenses. Another source of interpretations is connecting seemingly disparate issues for clients to show that their behaviors make sense if one considers varied aspects of their lives. An additional source of interpretations is existential concerns, given that all of us struggle with issues about death, freedom and responsibility, isolation, and the meaning of life.

When to Use Self-Disclosure

Self-disclosure can be useful in bringing clients to insights that they might have felt too threatened to admit if suggested directly through other interventions. With self-disclosure, helpers reveal some aspect of their personal experience that they think might help clients gain some greater self-understanding and think more deeply about themselves. Self-disclosure can be a powerful intervention, particularly when it allows clients to feel that they are not alone with their struggles. Empirical research shows that self-disclosure is perceived by clients as being very helpful, and it may be particularly helpful because experienced helpers use it infrequently. In contrast, beginning helpers often disclose too much because they overidentify with clients and are less skilled in keeping their unresolved issues from impinging on the helping process.

When to Use Immediacy

Immediacy is a useful intervention when there are problems in the therapeutic relationship such that therapeutic progress is impeded, or when the client's behavior in sessions is maladaptive and feedback would be helpful. Immediacy allows helpers to provide feedback to clients about how they are perceived in sessions and to gain some insight about why they act as they do. It is important that helpers admit their own feelings in addition to giving clients feedback about their behaviors. Discussing the relationship can provide a powerful learning experience because helpers are demonstrating to clients how to deal with interpersonal conflict in a respectful yet assertive manner. Thus, problems can be resolved, clients can gain some insight into the reasons for their behaviors, and clients can learn the skills to handle interpersonal conflicts better in relationships outside of the helping situation.

Caveats

Several caveats apply to the use of insight interventions. First, the therapeutic relationship must be solid before any insight skills are used. Clients must trust their helpers, and helpers must have a base of knowledge about clients from which to formulate insight interventions. A relationship can sometimes be established quickly, but at other times, a long period of testing is needed before the relationship can withstand insight interventions. In addition, helpers should always be attentive to client reactions to insight interventions. The most superb interventions are worthless if clients are not ready for them; relationships can be damaged by premature insight interventions.

Insight interventions need to be delivered with caring and empathy rather than judgment or blame. They should be preceded by and interspersed with exploration skills (i.e., reflection of feelings, restatement, and open questions). As clients contemplate what they have learned from insight interventions, they are in effect at a new level and need time and support to explore what they have discovered about themselves.

In addition, insight interventions often need to be repeated many times in diverse ways over long periods of time so that clients can begin to incorporate them, use them to change their thinking, and apply them to different parts of their lives. Altering ingrained ways of thinking is often difficult, and repetition often assists clients in coming to awareness and being able to use the new insights. We also stress that the process in the insight stage needs to be collaborative. Helpers and clients need to work together to construct understanding rather than helpers articulating all the insights for the clients.

Furthermore, although we postulate that clients need to understand the reasons for their current troubles and ways of being to improve their functioning, we recognize that not all clients are interested in or willing to search for insight. Thus, helpers will not pursue this deep understanding with all clients. Helpers might move more directly into action for clients who need an immediate sense of symptom relief, desperately need problem resolution, or have no interest in insight.

Helper countertransference can interfere with the helper's ability to deliver insight interventions effectively. *Countertransference* refers to thoughts and feelings about the helper's personal issues that are stimulated by clients. For example, a client talking about abortion or divorce might stimulate unresolved feelings about these issues on the part of a helper, or a helper who has problems dealing with anger might withdraw when a client becomes angry at her. We stress that helpers should seek supervision or personal therapy to help them work on their personal issues to ensure that these issues do not negatively influence the helping relationship.

DEVELOPMENT OF HYPOTHESES ABOUT CLIENT DYNAMICS

To make decisions about how to intervene in the insight stage, helpers rely in part on their perceptions and intuitions. They use themselves as barometers of what is going on in the relationship. They allow themselves to have their inner reactions and then question what they contribute and what the client contributes to their interactions. Helpers can ask themselves the following questions to begin to assess client dynamics.

- Are there discrepancies or contradictions in feelings, actions, or thoughts expressed by the client?
- What might be causing the client to behave this way at this time?
- What contributes to keeping this client from changing at this time?
- What are the client defenses, resistances, and transferences operating in this situation?
- How am I feeling in the therapeutic relationship and could others react similarly to this client?
- How do my unresolved issues contribute to the dynamics of this relationship?

Students can reflect about their hypotheses regarding the client's dynamics outside of the session. For example, in one training session, a client talked about not having been accepted into graduate school and feeling unsure about what he wanted to do—did he really want to go to graduate school or do something else with his life? After students provided their self-disclosures (and most students could relate to this topic), we stopped the interaction and discussed our emerging conceptualizations of this client. We wondered together whether the client had problems with committing himself in other areas. We speculated about family pressures with regard to attending graduate school. Such speculation can be helpful to identify other issues for consideration in the insight stage. It is important for helpers to begin to develop intentions for interventions by hypothesizing about the client's problem, the reason he or she is talking about the problem at this particular time, and what the helper can do to help. Conceptualization enables helpers to have a focus and intentions for interventions instead of just wandering around aimlessly in sessions.

DIFFICULTIES HELPERS EXPERIENCE IN THE INSIGHT STAGE

Becoming competent in the skills used during the insight stage is difficult; it often takes many years to master these skills. In addition, the skills cannot be applied in a rote, technical fashion to every client, which makes it challenging for instructors to teach and for students to learn these skills. Helpers have to use their intuition and rely on their experiences of clients, so there is more danger of countertransference interfering with the process. We encourage helpers to proceed slowly and observe client reactions to their interventions, but not to avoid doing insight interventions because they might miss helping clients understand themselves at deeper levels.

AN EXAMPLE OF AN EXTENDED INTERACTION

In the example below, the helper has already established rapport and explored the client's feelings about her relationship with her daughter. We start from where the helper enters into the insight stage:

Helper: "So you said that your daughter is not doing well in middle school and you're worried that she's going to flunk out of school." (The helper wants to tie together what the client has been talking about and so offers a summary statement.)

Client: "Yeah, she just never does her homework. She watches television all the time, talks on the phone to her friends constantly, and eats. She's not even doing any extracurricular activities at school. I just can't get her to do anything. She just got her grades, which she wouldn't even let me see at first, but I finally got them from her, and she's flunking two classes."

Helper: "Have you considered getting her a tutor?" (The helper jumps prematurely to the action stage here to offer suggestions for what to do about the problem.)

Client: "We keep trying to get her to a tutor, but she doesn't want one. Last year we made her see a tutor, but it didn't help. She still flunked the course, and we wasted a lot of money."

Helper: "You sound really frustrated." (The helper comes back to a focus on the client instead of on the client's daughter.)

Client: "Yeah, I really am frustrated. I just don't know what to do. I feel so helpless. School was so important to me, and I just feel like if she doesn't get a good education, she won't get anywhere in life." (The client really takes in the reflection and talks in more depth about her feelings about the problem with her daughter.)

Helper: "You know, in my experience with my kids, it was really hard to separate myself from them. I wanted so much for them to be perfect to show that I was a perfect parent." (Helper uses self-disclosure to stimulate client insight.)

Client: "Yeah, I get into that. I feel like I'm not a very good parent. Everyone else's kids are doing so well. They're all talking about their kids going to these expensive colleges. I want my kids to have all the things I didn't have and not feel as bad about themselves as adults as I do."

Helper: "You really want the best for your children." (Helper shows support through a restatement.)

Client: "Yeah. Education wasn't a big thing in my family. My parents pushed me on religion and health food. In fact, they were really pushy, well at least my mother was pushy about wanting me to be a missionary. We had such incredible fights when I was a teenager. They didn't even notice that I did well in school. So it was something that I could do on my own."

Helper: "Interesting—you wanted to be independent from your parents and make your own decisions in life, but you want your daughter to do what you tell her to do." (Helper challenges client with a contradiction of which the client seems to be unaware.)

Client: "Wow, you're right! I can't believe that I would be doing the same thing to her that my parents did to me. I guess it seemed like such a different thing. I want her to do well in school, and my parents wanted to control me about religion. But I don't know how to be any different. I really try hard to be a good parent. It's so important to me."

Helper: "I wonder if you think I'm judging you and maybe thinking you're bad for your parenting?" (Helper picks up on the client's self-blaming and wants to see if she feels negatively toward her, so helper uses an immediacy statement.)

Client: "Well, I don't know if you blame me. I blame myself. I just don't know how to quit doing what I'm doing with my daughter. I feel stuck. I don't know any other way to be a parent. I've tried as hard as I can."

Helper: "You're feeling very discouraged." (Helper reflects feelings to support client.)

Client: "When I was younger, I didn't want to be a parent because I thought I would be such a rotten parent. I thought people should have to pass tests before they could become parents. There are so many rotten parents out there. But I was in therapy for a lot of years, and I thought I had solved a lot of my problems. But I guess I didn't solve them all. You know it was so much easier when the kids were younger."

Helper: "Perhaps you're having problems now that your kids are teenagers because that's when you had your problems with your parents. You didn't get much of a model on how to be a parent of teenagers." (Helper interprets client's current difficulties as related to past experiences.)

Client: "Boy, that's really true. I sure didn't. You know, I still haven't forgiven my parents for some of the things they did. You wouldn't believe how controlling my mother was."

Helper: "You still have some anger at them. I wonder if you can identify with your daughter's anger?" (Helper reflects feelings and interprets a parallel of her feelings with her daughter's to help client get some empathy with daughter.)

Client: "Yeah, I know she feels angry at me. And you know, I feel good that she can express it. I used to just withdraw and get depressed when I was a kid. She at least can express herself pretty well sometimes. You know she does have a lot of spirit. She's different from me in some ways, yet in some ways she's a lot like me. School really is difficult for her. It's not fun for her to sit down and read a book like it is for me. She's just not academically oriented. But I guess she has to find her own way. She's not 5 years old anymore. Maybe I just have to trust that she will find herself. I have to accept her as she is just as I have to accept myself as I am. Maybe what I need to do is go back and do some more work on myself to see why I'm so controlling."

Helper: "You've done a really good job of focusing on yourself. You've gone from blaming your daughter to looking at your part in this whole situation." (Helper wants to reinforce client for all the work she's done.)

Client: "Yeah, it's not easy though. It's so much easier to blame her."

Helper: "How do you feel about the work we've done today in trying to understand your conflicts with your daughter?" (Helper asks how the client is feeling about their interaction.)

Client: "I think I have a new understanding of my issues with my daughter. I'm not sure yet that I'll be able to stop having the fights because they happen so quickly, but I do have more of an idea of what my part in the struggles is all about. I'll need to do a lot more thinking about what kind of relationship I want to have with my daughter."

What Do You Think?

- What would you have done differently as a helper in the previous example to help the client attain insight?

- Several of our students have noted how difficult it is to use the interventions in the insight stage. They have said that the exploration skills seemed easy, whereas now all of a sudden the insight skills seem hard. What is your experience?

- Many students forget to use the exploration skills when they are trying to use challenge, interpretation, self-disclosure, and immediacy. They revert to using lots of closed questions. What is your experience? What can you do to remember to integrate the exploration skills into the insight stage?

- How do you think clients react to the insight skills as compared to the exploration skills?

- Debate the advantages and disadvantages of the insight stage. Identify the benefits and possible problems with moving clients to deeper awareness.

IDEAS FOR RESEARCH

Many ideas need to be tested empirically in the insight stage. The following are a few suggestions that we hope stimulate thinking about research in this stage:

- What is the best timing for presenting challenge, interpretation, self-disclosure, and immediacy? What is the role of the therapeutic relationship, point in helping, and client readiness in relation to using these interventions?

- When is it useful to challenge a client before interpreting?

- If clients are very defended, what is the most effective way to challenge and interpret?

- How do clients respond to challenges and interpretations if presented tentatively versus absolutely?

- At what points in the helping process are different types of self-disclosure (e.g., disclosing feelings, disclosing insight, disclosing strategies) helpful?

- What types of helpers are uncomfortable or have difficulty delivering challenge, interpretation, self-disclosure, and immediacy?

- When does self-disclosure facilitate the development of the therapeutic relationship in cross-cultural situations?

- At what point does self-disclosure become harmful to the process and outcome of helping?

- What degree of disclosure is most helpful for different types of clients (e.g., does providing extremely personal information make compliant vs. resistant clients uncomfortable or damage their respect for the helper?)

- What is the best method of training to assist helpers in learning the skills in the insight stage?

- When should helpers provide insight, and when should they facilitate clients in coming to their own insights?

- What are the characteristics of emotional and intellectual insight? How are they similar and different? How can helpers assess the level of emotional and intellectual insight obtained by their clients?

- Do exploration and insight skills differentially influence emotional and intellectual insight?

- What is the course of the development of emotional and intellectual insight over the course of helping?

- How do transference and countertransference influence the use of the insight skills by helpers and the perception of the skills by clients?

Conducting research on the insight stage is more difficult than conducting research on the exploration stage. To study the exploration stage, researchers can use first or one-shot brief sessions because they are investigating the beginning of helping. In contrast, it is preferable for researchers interested in the insight stage to study relationships that are established. For example, helpers typically use challenge, interpretation, or immediacy depending on whether the relationship is strong enough to withstand the intervention. Furthermore, it is more difficult to use scripted interventions of the insight skills compared with the easier exploration skills because insight interventions need to be tailored to specific client dynamics. These issues make it difficult to study the insight skills. We propose that most studies of skills in this stage need to be naturalistic (i.e., study helping as it naturally occurs rather than experimentally manipulating the helping). We also suggest that qualitative methods can be useful in examining the inner experiences of participants in the insight stage (see Hill, Thompson, & Williams, 1997).

LAB 11 Integration of Exploration and Insight Skills

You are ready to integrate the skills that you have learned so far. In this lab, you will meet with a client and first use exploration skills to help the client explore. Then you will use both exploration and insight skills to facilitate the client gaining insight. Note that forms needed for this lab are at the end of chapter 11.

Goal: For helpers to participate in a 40-min helping session using the exploration and insight skills.

Helper's and Client's Tasks During the Helping Interchange

1. Each helper should be paired with a volunteer client whom they do not know.
2. Helpers should photocopy the necessary forms and bring them to the session: The session review form (Table 11.2), the helper intentions list (Appendix A), and client reactions system (Appendix D).
3. Helpers should bring an audio- (or video-) tape recorder (tested ahead of time to ensure that it works) and a tape. They should turn the recorder on at the beginning of the session.
4. Helpers should introduce themselves and remind clients that everything they say is kept confidential. Helpers should indicate exactly who will listen to the session (e.g., peer, supervisor).
5. Each helper should conduct a 40-min session with the client. Be as helpful to your client as possible. Use exploration skills to help the client explore for about 20 min, and then move to combining exploration and insight skills to help the client gain insight for about 20 min. Watch for the client's reactions to each of your interventions and modify subsequent interventions when appropriate.
6. Watch your time carefully. About 2 min before your time is up, let the client know that you need to stop soon. Let the client know when to stop by saying something like, "We need to stop now. Thank you for helping me practice my helping skills."

Supervisor's Tasks During Session

Supervisors should monitor sessions so that they can provide feedback to helpers about basic helping skills. Supervisors can use the supervisor rating form shown in Table 11.3 to record their observations and evaluations.

Helper's and Client's Tasks During the Postsession Review of the Tape

1. After the session, each helper should go over the tape with the client (review of a 40-min session takes about 90 min. Alternatively, helpers might just review 10 min of each stage). Helpers should stop the tape after each helper intervention (except minimal acknowledgments such as "mmhmm," and "yeah"). Helpers should write down the key words on the session review form so that the exact spot on the tape can be located later for transcribing the session.

(Continues)

2. Helpers should rate the helpfulness of the intervention and write down the numbers (from the helper intentions list; see Appendix A) of up to three intentions that they had for the intervention. Helpers should respond according to how they felt during the session rather than when listening to the tape of the session. Use the whole range of the Helpfulness Scale and as many categories as possible on the helper intentions list. Do not complete these ratings collaboratively with clients.

3. Clients should rate the helpfulness of each intervention and write down the numbers of up to three reactions (from the client reactions system; see Appendix D), circling any reactions that they hid from (i.e., did not share with) helpers during the session. Clients should respond according to how they felt during session rather than how they feel listening to the tape of the session. Clients should use the whole range of the helpfulness scale and as many categories as possible on the reactions system (helpers learn more from honest feedback than from "nice" statements that are not genuine). Do not collaborate with helpers in doing the ratings.

4. Helpers and clients should write down the most helpful and least helpful event in the session.

5. Helpers should type a transcript of their 40-min session (see sample transcript in Table 11.4). You can skip minimal utterances such as "okay," "you know," "er," "uh."

6. Divide the helper speech into response units (essentially grammatical sentences). See Appendix C for directions.

7. Using the helping skills system (see Appendix B), determine which skill was used for each response unit (i.e., grammatical sentence) in your transcript.

8. Indicate on the transcript what you would say differently for each intervention if you could do it again.

9. Erase the tape. Make sure that no identifying information is on the transcript.

Personal Reflections

- What did you learn about yourself as a helper from this experience?
- How did you feel about using the insight skills? Some helpers feel intrusive using the insight skills. Was this true for you? If so, speculate about what makes it difficult for you to delve deeply into inner dynamics.
- Which skills are you most and least comfortable using? What might you do to increase your comfort with skills that you were not comfortable using?
- Discuss how well you were able to select skills to match your intentions. How might you improve on this ability?
- Compare your performance of this session with your performance of Labs 1 and 6. What differences have you noticed? How do you account for the differences?
- Many students report difficulty integrating the different skills. How did you feel about your ability to choose from among the various skills?

IV ACTION STAGE

18 Overview of the Action Stage

The only way to make sense out of change is to plunge into it, move with it, and
join the dance.

Alan Watts

Consuela sought help because she was feeling vaguely uninterested in life. Through exploration
with her helper, she described her situation as being devoid of close friendships and feeling
isolated. She also indicated that she had not been doing well in her job since she was promoted
to a managerial position. She described her childhood as idyllic, with no major problems. After
further exploration, Consuela revealed that her parents had been killed in a car accident a year
ago. In the insight stage, the helper and Consuela began to piece together that Consuela had
not had a chance to grieve the loss of her parents because she felt pressured to perform in her
new job. Since she had moved to a new city to take the job right before her parents' deaths,
she had not made any friends who could have supported her in the aftermath. In addition,
Consuela's childhood did not sound as idyllic as she had initially indicated, in that Consuela
had gone through a rough adolescence with many fights with her parents. Through the helping
process, she was able to understand that she felt anger at her parents because they had been
so strict and had not allowed her to develop friendships outside the home. Although she still
missed her parents and the support they provided, Consuela came to realize that she needed
to move on. At this point, the helper felt that Consuela had some insight into her vague lack
of interest in life and decided to move into the action stage. Consuela indicated that she had
three areas in which she wanted to change: making new friends, dealing with the stress of her
job, and resolving her anger toward her parents. They decided to work first on assertiveness
training because that would help her to make friends and to deal with issues at work. After
several sessions, she had gained some confidence in dealing with friends and work; she was
then ready to work on her anger and unresolved grief over her parents' deaths.

DURING THE exploration stage, helpers work with clients to establish a relationship and
to examine the thoughts, feelings, and behaviors related to their problems. During the
insight stage, helpers collaborate with clients to construct an understanding of their problems. After helpers and clients have explored and obtained insight about the what and why
of the problem, they are ready for the action stage, which provides them with an opportunity to generate, explore, and choose options for addressing the problems and help clients
begin to make changes. Changes may be in thoughts (e.g., fewer self-defeating statements),
feelings (e.g., less hostility), or behaviors (e.g., less overeating). Thus, exploration leads to
insight, which leads to action.

Sometimes the newly gained insight leads spontaneously to thinking about action.
Clients begin to say things like, "I can see that I've been so angry at the world because it felt
unfair that I am not as smart and good looking as my brother. I don't need to feel so angry

now, because I can accept who I am and see that I have things to offer other people. I am going to do the things that I want to do with my life," or "It makes sense that I had a hard time in my job if I kept treating my boss like my father. I don't need to do that anymore. I'm going to stand up to him and ask him for a raise." Hence, moving on to the action stage comes naturally to some clients as they begin to talk about how they might apply what they have learned about themselves in the insight stage.

At other times, however, insight does not always lead spontaneously to action, perhaps because clients might not have gained an adequate amount of insight. They might feel stuck, understand the situation incompletely or only at an intellectual level, or not take personal responsibility for their role in the maintenance of the problem. For example, Stefan might realize intellectually that he is upset about being fired, but he might not have allowed himself to feel the humiliation of the loss or the anger at his boss for the injustice. He also might not have understood that he set himself up in self-defeating ways. Expressing, understanding, and accepting his feelings and his role in creating the situation are important tasks prior to moving to action.

Another reason that insight might not lead to action is that clients might not have the skills to move to action. For example, even though a client understands why she is not assertive and wants to change this behavior, she might not know how to stand up for herself. Clients cannot behave more assertively if they do not have the skills associated with being assertive (e.g., maintaining eye contact, stating needs directly without blaming) in their repertoire. Hence, they may need to be taught specific skills. They may need to practice and get feedback to develop the skills.

Even if clients understand themselves thoroughly and have the skills to change, however, they may lack motivation to change. Clients might feel blocked from changing because old habits are hard to alter and they are afraid of trying anything new (e.g., a client learning to be more assertive might be reluctant to confront a friend for fear of losing the friendship). They may feel demoralized and not believe they can change. They may need specific encouragement and practice trying out different behaviors.

In addition, clients cannot always make all the changes they might want or need to make because of limited talents and resources. For example, if Andrew is not very bright and has earned poor grades in college, getting into a high-ranking graduate program is an unlikely proposition. Hence, the goal of this stage is to enable clients to learn to make changes within the limits of the possibilities and to expand these possibilities as much as possible. In the earlier example, Andrew's helper might help him explore advanced training in a related field so that he can pursue a career related to his goals. Although this view does not fit with the idealistic notion that every person can do whatever he or she wants, it fits with the more realistic idea of realizing one's limits and maximizing one's potentials within the limits.

There are two important reasons for moving beyond insight to action. First, because most clients seek help to change specific behaviors, thoughts, or feelings, it is important to help them attain the goals that they choose after thorough exploration. Second, taking action is crucial for consolidating the new thinking patterns learned in the insight stage. Action concretizes the abstract insights for clients into more permanent schemas. Moreover, new understandings can be fleeting unless something is done to help the client consolidate them. Old thinking patterns and behaviors easily resurface unless new thinking and behaviors are practiced and incorporated. For example, Miguel's old thinking pattern might be that he is worthless unless he is perfect. When the helper challenges his thoughts, Miguel comes to realize that he does not have to be perfect to accept himself. Miguel also might come to the insight that he always acts needy and dependent because his parents never accepted him for who he was. They idealized his older, brilliant, successful brother because they never achieved much in their own lives. They had constantly put Miguel down for being only average in intelligence. He might come to realize that even though his parents do not accept him fully for who he is, he is still a worthy and lovable person. These insights are fragile and may erode unless the helper helps Miguel understand them on a deeper level and really incorporate the learning into a new pattern of behavior and thinking. Thus, the helper works with Miguel to accept himself. They devise a list of things that Miguel has always wanted to do (e.g., skydiving, Rollerblading, going back to school) and figure out how he can pursue these activities. Beginning to do things that he wants to do and at which he succeeds enables Miguel to feel better about himself. The helper also works with Miguel to help him develop friends who approve of what he does so that he can receive social support. When he feels better about himself, Miguel can begin to question the things he has told himself about needing to be perfect. Hence, Miguel cycles back to insight after making changes.

In the action stage, we focus on making changes in behaviors, thoughts, and feelings, but we also are involved in exploring feelings and examining values, priorities, barriers, and support in relation to change. Hence, helpers need to be just as empathic and supportive as they were in earlier stages. Mickelson and Stevic (1971) found that behaviorally oriented counselors who were warm, empathic, and genuine were more effective in generating information-seeking responses in their clients than were those who were low in these facilitative conditions.

This stage, then, is still very client centered, with helpers facilitating clients in thinking about change rather than imposing change on them. Helpers do not have to know the best action plans for clients. In fact, helpers rarely need to form an opinion about what clients "must" or "should" do. The goal for helpers in this stage is to provide a supportive environment and facilitate clients in resolving their problems and making their decisions. Furthermore, when clients decide for themselves what to do differently, they are more likely to take responsibility and ownership for their actions than if helpers tell them what to do. Having helpers tell them what to do, even if clients ask for advice, is not typically helpful, because clients become dependent on the helpers. Helpers cannot always be there for clients, so they need to teach clients how to motivate themselves to change and how to implement changes in their lives. Thus, rather than solving clients' problems, helpers seek to enhance clients' problem-solving capacities. With enhanced coping skills, clients can address the specific problems that led them to seek help and be better equipped to solve problems in the future.

Hence, helpers need to try to be uninvested in whether and how clients change. The client's change is not a reflection on the helper but a statement about the client. Thus, the helper's goal is to encourage clients to explore whether they want to change and, if so, to assist clients in making the changes they have identified as desirable. Although this objective stance is difficult to achieve, it is crucial that helpers not care which direction clients choose but still care for the client. Otherwise, it is too easy to replicate childhood patterns where clients act or do not act to get the attention of, please, or defy helpers as they did their parents. Instead, helpers need to collaborate with clients in making their own choices. Helpers thus serve as facilitators of the process rather than as experts who provide the answers and tell clients what to do. It is important for clients to understand the helper's role and to realize that helpers are not invested in a particular action plan.

At a minimum, we suggest that helpers ask what clients would like to do differently once they have gained some insight into their problems. In this way, helpers emphasize that insight is not enough and that change is necessary and possible. Initially, helpers might suggest that clients think about action (e.g., "What might you think about doing differently?" or "How would you like to be different if you could do anything that you wanted?"). Of course, helpers can go well beyond raising the issue of action. They also can actively facilitate clients in working on action: role-playing difficult situations, teaching clients specific skills, helping clients make decisions or solve problems, teaching relaxation, and so on.

We use an example to illustrate the need for the action stage and show how it is implemented. Kondja acted silly (e.g., giggled uncontrollably) when she went to dances because she was extremely nervous. Because Kondja felt so embarrassed and panicked when she acted silly, she would leave the dance early and then feel bad that she had missed all the fun. Through exploration and insight, she came to realize that her anxiety at dances was due to her fear of being with men. She was afraid that no one would like her because her brothers had made so much fun of her when she was a child. Her brothers had told her that she was ugly and had taunted her about her face and hair. Insight was not enough, however; Kondja needed something to help her deal with the anxiety in the situation. The helper taught her relaxation and then strategized with her about how to handle specific situations at dances. When she felt a "silly" attack coming on, she and the helper planned that she would take a time out in the bathroom, practice deep breathing, and watch what she was saying to herself. After practicing several times in sessions, Kondja was able to attend a dance and enjoy it. She was even able to let a man touch her and allow herself to think that she was attractive. Being able to master the situation made her feel better about herself. She could then begin to reevaluate whether she was indeed ugly and wonder what motivated her brothers to be so mean to her. Hence, insight led to action, which in turn led to more insight.

With some clients, helpers need to move to action more quickly and shorten the exploration and insight stages more than usual. Such clients need more direct interventions because they are in crisis, are not psychologically minded, or cannot articulate their concerns. For example, a person who has been kicked out of his house, has no job or food, and has delusions may need more immediate help in terms of housing, food, and medication before he can focus on understanding. To rephrase Maslow's (1970) statement, "people cannot live on bread alone unless they have no bread." For these clients, after they have received direct guidance about how to solve a pressing problem, they might be willing to go back and understand what contributed to the problem or work on other problems. However, not everyone values insight. Some clients just want something or someone to make them feel better. Helpers know that clients do not want insight when they respond negatively to insight-oriented interventions and resist all attempts to achieve deeper understanding of their issues (of course, helpers must question whether they have approached the insight stage appropriately in these circumstances). Hence, in some cases, action comes after exploration and may or may not be accompanied by insight.

COGNITIVE–BEHAVIORAL THEORIES

Cognitive–behavioral theories lay the theoretical foundation for the action stage. In this section, we discuss the assumptions of cognitive–behavioral theories, the principles of learning, and treatment strategies.

Assumptions

The various cognitive and behavioral theories share several basic assumptions (Gelso & Fretz, 1992; Rimm & Masters, 1979):

- They focus on overt behaviors (including cognitions) rather than unconscious motivations.
- They focus on symptoms and what maintains them currently rather than what caused them.
- They posit that behaviors (including cognitions) are learned.
- They emphasize the present as opposed to the past.
- They stress the importance of specific, clearly defined goals.
- They value an active, directive, and prescriptive role for helpers.
- They posit that the helper–client relationship is important but not sufficient.
- They focus on determining adaptive behavior for a situation rather than on personality change.
- They rely on empirical data and scientific methods in developing therapeutic interventions.

Principles of Learning

Because one of the defining characteristics of these approaches is that behaviors, emotions, and cognitions (both adaptive and maladaptive) are learned (Gelso & Fretz, 1992), we discuss how this learning takes place according to learning theory. We cover four types of learning: classical (or respondent) conditioning, operant conditioning, modeling (also called *observational learning*), and cognitively mediated learning. Although the four types of learning are not as distinct as it was once thought, it is still useful to be knowledgeable about all of the separate types.

Classical or Respondent Conditioning

Pavlov (1927) first identified classical or respondent conditioning in his work with dogs. Prior to conditioning, he noted, only some stimuli elicit involuntary responses (e.g., food elicits salivation or noise elicits a startle response). In classical conditioning terms, the unconditioned stimulus (e.g., food) elicits an unconditioned response (e.g., salivation). However, when a stimulus that was previously neutral is paired several times with an unconditioned stimulus, the new stimulus takes on the conditioning properties of the original stimulus. Hence, if a bell is rung immediately before food is offered for several trials, a dog salivates to the sound of the bell even when it is presented without the food. The bell is now a conditioned stimulus, and the response of salivation to the bell is a conditioned response. The previously neutral stimulus takes on the power to elicit the response. Furthermore, the organism (in this case the dog) learns to discriminate which stimuli lead to reinforcement (e.g., the bell) and which do not (e.g., a trumpet). Learning generalizes (i.e., transfers) from one conditioned stimulus to other similar ones (e.g., bells of different tones). However, the conditioned response (e.g., salivation in response to the bell) extinguishes (i.e., gradually lessens and disappears) if the conditioned stimulus (e.g., the bell) is presented repeatedly without at least an occasional pairing with the unconditioned stimulus (e.g., the food).

J. B. Watson and Rayner (1920) demonstrated that emotional responses also could be acquired through classical conditioning. They first observed that Albert, an 11-month-old boy, had a startle and fear reaction (an unconditioned response) to a loud noise (an unconditioned stimulus), although he had no fear when playing with a white rat. They then paired the rat with a loud noise. Whenever Albert reached out to touch the rat, the noise sounded and Albert was startled. After only seven pairings, Albert cried when the rat was presented without the noise. Hence, after conditioning, the conditioned stimulus (i.e., the rat) elicited the fear response. Furthermore, Albert's fear response generalized to other white furry things that he had not been afraid of previously (e.g., a rabbit, a dog, and a Santa Claus mask). Hence, the development of anxieties and phobias may be at least partially due to classical conditioning.

Operant Conditioning

Operant conditioning assumes that behaviors are controlled by their consequences, or the reinforcements and punishments (Kazdin, 1994; Rimm & Masters, 1979; Skinner, 1953). Reinforcement is anything that follows a behavior and increases the probability that the behavior occurs again. An event, behavior, privilege, or material object whose addition increases the likelihood of a behavior occurring again is called a *positive reinforcement*. Primary reinforcers (e.g., food, water, and sex) are biological necessities, whereas secondary reinforcers (e.g., praise or money) gain their reinforcing properties through association with primary reinforcers. An example of a positive reinforcer related to helping is an approval–reassurance given after a client talks about feelings. We should note that reinforcers are not always reinforcing (e.g., food is typically reinforcing only if a person is hungry) and that reinforcers are not the same for all individuals (e.g., a long bath may be reinforcing for one person but not another). Whether something is a reinforcer can only be determined by looking at whether the target behavior occurs in response to the reinforcer being administered. Thus, a helper cannot determine if something is reinforcing until the client response is observed.

For a behavior to be reinforced, it first must be performed. Hence, helpers often have to engage in shaping to get the person to emit the behavior. Shaping refers to the gradual training of a complex response by reinforcing closer and closer approximations to the desired behavior. Goldfried and Davison (1994) give the example of training a developmentally disabled child to make his bed by first reinforcing him for fluffing up his pillow, then pulling the top sheet forward, and so on. Each of these acts is a successive approximation of the final desired behavior. An example of shaping, related to learning helping skills, is when we practice first with repeating what clients said, then saying the main word, and then doing restatements.

An event whose removal increases the probability of the occurrence of the desired behavior is called a *negative reinforcement*. The removal can be by escape (e.g., leaving the room during a fight) or by avoidance (e.g., avoiding fights). Primary aversive stimuli are things that are inherently punitive (e.g., shock, noise, and pain), whereas secondary aversive stimuli (e.g., disapproval) are things that have gained their aversive quality from being paired with primary aversive agents. For example, if a child stops crying when the parent picks him or her up, the parent is more likely to pick up the child because picking up the child stopped the crying. Other examples are using an umbrella to avoid getting wet in the rain or putting on a seat belt to avoid the warning buzzer.

In contrast, punishment occurs after a behavior and reduces the probability that the behavior occurs again. Goldfried and Davison (1994) identified three punishment procedures: (a) presenting an aversive event (e.g., a frown when the client reports something undesirable), (b) removing a person from a situation where she or he would otherwise be able to earn reinforcers (e.g., a time-out in a room separate from the counselor who could provide positive reinforcement), and (c) reducing a person's collection of reinforcers (e.g., taking away candy). The purpose of punishment in clinical situations is to decrease the frequency of maladaptive behaviors.

To work, reinforcement or punishment must be contingent on, or linked directly to, the behavior (Rimm & Masters, 1979). An office worker who receives a raise every 3 months regardless of the quality of work is less likely to improve than one whose raise is contingent on good performance. However, it is especially difficult to deliver punishment contingent to behavior. Very often, what gets punished is being discovered rather than the behavior itself. Hence, when punishment is used as the primary mode of behavior management, people often figure out how to avoid getting caught rather than decrease the problematic behavior. For example, a child who steals cookies from the cookie jar feels great when he gets the cookies because they taste good, but he feels lousy several hours later when he gets caught because it does not feel good to get caught and be punished. Because the punishment is contingent with getting caught rather than eating the cookies, he figures that he should not get caught again. If he is clever, he figures out a way to get the cookies without getting caught.

Another important behavioral concept is generalization, which involves the transfer of learning from one situation to other, similar situations. For example, if kicking and hitting are punished with time outs and cooperative behavior is positively reinforced at school, one would expect the decrease in kicking and hitting and the increase in cooperative behavior to generalize to the home setting. These behaviors are most likely to generalize if they are punished and reinforced in the same manner in the home setting as in the school setting. Another example of generalization is when a person acts frightened by a teacher or helper because she or he was punished by authority figures in the past (a concept that is similar to transference).

Extinction reduces the probability of a behavior occurring by withholding reinforcers after the behavior is established (Goldfried & Davison, 1994). For example, if a parent's attention is maintaining fighting among siblings (when no other problems are apparent), a helper might instruct the parents to stop attending to the fighting (unless one child is in danger of getting hurt) in the hopes that it will extinguish. Goldfried and Davison noted that extinction often is facilitated by concurrently reinforcing an incompatible and more adaptive behavior. Thus, in the previous example, the parents might also praise the siblings when they play together constructively.

Although the concepts of operant conditioning sound relatively straightforward, it is often very challenging for helpers to use them because of the complexity of human nature and because helpers often have minimal control over the reinforcers and punishments in the environment. Furthermore, Goldfried and Davison (1994) noted that helpers typically do not reinforce the actual changes but rather the client's talking about making specific changes. Clients have to transfer the reinforcement of talking about changing to making the changes outside the session. Thus, helpers often act more as consultants to clients than as actual change agents, suggesting that clients actually have to be self-changers.

Modeling

People sometimes learn things even though they have never been reinforced for performing them. The explanation for this learning is through modeling or observational learning, which occurs when an individual observes another person (a model) engage in a particular behavior (Kazdin, 1994). The observer sees the model perform the behavior but does not perform the behaviors and does not receive any consequences while observing and learning. The observer also notices whether the actor receives reinforcement or punishment (Bandura, 1977). For example, children learn how to be parents by watching their parents and experiencing the effects of their child-rearing practices. Students learn how to be teachers by observing effective and ineffective educators. Helpers learn how to help by observing the behaviors of effective and ineffective helpers.

To understand how modeling works, we must distinguish learning and performance. A person can observe a model and learn a behavior. Whether the person actually performs the learned behavior, however, depends on the consequences at the time of performance. Bandura (1965) demonstrated this distinction between learning and performance with his classic Bobo doll study. Children observed a film in which an adult hit or kicked a Bobo doll (a life-size, inflatable, plastic doll that is weighted so that it pops upright after you punch it). The adult's behavior was rewarded, punished, or met with no consequences. When the children were put in the room with the Bobo doll, those who had observed the aggression being punished were less aggressive than those who had observed the aggression being rewarded or ignored. When an incentive was given for performing the aggressive behavior, there were no differences among conditions, indicating that the children in all conditions learned the aggressive behaviors equally well. Bandura concluded that the learning occurred through observation but that performance depended on whether the child perceived that the adult was rewarded or punished. Kazdin (1994) noted that imitation of models by observers is greater when models are similar to observers, more prestigious, and higher in status and expertise than observers, and when several models perform the same behavior.

Cognitively Mediated Learning

Early behaviorists believed in a stimulus–response (S-R) model, meaning that people respond directly to environmental cues (e.g., noise leads to a startle response). Cognitive theorists have introduced a stimulus–organism–response (S-O-R) model, suggesting that the organism (i.e., person) processes the stimulus prior to determining how to respond. Thus, we respond not to stimuli, but to our interpretation of stimuli. For example, how we react to a noise heard in the middle of the night is dependent on whether we think it is a benign noise (the house "settling") or made by a burglar. Theorists such as Ellis, Meichenbaum, and Beck suggest that it is not so much events that cause us to become upset, but what we think about the events.

Cognitive processes are of utmost importance to the helping situation. As discussed in chapter 3, much of the helping process takes place at covert levels. Helpers have intentions for their interventions as well as perceptions of clients' reactions that influence their subsequent interventions. In addition, clients have reactions to helpers' interventions as well as intentions for how to influence helpers. Hence, we are postulating a cognitively mediated model for understanding the helping process.

Another cognitive process that is important for helping involves thoughts about one's abilities. Bandura (1986) defined self-efficacy as "people's judgments in their capabilities to organize and execute courses of action required to attain designated types of performance" (p. 361). According to Bandura, self-efficacy relates to initiation of behaviors, persistence despite obstacles, and eventual success. For example, beginning helpers who lack self-efficacy in their helping skills might be very reluctant to role-play their helping skills in front of the instructor. They might use the slightest obstacle (e.g., a bad hair day) as an excuse to not attend class on the day that students are practicing skills. Their lack of confidence would then manifest itself in poor skill development and ineffective helping relationships. Obviously, self-efficacy also applies to the experiences of clients. Attention to the role of cognitions can enable helpers to understand a client's hesitance to try new behaviors. For example, a client who lacks confidence in public speaking might receive poor job evaluations for refusing to present his work in front of customers. Bandura would suggest that providing this client with small success experiences (e.g., having him present his work to you and to small groups of trusted friends) might enhance the client's self-efficacy and enable him to comply with the requirements of his job.

Treatment

Cognitive–behaviorists generally integrate classical, operant, modeling, and cognitive models of learning into their strategies. They focus on specific thoughts or behaviors, make changes in small steps, introduce reinforcers, and make necessary modifications to tailor strategies to clients. Helpers and clients work together collaboratively as scientists to determine what does and does not work. Several specific cognitive–behavioral interventions have been developed, some of which are described below.

Relaxation Training and Systematic Desensitization

An extensive amount of data show that relaxing one's muscles reduces anxiety (Jacobson, 1929; Lang, Melamed, & Hart, 1970; Paul, 1969) and that it is useful to teach certain (particularly anxious) clients to relax (Bernstein & Borkovec, 1973; Goldfried & Trier, 1974). The most commonly used method of relaxation in helping settings involves deep muscle relaxation. Essentially, the helper instructs the client to get comfortable and close her or his eyes. The helper then goes through the body systematically and teaches the client to tense a muscle set in the body (e.g., make fists for 30 s) and then relax (e.g., allowing the feelings of tension to flow out of the hands). The helper uses a very calm, slow, and almost hypnotic voice to take the client through the relaxation exercise, which requires about 45 min to cover all the muscle sets in the body. Helpers ask clients to rate the amount of relaxation they feel at several steps along the way (using something like a 10-point scale where 1 = *totally relaxed* and 10 = *extremely tense*), so that they can determine whether clients are relaxed and so that clients can begin to recognize and label the feelings of anxiety and relaxation in their bodies. Clients often are asked to tape the relaxation session and then practice relaxation on their own for at least 20 min a day.

When clients have mastered the deep muscle form of relaxation, helpers can teach them to relax just by letting go of each muscle group (instead of tensing and then relaxing each muscle group). After several weeks of training, clients can typically evoke the relaxation response just by thinking about relaxing. Clients can also be taught to induce relaxation by deep breathing and imagining a safe haven or relaxing spot (e.g., the beach on a warm summer day or sitting on the porch of a mountain cabin). Helpers can then ask them to imagine themselves in a stressful situation and evoke the relaxation response. Helpers can also encourage them to practice relaxation in actual (in vivo) situations.

A more structured approach to dealing with anxiety-producing situations is systematic desensitization (Salter, 1949; Wolpe, 1958). After teaching relaxation, a helper works with a client to develop a hierarchy, which is a personalized list of a series of increasingly stressful situations. For example, for a client with test anxiety, a situation low on the list might be being told at the beginning of the semester about a test. Midway on the list might be studying for the test the night before. High on the list might be the moment that the test is handed out and the client begins to read the directions. After the list is constructed for the individual client, the helper asks the client to relax and close her or his eyes and then visualize the scene that is lowest on the list. When the client visualizes the image completely, the helper asks the client to use relaxation techniques and relax. After the client is completely relaxed (as indicated by asking the client to choose a number from 1 to 10, with 1 = *completely relaxed* and 10 = *completely anxious*, or by asking the client to raise a finger when completely relaxed), the helper moves to the next item on the list. The helper goes through the complete hierarchy of anxiety-provoking situations, moving at a pace that is comfortable to the client, until the client is able to relax completely while imagining the most anxiety-provoking situation. Helpers then encourage clients to relax in the actual anxiety-provoking situations.

Operant Methods for Behavior Change

The first step in using operant methods for behavior change is to assess the problem carefully. (Recall from earlier in the chapter that operant methods are based on the assumption that behaviors are controlled by their consequences.) The assessment might involve first interviewing the client about the conditions under which the target behavior occurs. Then a helper typically would instruct a client to monitor his or her behavior over the course of 1–2 weeks to gather specific information about the antecedents, behaviors, and consequences. For example, a client who wants to reduce his overeating might be asked to write down all the food he eats, where he eats it, who he is with when he eats, and how he feels before and after eating. Clients often learn that their monitored behavior differs dramatically from what they reported earlier to helpers. For example, an overweight man who claims that he never snacks might learn that he consistently nibbles on something while watching television in the evenings. A person who feels lonely might discover that she never looks people in the eye and does not say hello when passing them in hallways.

When helpers have an idea of the baseline (i.e., typical) behavior, they can help clients determine realistic goals for how they want to change. For example, if an overweight person wants to lose 50 lbs in 1 month, the helper can work with the client to recognize that this goal is unrealistic. Often the goals that clients choose have to be modified to be more attainable. For example, instead of encouraging the overweight client to begin a severely restricted diet of 800 calories per day, the helper might encourage the client to walk 20 min a day in addition to eating more moderately (e.g., 1,500 calories per day) to facilitate gradual weight loss (which is most likely to be maintained).

Helpers also work with clients to identify reinforcers. For example, one client might find it reinforcing to look forward to going on a vacation to a Caribbean island if she can get straight As. Another client might need the more immediate reinforcement of being able to call his girlfriend after he studies for 1 hr.

When the target behavior is identified, baseline information has been gathered, realistic goals set, and reinforcers identified, the helper works with the client to figure out how to modify the behavior. They look for behaviors that need to be increased. For example, for a problem with social anxiety, the helper might identify that the client needs to make more overtures to others. The chosen behaviors must be observable, behavioral, and specific (e.g., smiling at strangers) rather than broad and vague (e.g., becoming more friendly) because specific behaviors are easier to work on and monitor for changes. In addition, helpers need to target specific behaviors to change (e.g., a certain amount of

homework) rather than trying to change the outcome (e.g., the final grade) because the specific behaviors are within one's control whereas the outcome is not always within one's control (e.g., one never knows how instructors will curve the grades). The principle of "baby steps" is also important here. Rather than expecting the client to make huge changes immediately, small changes are more reasonable to attain.

Behavioral Rehearsal or Role-Playing

Behavioral rehearsal or role-playing is used to help clients learn new ways of responding to specific life situations (Goldfried & Davison, 1994). Rather than talking about behavioral changes in the helping setting, new behaviors are taught through acting out situations in which the behaviors could be used. Because assertiveness is the most common problem focused on for behavioral rehearsal, we illustrate interventions designed to increase assertive behaviors.

According to Alberti and Emmons (1974), the goal of assertiveness training is to teach clients to stand up for their rights without infringing on the rights of others. Unassertive people let others walk all over them, whereas aggressive people walk all over other people. Both unassertive and aggressive people can be taught to express both positive and negative feelings more appropriately, although one cannot guarantee that clients get their way when they assert themselves. In fact, aggressive people who are used to getting their way are not likely to respond favorably to a previously unassertive person acting assertively. Hence, helpers also have to assist clients in thinking of ways to respond to escalated aggressiveness.

The first step in assertiveness training is to assess the actual behavior. Helpers might ask clients to describe a typical scene and then role-play exactly how they usually behave (with the helper playing the role of the other person). For example, a client might present with extreme awkwardness and unassertiveness in interactions with interesting men. The helper can role play a situation in which the client meets an attractive man at a party. The helper can observe exactly what the client does, noting particular things like eye contact, voice volume, statement of needs, and attitude. Helpers can also ask clients for self-evaluations of how assertive they were and how they felt in the situation.

Then helpers can work with clients to determine specific goals of how they would like to behave differently. Clients are much more likely to make change when they have specific, clear goals than if they have vague goals. To construct goals, helpers and clients can brainstorm different possible behaviors and determine which behaviors would feel comfortable to clients. We should note that there is no "right" way to be assertive, so this step is crucial in devising goals that clients can embrace. For example, one female client may want to learn how to ask an interesting man for a date, whereas another would not find this action desirable.

When the target behavior is determined, helpers can reverse roles with clients and provide a model of how clients could implement the new behaviors (e.g., the helper could show how she would ask an instructor for an extension of a deadline given a documented illness). Helpers then can ask clients to try the chosen behavior in a role-play, again observing the client's behavior carefully. After the role-play, helpers should provide some honest positive feedback. Even if the positive feedback is about something minor, clients need to feel that they are doing something well and making some progress. Helpers then can give corrective feedback about one or two things, remembering the behavioral principle of working on small, manageable steps. Helpers might also provide some coaching about what clients could try differently in the next role-play (e.g., "Okay, say it louder and with more conviction this time"). Role-plays can be continued until the client feels confident that she or he can perform the desired behaviors. Using videotape feedback can be invaluable because clients may be unaware of how they are perceived. During the role-plays, helpers might also discover that they need to do relaxation training or cognitive restructuring with clients to overcome obstacles to change.

Finally, helpers can encourage clients to try the new behaviors in real life. By examining what happens when clients change their behaviors, helpers can work with clients to modify their behaviors and deal with the reactions of others to their behavioral changes. We want to emphasize that helpers should start with relatively easy behaviors first (e.g., questioning a clerk in a store) rather than major behaviors (e.g., asking for a raise) to maximize the possibility of success. In our previous example, the client might initiate a conversation with a man in class and work up to asking him out on a date.

Cognitive Restructuring

Cognitive theorists have suggested that irrational thinking keeps people from coping effectively and makes them unhappy. Ellis (1962, 1995) suggested that people say irrational things to themselves, such as "I must be loved by everyone," "I must be completely competent and perfect to be worthwhile," "It is awful if things are not the way I want them to be," "There should be someone stronger than me who will take care of me," and "There is a perfect solution to human problems and it is terrible if I don't find it." Beck (1976) added that people make systematic errors in reasoning. He suggested that people draw conclusions without having adequate evidence (e.g., a person might conclude that she is an unlovable person just because she has no one with whom to eat lunch on one day). People also take details out of context (e.g., focus on one negative comment about a presentation in class and ignore several positive ones), develop general rules out of a few instances (e.g., because she made a mistake one time, a person generalizes that she cannot handle any responsibility), and make something more or less important than it is (e.g., perceive a person not saying "hello" as meaning that he is angry; minimizing the importance of failing a course). In addition, people attribute blame to themselves without any evidence (e.g., a secretary believing that a company's going out of business is due to her not coming into work one day), and engage in rigid, either–or thinking (e.g., a man may think that women are either goddesses or whores).

The main goal of cognitive restructuring is to help clients recognize their faulty thinking and change it. To enable clients to recognize their maladaptive thoughts, helpers such as Ellis (1962, 1995) use persuasion and challenges. They attack the irrational thoughts ("What are you telling yourself now?" "You are telling yourself that it would be awful if you did not succeed at being a physicist, but what would be the worst thing that would happen?" "What would be so horrible about that?" "You say you can't stand it, but is that true, would you fall apart?" "It might not be pleasant, but would it actually be catastrophic?"). It is important, however, that helpers attack the beliefs and not the person.

Ellis's approach is didactic, in that he teaches clients an ABC model, where A is the activating event, B is the irrational beliefs, and C is the consequent negative emotional reactions or behaviors. Whereas clients make the assumption that events (A) cause emotions (C), in fact it is the irrational beliefs (B) that lead to negative emotions (C). Hence, if we replace the irrational beliefs (B) with more rational cognitions (D), clients have more positive emotions (E). Ellis would also give clients homework to test out the validity of

their irrational beliefs. He might suggest that a client who worries about what everyone thinks should go out wearing two different colors of socks and see what kind of reaction she receives. He would encourage the client to record her irrational thoughts and combat them with more rational thoughts.

Beck and his colleagues (Beck, 1976; Beck & Emery, 1985; Beck & Freeman, 1990; Beck, Rush, Shaw, & Emery, 1979; Beck & Weishaar, 1995) have developed a cognitive theory that is slightly different from Ellis's theory. They postulated that automatic thoughts and dysfunctional interpretations are the major source of problems for clients. They said that clients miscontrue events on the basis of faulty logic and beliefs in the cognitive triad of the self, world, and future. Hence, clients often view themselves as defective, inadequate, or unlovable; the world as unmanageable, uncontrollable, or overwhelming; and the future as bleak and hopeless. Beck's gentle therapeutic approach is also quite different from Ellis's direct confrontational style. He recommended that helpers work collaboratively with clients as scientists to uncover faulty logic and examine its impact. Helpers ask a series of questions to help clients arrive at logical conclusions ("What happens when you say X to yourself?"). Helpers also actively point out cognitive themes and underlying assumptions that work against clients. In addition, they might devise homework assignments to help clients identify and correct dysfunctional thoughts, assumptions, and behaviors.

How Cognitive–Behavioral Theories Relate to the Three-Stage Model

Cognitive–behavioral theories fit well into the action stage of the helping model because they provide specific strategies for helping clients change. When clients have explored thoughts and feelings thoroughly and obtained insight about themselves, action allows them to determine how they would like to change their lives. Thus, helpers need to focus on action to help clients attain their goals. When used in an empathic and collaborative manner at the appropriate time, cognitive–behavioral treatment can be extremely helpful in facilitating change.

GOALS OF THE ACTION STAGE

The goals for the action stage are for helpers to encourage clients to explore possible new behaviors, assist clients in deciding on actions, facilitate the development of skills for action, provide feedback about attempted changes, assist clients in evaluating action and modifying action plans, and encourage clients to process feelings about action. Helpers need to spend sufficient time in the exploration and insight stages so that clients have enough insight and confidence to determine what actions assist them in attaining their desired outcomes. While in the action stage, helpers need to remember to maintain empathy and pace themselves according to the clients' needs. A stance of exploring action, rather than prescribing action, is typically most helpful.

SKILLS USED IN THE ACTION STAGE

The helping skills used primarily in the action stage are information (about the helping process; or data, facts, opinions) and direct guidance (process advisement or directives). If clients lack important knowledge, helpers can provide information. This educative function is one role of helpers in the action stage. If clients have trouble generating ideas and action plans, helpers might provide direct guidance (i.e., suggest what the client might do). These skills are covered in detail in the next two chapters.

The skills used most frequently in the action stage, however, are the skills used in the exploration and insight stages. Helpers rely on skills from the previous stages to assist clients in determining exactly what changes to make and what steps to take to implement these changes. In particular, open questions (and occasionally closed questions) are useful for obtaining information about what clients have tried before and how they felt about previous efforts. Restatement and reflection of feelings are important to uncover feelings related to change, to demonstrate helper support, and to ensure that helpers accurately hear what clients are saying. When clients are unable to take the actions that they want to take, insight skills such as challenge, interpretation, self-disclosure, and immediacy are useful to probe deeply for obstacles to action.

Unlike in the other two stages where the individual skills are important in and of themselves, the action stage requires combining skills into steps or sequences of interventions. Hence, helpers can integrate the action skills (information and direct guidance) along with the exploration and insight skills into specific steps for change. In addition, helpers can use specific strategies (sequences of steps for specific problems). For example, assertiveness training involves the use of questions to discover the details of the situations in which clients are unassertive, information to educate clients about the process, process advisement to direct clients about how to do the role-playing, reflection of feelings to mirror how clients are reacting, challenges to encourage clients to examine their defenses about changing, interpretations about how they came to be unassertive, and encouragement to reinforce clients for improvements in assertiveness. In chapter 21, we present the steps that helpers can use to guide clients through the action stage.

DIFFICULTIES HELPERS EXPERIENCE IN THE ACTION STAGE

Moving Too Quickly to Action

Some helpers move too quickly to action before they have established a firm foundation of exploration and insight. They might feel impatient with the long process of exploration and insight; they might feel that they "know" what the client should do; they might feel compelled to "do" something for the client. Unfortunately, when helpers move too quickly to action, clients often are "resistant," not attuned with the helper, unable to take responsibility for their changes, or unmotivated to make changes. Helpers need to remember to spend the majority of their time in exploration to establish the foundation for insight and action.

Too Much Investment in Client's Changes

Some helpers become so invested and feel so responsible for developing action plans that they try to make decisions for the client. They feel that things would be much easier if clients just did what helpers told them to do. However, taking over for clients is typically counterproductive (except in extreme cases of suicidal or homicidal ideation or intent) because clients become dependent and do not develop the skills needed to make changes in the future. In addition, what might work for the helper might not work for the client. Furthermore, if helpers become too invested in what they think clients should do, it is difficult for them to listen supportively but objectively to clients. Hence, helpers generally need to be uninvested in what action the client chooses (or does not choose) to pursue. Helpers must allow clients to make their own decisions, serving as guides and supporters rather than bosses.

Imposing One's Values on Clients

Sometimes helpers lose sight of trying to help clients uncover their values and instead impose their own beliefs and values on clients. It is sometimes difficult for helpers to accept that clients have different values, especially when the values differ significantly from the helper's cherished beliefs. For example, a client dying of a terminal illness might want to talk about the possibility of suicide. If helpers are rigid about the value of life, they might not allow clients to explore the possibility of suicide, thus limiting the client's ability to contemplate all the options thoroughly and make an informed decision.

Not Challenging Enough

Helpers may not challenge clients enough to make changes. Some helpers are worried about intruding on their clients and, thus, do not encourage them to change. They believe that it is not their place to challenge. We agree that clients need to be the ones who choose to change, but we believe that helpers can encourage and challenge clients when they are stuck and struggling. In addition, helpers are sometimes nervous about challenging clients because they are not sure what to do to help clients. In this case, we suggest that these helpers study the action skills carefully and practice more.

Not Being Supportive

Sometimes helpers become so involved in developing the action plan during this stage that they forget to be supportive. Encouragement and reinforcement are crucial both for actual change and for efforts to change. We suspect that when helpers remember aspects of their lives that are difficult to change, they are more sympathetic to clients having difficulties with changing.

Getting Stuck on One Plan

Helpers often remain committed to plans that they have developed, even when it is clear that the plans are inappropriate and that clients cannot or will not follow them. Perhaps these helpers have spent a lot of time thinking about what their clients should do and have become very invested in the action plans. However, helpers need to realize that helping requires flexibility; action plans often require adjustment. Rarely is the first action plan perfect, simply because helpers and clients are not aware of all the problems that can arise. They need to select and keep the parts that work and revise the parts that do not.

STRATEGIES FOR OVERCOMING THE DIFFICULTIES

Return to the Exploration Skills

When helpers get trapped in any of the pitfalls (moving too quickly to action, becoming too invested in clients' changing, imposing their values on clients, not being challenging enough, not being supportive enough, or getting stuck on one plan), we recommend returning to the exploration skills (open question, restatement, and reflection). In effect, clients are at a new point in the helping process and helpers need to make sure they understand the problem at this particular time. When clients feel misunderstood, helpers also need to rebuild trust and reassure clients that helpers can listen to them and collaborate with them. In addition, helpers can go back and use the management strategies suggested in chapter 5 for dealing with anxiety (e.g., relaxation, imagery, positive self-talk, focus on the client).

Deal With Problems in the Therapeutic Relationship

Helpers can ask clients how they are feeling about what is going on in the helping relationship, particularly when they have reached an *impasse* (defined by Elkind, 1992, as a deadlock or stalemate that causes helping to become so difficult that progress is not possible). Using immediacy to deal with the relationship and resolve problems is particularly crucial (see Hill et al., 1996; Petersen et al., 1998; Rhodes et al., 1994; and Safran & Muran, 1996). Helpers need to listen for feedback and be willing to hear how they can improve their work with their clients. If appropriate for the helping situation, helpers can talk about their own immediate feelings (without burdening clients with their personal problems). Acknowledging their part in the problems in helping relationships (e.g., apologizing if they have made a mistake) can be therapeutically beneficial. Helpers also can thank clients for sharing their feelings and working hard to make positive changes in their lives.

Self-Reflection

If helpers discover that they have become too invested in changing a client, they can take time to reflect and hypothesize about aspects of the situation that caused them to lose objectivity. Moreover, when overinvestment and overdirectiveness is typical across all clients, helpers can look inward to understand themselves so that they do not harm clients. If the overinvestment and overdirectiveness is directed to a specific clinical situation, helpers can examine the characteristics of the specific situation that elicited the behavior. Consulting with peers, seeking personal therapy, and receiving supervision are all helpful methods for coping with overinvestment.

CONCLUDING COMMENTS

We believe that action is the natural outgrowth of exploration and insight. However, because of the difficulty encountered in making changes, clients often need support and guidance to take action.

Some helpers are nervous and uncomfortable with pursuing action, so they ignore the action stage. We encourage such helpers to look at their own attitudes about action and to struggle to implement this stage. If clients do not make changes in their lives (in thoughts, behaviors, or feelings), helping has not been as successful as it could have been.

What Do You Think?

- What are your thoughts and feelings about the action stage? In your answer, consider whether you think that clients are naturally propelled toward action or whether they need help to change.
- What is the role of helpers in assisting clients in changing?
- Brainstorm ideas for how helpers can make the transition from insight to action.
- How can helpers think of ideas for action plans?
- How does a helper's manner of introducing action plans influence the client's acceptance of the plans?
- Who is responsible for client change, the helper or the client? Discuss what you mean by responsibility.
- In what instances and with what clients do you think specific interventions (e.g., relaxation training, systematic desensitization) would be useful?
- Which behavioral interventions (e.g., relaxation training, systematic desensitization) would you have the most and least difficulty implementing? Think about why these interventions would be difficult.
- Check which of the following obstacles you are most likely to face in your development of action skills:

  _____ moving too quickly to action

  _____ investing too much in clients' changes

  _____ imposing one's values on clients

  _____ not challenging enough

  _____ not being supportive

  _____ getting stuck on one plan.

- Which of the following strategies might help you cope with the obstacles in the action stage?

  _____ return to exploration skills

  _____ address issues related to the therapeutic relationship

  _____ self-reflection

  _____ consultation with supervisors, peers, or teachers.

19 Information

> Ideal teachers are those who use themselves as bridges over which they invite
> their students to cross, then having facilitated their crossing, joyfully collapse,
> encouraging them to create bridges of their own.
>
> *Leo Buscaglia*

Jane realized that her fears about leaving her house and returning to the university were because she had never gotten over a brutal rape and beating that had occurred on campus. She asked her helper what her condition was called. The helper responded, "it is called agoraphobia, and it is quite common after a trauma such as you have experienced. There are a number of interventions that we could implement to help you cope." Thus, the helper gave information to educate Jane about her condition and possible treatments. This information reassured Jane.

GIVING INFORMATION can be defined as providing specific data, facts, resources, answers to questions, or opinions to clients. One type of information (information about the helping process) is presented in the exploration stage. Helpers also use information about the helping process in the action stage to explain their intentions and goals for this stage (e.g., "We will explore what you've done in the past about this problem, brainstorm some ideas for what you could do differently, make some choices about what you want to do, try out your choices, and then evaluate how you feel about your choices"). In this chapter, we discuss two additional types of information that are used primarily to promote action: (a) facts, data, or opinions and (b) feedback about the client (see Exhibit 19.1).

TYPES OF INFORMATION

Facts, Data, or Opinions

Helpers often use their wisdom, knowledge, experience, and expertise to provide facts, data, or opinions to educate clients. As an example, helpers sometimes provide information about psychological tests that clients have taken (e.g., "The Strong Interest Inventory measures a person's interests and compares those interests with interests of people happily employed in a variety of occupations").

Helpers might also give their opinions or specialized knowledge from their education or life experience. Examples include "Having a specific place to study allows students to concentrate better on their studies without distraction," "A moderate amount of stress is typically helpful to motivate a person, but too much or too little stress can be counterproductive," or "Many women become depressed after giving birth; it's called postpartum depression."

■■■■ **EXHIBIT 19.1. OVERVIEW OF INFORMATION**

Definition	Giving *information* refers to supplying data, opinions, facts, resources, answers to questions, or opinions
Subtypes and examples	*Facts, opinions, or answers*
	Client: "I don't know where to go to find information about careers."
	Helper: "Both the career center and counseling center have lots of information about careers."
	Client: "What do we do next?"
	Helper: "Now that we have some basic understanding of your problem, the next step is to figure out what you would like to do differently."
	Feedback about the client
	Client: "How did I do that time?"
	Helper: "You maintained good eye contact during the role-play, but your voice sounded hesitant when you told your partner that you were leaving the relationship."
Typical intentions	To give information, to promote change (see Appendix A)
Possible client reactions	Educated, new ways to behave, hopeful, no reaction (see Appendix D)
Desired client behaviors	Agreement, therapeutic changes (see Appendix E)
Difficulties helpers experience in giving information	Desiring to be viewed as the expert who has important information
	Needing to know all the relevant information
	Believing that helpers should provide a lot of information to be perceived as helpful
	Being judgmental when giving feedback
	Providing information before client has explored thoroughly
	Implying direct guidance (telling the client what to do)

Note. Another type of information (information about the helping process) was presented in chapter 10.

Helpers also sometimes provide answers to questions if they judge that it is therapeutically appropriate to do so. For example, if a client asks for information about how to become a helper and the helper judges that the client is doing it for appropriate reasons, the helper might inform the client about graduate programs.

In addition, helpers often educate clients about their psychological condition. They teach clients about the course of depression, explain the effects on performance of not getting enough sleep, describe how psychotropic medications work, explain the influence of transference on helping relationships, and so on. Thus, they are imparting information that could help clients understand more about themselves and how they function.

Feedback About the Client

Helpers sometimes provide feedback to clients about their behaviors. Brammer and MacDonald (1996) suggested that effective feedback can increase client self-awareness, which can lead to behavior change. Examples of feedback include the following: "You expressed yourself very clearly and concisely in the role-play," "You are smiling a lot and seem more open to making changes," or "I wonder if you are aware that you were tapping your foot when we were working on the relaxation exercise?"

Feedback about the client is similar to immediacy. Both are feedback about the client, except that feedback about the client is only about the client (e.g., "you") individually, whereas immediacy is about the interaction between helper and client in the therapeutic relationship (e.g., "we" or "you and I"). In addition, whereas immediacy is used in the insight stage to promote insight and deal with problems in the therapeutic relationship, feedback about the client is typically used in the action stage to assist clients in generating, implementing, and maintaining changes in thoughts, feelings, and behaviors.

INTENTIONS

The intent of providing information is typically to educate, instruct, or teach so that clients can change their behaviors, thoughts, or feelings. Sometimes clients need to know facts or information to make decisions, to be prepared for action, or to educate themselves. Information about how a system operates, how to obtain what they need, or how they come across can assist clients in following through on their action plans. Thus, helpers can serve as resources for clients. Helpers obtain their knowledge from their education, from experiences in their lives, from making themselves aware of the resources in the community, and from knowing whom to ask for help. Information fits into the action stage in that clients sometimes need specific information to make changes.

WHY GIVE INFORMATION?

In the action stage, helpers sometimes shift into a teacher role. A teacher's role is typically to provide information. Helpers thus act as educators, especially if the information is given in a caring manner when clients need information and are ready to listen. Hence, helpers educate clients about their mental condition or about what to expect in different situations. For example, helpers might explain what happens during panic attacks as a way of teaching clients that the physical sensations that they experience (e.g., heart palpitations) are due to anxiety rather than a heart attack. Such information can lead to change when clients are open to learning.

It is within a helper's role to provide information to clients about what to expect from the helping process. Helpers often provide information about the limits of the helping relationship and the roles of the client and the helper. In addition, helpers might explain the three-stage helping process to clients, so that clients can know what helpers are doing and thus can participate more collaboratively in the process. Although education about the general helping process occurs early in the exploration stage, helpers also educate clients about strategies in the action stage. Hence, if helpers believe that systematic desensitization would be useful, they might explain what is involved in the procedure and then teach the technique to the client. If a helper thinks that a role-play might be beneficial, he or she might describe the role-play so that the client can participate actively and appropriately. In other situations, the helper might give information about how to implement action steps that the client has decided to take. For example, if clients are seeking new jobs, helpers might provide information about resources in the community for resume writing, job listings, interview consultants, and clothing consultants. Or helpers might provide the phone numbers of battered women's shelters to clients who seek to leave abusive relationships.

Information is not always the most appropriate intervention in a situation, even when the client has requested this type of assistance. Sometimes clients need to explore how they feel about situations without being told what is "normal" or typically expected. Other clients need to seek out their own information without having the investigative work done for them. Some clients need to be encouraged to think about why they do not already have the desired information or what motivates them to rely on others to give them information.

EMPIRICAL EVIDENCE

In studies (Barkham & Shapiro, 1986; Hill, Helms, Tichenor, et al., 1988), information sharing by therapists accounted for 11% to 24% of all response modes. Given that it is one of the most typical helper interventions, it is interesting that Hill et al. found that information was rated by clients and therapists as not being very helpful. Clients reported feeling supported but not feeling challenged in response to receiving information from helpers.

Hanson, Claiborn, and Kerr (1997) investigated delivered versus interactive styles of feedback for tests. In the first of three sessions, helpers gathered information about the clients, set goals, and then asked clients to take a personality and a vocational interest test. In the second session, helpers asked about client reactions to the first session and to taking the tests, provided information about what the tests measured, and then began the experimental condition. In the *delivered* condition, students were given descriptions of scales on which they had scored particularly high or low and were given behavioral examples of the meaning of the scale (e.g., *autonomy* means that you need to be free to come and go as you please, to work on your own). At the end of the session, counselors summarized test results and restated results if clients had questions. In the *interactive* condition, clients were asked to note which of their scores were particularly high or low. Clients then were given descriptions of these constructs and were asked to think of one or two behavioral examples for the scale. If examples were inappropriate, counselors provided modifications. At the end of sessions, counselors asked clients to summarize the results and indicate what they had learned about themselves. Hanson et al. found that clients evaluated the interactive condition more highly than the delivered condition. The authors suggested that when clients play an active part in generating and supporting conclusions, they are more likely to change their attitudes, a conclusion that is supported by the literature on persuasion and attitude change (e.g., Petty & Cacioppo, 1986). These results suggest that helpers should be mindful about involving clients when they offer information.

In summary, we know that information is one of the most frequently used interventions within helping, which is surprising considering how little attention has been paid to the use of this skill on a theoretical level. Apparently, helpers often take on an educative role with their clients, even though we know little about the most appropriate time and manner for disseminating information. We also know that information seems to be most effective within the context of collaborating with clients. Unfortunately, minimal research has been done on the timing of providing information or on the effects of different types of information, so we cannot turn to the empirical literature for much guidance. Clearly, more research is needed about the usefulness of information and the most appropriate manner for delivering information in helping sessions.

HOW TO GIVE INFORMATION

Helpers should think carefully about their intentions before supplying information. What is motivating you to want to give information at this particular point? For whom (the client or you) is this information helpful? Do you want to stop exploration? Reduce client anxiety? Educate the client? Show the client how much you know? Normalize the experience? Explain what is happening in the session? Examination of intentions is critical to ensure that information is delivered appropriately.

If a client requests information, helpers need to try to understand what is motivating the client to ask for information at this particular point in the therapeutic process. Helpers should be aware of issues in the dynamics of the relationship when clients request information. Is the client trying to make you feel needed or like an expert? Is the client trying to avoid exploration or insight? Is the client resorting to familiar defenses of being dependent on others? Does giving information foster further dependency in the client? Does the client expect you to be like a medical doctor who asks questions about the problem and then gives a diagnosis and a course of treatment? Helpers need to answer these questions before deciding whether to provide the requested information. We recommend that helpers pause and consider all requests for information. If the issue is straightforward and not motivated by inappropriate needs, helpers can provide the information. If other motives are behind the request for information, helpers need to address these other motives directly. Helpers might ask clients what is motivating them to ask for information, what they want to do with the information, or what they hope the helper will do for them. In other words, helpers can use their immediacy skills to process what is going on in the relationship. Not providing requested information or dealing with the resulting issues can lead to a power struggle, so helpers need to think carefully about how to handle such situations.

Prior to giving information, it is often useful for helpers to ask what information clients possess. Thus, rather than assuming that clients need information, helpers assess the client's knowledge base. They can also ask clients what strategies they have used to gather information. Providing too much information prematurely can create dependency rather than build self-efficacy.

If helpers determine that giving information is appropriate, they should not provide too much information at one time. Meichenbaum and Turk (1987) noted that patients remember very little of the information that medical doctors give them. In fact, ironically, the more information given to patients by doctors, the less patients remember. When clients are anxious, it is very easy for them to forget information. Crucial information, such as referral numbers or homework assignments, should be put in writing to assist clients in accessing the information later.

In addition, feedback about the client must be given cautiously with the clear understanding that the helper is offering his or her personal observations about the client's behavior. Making the statements descriptive (e.g., "You spoke very softly") rather than evaluative (e.g., "You aren't taking this role-play very seriously") and emphasizing strengths (e.g., "You effectively articulated your feelings") rather than weaknesses (e.g., "You didn't do that role-play very well") can make it easier for clients to hear the feedback. It is also important to give feedback (a) about things that clients can change (e.g., nonverbal behaviors, actions) rather than about physical characteristics or life circumstances that cannot be changed (e.g., height, personality) and (b) as closely as possible to the behavior (e.g., "You spoke with more assurance that time") rather than waiting for a long time and then trying to recreate the situation (e.g., "A while back you looked away from me and wouldn't say anything").

When delivering information, helpers should be empathic, gentle, and sensitive to how clients are reacting. The role of information is not to lecture clients but rather to educate clients when they are ready to learn. Sharing the information in a collaborative manner, although challenging for helpers, communicates respect and valuing of the client's contribution to the process. Finally, it is important to observe the client's reactions and ask for feedback about the intervention.

The following example is provided so that helpers can get an idea of how to use information (in italics) within a helping session.

Client: "So tell me all about your class. I think I want to take it next year."

Helper: "It sounds like you would be interested in learning helping skills."

Client: "Yeah, I've always had the idea that maybe I might want to be a social worker. But on the other hand, I'm not sure I would be very good at helping."

Helper: "What concerns do you have about learning helping skills?"

Client: "I'm afraid of getting too involved with the clients. I feel so responsible for my friends when they talk about their problems. I feel like I have to solve all their problems and tell them exactly what to do."

Helper: "So maybe you're worried that you won't be able to have any distance from clients in a helping setting."

Client: "Yeah, do they talk about how to deal with that in the class?"

Helper: "Sounds like you really need some help with that."

Client: "I do. I had a friend talk to me just yesterday, and I felt totally depressed when we were done because I felt like I had done nothing to help her. I'm afraid that she felt worse when we were done. It reminded me of my mother and father who both keep wanting to talk to me ever since they divorced. Both want me to be on their side. Sometimes I feel split in half."

Helper: "I can see why you'd be nervous about the helping situation after having to be a helper with your parents."

Client: "Yeah. What was it like for you?"

Helper: *"I have had a good experience in the class. The professor has talked a lot about how we have to get personal issues dealt with in our own therapy or else it is difficult to help clients with their issues.* I wonder if you have ever explored the idea of getting therapy?"

Client: "Not really. I don't know much about it."

Helper: *"There's a counseling center on campus that offers 12 sessions of free therapy for students."*

Client: "Really? That sounds great. Maybe I'll check it out."

EFFECTS OF GIVING INFORMATION

Helpers can observe their sessions and use the following 3-point scale to determine the effects of giving information on clients.

1 = At the unhelpful end of the spectrum, clients probably do not exhibit any reaction to information. They might retreat into a passive stance similar to that of students listening to a lecture by an authority. Their eyes might glaze over and their attention might wander. They might look like they are listening when in fact they hear

nothing. One dissatisfied client told us that he avoided talking by asking the helper a question—the helper would start talking and provide overwhelming amounts of information and the client could relax because he knew he would not have to do any more work in that session. On the other hand, clients might become dependent on helpers and expect that they can get all their information from them.

2 = At moderate levels of helpfulness, clients might listen and take in all the information shared by the "expert" but not become very involved in the process. They might be grateful to someone for explaining what they need to know, but they might not feel a need to respond, participate in the information-generating process, or make any changes as a result of obtaining the information.

3 = At the helpful end of the spectrum, clients collaborate with helpers in response to being given information. They ask questions of helpers, challenge helpers, and contribute their own ideas. In addition, they describe when and how they could use the information and how they could collect additional information.

DIFFICULTIES HELPERS EXPERIENCE IN PROVIDING INFORMATION

Providing information gratifies some helpers' needs to be viewed as experts. Some helpers like being perceived as "knowing it all" and enjoy having clients admire them. We would caution these helpers that they might be looking expert at the expense of encouraging clients to seek out their own information. Other helpers might embrace the role of expert because they want to assist clients and they believe that helpers should provide all the answers and give lots of helpful information to clients. Both types of helpers do a disservice in neglecting the client role in the information-generating process.

Other helpers feel that they must know everything before they can be adequate helpers. In this world of rapidly expanding knowledge, however, it is simply not possible to have all the information about any topic. Even when helpers do not know everything, they still can assist clients because providing information is only one small part of the helper role. Helpers can always refer clients to other sources to get information.

Another problem helpers have in giving feedback is becoming judgmental. Helpers can imply that they know more than the client and thus be patronizing (e.g., "I'm telling you this for your own good"). Such helpers make judgments about the goodness or badness of clients. For example, the helper who tells a client that she does not smile enough may be doing so because he wants all women to appear happy. Helpers always need to be attentive to their own issues and needs and try to minimize their effect on clients.

Moreover, information can be provided too soon in the helping process before clients are ready to hear and use the information. For example, some volunteers in battered women's shelters immediately provide information to women when they come in about how to make it on their own. At this point, clients more often need to explore their feelings about being in an abusive relationship. They are not ready yet to use information, no matter how helpful or well intentioned it is.

▬▬ HELPFUL HINTS

- Determine the appropriateness of giving information and think about what is motivating you to provide information.
- Make sure the client wants and needs information.
- Check whether the client has explored the situation thoroughly.

- Ask what the client knows already and build on that information to reinforce the client as a person who can seek his or her own information. Encourage clients to seek out information and teach them how to participate actively in obtaining knowledge.

- Don't overwhelm the client with too many facts. Write down information that you want the client to remember.

- Be gentle, empathic, and respectful in the information-giving process.

- Be collaborative and interactive with the client and act as a resource when providing information rather than delivering it as the authority who knows everything.

- Note the client's verbal and nonverbal reactions to the provision of the information. Be ready to modify your interventions if the client is not responding well.

PRACTICE EXERCISES

Recall that the typical intentions for giving information are to give information and to promote change. Read each of the following examples with the assumption that you have spent an adequate amount of time with the client exploring and gaining insight and that the client is ready to hear information. Indicate your intention(s) and then write an informational statement that you might use if you were the helper:

Statements

1. **Client:** "I just came into town, and I've been staying at this horrible guest house. I need to get an apartment close to the university, but I haven't been able to find out where they are advertised. Where would I find out about apartments?"
   Helper intention(s): _____
   Helper response: _____
   _____

2. **Client:** "I want to go to graduate school but I don't know how to go about applying. What are the steps involved?"
   Helper intention(s): _____
   Helper response: _____
   _____

3. **Client:** "I want to be more assertive the next time I have to confront my roommate about borrowing my clothes. Can you give me some feedback about how I come across?"
   Helper intention(s): _____
   Helper response: _____
   _____

Possible Helper Responses

1. "There is an office for housing that you might check." (intent: to give information)
   "You might read the ads in the university newspaper." (intent: to give information)
   "Apartments near the university are hard to find and are very expensive. They are cheaper if you're willing to live further away from campus." (intent: to give information)

2. "First you take the GRE; then you write for application materials." (intent: to give information)

"I'm not sure about the exact procedures, but I know who you could ask to find out." (intent: to give information)

3. "Your voice was strong, but you didn't sound real sure of yourself when you spoke." (intent: to give information, to promote change)

"I thought you did a good job of being assertive. I would listen if I were your roommate." (intent: to give information, to promote change)

What Do You Think?

• Clients often ask for information. How would you decide when to give clients the requested information and when to probe them for their ideas?

• Helpers often feel a need to know everything and be an expert. Describe what it might be like for you to tell clients that you do not know the answer to their questions. How might not knowing an answer influence the client's perception of the helper?

• Describe the types of information helpers need to know to be adequate helpers.

• How do you feel about receiving information from other people? What feelings do you have when you seek information or when people ask you for information?

• What might happen to the therapeutic relationship if helpers withhold information from clients?

LAB 12 Information

Goals: For helpers to have another chance to practice exploration and insight skills and then to use information when appropriate. Divide into groups of three people, with each person taking a turn as client, helper, and observer.

Helper's and Client's Tasks During the Helping Interchange

1. Clients should talk about something that they understand at least somewhat and for which they have decided they need to take action (e.g., need to study more, diet, or exercise).
2. The helper should use basic helping skills with the client for about 5–10 min, allowing the client to explore. The helper should use primarily open questions, restatements, and reflections of feelings.
3. When the client has explored and the helper feels ready to move on to deeper levels of insight, the helper should begin interspersing challenges, interpretations, self-disclosures, and immediacy with open questions, restatements, and reflections of feelings (thinking carefully first about his or her intentions).
4. When the client has gained some insight, he or she should ask for information.
5. Helpers should pause and take their time to think about their intentions and what the client has contributed to the process. Helpers should ask themselves "What would I do in this situation if I were the client?," "What might be good for the client to know or to try?," "Why am I giving information right now?"

(Continues)

When helpers have clarified their intentions and have decided that the time is right for information, they should give the information.

6. The client should respond to the information provided by the helper, and the helping sessions should continue for 5–10 more interchanges so that helpers can observe the client's reactions to the information.

Observers' Tasks During the Helping Interchange

The observer should take extensive notes throughout the session about the effectiveness of all of the interventions. Did the helper establish a good foundation of exploration and insight prior to giving information? What was helpful and not so helpful about the way the helper delivered information? How did the client respond? What is one thing that the helper should continue to do in future sessions? What is one thing that the helper should try to change or do better in future sessions?

After the Helping Interchange

After the session, the helper should talk first about how he or she felt about the session, particularly about giving information. Then the client can talk about what was most and least helpful and why. Finally, the observer should give feedback to the helper about his or her observations.

SWITCH ROLES

Personal Reflections

- What were your intentions for giving information?
- Describe your strengths and areas needing improvement in terms of giving information.
- How can you deliver information that clients can hear and absorb without inhibiting the client from joining in the collaborative process of the action stage?
- How might you react if a client demanded that you give information and you did not think it was appropriate?
- How might you feel if a client rejected your information after asking for it?
- How do you feel when people give you information? What factors contribute to your accepting versus rejecting information?

20 Direct Guidance

We go quickly where we are sent when we take interest in the journey.
(African [Wolof] proverb)

Through a dream interpretation, Yelin came to realize that he allowed his mother to dominate his life. When Yelin was 16, his father died after asking Yelin to take care of his mother. His mother, though only 45 years old and healthy, depended on Yelin to drive her everywhere. She refused to learn English, make friends, or work, and she clung to hopes of returning to her country. At the age of 20, Yelin felt like he would never be able to marry or have his own life. Consequently, he was beginning to drink several beers each night and isolate himself from his peers. After thorough exploration and insight, the helper suggested that Yelin go to Alcoholics Anonymous (AA) and begin to think about moving away from his mother. The helper asked Yelin how he felt about these options. Yelin responded that he wanted to move away from his mother and would prefer to work on that first. He thought that AA might be worth trying, but he said that he would rather continue in individual therapy for the time being because he didn't like groups. Thus, these directives helped Yelin determine which changes he wanted to make in his life.

DIRECT GUIDANCE can be defined as helpers making suggestions, giving directives, or providing advice for what they think clients should do. Whereas giving information just provides facts or data but does not suggest the actions clients might take, direct guidance indicates what a helper thinks a client should do. Contrast the effects of "The counseling center is in the Shoemaker Building" (information) versus "You should go to the counseling center" (direct guidance). Information often has an implied directive about what the client ought to do (e.g., "In my opinion, students earn better grades when they get a full night of sleep before taking a test"), but it does not state directly that the client should take a particular action (e.g., sleep 8 hr before taking a test). In summary, information provides facts or opinions, whereas direct guidance suggests actions for clients.

TYPES OF DIRECT GUIDANCE

Two types of direct guidance can be used to promote action: (a) process advisement and (b) directives. In addition, direct guidance can also be implemented through disclosing strategies that the helper has tried (see Exhibit 20.1).

Process Advisement

With process advisement, helpers direct clients to do things within helping sessions (e.g., "Show me how you acted when your roommate asked to borrow your new

291

Definition	*Direct guidance* refers to helper suggestions, directives, or advice for the client
Subtypes and examples	*Process advisement within sessions*

> Client: "I don't know what to say when he yells at me like that."
> Helper: "Let's try a role-play to practice a new way of acting in that situation."

Directives for outside sessions

> Client: "I get upset when I have a recurrent nightmare about an intruder."
> Helper: "When you have the nightmare the next time, wake yourself up and imagine a new ending where you get angry at the intruder and chase him out of the house."

Discloses strategies

> Client: "I don't know how to talk to my mother when I've made a mistake."
> Helper: "When I have been in similar situations with my mother, I call her and ask to talk. I try to be as honest as possible and let her know that I messed up. Usually she is pretty understanding."

Typical intention	To promote change (see Appendix A)
Possible client reactions	Educated, unstuck, new ways to behave, hopeful, confused, misunderstood, no reaction (see Appendix D)
Desired behaviors	Agreement, therapeutic changes (see Appendix E)
Difficulties helpers experience in using direct guidance	Using direct guidance to meet the needs of the helper to feel expert and in control
	Using direct guidance without knowing enough about the situation
	Shifting the focus to the helper's experience
	Not collaborating with the client in developing action plans

Note. "Discloses strategies" is listed under "self-disclosure" in the helping skills system.

---

dress" or "Play the part of the man in your fantasy"). Helpers are experts on how to facilitate the helping process and, hence, often have suggestions about what clients can do in sessions to facilitate the change process. Clients, in contrast, are not experts in the helping process and consequently rely (within limits) on helpers for judgments about the best procedures to follow in sessions.

Some clients do not know how to express their emotions in an appropriate manner. These clients need a safe and supportive environment in which to learn how to identify, express, and explore their feelings. Experiential exercises allow clients to express and come to accept their inner experiencing. We strongly recommend, however, that helpers approach these exercises carefully because they can be very powerful. Helpers should pay attention to clients' nonverbal cues to see if they are ready to try these exercises. In addition, helpers might want to read several texts first and then practice the exercises under careful supervision before using them with clients.

Greenberg et al. (1993) presented a number of experiential interventions. We focus only on the two-chair technique because it is the best known and empirical research supports its effectiveness (see the review chapter by Greenberg, Elliott, & Lietaer, 1994). A two-chair intervention can be used when a client presents a conflict between two parts of self (e.g., "I want to travel abroad but I should finish school first and I just can't decide what to do" or "I am so confused because I want to retire but I feel an obligation to finish my term at work" or "I should lose weight but I don't want to exercise regularly"). The client might be experiencing a conflict between emotional reactions, needs, or wants on the one hand and irrational thoughts, standards, and values on the other hand. Two-chair work can also be used to address conflicts with another person (e.g., a dispute with a friend). Two-chair work involves an active expression of both sides of the conflict with both sides listening to the other so that the person can fully hear and experience both sides of the conflict rather than shutting down as most people do. Change typically involves clients acknowledging and accepting the thoughts and feelings of both sides and negotiating a resolution between the two sides in a manner acceptable to their values and standards.

To begin the process using the first example about travel, the helper might say something like, "What I'd like you to do is experience both sides of this conflict. Be the side that wants to travel and talk to the other side of you who thinks you should stay in school as if that side is sitting in this other chair." When the client expresses one side, the helper asks the client to move to the other chair and play the other role. In the next interaction, the helper might ask the client to respond from the first side and then the second side and to experience the emotions more deeply. Helpers might encourage clients to provide more specific examples and details using an expressive manner and feeling (e.g., finger pointing, curled lip, passive voice). As clients begin to express themselves in each chair, new feelings typically begin to emerge (e.g., hurt, abandonment anxiety, loneliness). As the two sides listen to each other, they begin to hear, understand, and accept the different feelings. The formerly critical chair begins to soften and becomes more friendly toward the want–need chair. The want–need chair begins to express its feelings in a more assertive manner. Resolution occurs when the two sides compromise and negotiate a new position. Clients might discard the "shoulds" completely, come to a balance between the two sides, or give up the wants or needs that cause problems.

Helpers are often anxious about introducing two-chair work, because they fear that clients think it is silly and feel self-conscious playing the different parts. Our experience is that clients are often quite willing to do what helpers suggest if the exercise is introduced logically and without apology and the benefits are explained. Clients typically expect that helpers suggest different things to help them. Some clients feel awkward initially, but if helpers are nonjudgmental, clients soon can allow themselves to relax and participate in the exercise. We do suggest that helpers try this exercise first under supervision (see the lab at the end of this chapter).

Process advisement, particularly the experiential exercises, can also be used during the exploration stage to facilitate deeper experiencing of emotions. We present it during the action stage, however, because process advisement is very useful during behavior rehearsal and role-plays and in helping clients make decisions.

Directives

Helpers also sometimes advise clients about doing things outside of sessions (e.g., "Practice this relaxation tape every day for 20 minutes" or "Take control of your life"), which we call *directives*. They might suggest that clients do homework (e.g., monitor exercise and eating behaviors, read a self-help book, seek information, practice being assertive, or record dreams). Homework allows clients a chance to practice what they are learning in helping, determine whether they can use it outside of the helping setting, and see what modifications are needed to fit their style and situation. Homework can be particularly useful as a way of helping the client keep involved in the change process in between sessions. Homework is a major intervention in cognitive–behavioral therapies because it allows clients to practice what is being learned in helping and thus speed up the process considerably as well as get clients acting on their own.

DIRECTIVES THROUGH SELF-DISCLOSURE

Helpers can also make suggestions through disclosing strategies that they personally have tried in the past (i.e., another form of self-disclosure). In effect, rather than telling clients what to do, helpers instruct through modeling what has worked for them previously. Hearing what another person has done can both provide specific ideas for new behaviors (e.g., "I brush my teeth as soon as I have finished eating so that I don't forget to do it or am too tired to do it") and can also encourage clients to think of novel action plans (e.g., "I treat myself to a cruise each year as a reward for working hard all year. I wonder what you could do?"). Disclosing what has worked for the helper is also somewhat disarming—rather than telling clients what to do, helpers communicate that they do not have the answers but are willing to share what has worked for them. By disclosing strategies, helpers are able to provide more ideas for clients without imposing the type of demands that may result from directives. Helpers should be aware, however, that clients might be unduly influenced by the helper's disclosure to adopt a similar action plan. Hence, helpers have to be careful not to suggest that clients must do what they did but rather offer their actions as alternatives. In addition, helpers need to be careful not to slip into disclosures aimed at relieving their own feelings so that the focus shifts from the client to the helper (e.g., "Let me tell you all about what I did because it's so fascinating and interesting").

INTENTIONS

The most typical helper intention for direct guidance in the action stage is to promote change. Direct guidance is appropriate to use after clients have explored issues, come to some insight, and have decided how they want to change. When appropriate, helpers can give their opinions about what actions clients should take so that they have more alternatives to consider, always expecting that clients make the final decision about what to do with their lives. For example, helpers might suggest homework if they think clients would benefit from this intervention or they might encourage clients to seek information about occupations in which they are interested.

WHY GIVE DIRECT GUIDANCE?

Ann Landers, Dear Abby, Susan Forward, Dr. Laura Schlessinger, and others give advice to millions of people. Many people (including the authors) read the newspaper columns and listen to the radio shows, which have become immensely popular because they are so entertaining. Providing advice probably is as old as human speech, but what are the consequences? Do people follow the direct guidance, and if so, is the direct guidance helpful or harmful? Unfortunately, we do not have the answers to these concerns, except anecdotally. Our main concern about direct guidance given in these entertainment formats is that clients do not make their own decisions but rely on someone else to direct them. Some people seek guidance from many people and then either become totally confused or consider only the opinions that they want to hear. It certainly can be valuable to gain input from many people, but hearing advice can make it difficult for clients to know what they want to do. Clients may also follow others' direct guidance out of fear of hurting their feelings. We encourage helpers to work collaboratively with clients to help them choose actions that are driven by the needs, issues, and values of the client.

Direct guidance can sometimes be very helpful, especially when given by a trusted helper whose expert opinions are based on solid knowledge and experience. Examples include providing suggestions to parents who are exploring ways of dealing with bed-time for a young child, helping a client think of coping strategies after a hospitalization, or assisting a client in thinking of alternatives for dealing with an elderly parent with Alzheimer's disease. For example, Dorothy asked her helper for advice on negotiating her salary for her first job in an academic setting. Clearly, this was something that her helper knew something about, given that she had worked in an academic setting for some time, although she did not know the politics of the specific department with which Dorothy was negotiating. They talked about the information that Dorothy had gathered about the salary range of other recent hires, what her values were, and what she wanted. They then discussed options about how Dorothy could navigate the negotiation process. The helper suggested that Dorothy not name a specific salary but say that she was dissatisfied with what had been offered. They talked about that possibility, and Dorothy modified it to fit her style. It is important to note that the process was collaborative because the helper very much respected Dorothy's right and ability to make her own decisions. The helper was not invested in which strategy Dorothy chose but rather was interested in presenting alternatives for Dorothy to consider so that she could develop a plan that worked for her. Although the strategy did not work as planned, Dorothy was able to modify it during the negotiation. She accepted the job at a competitive salary and started her new job soon afterwards.

Most clients are competent enough to make their own decisions, but some lack competence and need explicit guidance. When clients are suicidal, for example, they often have "tunnel vision" that prevents them from seeing options other than death. Helpers may need to intervene in such situations and try to ensure that clients do not harm themselves. (See chapter 11 for more discussion on dealing with suicidal clients.) It is important to emphasize that other than in extreme cases (e.g., child abuse or suicidal or homicidal risk), helpers should not dictate what clients should do.

Helpers also need to be aware that they can offer help but cannot force clients to take it. Helpers are not taking over for clients, but are providing options for clients to consider. Clients have to decide for themselves what to do, even in the most desperate of circumstances. Furthermore, helpers have to know limits of how much they can offer. Friedman (1990) recounts a fable about a rescuer who holds a rope over the rail of a bridge to save a drowning person. The drowning person grabs the rope but refuses to climb up. After a while, the rescuer holding the rope cannot hang on any longer because the person is so heavy. The rescuer has to make a decision about letting go or falling from the bridge himself, which clearly does not help the drowning person. Helpers can offer the direct guidance, but clients must choose their actions.

EMPIRICAL EVIDENCE

Direct guidance (not subdivided into process advisement and directives) has not been used very frequently by therapists in most studies (Barkham & Shapiro, 1986; Hill, Helms, Tichenor, et al., 1988), averaging about 5% of all helping skills. Hill, Helms, Tichenor, et al. found that direct guidance was rated by clients as not being very helpful but was rated by helpers as being moderately helpful. In addition, direct guidance led to low levels of client experiencing (i.e., talking about their feelings).

Several studies show the effectiveness of the two-chair technique (Greenberg, 1979; Greenberg & Clarke, 1979; Greenberg & Dompierre, 1981; Greenberg & Webster, 1982). For example, Greenberg and Webster found that clients who resolved a decisional conflict were less anxious and undecided after treatment as well as more improved on target complaints and behavior change.

Several studies (Bischoff & Tracey, 1995; Gillespie, 1951; Mahalik, 1994; Patterson & Forgatch, 1985) show that when therapists are directive, however, clients are likely to be resistant and uncooperative. Thus, helpers need to be careful not to use too many directives and to be very aware of how clients respond.

Fortunately, some research shows which types of homework are most likely to be accepted by clients. Conoley, Padula, Payton, and Daniels (1994) found that clients were most likely to follow helper recommendations for homework that matched the problem, was not difficult to implement, and was based on the client's strengths. They gave an example in which the client was depressed and angry. He said in the session that he wished that he had written down instances when he felt bad during the previous week, so that he could remember them to talk about them in helping. For homework, the helper asked the client to write down instances when he felt badly, recording what he was thinking, doing, and feeling and what the situation was. The helper gave the rationale that the homework would help them discuss the problem more specifically in the next session. After the homework was presented, the client responded favorably, saying that he liked to write and that writing had helped him in the past. Thus, the recommendation was rated as not difficult because it involved only a small amount of time, was not anxiety producing, and was clear. In addition, it was based on the client's strengths because he had indicated that he liked to write. Furthermore, it clearly matched the client's stated problem because it facilitated the client in remembering situations in which he was depressed and angry. During the next session, the client indicated that he had implemented the recommendation.

In summary, although directives can lead to resistance, we have some preliminary evidence that the manner in which homework is presented and the type of homework recommended are important. Helpers need to make sure that the homework they assign fits the needs and strengths of clients.

HOW TO GIVE DIRECT GUIDANCE

Helpers should think about their intentions before using direct guidance. They should make sure that they are using this intervention because clients are ready to change and are working collaboratively to explore the changes. As with information, helpers should not give direct guidance until they have assessed client motivation.

When clients ask (or sometimes even beg) for direct guidance, helpers have to be particularly careful to distinguish between the honest and direct request for direct guidance and the expression of dependent feelings. When in doubt, it is probably best to deal first with the feelings involved (e.g., "You seem pretty desperate to get some advice.

I wonder what's going on for you?"). After such exploration, helpers have additional data to consider how to deal with the request. Helpers also have to assess their own motivation and ensure that their needs to take care of others do not interfere with allowing clients to make their own decisions. We stress also that clients often have negative reactions if helpers ignore their requests for advice. Some clients want direct guidance and are angry when helpers refuse to tell them what to do. An example is a case presented in Hill (1989), where a woman wanted direct guidance about family issues in the early sessions, and the helper did not give it to her because she wanted to do insight-oriented helping. The client felt disregarded by the helper and became less invested in the therapy thereafter. Openly addressing the client's feelings using immediacy skills may help repair such breaches in relationships when clients become angry at helpers for not providing direct guidance.

Helpers also must be attentive to signs of resistance from clients not wanting to follow process advisements. We have noticed that sometimes when clients are reluctant, helpers have not presented the task well. Helpers are sometimes apologetic (e.g., "I don't suppose you'd want to do this exercise that my supervisor suggested?") and defeat the possibility of gaining client cooperation. Or sometimes helpers are not clear about their suggestions or do not provide a rationale for them. Clients are generally agreeable to trying things that helpers deem appropriate if they are presented with a credible rationale for why the exercises are helpful (e.g., "Let's try this role-play to help you learn how to be more assertive. It may feel silly at first, but it can be helpful").

Sometimes clients simply do not want to do what the helper has suggested, either within or outside of the session. Some clients are resistant to suggestions, no matter how skillfully they are presented. At all times, helpers need to respect the client's decision not to participate in an exercise or not to change (unless the decision involves harm to another person—in which case, see chapter 4 for guidelines about what to do). Perhaps the worst thing to do with reluctant or resistant clients is to get into a control struggle over what action the client should take. Control struggles tend to escalate, sometimes leading to disastrous consequences with both people feeling that they lose "face" if they back down. Rather, we suggest that helpers use the basic listening skills to understand why clients are reluctant and perhaps resistant to change. Helpers can also work with clients to accept themselves for not changing. For example, after having struggled for years with trying to be assertive with her boss only to be punished and ridiculed in front of her coworkers, Sandra decided not to fight back any longer against her boss' inappropriate behaviors. The helper (who was initially overly invested in the client being assertive) had to respect this decision and assist the client in developing coping skills (and in pursuing another job).

When giving direct guidance, we suggest that helpers remember that it is easier to make small specific changes rather than huge changes. Hence, helpers should be very specific about what small steps are to be done and when they are to be done, and they should reinforce approximations toward the desired behaviors. For example, rather than suggesting that an inactive client try to lose 5 lbs in the next week (which is not completely under the client's control), the helper might suggest that the client walk 15 min three times in the next week and reinforce herself by taking a hot bath after each walk and allowing herself to read a novel (something the client has said she enjoys doing).

We also suggest that helpers write down homework assignments so that clients remember them. It is often difficult to remember everything that happened in sessions. Furthermore, clients are more likely to take written assignments seriously. In addition, following up on homework assignments in subsequent sessions is important or clients might feel that such assignments were frivolous and not to be taken seriously.

The following is an example of how direct guidance (in italics) could be used in a session.

Client: "Our 3-year-old daughter has gotten into the habit of coming into our bedroom in the middle of the night every night and climbing in bed with us and wanting to stay until morning. At first it seemed okay because she seemed to need comforting, but it has gotten out of hand. We only have a double bed, and my husband takes up more than his half, so I end up not being able to sleep because I can't move. When I try to move her, she doesn't want to leave. So we've got to do something."

Helper: "You sound frustrated."

Client: "I am. We can't figure out what to do. I don't want to traumatize her if she needs comforting. She seems to really like sleeping with us."

Helper: "What have you tried so far?"

Client: "Nothing really. It just started getting intolerable. So now I know we have to do something. Plus I think she's getting a little too old to be doing this."

Helper: "What is your goal?"

Client: "When she wakes up and is upset, I'd like to comfort her and then have her go back to her bed. I don't want her to get into our bed. Once she gets in, it's too hard to get her out."

Helper: "What are your usual strategies for dealing with problems with kids?"

Client: "We talk things out ahead of time so that the kids are prepared and are in on it."

Helper: "*Maybe that would work here if you talked with her ahead of time about what you are planning to do.* How would you do it?"

Client: "Before bedtime, I could tell her that during the night when she wakes up, she can't come into our bed anymore. But I'm afraid there's not something positive to replace it with."

Helper: "That's a good point. *What if you were to lay down next to her on her bed until she went back to sleep and then you could go back to your bed.*"

Client: "That sounds like a good idea. So when she comes into our room, I just take her back to her room and lay down with her for awhile until she's asleep and then go back to my bed. I think that would work, especially if I tell her about it ahead of time. I might miss some sleep but not as much as I'm missing not being able to sleep the rest of the night."

Helper: "Sounds good. Do you see any problems?"

Client: "Well, I might fall asleep on her bed, but probably not for long because it would be uncomfortable there too. I might also be groggy in the middle of the night and just let her in out of habit."

Helper: "*Well, it probably would only take 3 to 5 nights, so you could tell yourself that if you can just do it for that long, the habit will be broken.*"

Client: "Good point. I'm going to do it. It fits with the way I like to do things, so I know it will work."

EFFECTS OF DIRECT GUIDANCE

Helpers can observe sessions and use the following 3-point scale to determine the effects of their direct guidance on clients.

1 = When direct guidance is unhelpful, clients typically show resistance. They might flatly refuse to do what the helper suggests, become angry that the helper provided direct guidance, passively ignore the direct guidance, or not even hear the direct guidance. They often say "Yes, but ..." and list all the reasons that they cannot follow the guidance. Direct guidance given in the form of "father knows best," strong persuasion, or with a strong investment by the helper is often offensive to clients and can lead to hostility or passive–aggressive behavior.

2 = When direct guidance is moderately helpful, clients might listen, hear, think about it, and maybe even use it. However, they tend not to become actively involved in the process of generating action ideas. They more compliantly accept what the helper provides without personally owning it or contributing their ideas or thinking about what they want to do.

3 = When direct guidance is very helpful, clients actively engage with helpers in a collaborative process of choosing and implementing the guidance. Helpers might suggest action, which clients modify according to their thinking. Clients might then contribute an idea to which helpers react and give feedback. Alternatively, clients might reject the helper's guidance completely but explore what causes it to be unacceptable. When clients disagree with helpers, clients feel comfortable enough with helpers and invested enough in change to discuss the situation and generate more appropriate alternatives. Thus, the process is collaborative, with both helpers and clients searching for ideas and respecting each other's opinions.

DIFFICULTIES HELPERS EXPERIENCE IN USING DIRECT GUIDANCE

Some helpers believe that they know what is best for clients. These helpers think that their clients would be well-advised to follow whatever course of action that they (as the experts in the field) have prescribed. These helpers do themselves and their clients a disservice by overlooking the clients' ability to generate ideas or solutions. Clearly, we believe that these attitudes lead to disastrous outcomes in helping, and we recommend that individuals with these attitudes recognize the importance of adopting a more client-centered approach. We agree that helpers might know more about helping than their clients, but they do not know more than clients about the client's inner experiences or what actions the client should implement.

Some helpers give direct guidance before they know enough about the client's situation. They might jump quickly to a solution before exploring the complexity of the situation—and most problems are quite complex when the client's feelings and values are examined. Furthermore, it can appear disparaging to clients for helpers to jump to quick solutions and imply that they were inept for not knowing how to solve such simple problems. If problems were so simple, clients would have solved them on their own. In contrast, other helpers give no direct guidance because they fear being too intrusive or giving bad or ill-timed advice. They are too passive when they might have ideas for action that could be beneficial to clients.

Another problem with direct guidance is that it can foster dependency by shifting the responsibility for solutions from clients to helpers. Clients can become passive and helpless if helpers insinuate that they are not competent enough to solve their problems. Furthermore, when helpers rather than clients are responsible for the guidance, clients can feel free to blame the helpers when things do not go so well. In addition, when helpers use too much direct guidance, it can lead to tension, resistance, or rebellion if clients choose to ignore helpers who demand that clients pursue their advice. Hence, direct guidance can cause problems in therapeutic relationships if it is not done collaboratively so that helpers and clients together construct the direct guidance.

▬ HELPFUL HINTS

- Determine if direct guidance is necessary and appropriate.
- Discuss openly the feelings and issues that arise when a client wants direct guidance but the helper deems this request to be inappropriate.
- Think about your intentions and motivations for giving direct guidance. Watch for overinvestment; check to see what's going on for you in wanting to provide direct guidance.
- Check to see if the client has explored the problem adequately, accepted his or her feelings about the problem, and understands the problem.
- Pick direct guidance that matches the problem, is not difficult to do, and is based on the client's strengths.
- Give the direct guidance gently rather than forcefully or in a demanding manner.
- After suggesting some action, observe and listen to the client's reactions. Was the client enthusiastic about trying the ideas? Did the client respond by sharing ideas about how to implement the suggestion? If so, the direct guidance was probably appropriate. Alternatively, did the client list all the reasons that the suggestion could not possibly work? Or did the client not respond at all? If so, the client was probably resistant, and you need to try something else. Use exploration skills (restatements, open questions, and reflections of feelings) and try to understand how the client feels.
- Direct guidance can sometimes be phrased as self-disclosures. In effect, helpers disclose what they have tried in similar situations. By discussing their strategies, helpers offer suggestions without imposing their opinions on clients. After giving such a disclosure, the helper can turn the focus back to the client (e.g., "I wonder if something similar might work for you?").

PRACTICE EXERCISES

Recall that the typical intention for using direct guidance is to promote change. For these examples, assume that you have spent an adequate amount of time with the client exploring and gaining insight into the problem and that the client is now ready for direct guidance. Specify your intention(s) and then write a direct guidance that you would offer the client:

Statements

1. **Client:** "I get real anxious when I have to be the helper in these sessions. I'm real afraid of doing the session with a client next week. I just freeze when I'm supposed to come up with a reflection of feelings. I know that the reason I'm anxious is because I'm afraid of evaluation. My parents were always really critical of whatever I did in public. I remember when I was on the diving team, and they would criticize everything I did so much that I just couldn't perform. They were

embarrassed because they thought that whatever I did was reflected on them. So I know why it's so difficult for me, but I'm still having a hard time with it."
Helper intention(s): _____
Helper response: _____

_____

2. **Client:** "I wonder if I should break up with my boyfriend. He's been beating up on me lately. For a while everything will be okay, then all of a sudden he'll get into a rage and start hitting me. Afterwards, he gets real apologetic and says he'll never do it again. He brings me flowers and is real sweet for awhile. But then it all starts over again. I've about reached the end of my rope. But I'm just not sure what to do."
Helper intention(s): _____
Helper response: _____

_____

3. "I just let myself get stepped on in all my relationships. I don't know how to stand up for myself. Yesterday, my roommate came in and said that she wanted to borrow my brand-new dress and I didn't even say anything. I just let her take it. I am so disgusted with myself."
Helper intention(s): _____
Helper response: _____

_____

Possible Helper Responses

1. "Perhaps we could work on some relaxation skills today in our session to prepare you for the next session." (intent: to promote change)
   "Maybe you should go to the counseling center and get some help for your anxiety because it sounds pretty overwhelming." (intent: to promote change)
   "When I'm anxious, I take a deep breath and it relaxes me." (intent: to promote change)
2. "Perhaps you might look at how your decision to stay in the relationship negatively affects your mental health. Let's role-play the part of you that wants to leave and the part of you that wants to remain in an abusive relationship." (intent: to promote change)
   "You should leave him. No woman should stay in a relationship where she's getting hurt. Let me take you to the battered women's shelter." (intent: to promote change)
   "I was in a similar situation, and it took me a long time to get out, but once I left, I felt so much better about myself." (intent: to promote change)
3. "Let's role-play what you could do differently. First, I want you to show me exactly how you behaved in that situation yesterday. I'll be your roommate and you be yourself. Ready? 'Hey, can I borrow this dress—I'm going out on a big date tonight and I don't have anything to wear.' What would you say?" (intent: to promote change)
   "Read this book about assertiveness training and try out the suggestions." (intent: to promote change)
   "When my roommate did that, I had to work myself up to it but I finally said something to her, and I was surprised about how well it worked. Let's try practicing how you might talk to her." (intent: to promote change)

What Do You Think?

- What do you think needs to be present in a helping relationship for direct guidance to be an appropriate skill for helpers to use with their clients?
- What problems might helpers encounter when giving direct guidance?
- Debate the pros and cons related to radio talk show psychologists giving direct guidance after having spoken only briefly with callers. What do you suppose are the consequences of this type of direct guidance? What types of people are helped by radio talk show psychologists?
- How can you determine whether clients really want or need direct guidance?
- Argue for or against the opinion presented in this book that direct guidance should generally be given with caution and only after thorough exploration and insight.

LAB 13 Process Advisement

Goals: For helpers to continue to practice exploration and insight skills and to have helpers gain experience with actions skills by implementing the two-chair technique.

Students should be arranged in groups of 4–6, with one person being the client, one person the helper, and the rest observing and being ready to switch into the helper role if needed. A lab leader should be in charge of organizing and directing the session.

Helper's and Client's Tasks During the Helping Interchange

1. The client should talk about an unresolved conflict that she or he has with another person (e.g., parent, friend, partner). Alternatively, the client could discuss an internal conflict. For example, Nora was struggling with a decision to attend graduate school or join the Peace Corps. The helper asked Nora to play the part of herself that wants to go to graduate school when sitting in one chair and then switch chairs and play the part of herself that wants to join the Peace Corps.

2. The helper should use exploration skills (restatement, open question, reflection) to encourage the client to explore feelings, thoughts, and behaviors related to this conflict (for at least 5 min). Once the problem has been explored, the helper can move to insight (using challenge, interpretation, self-disclosure, immediacy) for at least 5 min. Another class member should be the helper.

3. When it is clear that there are two polarities that the client needs to understand and resolve, the lab leader can direct another helper to begin the two-chair exercise. The helper can invite the client to participate in the two-chair technique. The helper should explain that this technique is often used effectively to help clients gain insight about a conflict with another person or a conflict within oneself. These insights can then inform the actions that clients plan to take to resolve or gain closure regarding the conflict. The helper should place two chairs facing each other and ask the client to sit in one of these chairs. (The helper can sit next to the client in a third chair.) The helper then can ask the client to imagine that the person with whom the client has a conflict is seated in the empty chair. The helper can invite the client to share feelings

and thoughts with the imagined person in the chair. The helper facilitates deep and appropriate expression of feelings by encouraging the client to continue to talk to the chair (e.g., "Yes, go on, tell your partner more about your feelings of disappointment and hurt"). If the helper has difficulty presenting the exercise or facilitating the client in expressing feelings, another person can switch into the role of helper.

4. After the client has expressed feelings about the conflict, the helper invites the client to move to the empty chair and imagine that she or he is the other person. The helper should direct the client to respond to what he or she said in the first chair. If the client feels uncomfortable, the helper can gently encourage the client to give this intervention a try, although it is important to end the intervention if the client exhibits significant discomfort. The helper probably needs to provide encouragement and offer process advisement as the client plays the part of the other person (e.g., "Stay in the role of your partner. Have your partner address your hurt and disappointment").

5. Ask the client to switch chairs again and continue this procedure, expressing the full extent of feeling in each chair, until the client appears to have gained some insight about the conflict (especially insight regarding how the client may have contributed to the conflict and how the significant other might feel in this situation). Encourage the client to process possible actions that might be taken to resolve or reach closure regarding the conflict (e.g., "Talk to your partner about how you would like to resolve this conflict"). The helper should remain an active participant, intervening when the client seems to be rambling, moving off topic, or recounting problems. Try to keep the client focused on expression of immediate feelings, the development of insight, and potential action plans in this intervention.

6. Helpers should then ask the client to stop the two-chair conversation and share her or his insights about the conflict situation and the best course of action that emerged from these insights. Then, helpers can facilitate a discussion with the client about feelings related to participation in this intervention.

Observers' Tasks During the Helping Interchange

The observer should take extensive notes throughout the session about the effectiveness of the two-chair intervention. Did the helper establish an adequate foundation of exploration prior to implementing the two-chair technique? What could the helper have done to improve on the use of exploration and insight skills in this exercise? Note the way in which the helper described the two-chair intervention to the client. How did the client react to this intervention? Did the helper remain an active participant while facilitating the "discussion" between the two sides or two people engaged in this conflict? Note several things that the helper did well in this practice session and provide specific recommendations for how the helper might improve in future sessions.

After the Helping Interchange

After the session, the helper should talk first about how she or he felt about the session, particularly about facilitating the two-chair exercise. The client

(Continues)

can then discuss the most and least helpful aspects of the session. Finally, the observers can provide feedback to the helper to assist the helper in improving her or his skills for implementing the two-chair technique.

SWITCH ROLES

Personal Reflections

1. What was it like to be the helper, client, and observer for the two-chair technique?
2. Describe your strengths and areas needing improvement when implementing the two-chair technique.
3. How might you react if your client refused to participate in this intervention and you thought the two-chair technique would be helpful in resolving the conflicts experienced by the client?
4. How might your reluctance or discomfort with implementing a new technique affect the client's willingness to participate in alternative interventions like the two-chair technique?
5. What possible problems might emerge when implementing the two-chair technique?
6. What conflicts might you try to resolve in your life using the two-chair technique? Discuss your thoughts about how important it is to have a helper facilitate this process.

21 Integrating the Skills of the Action Stage

> It is movement, not just insight, that produces change.
> *Waters and Lawrence* (1993, p. 40)

Debi was 40 years old when she first came to the homeless shelter. A helper listened to her expressions of rage, feelings of powerlessness, and sense of humiliation that she had been evicted from her home. The helper challenged her irrational thoughts that she was worthless and a social outcast. The helper self-disclosed about her experiences with poverty and losing her job and how she had been forced to figure out how she wanted to live her life. Debi felt much better after expressing her feelings and gaining new insights about how she had gotten to this situation, but she also wanted to learn skills so that she would never have to be homeless again. The helper asked her more about how she had come to lose her job and her apartment. Debi had been fired from her job because of downsizing and had become discouraged about getting another job after having been turned down by 15 places. The helper gave Debi some tests to figure out her interests, helped her write her resume, and did role-playing with her about how to handle an interview. Debi applied for several more jobs while living at the shelter and finally was offered one that she liked.

FOR HELPERS, the action stage is often the most challenging of the three stages. Helpers tend either to avoid action in favor of being empathic and insightful or to become overly directive and authoritarian while neglecting their empathic skills. Leaving enough time for action can also be difficult for helpers who have trouble planning sessions.

Change is also difficult for clients. Demoralization and hopelessness are major hurdles that must be overcome for clients before they can change (Frank & Frank, 1991). Clients often feel discouraged or defeated about their ability to change because they have had bad experiences in the past with such attempts. Accordingly, helpers might need to take "baby steps" when exploring change, recognizing how hard it is to change. Remembering how difficult it is for them to make changes in some areas of their own lives can assist helpers in being empathic with clients who are struggling to change. Helpers also need to remember that clients developed their problems over many years, and changing ingrained patterns is difficult.

Although the action stage presents many challenges for both helpers and clients, helpers should not neglect assisting clients in making positive and lasting changes in their lives. They do, however, need to approach action with appropriate caution, self-awareness, and empathy for their clients.

STEPS TO TAKE IN THE ACTION STAGE

Several steps can be used in the action stage. Helpers need not go through every step with every client or follow the steps in a particular order. Furthermore, most helpers do not complete all the steps in a single session. To facilitate change, however, helpers need to be aware of the general outline of the steps so that they can determine which ones are appropriate for their clients at different points in time.

Helpers use the action stage in every session, but they use it somewhat differently at different times. In initial sessions, the focus of the action stage is usually on exploring the possibility of changing and helping clients think about whether and what they might want to change. In later sessions, the focus of the action stage moves to discussing specific action plans, the positive and negative consequences of the changes the client has tried to make, making modifications in action plans, and planning for termination of the helping relationship.

Flexibility and creativity are critical in the action stage. Helpers can use an endless number of cognitive–behavioral interventions that seem appropriate from their assessment of client needs. If one intervention does not work, helpers can try something else. If several interventions are unsuccessful or the client continually says, "Yes, but ... " in response to interventions, helpers should explore how clients feel about the therapeutic relationship or the process of change. Helpers also can use insight skills to help clients understand their resistance to change. We stress the continued need for empathy and support throughout the action stage because of the difficulty that clients face when implementing change.

As we describe each of the steps, we discuss the helping skills that can be used to implement the step. See Table 21.1 for a summary of when to use the various skills and Exhibit 2.1 for a summary of the steps and possible interventions.

Step 1. Explore Action

Our first step is to explore action. Not every client is ready to change behaviors. Some are reluctant to give up familiar patterns, others are scared, and others see no benefit to changing. Recall in chapter 3 that we listed six stages of client readiness for change: precontemplation, contemplation, preparation, action, maintenance, and termination (Prochaska et al., 1992). Assessing the client's stage is important prior to determining how to proceed in the action stage. In the precontemplation and contemplation stages, clients typically require more time to explore their feelings and develop insights before making a commitment to change, whereas clients in the preparation and action stages often are more ready to move directly into action. Clients in the maintenance and termination stages probably are more interested in stabilizing the changes that they already have made.

It is, of course, entirely up to clients to decide whether they want to change. Helpers should not be invested in whether clients change, but they should assess client readiness to change before proceeding to develop action ideas. If helpers plunge too quickly ahead into action with clients who are not ready, they typically hear "Yes, but ... ." These clients will have all kinds of reasons why action is not possible. Alternatively, some clients might simply withdraw and act compliant but have no intention of following through on the action. To assess client readiness to change and how clients feel about changing, helpers can ask open questions.

- "What would you like to do about this problem?"
- "What are the positive and negative aspects of staying as you are?"
- "How would changing make you feel?"

TABLE 21.1. A Guide for Which Helping Skills To Use During the Action Stage

Marker in session	When helper intends to	Helper might try
At all points	Support	Appropriate attending behaviors Listening attentively Approval and reassurance Reflection of feeling
When the client has explored and has an understanding of the presenting problem	Promote change	Assessing the client's motivation to change through open questions
When the client needs specific information or education about the outside world	Give information	Providing information in the form of facts, data, or helper's opinion
When the client needs feedback about her or his behavior	Give information and identify maladaptive behaviors	Feedback about the client Open questions Reflection of feelings
When the client would benefit from engaging in a specific task during the session	Promote change, identify maladaptive cognitions, identify maladaptive behaviors, and encourage self-control	Process advisement
When the client would benefit from suggestions from helper for behavior outside session	Promote change and encourage self control	Directives for outside session
When a specific issue has been identified that can be dealt with through behavioral techniques	Promote change and encourage self-control	A behavioral strategy such as relaxation training, systematic desensitization, behavioral rehearsal, cognitive restructuring, or problem-solving training
When the client needs to get in touch with feelings about changing or deal with a conflict within himself or herself about changing	Identify or intensify feelings, promote insight, and promote change	Open question Restatement Reflection of feelings Immediacy Challenge An experiential exercise such as the two-chair technique
When the client has made a change or needs encouragement to change	Reinforce change and instill hope	Approval and reassurance and offer feedback about behavior

(Continues)

TABLE 21.1. *(Continued)*

Marker in session	When helper intends to	Helper might try
When the client does not do assigned task in or outside of session	Deal with resistance, deal with therapeutic relationship, clarify, and promote insight	Approval and reassurance, open question about feelings, reflection of feelings, or immediacy
When the client is in crisis	Promote change, encourage self-control, and provide support	Open and closed questions Reflections of feelings Restatements Directives for outside session (e.g., help client plan the next few hours, develop a contract so that the client promises not to attempt suicide, give client the phone number of a crisis hotline)

The helper also can facilitate clients' talking about feelings regarding change through reflection of feelings.

- "You sound unsure about whether you want to change."
- "It's exciting for you to think about doing something new."

If a client is ambivalent about changing, the helper can facilitate an exploration of the client's feelings. The goal is to encourage clients to express their thoughts and feelings about action, rather than forcing clients to make changes. Helpers can maintain an attitude of curiosity and ask open questions.

- "What keeps you from changing?"
- "What goes through your mind as we talk about changing?"
- "What feelings are you having when you contemplate making changes in your life?"

Hence, the primary interventions at the beginning of the action stage are open questions and reflection of feelings. Open questions are useful to begin the discussion, which the helper then can facilitate by reflecting feelings, thereby drawing the client into a discussion of values, needs, and problems related to change.

After weighing all the options, some clients might choose not to change. They might decide that the costs of changing are not worth the benefits. Helpers need to respect clients' choices about whether or not to change. Rather than perceiving that their success as a helper is based on clients making radical changes, helpers need to view their success as based on helping clients decide what is best for them to do. Sometimes change is too painful, and sometimes clients discover that their current life is not so bad. Choosing not to change can be just as valid a choice as deciding to change.

▬▬▬ **EXHIBIT 21.1. STEPS OF THE ACTION STAGE**

Step	Possible interventions
1. Explore action	"What would you like to do about this problem?"
	"What are the positives and negatives for staying as you are?"
	"How would changing make you feel?"
	"You sound unsure about changing."
	"It's exciting to think about doing something new."
	"What keeps you from changing?"
	"What are you thinking about as we talk about changing?"
	"What feelings are you having when you contemplate making changes in your life?"
2. Assess what the clients have tried before	"What have you tried before?"
	"What strategies have you used in trying to change?"
	"What has worked?"
	"What hasn't worked?"
	"What problems have you encountered that made change difficult?"
3. Set specific goals	"What do you want to change in your life?"
	"Describe your dreams for the future. What changes would you need to make for those dreams to come true?"
	"What are the goals you want to work on here?"
4. Brainstorm possible ways to reach goals	"What alternatives have you thought about trying?"
	"If there were no restrictions, how would you try to change this problem behavior?"
	"What would you suggest to someone else?"
5. Explore the different options	"Which option seems most appealing? Why?"
	"Which option seems least appealing? Why?"
	"What are your values about the different alternatives that you might try?"
	"What changes would you not want to make because they go against your values or beliefs?"
	"What things would help you in making changes?"
	"What prevents you from making changes?"
6. Decide on actions	"Which action would you like to do right now?"
	"What problems do you foresee with this choice?"

(Continues)

Step	*Possible interventions*
	"How could you resolve the problems that might come up with the action choice?"
7. Implement actions	Teach specific skills (e.g., relaxation, assertiveness, behavior modification)
8. Modify actions on the basis of experience	"What worked when you tried your action plan?"
	"What did not work when you tried your action plan?"
9. Give feedback	"You used a lot of eye contact."
	"You were smiling the whole time. Let's try it again, and try not to smile so much."
Overall step: Give support throughout	"You did a great job of trying to do the homework."
	"Let's see how you might get more support in your environment."

Step 2. Assess What Clients Have Tried Before

When helpers have established that clients want to change, they can assess what changes, if any, clients have already tried to make. Finding out previous strategies can help to avoid encouraging actions that have not worked in the past. After all, clients have usually had lengthy experiences with their problems and have undoubtedly tried, and have many feelings about, various alternatives. Rather than spinning their wheels, helpers need to assess this information. Discovering what clients have done before also lets clients know that helpers are aware that they have been attempting to solve problems, albeit not always in effective ways. Helpers thus act as consultants with clients, collaboratively working with them to learn what they have tried and how these strategies have worked. The following are examples of open questions to assess previous efforts.

- "What have you tried before?"
- "Describe the strategies that you have used in trying to change."
- "What has worked?"
- "What hasn't worked?"
- "What problems did you encounter that made change difficult?"

Step 3. Set Specific Goals

Sometimes it is helpful at this stage for helpers to work with clients to set specific goals. Research suggests that setting small, achievable goals makes accomplishing change more likely. Open questions that can be used to set goals include the following.

- "What do you specifically want to change in your life?"
- "Describe your dreams for the future. What changes would you need to make to ensure that these dreams become a reality?"
- "What are some of the goals that you want to work on here?"

Oscar Wilde said that the only thing worse than not getting what you want is getting what you want (from *Lady Windemere's Fan*, Act 3; Murray, 1989). Helpers need to help clients think carefully about what they want, because there are advantages and disadvantages to every change. Clients may not be sure that they actually want the changes when they have thought carefully about them. For example, Joan might want her husband to become more in touch with and expressive of his feelings. However, if he does this, he is likely to express some feelings about ways in which he would like Joan to change. Joan might realize that she liked him more when he was less expressive of his feelings.

Step 4. Brainstorm Possible Ways to Reach Goals

One of the biggest benefits for clients of working with helpers is that they can brainstorm together. Through collaboration, more ideas can be produced than can be generated by either person alone. The idea is initially to generate as many ideas as possible to enable clients to see many alternatives. Reality can come later when deciding among the possibilities, but the ideas must first be generated.

To aid brainstorming, helpers can ask clients to think of whatever action comes to mind, no matter how unlikely or silly it might initially sound. It is important for clients to lift restrictions on themselves while brainstorming and to suspend judgment about what is possible so that they do not censor any possibilities. Helpers can add ideas of things that they have heard about, thought about, or tried. One useful strategy is to set a specific time limit, such as 2 min, and alternate with the helper and client coming up with as many ideas as each can in the time period.

- "What alternatives have you thought about trying?"
- "If there were no restrictions, how would you try to change this problem behavior?"
- "What would you suggest to someone else in this situation?"

Step 5. Explore the Different Options

During brainstorming, the idea is to generate as many ideas as possible without judgment or restrictions, but when brainstorming has been completed, helpers should work with clients to think through the options systematically. Helpers can ask about which options seem appealing and why and which options do not seem appealing and why. Helpers also should determine whether any of the options violate the client's values. For example, even though a quick way to obtain money might be to rob a bank, clients (one hopes) have values against theft.

- "Which option seems most appealing? Why? Which option seems least appealing? Why?"
- "What are your values about the different alternatives that you might try?"
- "What changes would you not want to try because they go against your values or beliefs?"

Helpers also need to work with clients to identify potential aids and blocks to each of the ideas for action. Helpers can assist clients in understanding the restraining forces (the forces that work against change) and the facilitating forces (the forces that promote change). For example, a woman thinking about leaving her husband might identify the restraining forces as financial concerns and loneliness and the facilitating forces as reduction in tension and potentially increased self-efficacy.

- "What things would help you in making changes?"
- "What things would prevent you from making changes?"

Step 6. Decide on Action

Helpers should focus on one problem at a time in developing action plans. Dealing with too many problems simultaneously can be confusing and diffuse any efforts at changing. Hence, one could, for example, first teach relaxation and then move on to social skills. Choosing which problems to focus on first can be quite a challenge, but generally we suggest focusing initially on easier (but still meaningful) problems so that clients can gain a sense of accomplishment when they change. Furthermore, accomplishing small changes can provide clients with confidence to pursue additional challenges.

Through the previous two steps, clients probably have generated some ideas about what changes they would like to try to make in their lives. Helpers then begin to work with clients to choose which ideas they want to implement, selecting ones that are specific, realistic, within the realm of possibility, and consistent with the client's values. Helpers do not want to put a damper on enthusiasm, but neither do they want to encourage clients to pursue changes that are not feasible, because that could result in failure. For example, it is highly unlikely that a 40-year-old bricklayer with no previous theater experience will be able to become a movie actor, and it could be a mistake to encourage such a pursuit without caution. Clients can be asked to list the advantages and disadvantages of each action idea (with helpers adding their opinions if appropriate). If the disadvantages outweigh the advantages, it is unlikely that the client can implement this plan effectively. In this case, the helper can assist the client in altering the plan to make it more feasible.

Helpers might need to assist clients in making a commitment to change because it is important that clients feel invested in the action plan. If clients are ambivalent about the different action ideas and have a hard time making a commitment, more work might be needed to understand the reluctance. Helpers might find it helpful to cycle back to the exploration and insight stages to assist clients in exploring feelings about change and to understand what contributes to the client's ambivalence about the action plans.

- "Which actions would you like to do right now?"
- "What problems do you foresee with this action choice?"
- "How could you resolve the problems that might come up with this action choice?"

Egan (1994) suggested that helpers challenge clients to imagine obstacles in their action plans and then to imagine how to deal with these obstacles. Many clients are unrealistic and develop plans that never work. For example, Elena might decide to lose weight before the holidays and resolve to eat only carrot sticks at every party she attends. Preparing clients ahead of time for possible problems can help them figure out how to deal with adversity. In the previous example, the helper might suggest a more realistic plan in which Elena has small portions of food at each party as opposed to eating only carrot sticks. Egan noted that there is a fine line between preparing clients for problems and giving them permission to make mistakes by implying that mistakes are inevitable—one is proactive whereas the other is providing excuses. Helpers need to be careful about their intentions and what they communicate to clients.

Step 7. Implement Action

When helpers and clients have selected an action idea, they begin to implement the idea. For example, if helpers have assessed the problem as being a lack of skills, they could teach clients specific skills through role-playing or modeling. If anxiety is interfering, helpers could teach relaxation techniques. If the problem is a lack of confidence, helpers might provide verbal support. If other people (e.g., family) are interfering with progress, helpers might teach the client problem solving skills and coping strategies. Strategies for specific problems are discussed in chapter 18.

In action plans, establishing small steps of change and determining what is realistic to change in a specific time period is important so that clients are more likely to attain their goals. Hence, rather than merely telling clients to start studying better, helpers need to break the action down into small concrete steps to make change easier to accomplish (e.g., study no more than 15 minutes at a sitting and take a short break as soon as you cannot concentrate). Rather than encouraging clients to make major changes immediately, which is rather unrealistic, helpers can encourage clients to "go slow." This intervention can have a paradoxical effect (Watzlawick et al., 1974) with clients who are reluctant to change by suggesting that they do not need to change rapidly. It is paradoxical because the reluctant clients are given permission to continue as they have been, which can sometimes free them up to not be oppositional. However, it also can be very directly reassuring to clients that they do not have to change overnight. From a behavioral perspective, it is easier to make small changes ("baby steps") than major changes. We have heard it said that it takes 21 days to establish a new behavior (e.g., implementing a new exercise program). Clients sometimes get discouraged by thinking that they should be able to change immediately, so it can be useful to inform clients that it takes time and practice to make lasting changes.

Helpers also should work with clients to find incentives and rewards for making changes. As discussed in chapter 18 on behavioral theory, reinforcers increase the probability that a behavior occurs again. However, it is important to emphasize that reinforcers are unique for each person, so helpers must work with clients to identify reinforcers that work for them. For one person, watching television for 30 min after studying for 30 min would be a reinforcer, whereas another person might choose talking on the telephone or going for a run.

Helpers can practice new behaviors with clients in sessions and then encourage clients to try these behaviors in between sessions. For example, a helper might suggest that, after practicing assertiveness in sessions, a client try being more assertive the next time she is at a store. Note that it is typically better to practice new skills in a safe or insignificant setting before trying them out in a difficult setting. Or, after discussing study skills, a helper might make a contract with a client to study at least 30 min a night at his desk, after which he can reinforce himself by getting a soft drink and calling his girlfriend. Assigning homework can be particularly effective in providing additional opportunity for clients to practice newfound skills in other settings (e.g., practicing small talk with classmates after practicing it in sessions). As with direct guidance in general, helpers need to remember to be collaborative in developing homework assignments with clients. If helpers are too insistent about assigning homework, clients can become reluctant to comply with the assigned tasks. We also should add that clients might be resistant to the idea of doing "homework" in between sessions because it makes helping seem like school. Helpers might use other terms such as *tasks* or *action assignments*.

Let us give some examples of how this step can be implemented. Charlie, a 25-year-old, had tremendous anxiety about leaving home and getting a job. Our work in the exploration and insight stages suggested that Charlie was anxious about leaving home because he was extremely shy and also because he was worried about his parents' fighting. We laid out a plan first to deal with his shyness. We focused on relaxation training and systematic desensitization for several sessions to help Charlie deal with his anxiety about meeting new people and getting a job. Then we used assertiveness training and role-plays focused on small talk to help him deal with his anxiety around strangers. In additional sessions, we helped Charlie develop skills to hunt for apartments and do job interviews. We then turned to issues related to his feelings about his parents and asked Charlie to bring his parents in for a couple of sessions. As we observed Charlie communicating with his parents, we helped him tell them how upset he becomes when they fight. We also suggested that his parents seek couples counseling so that Charlie can be extricated from having to mediate their fights.

For Charlene, a 30-year-old homemaker who was depressed and overweight, we structured a very different action plan. Through the exploration and insight stages, we discovered that Charlene was frustrated about staying home but felt that it was her duty to take care of the children full time. She came to the insight that she thought she should be a stay-at-home mom because she believed that was the only way her husband would love her. She recounted memories of her parents having an awful relationship and her dad resenting her mom for having a successful career. She came to understand that she could achieve in her own career without destroying her husband. At this point, however, she realized that she had been unemployed outside the home for so long that she did not know how to cope with the world of work. We first worked on a plan to get her back in shape physically to gain some confidence. She decided to take a 30-min walk with her husband each day (both to lose weight and have some private time with her husband). We also suggested that she monitor her caloric intake and eat more moderately. Once we had some success with these two issues, we taught Charlene career exploration skills so that she could determine what type of job she would like to obtain. We then taught Charlene to speak up for herself and practice interview skills.

Step 8. Modify the Action on the Basis of Experience

Even when helpers and clients have practiced skills in sessions or have generated a plan of action that the client can try outside sessions, problems often arise when clients try to implement actions. Changing is often more difficult than anticipated and may include obstacles that were not apparent initially.

On the basis of experiences that clients have had trying out action plans in the real world, helpers can work with clients in subsequent sessions to modify action plans. Helpers need to determine what works and what does not work without judging clients for their efforts. Helpers also need to encourage clients to talk about what aspects of the plan are not working, so that modifications can be made. Helpers can think of themselves as uninvested observers or scientists, who observe what does and does not work, so that they can help clients modify the plans to make them more effective.

Developing effective action plans is a process of trial and error—figuring out what does and does not work for the individual client and gradually approaching a good plan.

Rather than becoming angry with clients for not implementing their plans perfectly, helpers should view modifications as a natural part of the process. Often clients are not aware of all the barriers in their environment until they try to change.

Clients often become discouraged with relapses. Brownell, Marlatt, Lichenstein, and Wilson (1986) noted that a slip or lapse need not lead to a relapse. Helpers can work with clients to help them adopt an attitude of forgiving themselves for lapses and learning from them. For example, when Frank drinks too much at a party after having been sober for 6 months, he might learn that he cannot drink even in moderation. This learning might lead him to take steps to determine how to handle parties in the future. If Frank beats himself up too much for the relapse, he might feel even worse about himself and not be able to cope productively with the problem.

Step 9. Give Feedback

Helpers also can give clients feedback about their progress. Clients need to know how well they are performing (e.g., "You did a really good job of recording how many times you yell at your daughter and what provokes you to do it, and now you can start to try to figure out other ways to behave when you get angry"). The purpose of feedback is not to pass judgment but to provide guidance, support, and challenge (Egan, 1994). Egan noted that confirmatory feedback reinforces clients for doing well (e.g., "Congratulations on being able to keep organized this week"), whereas corrective feedback tells clients that they are not on the right track and need to make some changes (e.g., "It seems that you had some trouble keeping up your end of the bargain about getting home before the curfew several times this week"). Egan noted that corrective feedback should be given in a caring manner and paired with confirmatory feedback. He also suggested that corrective feedback be brief and to the point, focus on client behavior rather than personality characteristics, and be given in moderate doses to not overwhelm the client. Egan also noted that clients should be invited to comment on and expand on the feedback when necessary and helped to discover alternative action plans.

Overall Step: Offer Support Throughout

Clients need a lot of support and encouragement throughout the entire action stage, even if they have only accomplished one small step in the action plan. Making changes can be difficult, and clients can be supported by feeling that helpers are on their side. Clients appreciate knowing that their helpers are benevolent coaches or guides rather than harsh parents or dictators.

In addition, clients who do not have adequate support systems outside of the helping setting can be aided to find sources of support in the community (Sarason, Sarason, & Pierce, 1990). Because the therapeutic relationship does not last forever, it is incumbent on helpers to encourage clients to develop other support systems. Breier and Strauss (1984) noted that the benefits of a social support system include a forum for ventilation, reality testing, support and approval, integration into the community, problem solving, and constancy. Continuing our previous example, Frank might find it useful to attend Alcoholics Anonymous meetings to meet and talk with others who are facing similar challenges so that he can receive encouragement for continuing with his action plan and can begin to develop a healthy support system. Obtaining additional support might be especially important for clients who belong to marginalized groups in our society. McWhirter (1994) suggested that helping clients connect with similar others in their community can empower clients and provide needed support. Undoubtedly, the success of Alcoholics Anonymous and similar groups can be at least partially attributed to the benefits of social support.

AN EXAMPLE OF AN EXTENDED INTERACTION

An example is presented below to illustrate the action stage. In this example, the helper has already explored with the client, Sam, his feelings about his recent diagnosis of terminal cancer. They have come to the insight that his depression over the diagnosis is due to feelings that he has not yet lived fully. They have traced his passivity back to his having controlling parents who told him how to live his life. He now recognizes that no matter what his childhood was like, he is the one responsible for the rest of his life and he cannot blame anyone else. He is eager to alter his lifestyle but feels uncertain how to make the desired changes.

Helper: "You've been talking about how you want the remainder of your life to be different. What would it mean for you to make changes at this time?" (Helper wants to explore Sam's perceptions about change and so first restates his thoughts and then asks an open question about the meaning of change for the client.)

Client: "It would be scary because I've been resistant and angry and blaming my parents for so long, but I want to try."

Helper: "You sound sure of wanting to change." (The helper wants to support Sam's desire to change and so offers a reflection of feeling.)

Client: "Yeah, I am, even though I know it's going to be difficult. Maybe if I take it slowly, it will be easier. But I don't have much time left, so I want to get started."

Helper: "Okay, well let's take the issues one at a time. First, you indicated that you want to have more meaningful relationships. What have you tried in the past?" (The helper wants to slow Sam down and take the issues separately to make sure that a small change can be accomplished, so the helper first restates Sam's goal and then asks an open question to assess what Sam has tried before in just one of the areas of concern.)

Client: "Well, I'm pretty shy. It's not easy for me to make friends. I never really joined groups or clubs or anything. I guess I hoped that people would come to me. My parents always pushed people on me, so I never took an active role in making friends."

Helper: "What would your goal be in terms of relationships?" (To set goals, the helper asks Sam an open question.)

Client: "I don't need a lot of friends. I would be more interested in having two or three close friends—people I could really count on."

Helper: "Okay, let's brainstorm how you might go about making some new friends. What ideas do you have?" (The helper wants to help Sam brainstorm about ways to obtain the goal and so explains the process and then asks Sam for ideas.)

Client: "I thought about joining a cancer support group. There would be a lot of people there who are going through the same thing I am and would understand me. Also, my neighbor suggested that there's a poker game starting with a bunch of guys in the building. It's only once a month, but I like playing poker. I always wanted to do something like that, but I thought I should be working. Oh, I just remembered that a person who I used to be friends with in college moved back to town. Maybe I could get together with him."

Helper: "Those sound like terrific ideas. Are some of them more appealing than others?" (Because the helper first wants to reinforce Sam for coming up with lots of good ideas, he uses an encourager. Then the helper wants to help Sam choose among the ideas to make sure that Sam leaves with a definite plan, and so asks an open question about evaluating the ideas.)

Client: "Actually, I think I could easily do all of them. The cancer support group is once a week and it's not far away. The poker game is only once a month. And I've been meaning to call my friend anyway. So that doesn't seem like too much at all. I definitely want to do those things. But it still leaves one empty spot. I would like to have a good relationship with a woman before I die. I wonder, you know, I've been thinking a lot about my ex-wife lately. I think that a lot of the problems in our marriage were because of my passivity and never having resolved things with my parents. Now that I have some understanding of my relationship with my parents, I think I could be different with my ex-wife. I realize now that she is not my mother. She does have some quirks, but I do still care for her."

Helper: "Well, it's certainly worth checking out to see whether she's still available and interested." (The helper wants to encourage Sam in pursuing a good idea and so offers his opinion that the idea is a good one.)

Client: "I know that she's not with anybody. Because of our daughter, I have a pretty good idea what's going on in her life. And if I got back together with my ex-wife, I could also spend more time with my daughter, which is something I really want to do."

Helper: "It sounds like that might work. But I need to caution you that things might not be so smooth given all the past history that you and she had. You were very passive and might still have a tendency to fall into those behaviors. I think we need to work on some assertiveness training for you to be able to stand up to her better and say what's on your mind." (Helper wants to support Sam but also challenges Sam to be aware that things may not be as smooth as he hopes. Helper also wants to make suggestions for what might help Sam with these issues so gives a directive.)

Client: "That would be helpful. Could we begin today?"

Helper: "Sure, give me an example of a recent situation with your ex-wife in which you were passive and you wished that you had behaved differently." (Helper starts out asking for a specific example of an interaction.)

Client: "She might say something like that she thinks I ought to be spending more time with our daughter. She gets mad that I don't take more responsibility. She has her ideas of exactly what I ought to be doing and doesn't mince words. Yesterday she called and wanted to know exactly what I planned to do about the babysitting situation. I just said I didn't know, I hadn't really thought about it, and I was really busy right then. I felt irritated that she was bringing it up and was so bossy that I shut down and wouldn't give her any satisfaction."

Helper: "Okay, let's role-play that so I get a clear idea of what happened. I'll be your ex-wife and you be you. I want you first to role-play exactly what you did in the situation." (The helper wants to get a clearer idea of what actually happens in a specific situation and so uses a process advisement.)

Helper: "Okay, I'm your ex-wife. Mark, I want you to take more responsibility for our daughter. I just can't handle it all. I'm supposed to be working full time and I can't be the one to take off for everything. I'm going to lose my job if I keep having to take off every time she gets sick or needs to go to the doctor. You know that the day care center won't let her come if she has even the slightest sniffle. Plus, she needs to see her father more. She needs to have you around." (The helper plays the role of the client's ex-wife to provide a stimulus to which the client can respond.)

Client: (whines) "Well, I just can't do more right now. I'm so busy at school."

Helper: "Okay, let's stop there. What were you aware of feeling?" (The helper feels that something significant has happened and so stops the role-play and asks Sam to become aware of his inner experiencing.)

Client: "I felt resentful. She's bossing me around again, and I don't like it. She's right of course, that I ought to spend more time taking my share of the burden, but as soon as she starts up, I just don't want to do anything. I hear my mother's voice nagging me, and I shut down."

Helper: "That's great, you can really identify what's going on inside you. And did you notice your tone of voice?" (The helper first wants to reinforce the client for making connections and then asks more about the client's nonverbal behaviors to make Sam more aware of his feelings.)

Client: "Not really. I didn't notice anything."

Helper: "You sounded totally different from before. You actually started whining. Before, in talking with me, you were talking like an adult, but as soon as you role-played talking with your ex-wife, you sounded like a whiny child" (illustrates). (The helper gives Sam feedback about his behaviors.)

Client: "Wow, that's incredible. That's exactly what I do with my mother. I can't believe that it came out so quickly without my awareness. That's scary. And you played it exactly the way my ex-wife does—so bossy and controlling. I hate it when we get into these power struggles. Neither of us wins. But I can see how she feels that she has no choice but to get bossy and controlling when I get so passive and withdrawn."

Helper: "Now what would you like to say to her instead?" (The helper uses process advisement to direct Sam to think of a new way of behaving.)

Client: "I would like to say that she's right and that we need to work out a schedule because I really do want to do my part. I want to spend more time with my daughter—that's really not a chore. But I wish that she wouldn't treat me like a child. Perhaps if we could work on this like two equal adults, we could resolve this problem. I recognize my side of it, but she's got to see what she's doing too."

Helper: "Wow! That sounds great the way you said that. It sounded firm but not nasty. You weren't whiny. You sounded more in control of the situation, and I believed that you wanted to work it out with her. I think if I were your ex-wife, I would be willing to talk with you rationally. Do you think that you could say that to her?" (The helper reinforces Sam, gives him feedback about his behaviors, and asks an open question to assess the likelihood of his being able to do these behaviors.)

Client: "I think I could. I would have to overcome a lot of past experiences with her. But I think I could do that. I want to because I want things to change."

Helper: "Well, you were able to do it here, so I have confidence that you could be assertive with her. One thing that might help is if you took a deep breath before you say anything to her. Think about what you want to say, what you want to accomplish. Remind yourself that you are an adult and that she's not your mother." (The helper encourages Sam and gives him some direct guidance to offer further suggestions.)

Client: "Yeah, I think that would work. And I think if I told her ahead of time what I was trying to do, she would be very understanding. She often has said that we get tangled up in these situations that we can't seem to resolve. I think she knows that she gets bossy and doesn't want to but just feels really frustrated with the situation."

Helper: "Let's role-play it one more time to make sure you have it down. Again, I'm your ex-wife" (pause). "Mark, I want you to take more responsibility for our daughter. I want you to spend more time with her and help me out more when she needs to go to the doctor. I can't keep taking off work every time she needs to be taken out of day care" (pause). "Now remember to take a deep breath, Mark, and think about what you want to say to her." (The helper role-plays the ex-wife and then coaches Sam about relaxing and thinking before he starts talking.)

Client: "You know, you're absolutely right to be angry at me. I haven't done my share in the past, and I want to start doing my share now. But we need to step back and talk about how you and I are going to handle this situation. I want to quit acting like the bad child and forcing you to play the nagging mother to increase my involvement with our daughter. I'd like us to work on this like equal adults because I want to have a better relationship with you."

Helper: "That's great. You didn't have any whine in your voice. You assertively told her what you would like to happen rather than blaming her." (Helper reinforces Sam and gives specific behavioral feedback about what Sam did well.)

Client: "Thanks, it felt good. I might have to practice it a couple more times, but I liked how it felt. I think it would work with her too."

Helper: "Unfortunately, we are almost out of time for today. But I wanted to check in with you about how you felt about the ideas we came up with for you to make some changes." (The helper warns Sam that the end of the session is approaching and then asks for feedback about how Sam felt about what they did.)

Client: "I am really excited because I think this is something I can try. I feel hopeful about being able to have a better relationship with her."

▬▬▬ **What Do You Think?**

- What would you have done differently in the previous example to facilitate the exploration of action?
- How do you know when to move from one action step to another? How do you know when you have spent enough time in each of the steps?
- How do helpers decide which of the many action possibilities to pursue in a given situation?
- What might helpers do when clients say "Yes, but ..." frequently?

IDEAS FOR RESEARCH

Minimal research has been conducted on the helping skills in the action stage (although more has been done on the effects of specific strategies such as systematic desensitization). Research is needed to understand what works, with whom, and at which point in the action stage. A few of the issues that could be researched in the action stage include the following:

- Does action develop naturally? What might helpers do to encourage clients to move to action?
- When is insight necessary prior to action? Is action that develops without insight less permanent or less effective than action that develops with insight? How could you test your hypothesis about insight and action?
- Which approaches to action (e.g., directive vs. nondirective) work best with which types of clients?
- Helpers often have some resistance to moving into the action stage. What training procedures would be most useful for training resistant helpers?
- How does a helper decide which of the many action procedures to use?
- How would you follow up with clients to determine whether they have completed their action assignments?
- Clients vary in their readiness to pursue actions to change troubling behaviors. What personal characteristics of clients assist or impede movement to action? What personal characteristics of helpers assist or impede clients' movements to action?

LAB 14 Steps of the Action Stage

Goals: To teach helpers about how to do the steps of the action stage.

Divide into groups of four to six people, with one person taking the role of the client. The other people will alternate in the role of helper. A lab leader should direct the flow of the session. Helpers are encouraged to bring in a sheet outlining the steps (perhaps Exhibit 21.2), so that they remember what to do in each step.

Helper's and Client's Tasks During the Helping Interchange

1. Clients should talk about something that they understand at least somewhat and for which they know they need to take some action (e.g., increasing amount of study or exercise).
2. The helper should use basic helping skills with the client for about 5–10 min allowing the client to explore. The helper should use primarily open questions, restatements, and reflections of feelings.
3. When the client has explored, a second helper should take over and do the insight stage for 5–10 min. The helper should intersperse challenges, interpretations, self-disclosures, and immediacy with open questions, restatements, and reflections of feelings (thinking carefully first about his or her intentions).
4. When the client has gained some insight, another helper should take over and do Step 1 (explore action) with the client. Remember to assess the client's motivation to change.
5. A different helper should now do Step 2 (assess previous attempts to solve problem) with the client.
6. Another helper should do Step 3 (set specific goals) with the client.
7. Another helper should do Step 4 (brainstorm possible ways to reach goals) with the client.
8. Another helper should do Step 5 (explore the different options) with the client. Remember to explore values related to the different options and to examine the restraining and facilitating forces for each action.
9. Another helper should do Step 6 (decide on a specific action) with the client. Remember to come up with a specific, concrete action. Remember to assess the obstacles in performing the action and to develop methods to deal with the obstacles.

When helpers have trouble completing an individual step, the lab leader can prompt them about what is expected and how they might proceed differently.

Processing the Helping Interchange

The "client" can talk about what the experience was like and which steps were most helpful. The helpers can talk about how they felt trying to do the different steps. The lab leader can give specific behavioral feedback about the helpers' skills during the different steps.

(Continues)

Personal Reflections

- What are your strengths and areas that need improvement in terms of doing the action steps?
- Were you able to maintain empathy with the client while going through the steps?
- How familiar are you with various cognitive–behavioral interventions (e.g., relaxation training, assertiveness training)? How could you improve your familiarity with these approaches?
- How could you apply the behavioral principles to improve your skills as a helper?

LAB 15 Integration of Exploration, Insight, and Action Skills

You are ready to integrate the skills that you have learned so far. In this lab, you meet with a client and first use exploration skills to help the client explore. Next, you use exploration and insight skills to facilitate the client gaining insight. Then you use exploration and action skills to assist the client in deciding what type of action to take.

Goal: For helpers to participate in a 50-min helping session using all of the helping skills.

Helper's and Client's Tasks During the Helping Interchange

1. Each helper should be paired with a volunteer client whom they do not know.
2. Helpers should photocopy the necessary forms and bring them to the session: the session review form (Table 11.2), the helper intentions list (Appendix A), and the client reactions system (Appendix D).
3. Helpers should bring an audio- (or video-) tape recorder (tested ahead of time to ensure that it works) and a tape. They should turn the recorder on at the beginning of the session.
4. Helpers should introduce themselves and remind clients that everything they say is kept confidential. Helpers should indicate exactly who will listen to the session (e.g., peer, supervisor).
5. Each helper should conduct a 50-min session with the client. Be as helpful to your client as possible. Use exploration skills to help the client explore for about 20 min, then move to combining exploration and insight skills to help the client gain insight for about 15 min, and then combine exploration and action skills to help the client determine a course of action for about 15 min. Watch for the client's reactions to each of your interventions and modify subsequent interventions when appropriate.
6. Watch your time carefully. About 2 min before you need to stop, let the client know that you need to stop soon. Let the client know it is time to stop by saying something like, "We need to stop now. Thank you for helping me practice my helping skills."

Supervisor's Tasks During Session

Supervisors should monitor sessions so that they can provide feedback to helpers about basic helping skills. Supervisors can use the supervisor rating form (Table 11.3) to record their observations and evaluations.

Helper's and Client's Tasks During the Postsession Review of the Tape

1. After the session, each helper should review the tape with his or her client (review of a 50-min session takes about 90–120 min); alternatively, helpers might just review 10 min of each stage. Helpers should stop the tape after each helper intervention (except minimal acknowledgments such as "mmhmm," and "yeah"). Helpers should write down the key words on the session review form (see Table 11.2) so that the exact spot on the tape can be located later for transcribing the session.

(Continues)

2. Helpers should rate the helpfulness of the intervention and write down the numbers of up to three intentions that they had for the intervention. Helpers should respond according to how they felt during the session rather than when listening to the tape of the session. Use the whole range of the Helpfulness Scale and as many categories as possible on the intentions list. Do not complete these ratings collaboratively with clients.

3. Clients should rate the helpfulness of each intervention and write down the numbers of up to three reactions, circling any reactions that they hid from helpers during the session. Clients should respond according to how they felt during session rather than how they feel listening to the tape of the session. Clients should use the whole range of the Helpfulness Scale and as many categories as possible on the reactions system (helpers learn more from honest feedback than from "nice" disingenuous statements). Do not collaborate with helpers in doing the ratings.

4. Helpers and clients should write down the most helpful and least helpful event in the session.

5. Helpers should type a transcript of their 50-min session (see sample transcript in Table 11.4). You can skip minimal utterances such as "okay," "you know," "er," and "uh."

6. Divide the helper speech into response units (essentially, grammatical sentences).

7. Using the helping skills system (Appendix B), determine which skill was used for each response unit (i.e., grammatical sentence) in your transcript.

8. Indicate on the transcript what you would say differently for each intervention if you could do it again.

9. Erase the tape. Make sure that no identifying information is on the transcript.

Personal Reflections

- What did you learn about yourself as a helper from this experience?
- Were you able to work with the action stage successfully? What problems did you have getting the client to think about action?
- Were you able to move smoothly from exploration to insight to action?
- Which skills did you and the client find to be most helpful?
- How often did your intentions match your skills? Provide examples of when your intentions did or did not match your helping skills and think about why they did or did not.
- How did you feel about giving information and direct guidance?
- How did your client react to moving to action?
- How might you handle feeling too invested in the client doing whatever you wanted him or her to do?

V FINAL THOUGHTS

22 Putting It All Together

Whatever you do or dream you can do—begin it. Boldness has genius and power and magic in it.

Johann Wolfgang von Goethe

Josh was an honors student in psychology and had volunteered at a hot line before taking our helping skills course. He thought he knew how to be a helper when he started, but he quickly became discouraged after the first few labs when he had difficulty doing and integrating the skills. He considered giving up on his dream of being a counseling psychologist; the helping skills were more complicated and challenging to implement than he had ever imagined. After his first session with a client, however, Josh received positive feedback from his peers and lab leaders and began to feel like he was understanding what being a helper is all about. By the end of the course, Josh felt confident that with continued practice and graduate school experiences, he could develop the skills that he needed to help others.

CONGRATULATIONS, YOU have learned all the skills required to be an effective helper. Now comes the tough part. In this chapter, we review techniques related to managing sessions. We also discuss several issues related to integrating the helping skills in the three stages: conceptualizing clients, referral, and termination. Finally, we provide two examples of integrating the three stages.

HOW TO MANAGE SESSIONS

How to Begin Sessions

Helpers need to do several things at the beginning of the first session: introduce themselves, explain the structure of the helping process, discuss limits to confidentiality, and then ask the client what he or she wishes to focus on in the session. For further discussion of these tasks, refer to chapter 11.

At the beginning of subsequent sessions, helpers might sit quietly and wait for clients to talk about what is on their minds, or they might ask what clients would like to talk about that day. Helpers cannot assume that clients will continue talking about what they discussed the previous session or that clients have the same feelings that they had during the previous session. Many beginning helpers spend a great deal of time debriefing after sessions and approach subsequent sessions prepared for what to do differently to help clients with problems they discussed the previous session. Helpers are often surprised, however, when clients are not concerned with or interested in talking about the same issues. When clients leave the helping setting, many things happen that change the way that clients feel. They may have spent time thinking about the issues and may feel more resolved than when they left the previous session. In addition, other issues might have become more salient, or significant others might have had reactions to changes that clients made. Thus, helpers have to be prepared to respond to clients in the moment. Being prepared yet flexible is one of the biggest challenges of helping.

How to Develop a Focus

It is typically best for beginning helpers to focus on one problem at a time. Otherwise, there is a danger of becoming so diffuse that nothing gets accomplished. A clear focus typically involves a specific incident or behavior such as a fight with a roommate, procrastination over completing assignments, or concern over how to communicate with a parent. The focus should be neither too vague nor too diffuse. To develop a focus, helpers typically ask clients what is troubling them now. It may take a few minutes to determine what the most pressing issue is, because clients often start with one concern whereas another issue is actually more critical. For example, Michael initially said that he was concerned about his grandmother's imminent death. After talking for a few minutes, it emerged that Michael was far more concerned about the breakup of a relationship with a woman whom he had been dating for 4 years. So we focused on his feelings about the breakup for the rest of the session. If one cannot develop a focus, the lack of focus can become the focus of the exploration stage, with one possible outcome being that clients decide that they are not willing to engage in the helping process.

Once a focus is established, helpers begin the exploration stage with the goal of learning about the identified issue from the client's perspective. The helper's goal is to understand the client's experience of this concern. Although the focus stays on the problem, helpers also explore how the concern is affected by and influences other parts of the person's past, current, and future life. When the dyad has explored the client's experiences of the concern, they delve into reasons and try to develop insight into how the problem developed and what contributes to the maintenance of the problem. Finally, armed with insight, the dyad moves to thinking about what the client wants to do about the problem. If the client is not yet ready to change, the action might be on thinking about change (e.g., "If you could change, how would you like to be?" or "Would you like things to be different?"). However, if clients are ready to change, helpers might work with them to develop specific action plans or to modify existing action plans. Thus, clients leave each session with specific insight and action about the focal concern.

In subsequent sessions, we remind helpers that clients may have new concerns that they need to explore. The presenting problems might be the same, but clients might have changed their perspectives from having thought about their concerns over the intervening time. Alternatively, clients' problems might be entirely different because other things might have become more pressing. Hence, clients might spend one or more sessions on one problem. Helpers must respect client decisions about the focus of the sessions. For example, Judy initially sought help for academic underachievement. Once she understood her difficulties with studying and changed her study skills, she wanted to work on problems in interpersonal relationships with friends. Later Judy wanted to examine her relationships with her parents and her feelings about religion. Helpers should be aware of and assess the possibility, however, that clients may be switching topics each session to avoid making changes in their lives. Should this occur, helpers can use immediacy and challenge to help clients explore their difficulty with changing.

How to Develop Appropriate Boundaries

Helpers need to learn how to manage the boundaries of helping (i.e., the ground rules and expectations about the roles of participants). Boundaries can be about the structure of helping (e.g., length, fees, policies about touching and violence, confidentiality) or about the interpersonal nature of the interaction (e.g., no sexual intimacies, friendships or other types of relationships with clients outside of helping). It is interesting that theorists have not written much about boundaries, so helpers have had to figure out through clinical lore and experience which boundaries are most appropriate. Research about the practices of experienced helpers (Borys & Pope, 1989; Conte, Plutchik, Picard, & Karasu, 1989; Epstein, Simon, & Kay, 1992; Holroyd & Brodsky, 1977; Nakayama, Thompson, Knox, & Hill, 1998) and the ethical considerations discussed in chapter 4 provide some ideas about which boundaries are important.

Initially, helpers need to clarify the rules about confidentiality, the length of the helping, and any fees involved. Helpers typically choose to avoid involvement in social activities with clients outside of sessions, because such activities may make it difficult for helpers to be objective and for clients to feel comfortable disclosing in the helping setting. We encourage beginning helpers to provide a phone number of a work setting so that clients can reach them for emergencies but that they not give a home phone number unless clients are actively suicidal. Our reason for suggesting that helpers not give out their home phone number is because some clients take advantage of beginning helpers, who have difficulty setting limits and not talking on the phone. One graduate student helper vividly recalled her first client calling for several nights at midnight because she had not clarified that calling was not appropriate. When she finally let the client know after several nights that she could not keep calling every night, the client felt quite hurt and the therapeutic relationship was damaged. These issues are better discussed initially so that clients are clear about the rules and know the appropriate behaviors for the helping relationship.

Developing appropriate boundaries is often quite difficult. We recommend that helpers start out being overly cautious and then relax their boundaries as they gain experience. A consultation with one's supervisor can be helpful when a helper is in doubt about which boundaries are appropriate.

How to End Sessions

Helpers need to be aware of the time in sessions so that they keep to the contract of how long they meet with clients. Five to ten minutes before the end of the session, helpers might advise clients that the session is almost over. Mentioning the approaching end of the session allows clients time to prepare themselves for leaving the session and to reflect on what they have accomplished in the session. Some clients wait until a couple of minutes before the end of session to bring up important feelings. They could be anxious about the helper's reaction, ambivalent about discussing the topic, or trying to manipulate the helper into extending the session. Although we cannot make any general statements about why clients wait until the last minute to raise important topics, helpers should try to understand this behavior in their clients.

As a way of beginning to close the session, helpers might ask clients how they felt about the session and the work that was done. This processing of sessions is important so that helpers can become aware of how clients reacted to various interventions. As we mentioned in chapter 4, clients often do not reveal their feelings about the helper and the helping process unless asked explicitly. For helpers to be able to plan the next sessions, they need to know what worked and what was not effective. Helpers should not, however, ask only for client reactions to elicit platitudes about their skills. In fact, they should be suspicious if clients repeatedly talk about how wonderful helpers were. Instead, they should be genuinely interested in hearing both positive and negative reactions.

Helpers might reinforce clients for what they have done in sessions and encourage them to think about and make changes outside sessions. Some helpers assign homework (e.g., practice smiling and saying hello to one new person) or ask clients to summarize what they learned in the session. Summarizing can reinforce what has been accomplished. In closing, helpers sometimes shake hands or engage in a small amount of social pleasantries (e.g., "Have a good week," "Enjoy the holiday"), which can serve as a transition for clients in returning to their everyday life.

CONCEPTUALIZING CLIENT PROBLEMS

Helpers need to think about their clients between sessions to try to conceptualize their problems. Specifically, they need to think about the origins of the problems, the underlying themes in the problems, and appropriate interventions to help clients. One way to facilitate this conceptualization process is for helpers to make extensive process notes after each session to help them remember the salient issues that were covered during the session. In the process notes (see form in Appendix F), which are best done as soon as possible after sessions, helpers can use their experience and perceptions to write about the following areas (Mary Ann Hoffman, personal communication, January 9, 1998): (a) manifest content (what the client talked about), (b) underlying content (unspoken meanings in what the client said), (c) defenses and barriers to change (how the client avoids anxiety), (d) client distortions (ways in which the client responds to you as she or he has to other significant persons in her or his life, i.e., transference), (e) countertransference (ways in which your emotional, attitudinal, and behavioral responses may have been stimulated by the process), and (f) personal assessment (your evaluation of your interventions; what would you do differently and why).

These process notes can be given to the supervisor before supervision sessions. We recommend that helpers listen to the audiotapes or, even better, watch the videotapes of their sessions before they complete the process notes so that they can recreate what they were thinking and feeling and observe the client's reactions to their interventions.

Helpers should look for underlying themes and recurring patterns across all the problems that clients raise. For example, the client is always the passive victim in every encounter, the client idealizes everyone, or the client is always angry. These themes provide important clues for the underlying personality problems that need attention in helping.

Ideally, helpers should meet with supervisors for assistance in conceptualizing clients. Supervisors can aid helpers in thinking about various hypotheses about what caused and maintained problems as well as possible interventions to help clients. Supervisors can provide a different perspective to aid helpers when they become stuck in their perceptions and countertransferences.

Helpers also need to educate themselves about theories and research to obtain a framework through which to understand client dynamics (i.e., what causes and maintains problems). We are not so concerned about which theories or research helpers choose as long as they select a theoretical framework and read current research so that they can think carefully about their underlying theories and use these theories to intervene effectively with their clients.

TERMINATION

Because helping sessions do not continue forever (even in long-term psychoanalytic therapy), separation is inevitable. After helpers and clients have finished as much as they can accomplish within the confines of their contracted relationship, the time comes to terminate the helping relationship. They might have gone through several cycles of exploration–insight–action dealing with several different problems until clients felt ready to apply what they learned in sessions to managing their lives and problems independently. One goal of helping is to prepare clients to leave helping and become self-reliant. Just as parents raise children to grow up and leave home to function on their own, helpers teach and encourage clients to cope on their own.

When to End Helping

How can helpers determine when to terminate the helping relationship? Sometimes the end is imposed by external time limits (e.g., beginning helpers often are only allowed to provide 1–3 sessions; some counseling centers on university campuses allow only 6–12 sessions). In these situations, helpers have to determine what they can accomplish with clients in a limited number of sessions (e.g., specific goals such as symptom relief or increased study skills) and what cannot be accomplished (e.g., working through childhood sexual abuse, engrained interpersonal deficits, or personality change). Often, beginning helpers refer clients who need additional assistance to experienced helpers who can work with them for an unlimited number of sessions.

In contrast, in open-ended long-term therapy, helpers and clients decide when they are ready to terminate the relationship. Rarely is there such a thing as a "cure" because cure implies a static state rather than the process of living, which involves continual change and new challenges. Most often, clients decide they are tired, have reached a plateau and are ready for a break, or have accomplished as much as they can with a particular helper. Often clients signal to helpers that they are ready to terminate, whereas at other times helpers have to tell clients that they think they are ready to terminate. According to the ethical standards for psychologists, helpers should terminate with clients when they feel they are no longer working productively. Sometimes helping goes on interminably because neither therapist nor client knows when and how to end. We believe that helpers need to be very mindful of continuing helping sessions only when they are productive and when clients are benefiting.

Budman and Gurman (1988) proposed that helpers adopt a model like that of family doctors. Just as no one would expect that antibiotics given by a doctor to cure fevers would inoculate patients for the rest of their lives, they argued, we should not assume that one therapy experience cures a client for life. They suggested that it makes more sense to see clients on an intermittent basis, such that helpers see clients for a few sessions until the current issues or crises are resolved and then see them again when other crises or life transitions arise. With such a model, termination is not typically as difficult because clients know that they can return to their helpers when they need further help (if that helper is still available).

How to Terminate

Mann (1973) considered termination to be the most important task of all of therapy because loss is an existential fact of life and everyone must cope with loss. He recommended that considerable time be spent in planning and preparing for termination in both short- and long-term therapy. He suggested that helpers discuss termination in every session and continually remind clients of where they are in the process (e.g., "This is our eighth session; we have four sessions remaining. How do you feel about being almost through with this process?").

Clients sometimes think that helpers are exaggerating the concerns about termination because they cannot anticipate how they will feel when they leave the helping relationship. Once they have terminated, they have an understanding of the feelings involved, but then it is too late for helpers to process the feelings of abandonment and loss with clients. Hence, prior to termination, helpers must assess whether clients might have strong feelings about ending the relationship so that these feelings can be addressed adequately.

There are three main steps to effective termination of helping relationships: (a) looking back, (b) looking forward, and (c) saying goodbye (Dewald, 1971; Marx & Gelso, 1987; Ward, 1984). In looking back, helpers review with clients what they have learned and how they have changed. Clients also can provide feedback about the most helpful and least helpful aspects of the helping process. Reviewing the process can help clients consolidate their changes and provide clients with a sense of accomplishment. In looking ahead, helpers and clients set an ending date, discuss future plans, and consider the need for possible additional counseling. Helpers review with clients the issues that they still want to address. No helping process is ever complete. We keep changing (for better or worse) until we die. The task for helpers is to assist clients in identifying the ongoing issues, determining how they will address these issues, and clarifying how they can find support in their lives for making changes. If such plans are not realistic, helpers need to confront clients so that they do not set themselves up for failure. Finally, in saying goodbye, clients express their thanks to helpers, both share their feelings about ending, and both say their farewells.

Termination is often challenging for both helpers and clients. Once two people have spoken about many deep and personal issues, it is often difficult for them to think of not seeing each other again. Termination thus often brings up issues of loss for both helpers and clients. Some evidence shows that helpers and clients who have the most trouble with termination are those who have a history of painful losses (Boyer & Hoffman, 1993; Marx & Gelso, 1987). If loss has been painful in the past, it is difficult to go through again. Other clients may not experience intense sadness but may struggle with how to thank the helper and show appreciation for the helper's role in their process of change. Other clients (and helpers) may feel disappointment about not having received the "magic cure" and may feel upset that they still have unresolved problems. Helpers need to talk openly about the client's feelings about the separation. Furthermore, they need to anticipate the separation well ahead of time so that they have time to deal with the feelings that arise from ending the relationship.

Making a Referral

Clients' needs are sometimes beyond what helpers are qualified for or capable of delivering. For example, a client might have an eating disorder or a substance abuse problem and the helper might lack expertise in that area. Sometimes the helper and client have accomplished as much as they can together, but the client needs a different kind of help. Referrals also are common when an agency has a time limit but clients still need more assistance, or when clients need marital or family therapy and the helper is trained only in individual therapy. Family treatment is typically more beneficial than individual treatment if clients are having difficulties with family members (see Haley, 1987; Minuchin, 1974; Nichols & Schwartz, 1991; Satir, 1988). In addition, clients might need referrals for medication, long-term therapy, assessment of learning disabilities, financial assistance, housing information, spiritual guidance, or legal advice.

Helpers need to be careful to explain to clients the reason for the referral. Otherwise, clients could easily feel that they are hopeless, need endless treatment, or are "bad clients." If helpers do a thorough job of the three steps of termination discussed above, clients are less likely to have negative feelings about being referred.

EXAMPLES OF AN EXTENDED INTERACTION

Career Concerns

Two examples are presented to illustrate working through all three stages. For ease of presentation, these examples present all three stages in single sessions, although working through all three stages often requires more than a single session.

The first example is a session with a young woman, Maria, who sought assistance because she could not decide on a major. Career concerns are common issues that many people struggle with throughout the life cycle (Brown & Brooks, 1991; Zunker, 1994). However, career difficulties are not as simplistic as psychologists once thought. It is not simply a matter of deciding on one's talents, interests, and skills. Our career identities are intertwined with our personal lives (Blustein, 1987; Brown, 1985; Hackett, 1993; Herr, 1989; Richardson, 1993; Savickas, 1994; Spokane, 1989), and hence both must be addressed in the helping process.

Exploration Stage

Helper: "Tell me a little about yourself and why you came for helping today." (The helper uses an open-ended question to start the interaction and to allow Maria to communicate her most pressing concerns.)

Client: "I'm a junior at the university. I should have declared a major already, but I just cannot decide what I want to do. I feel stuck, and they're trying to force me to declare something in the next couple of weeks. I don't want to just put something down and then have to shift after a semester or two. But I just don't have anything that I'm particularly good at. You know in high school when everyone else was in plays or orchestra or dancing or sports, I wasn't really doing anything. I just don't have any major talents. I seem to be mediocre in everything."

Helper: "You sound anxious about having to declare a major so quickly." (The helper wants to focus Maria on her feelings about the urgency of the situation.)

Client: "I am really anxious. You wouldn't believe how anxious I am. I haven't been able to sleep at night. I just keep trying to figure out what I want to do with my life. I guess I have never had any major ambitions."

Helper: "I wonder if you have feelings about trying to figure out who you are?" (The helper wants to determine how much of Maria's life is influenced by this issue.)

Client: "I have been feeling out of sorts. But I guess it's really hard to tell how much of it is because of trying to choose a major and not knowing who I am or where I'm going, and how much of it is due to feeling badly that I have never had a boyfriend and also feeling under stress that my parents are going through a divorce."

Helper: "Wow! Sounds like you have a lot of difficult things going on right now." (The helper wants to support Maria.)

Client: "Yeah, it's been a rough semester. I just found out that my parents were going to get a divorce over the holidays. They said that they stayed together until my younger sister went to college. I'm not sure that their staying together was actually so good for us because they were always fighting. Each of my parents has always talked to me about how horrible the other one was. I feel like I've always been the mediator, trying to help each of them understand the other."

Helper: "How was it for you being the one in the middle?" (The helper wants to allow Maria to explore her feelings more deeply.)

Client: "Part of me liked it because they both needed me. But it was also pretty bad because I felt like they both depended on me too much and I couldn't live my own life. I was glad to get away to college, but then I felt guilty about leaving. I go home a lot. I also feel like I have to take care of my little sister and shield her from the pain. I don't want her to end up feeling as badly about herself as I do about myself."

Helper: "It sounds like you feel pretty overwhelmed right now." (The helper wants to help Maria become aware of her feelings.)

Client: "I do. I feel about 20 years older than the other kids here. They are always talking about parties and drinking. It all seems so trivial."

Helper: "You mentioned that you have to choose a major soon. You also said that there's nothing you're particularly good in. Tell me more about that." (The helper wants to guide Maria back to exploring her problem in choosing a major.)

Client: "Well, I think I'm an average student. I get *B*s in most of my courses. I probably don't put as much time in as I could but I just can't get into studying."

Helper: "Tell me something about the courses that you have enjoyed." (The helper wants to help Maria explore specific interests.)

Client: "Well, I'm rotten at math and science. I almost flunked biology last semester. I guess the classes I have enjoyed most are my psychology courses. I like trying to figure people out. You know, I'm always the person whom people talk to about their problems. I'm taking this class in helping skills and am excited about it. I think I'm pretty good at helping. At least I enjoy being a helper."

Insight Stage

Helper: "What do you think got you so excited about learning helping skills?" (The helper wants to assist Maria in thinking about her motives.)

Client: "Everyone has always come to me with their problems, and I feel like I'm good at listening. And I was able to help my sister when she got so upset."

Helper: "I wonder if operating as a helper in your family helped you become interested in the helping field?" (The helper tries an interpretation to see whether Maria can engage in the interpretive process.)

Client: "You know, you may be right. Maybe helping my sister and mediating my parents' arguments helped me develop effective helping skills. It's funny that I've never really thought about majoring in psychology before. I guess my parents have always looked down on psychology. They would never go to a therapist because they have always said that people should solve their own problems. Well, they didn't do too good a job on their own. But I don't know, what do you think I should do? Why did you choose psychology?"

Helper: "I really liked to help other people with their problems. I also found that all my friends turned to me to talk about their problems." (The helper uses self-disclosure to reassure Maria that her feelings are normal.)

Client: "That's interesting. Do you like the field?"

Helper: "Yes, I like it a lot. Tell me more about your thoughts about psychology." (The helper wants to turn the focus back to Maria.)

Client: "Well, I think I might like to do it, but I don't know if I'm smart enough for it. I've heard an awful lot about how you have to be really smart to get into graduate school in psychology. I might not be able to make it."

Helper: "You know, you say you're not really smart, but I haven't heard much evidence for that." (The helper challenges Maria about her lack of self-efficacy.)

Client: "Well, I haven't gotten very good grades in college. I did get pretty good grades in high school though, and my SAT scores were pretty high. In fact, I was close to the top of my class."

Helper: "So something has happened during college to make you lose your confidence and not do as well in your classes. What might have contributed to your inability to study?" (The helper wants to facilitate Maria to think about insight and so restates and then asks an open question.)

Client: "Well, I'm not sure. Perhaps it has to do with my family, but I'm not sure how."

Helper: "Perhaps your concern about your parents and leaving home has distracted you from your ability to study." (The helper works with Maria to stimulate insight. Maria had a glimmer that her difficulties were related to her family, so the helper gives an interpretation that goes just beyond what Maria has stated.)

Client: "Hmm, I had never thought about that, but you're probably right. I've been so concerned about everyone else that I haven't had time to take care of myself. It's not really fair that my parents messed up my life just because they cannot get their act together."

Helper: "Yeah, you seem angry at them." (Maria has responded well to the interpretation, so the helper wants to help her explore her feelings about her discoveries.)

Client: "I am. I have been so worried about leaving my sister at home and not being able to calm my parents during their horrible arguments. These are supposed to be the best years of my life. And all I'm concerned about is them. When do I get my chance?"

Helper: "I wonder if your parents really need you as much as you think they do?" (The helper challenges Maria about her assumed need to be in the middle.)

Client: "Maybe they don't. In fact, maybe if I quit interfering, they would be able to make a decision about what they need to do. And you know my sister is not a kid anymore. She's 18 years old. I mean, I love them, but maybe I've just been doing too much, going home all the time."

Action Stage

Helper: "So what would you like to do differently?" (The helper wants to move Maria into thinking about how to make changes in her life.)

Client: "Well, I think I'm going to tell my parents that I am going to stop listening to each of their problems. I am going to suggest that they go to a therapist. It's been so helpful talking to you. That's what I think they need to do. If they don't do it, that's their problem, but I've got to get out from the middle."

Helper: "What feelings might come up for you in telling your parents your decision not to be in the middle?" (The helper wants to have Maria explore her feelings about this change.)

Client: "I think I'm pretty fed up right now, so I think I could do it. The difficult part will come when my mom calls late at night crying and says I'm the only one who really understands her. You wouldn't believe how many times she's done that right before a major exam."

Helper: "What could you do when that happens?" (The helper wants to guide Maria into problem solving what to do in the specific situation.)

Client: "Well, I could go to the library to study when I really need to focus on my work. Then my mom couldn't reach me. I really study better at the library anyway because the residence hall is so noisy."

Helper: "That's a great idea." (The helper reinforces Maria's feelings.)

Client: "Yeah, I don't know why I didn't think of that sooner. I guess I was just stuck in thinking I was the only one who could help my mom. You know, maybe I even kept her from going to a therapist because she could always talk to me. In fact, maybe I wanted her to talk to me because it made me feel so important and helpful."

Helper: "Yeah, that might be hard to give up. You feel pretty special when you believe that you're the one who can make everyone feel better." (The helper wants to warn Maria that it might be hard to change.)

Client: "Yeah, it could be hard. But I think it's time to start living my own life instead of living in their world."

Helper: "What could you do to make the transition easier?" (Again, the helper wants to prepare Maria for the difficulties involved in changing.)

Client: "Well, I would like to continue to talk with you. Would that be possible? I think if I had your support, it would be easier to change."

Helper: "Sure, we could arrange for eight sessions. That's the limit of the number of sessions I can offer to you through the counseling center." (The helper wants to let Maria know the limits of her availability.)

Client: "That would be great. Thanks."

Helper: "Now back to the major. What are your thoughts about what you would like to do about that at this point?" (The helper wants to bring some closure to the topic about the major since that was Maria's presenting concern.)

Client: "I'm leaning toward psychology. I get excited about some of the psychology courses that I've had, particularly the ones that involve personality and helping people. But I'm also interested in English. I've always liked to write. I've kept a journal for years. I have a fantasy of some day writing a novel or working on a newspaper."

Helper: "Perhaps you can do some more thinking about your likes and dislikes before the next session. It would also be a good idea to gather some information about majors and careers. There's some excellent information in the career center on campus. Perhaps you could go there before our next session. I'd also like you to take some vocational interest tests so that we can determine more about your interests. What do you think?" (The helper wants to give Maria specific guidance about how to proceed with this issue, but does not want to be seen as being too pushy.)

Client: "Terrific. Sounds like a great idea. Where do I take the tests?"

Helper: "I'll take you down and show you where to sign up after the session. How are you feeling about what we've done today?" (The helper wants to give Maria specific information about how to find the tests and also wants to assess how Maria felt about the session.)

Client: "I feel better than I've felt for so long. I actually have energy. I can't wait to take the tests. I can't wait to talk to my parents. I think they are going to understand that I need to do this for myself. They've been worried about me. It's not like me to be as upset as I've been. I can see some light at the end of the tunnel. It's very exciting."

Helper: "Good for you. So let's plan on meeting next week at the same time?"

Dream Interpretation

The three-stage model can be used with any type of problematic event. Hill (1996) has applied the three-stage model to working with dreams in psychotherapy. In the exploration stage, helpers encourage clients to retell the dream, provide rich description about dream images, associate to dream images, determine the triggers for the dream in waking life, and work with affect and conflict to heighten exploration. Exploration leads to the insight stage, in which helpers work with clients to understand the meaning of the dream in at least one of four levels: the phenomenological experience of the dream, how the dream relates to waking life, how the dream relates to past memories, or how the dream relates to parts of self. Insight leads to the action stage, in which helpers work with clients to determine what they would like to do differently (in the dream, in life, or in continued work on issues raised by the dream) because of what they learned in the dream interpretation. A number of studies (see most recently Hill et al., 1999) have found that dream interpretation is particularly effective for building a strong working alliance quickly and for helping clients develop insight, so helpers might consider using it in the helping process.

The following is an example of a single session with Joan, an older woman in the community, focused exclusively on dream interpretation.

Exploration Stage

Client: "I had a dream last night that really bothered me. It's a dream I've had several times, although it's often in a slightly different form. I would really like to understand it because I keep thinking about it."

Helper: "Great. Here's what we'll do. We will work with your dream by first exploring the individual images, then we will try to understand the dream as a whole, and then we will try to determine what you would like to do differently in your life based on what you learned about the dream. Why don't you start by telling me your dream in the present tense as if you are experiencing it right now." (The helper informs Joan about the structure that they will be following for the dream interpretation so that she can participate in the session more fully and then directs her about where to start. The helper asks Joan to tell the dream in the present tense, so that she can begin to immerse herself in the dream.)

Client: "In my dream, I have a few undergraduate classes left that I have not finished because I flunked them and have to take them over. So I have to go back to the university, even though I was supposed to have graduated. My old roommate's not there anymore, so I have to find a place to live by myself. I go and try to find my old apartment, but I can't find it. The city seems real industrial now, not like the little town it was before. I can't figure out how to find a new apartment. I think about alternatives. I think about asking my old roommate if I can go where she is and finish my courses there, but for some reason I can't ask her because we're not close friends anymore. I finally decide to go and live with my parents and go to a nearby university to finish. I've kind of resolved myself to this alternative, even though it seems rather disgusting. Then I realize that there's a residency requirement and I have to finish my courses at the university where I started. I feel defeated and wake up."

Helper: "What was your major feeling during and after this dream?" (The helper, wanting to facilitate Joan in reexperiencing the dream, asks an open question about feelings.)

Client: "The defeated feeling. I just felt like there was nothing I could do right. Everything seemed so hard. This is a recurrent dream. It's not exactly the same each time, but in each one I'm flunking out of some undergraduate classes, although usually it's a math class. The strange thing is that I successfully completed college several years ago. So I don't know why I keep having this kind of dream."

Helper: "You sound puzzled about why you would have the dream." (The helper wants to focus on Joan's feelings and uses a reflection of feelings.)

Client: "I am puzzled. I'd like to get whatever it is straightened out so that I could get on with my life and stop having these dreams."

Helper: "Well, maybe we'll figure that out as we work on the dream. Let's go back through the dream and look at each of the individual images. I'd like you to describe each image thoroughly and then associate, or say the first thing that comes to your mind, when you think of that particular image. Let's take undergraduate classes. What are your associations to undergraduate classes?" (The helper wants to stay with the dream because they haven't explored enough to determine the meaning of the dream or what Joan could do differently in her life. The helper informs Joan about the next step of the process and then asks an open question to get her associations to the first image.)

Client: "I didn't do so well in undergraduate school. I mean I did okay, but studying was not my first priority. I came from kind of a repressed family background. They wanted me to go to a church college and I didn't want to do that. I went to a university and ended up having to pay my own way. I kind of let loose while I was there. I ended up getting kind of wild, at least what was wild for me. It was actually pretty tame now that I look back on it, compared to what other kids were doing then. I guess I kind of made up for lost time in terms of socializing, so classes came in second. I remember one calculus class I had. I didn't go to class much and it met five times a week and counted for five credits. I just couldn't get it—not too surprising given that I didn't go to class much and didn't ask for any help. It is interesting that I had the same overwhelmed feeling from that class that I did in the dream—just like swimming through mud. Yuck. Anyway, the night before the final exam, I stayed up all night studying. Finally, right before dawn, I finally started to get it—it started to make sense. It was incredible. But of course, it was too late by then. But I got a *D* instead of flunking."

Helper: "What about your roommate?" (The helper asks for associations to another image.)

Client: "I roomed with her for 3 years. We were very close. I stayed on to go to graduate school, but she left to go to another university to get her master's degree. She started pulling away. She got angry at me. I can't recall after all these years quite what happened, but I felt bad to lose her friendship. It's interesting, she just started making contact with me recently and it feels good to have her back in my life."

Helper: "How about the old apartment?" (The helper asks for associations to another image.)

Client: "We had a lot of fun there. I remember parties. Walking home from the library where we used to study—it was a great place to see people. We always had conflicts with roommates because there were usually three of us living together. We had good friends next door. Those were good years."

Helper: "You said the city seemed industrial. Can you associate to that?" (The helper restates the dream image and then asks Joan for associations.)

Client: "Yeah, the city that the university was in was really small. It was one of these places that was really just a university town. It was real old fashioned. We went back recently and it was incredible how it has changed. The small town that used to have just one main street now has several big shopping centers. It was disorienting. I couldn't even find our old apartment when we went back. Hmm, that's interesting that there's a parallel."

Helper: "In the dream, you decide to go to your parents' home but that feels disgusting. What's that all about?" (The helper restates the dream image and then asks Joan for associations.)

Client: "Like I said, I didn't get along so well with my parents. Going back home would be like failing. I failed the classes and had to go home. I just can't imagine going back to live there. I had gotten out. I had broken free. To go back just seems like such a comedown. To live in that atmosphere again would be awful. Even thinking about it now, I get claustrophobic—afraid I won't be able to get free or be myself. You know, I have always had a hard time expressing my identity or even feeling like I know who I am. I can feel myself getting sucked back into the family and the church and sinking, just losing myself completely. It feels scary."

Helper: "Then you find there's a residency requirement and you have to go back to your first university to graduate. Say more about that." (Again, the helper restates and asks Joan for associations.)

Client: "Like I said, I just feel defeated. Nothing seems to be working right."

Helper: "I hear you feeling discouraged. Let's try to figure out what might have triggered this dream at this point in your life." (The helper acknowledges the feelings with a reflection and then informs Joan that they will be moving to the next step of looking for triggers in waking life.)

Client: "Boy, that's a good question. I feel pretty successful. Things are really going pretty well in my life. Good job. Family. But you know, I never feel secure. I feel like I'm always trying to prove something. I'm always running hard to try to succeed. I don't know when I will feel okay to settle down and just accept myself."

Helper: "Was anything specific going on at the time you had the dream?" (The helper asks for more information about current waking life to facilitate Joan in making the links.)

Client: "Yeah, now that you mention it, I was on a committee that was determining salary raises for everyone in our company. I wanted to get top ratings. I was really aware of every imperfection in my case. I haven't done this or that. I really want everyone to like me and to respect me. Boy, I sure do hate that about myself. I feel so needy."

Insight Stage

Helper: "Let's try to put the dream together then and see if we can come to some understanding of it. What do you think the dream means?" (Sensing that they have done an adequate amount of exploration for the amount of time they have, the helper informs Joan that they are moving on to the insight stage. Because the helper wants to hear Joan's initial ideas, he asks her what she thinks the dream means.)

Client: "Well, I think it's related to my desire to achieve. I'm trying to prove myself to all those people in the company. I want to pass and get their approval. You know I've noticed that I have this 'flunking out of college' dream whenever I'm under some kind of pressure. I often have it when I have to give a talk or when I'm feeling insecure."

Helper: "Okay. So it's clearly related to your current waking life. It sounds like you understand that pretty well. Let's go a little deeper, though, and try to understand how it might be related to your childhood." (The helper reinforces Joan for her initial interpretation and then challenges her to go a bit deeper and see if there are other alternative meanings.)

Client: "Well, I think it is. I was the youngest of four. Well, actually, I had a younger sister who died when she was very young. They always said something vague like she was 'weak.' My parents were really poor and probably didn't have enough money to really take care of her very well. The scary thing is that they called me 'weak' too. They were worried about my health when I was young. My aunt, who was a kind of doctor, expected that I would not be doing well by the time I was 25. I think I must have worried at some level that I was going to be the next to die off. I also felt that my siblings got a lot more attention than I did. My sister got my mother's full attention. She may not have liked it, but at least she got attention. My two sisters are so much more articulate than I am. Even now I feel like I just am incapable of speaking very well. I am better educated but I feel inadequate in comparison to them. And in comparison to everyone in my company, I feel inadequate. I can't believe I have the job I do where I have to do so much speaking in public."

Helper: "So you felt inadequate as a child." (The helper reflects Joan's feelings.)

Client: "Yeah."

Helper: "But in fact, are you inadequate now? You mentioned that you're doing pretty well in your job." (The helper challenges the accuracy of Joan's perception of herself.)

Client: "Yeah, I am. It's just that it's never quite enough. I keep thinking I have to do more and more."

Helper: "How does this interpretation fit so far for you?" (The helper checks out with Joan how well the interpretation fits.)

Client: "It does. I think I'm feeling anxious and inadequate right now in my job."

Action Stage

Helper: "Okay. Let's move to talking about what you'd like to do about what you've learned from your dream. First, how would you change the dream if you could?" (The helper informs Joan that they are moving into the action stage and asks her how she would change the dream, which is often an easy first step to thinking about change.)

Client: "I would like to have done well in all my undergraduate classes. I would like to have felt like I knew exactly what I wanted and went about getting it. You know graduate school was a lot easier for me than undergraduate school. I began to come into my own during graduate school. I would like undergraduate school in my dream to be more like that."

Helper: "Tell me more about what graduate school was like." (The helper follows up on Joan's statement about graduate school and asks her to describe what a good period of her life was like so that he can assess her strengths.)

Client: "I was more confident. I began to feel smart for the first time in my life. I really enjoyed what I was studying. I liked my classmates and the program. It all seemed like so much fun. The faculty treated us like colleagues, and I began to feel like I belonged."

Helper: "So it was a real different experience from being in your family." (The helper points out the discrepancy of graduate school and Joan's family experiences to highlight the positive experience for Joan.)

Client: "You're really right. I felt like I fit."

Helper: "How about now? Do you feel like you fit in your job?" (The helper brings the comparison to the present and asks about whether Joan is comfortable where she is currently.)

Client: "Sometimes I do, but lots of times I feel like I'm trying really hard but not quite making it."

Helper: "So you'd like to feel more like you did in graduate school?" (The helper makes a connection back to the graduate school experience so that Joan can begin to shape her goals of how she might like to live her life.)

Client: "Yes, I would. That's so interesting. I hadn't really made that connection before. You're right. I felt so much better about myself then. Anything seemed possible."

Helper: "How could you make that happen?" (The helper pushes Joan to think about changing her current situation.)

Client: "Hmm, that's a good question. I don't know. I need to think about that. You're right that I do need to make some changes. It's pretty scary to think of making changes in my job. Actually, I usually tell myself that I'm pretty happy there. Maybe I need to make some changes in the way I do my job. It makes me anxious even thinking about this right now. Aren't we out of time yet? The hour must be up."

Helper: "Yeah, I can tell you're really anxious. Perhaps we should continue our discussion next week. It sounds like you've got a lot to think about it. How could you continue to work on your feelings of inadequacy?" (The helper acknowledges Joan's anxiety but wants to leave her with something to think about so suggests further work.)

Client: "Well, it helps talking about it. I think I'll keep track of my dreams. I'm also going to do some thinking about my lifestyle. I guess the important thing is that I want to accept myself for who I am."

Helper: "Those things sound really good. I wonder it if would help to talk to some of your colleagues about this and see what their perceptions are of you?" (The helper reinforces Joan and then suggests additional action ideas.)

Client: "No, I don't think so, but I will talk with my husband. He usually has a pretty good perspective. Hey, I just thought of something—it's like I'm trying to get my colleagues' approval just like I tried to get my parents' approval."

Helper: "That sounds very plausible. Does that interpretation fit for you?" (The helper reinforces Joan for coming up with additional insights and asks an open question to encourage Joan to understand herself more.)

Client: "Yeah, it does. It's interesting, I've often thought that I felt like a kid in meetings. My colleagues are mostly older, and I've felt like the little kid. That's good."

Helper: "What implications does that have for changes you'd like to make?" (The helper goes back to asking Joan to think about action.)

Client: "Well, just like it was impossible to get more of my parent's attention, it's even more impossible to get my colleagues' attention. I don't really want it. I feel better when I focus in on what I want to do. I need to get centered on who I am and what I want from my life. I need to keep asking myself, 'What do I want?'"

Helper: "That sounds good. I wonder if it would be easier to do that if you took some specific time each week to ask yourself 'What do I want?' Maybe set aside an hour for yourself each week?" (The helper reinforces Joan and then makes another suggestion but is not dogmatic about it.)

Client: "No, that doesn't really work for me. But I will remind myself. I'll put a sign on my wall where I see it all the time to remind myself. That's a good idea. Thank you. This has been very helpful."

CONCLUDING COMMENTS

We hope that this book has provided you with the essential tools to begin your journey toward becoming a helper. We would appreciate any feedback (on the form at the very end of the book) that you might have about this text as we will continue to revise this text and work on improving our skills as teachers and helpers.

As a result of learning about helping skills, many of you may have decided that you would like to pursue a career that involves extensive use of helping skills, and others may have decided not to pursue such a career. Regardless of the career that you have chosen, we believe that these helping skills can be used to enhance your personal and professional functioning. We encourage each of you to set specific goals as to how to continue to develop these skills, given that this text and these practice exercises provide only a foundation on which your skills can be cultivated. Many sites are available for advanced training in helping skills (e.g., graduate programs in psychology, social work, counseling, psychiatry, psychiatric nursing). Volunteering at nonprofit agencies also provides a useful setting for obtaining additional practice for your skills while assisting people with pressing concerns. Whatever your path, we hope that it involves continued exploration of your feelings, increased insight regarding yourself, and positive changes that enable you to fulfill your potential and succeed in your interpersonal relationships and in your career.

What Do You Think?

- Compare and contrast the two examples of using the three-stage model. What did you learn? What would you have done differently if you were in the helper role?
- Which helping skills (e.g., open question, interpretation) and stage (exploration, insight, or action) do you prefer and feel most comfortable using as a helper? What is the relationship between the skills and stage you prefer and feel most comfortable with and the values you learned in your family, educational system, and culture?
- Evaluate your skills in terms of being able to deliver the skills in all three stages.
- How do you know when to terminate?

- Brainstorm several ways in which helpers can effectively end sessions.
- Discuss the feelings that you have when you end relationships.
- Who should decide that it is an appropriate time to terminate and what marker should help them decide that termination is appropriate?
- How might you react if a client decided to end the relationship before you thought the client was ready?
- What goals do you have for the continued development of your helping skills?

LAB 16 Conceptualizing Clients

Goals: To teach helpers about how to conceptualize clients and to think more about the timing of interventions.

Tasks

This lab is meant for advanced students who are seeing "real" clients. Within a classroom setting of 5–10 students, one student should role-play a client that he or she is seeing. The student who is doing the role-playing should provide only a very brief description of the client (age, gender, occupation, involvement in relationship with significant other, presenting problem) because the rest will be learned through the role-play. Another student should begin taking the role of the helper doing the exploration stage. Other students can take over the role of helper whenever necessary to continue the exploration.

When the leader determines that enough exploration has occurred (about 10–15 min), he or she can stop the process and ask the students to conceptualize the client's problems. They can talk about what they have learned so far about the client and what they do not know.

Then all the students can take turns being helpers and try using challenge, interpretation, self-disclosure, or immediacy. Each helper can interact with the client for two or three exchanges to see how the interaction works. The "client" should stay in the role and refrain from talking about interventions that he or she used with the real client or providing more information about the real client.

When the leader determines that an adequate amount of time has been spent in the insight stage, she or he can stop the process and ask the students to conceptualize the client's problems again. Helpers can discuss what they have learned through the insight stage. Helpers can talk about the theories that they think best explain how the client developed and maintains his or her problems. Furthermore, the leader can ask helpers to share what feelings and reactions were evoked in them by the client (e.g., boredom, anger, irritation, sexual attraction, deep empathy). Helpers can then turn their attention to discussing the action stage. Do they think the client is ready for action? If not, why not? What else needs to be done? If yes, what actions might be appropriate? How could the helper implement the desired interventions?

Again, one helper can begin the action stage with the "client," going through the first seven steps outlined in chapter 21 (explore action, assess what clients have tried before, set specific goals, brainstorm possible ways to reach goals, explore the different options, decide on an action, and implement the action). Other helpers can take over when one helper needs assistance.

Processing the Helping Interchange

The "client" can talk about what the experience was like and about what he or she learned that will help in working with the real client.

(Continues)

Personal Reflections

- What are your strengths and areas needing improvement in terms of conceptualizing clients?
- What are your strengths and areas needing improvement in being aware of your feelings and reactions toward clients? Identify and describe specific issues that tend to "hook" you most and make it most difficult for you to respond objectively to clients (e.g., hostility, sexuality, passivity, loose thinking, dependency)?
- What are the skills that you need to work on next in terms of your personal growth? Describe how you might gain more experience with the skills.
- What theoretical orientation is emerging for you? Describe your goals for learning more about this theoretical orientation.

References

Ainsworth, M. D. S. (1989). Attachments beyond infancy. *American Psychologist, 44,* 709–716.

Ainsworth, M. D. S., Blehar, M. C., Waters, E., & Wall, S. (1978). *Patterns of attachment: A psychological study of the strange situation.* Hillsdale, NJ: Erlbaum.

Alberti, R. E., & Emmons, M. L. (1974). *Your perfect right.* San Luis Obispo, CA: Impact Press.

Andersen, B., & Anderson, W. (1985). Client perceptions of counselors using positive and negative self-involving statements. *Journal of Counseling Psychology, 32,* 462–465.

Archer, D., & Akert, R. M. (1977). Words and everything else: Verbal and nonverbal cues in social interpretation. *Journal of Personality and Social Psychology, 35,* 443–449.

Arlow, J. A. (1995). Psychoanalysis. In R. J. Corsini & D. Wedding (Eds.), *Current psychotherapies* (5th ed., pp. 15–50). Itasca, IL: Peacock.

Atkinson, D. R., Morten, G., & Sue, D. W. (Eds.). (1993). *Counseling American minorities* (4th ed.). Madison, WI: Brown & Benchmark.

Auld, F., & White, A. M. (1956). Rules for dividing interviews into sentences. *Journal of Psychology, 42,* 273–281.

Bachelor, A. (1995). Clients' perception of the therapeutic alliance: A qualitative analysis. *Journal of Counseling Psychology, 42,* 323–327.

Bandura, A. (1965). Influence of models' reinforcement contingencies on the acquisition of imitative responses. *Journal of Personality and Social Psychology, 1,* 589–595.

Bandura, A. (1969). *Principles of behavior modification.* New York: Holt, Rinehart, & Winston.

Bandura, A. (1977). *Social learning theory.* Englewood Cliffs, NJ: Prentice-Hall.

Bandura, A. (1986). *Social foundations of thought and action: A social cognitive theory.* Englewood Cliffs, NJ: Prentice Hall.

Barkham, M., & Shapiro, D. A. (1986). Counselor verbal response modes and experienced empathy. *Journal of Counseling Psychology, 33,* 3–10.

Barrett, M. S., & Berman, J. S. (in press). Is psychotherapy more effective when therapists disclose information about themselves? *Journal of Consulting and Clinical Psychology.*

Basch, M. F. (1980). *Doing psychotherapy.* New York: Basic Books.

Basescu, S. (1990). Tools of the trade: The use of self in psychotherapy. *Group, 14,* 157–165.

Beauchamp, T. L., & Childress, J. F. (1994). *Principles of biomedical ethics* (4th ed.). New York: Oxford University Press.

Beck, A. T. (1976). *Cognitive therapy and the emotional disorders.* New York: International Universities Press.

Beck, A. T., & Emery, G. (1985). *Anxiety disorders and phobias: A cognitive perspective*. New York: Basic Books.

Beck, A. T., & Freeman, A. (1990). *Cognitive therapy of the personality disorders*. New York: Guilford Press.

Beck, A. T., Rush, A. J., Shaw, B. F., & Emery, G. (1979). *Cognitive therapy of depression*. New York: Guilford Press.

Beck, A. T., & Weishaar, M. (1995). Cognitive therapy. In R. Corsini & D. Wedding (Eds.), *Current psychotherapies* (5th ed., pp. 229–261). Itasca, IL: Peacock.

Bernieri, F. J. (1988). Coordinated movement and rapport in teacher–student interactions. *Journal of Nonverbal Behavior, 12,* 120–138.

Bernieri, F. J., Davis, J. M., Rosenthal, R., & Knee, C. (1994). Interactional synchrony and rapport: Measuring synchrony in display devoid of sounds and facial affect. *Personality and Social Psychology Bulletin, 20,* 303–311.

Bernieri, F. J., & Rosenthal, R. (1991). Interpersonal coordination: Behavioral matching and interpersonal synchrony. In R. S. Feldman & B. Rime (Eds.), *Fundamentals of nonverbal behavior* (pp. 401–431). New York: Cambridge University Press.

Bernstein, D. A., & Borkovec, T. D. (1973). *Progressive relaxation training*. Champaign, IL: Research Press.

Bibring, E. (1954). Psychoanalysis and the dynamic psychotherapies. *Journal of the American Psychoanalytic Association, 2,* 745–770.

Bischoff, M. M., & Tracey, T. J. G. (1995). Client resistance as predicted by therapist behavior: A study of sequential dependence. *Journal of Counseling Psychology, 42,* 487–495.

Blanck, G. (1966). Some technical implications of ego psychology. *International Journal of Psychoanalysis, 47,* 6–13.

Blustein, D. L. (1987). Integrating career counseling and psychotherapy: A comprehensive treatment strategy. *Psychotherapy, 24,* 794–799.

Bordin, E. S. (1979). The generalizability of the psychoanalytic concept of the working alliance. *Psychotherapy: Theory, Research, and Practice, 16,* 252–260.

Borys, D. S., & Pope, K. S. (1989). Dual relationships between therapist and client: A national survey of psychologists, psychiatrists, and social workers. *Professional Psychology: Research and Practice, 20,* 283–293.

Bowlby, J. (1969). *Attachment and loss: Vol. 1. Attachment*. New York: Basic Books.

Bowlby, J. (1988). *A secure base*. New York: Basic Books.

Boyer, S. P., & Hoffman, M. A. (1993). Counselor affective reactions to termination: Impact of counselor loss history and perceived client sensitivity to loss. *Journal of Counseling Psychology, 40,* 271–277.

Brainerd, C. J., & Reyna, V. F. (in press). When things that never happened are easier to remember than things that did. *Psychological Science*.

Brammer, L. M., & MacDonald, G. (1996). *The helping relationship: Process and skills* (6th ed.). Boston: Allyn & Bacon.

Breier, A., & Strauss, J. S. (1984). The role of social relationships in the recovery from psychotic disorders. *American Journal of Psychiatry, 141,* 949–955.

Brown, D. (1985). Career counseling: Before, after, or instead of personal counseling. *Vocational Guidance Quarterly, 33,* 197–201.

Brown, D., & Brooks, L. (1991). *Career counseling techniques*. Boston: Allyn and Bacon.

Brownell, K. D., Marlatt, G. A., Lichenstein, E., & Wilson, G. T. (1986). Understanding and preventing relapse. *American Psychologist, 41,* 765–782.

Budman, S. H., & Gurman, A. S. (1988). *Theory and practice of brief therapy*. New York: Guilford Press.

Bugental, J. T. (1965). *The search for authenticity*. New York: Holt, Rinehart, & Winston.

Burke, H. F. (1989). *Contemporary approaches to psychotherapy and counseling: The self regulation and maturity model*. Pacific Grove, CA: Brooks/Cole.

Burton, M. V., Parker, R. W., & Wollner, J. M. (1991). The psychotherapeutic value of a "chat": A verbal response modes study of a placebo attention control with breast cancer patients. *Psychotherapy Research, 1,* 39–61.

Cappella, J. N. (1981). Mutual influence in expressive behavior: Adult–adult and infant–adult dyadic interaction. *Psychological Bulletin, 29,* 101–132.

Carkhuff, R. R. (1969). *Human and helping relations* (Vols. 1 & 2). New York: Holt, Rinehart, & Winston.

Carkhuff, R. R., & Anthony, W. A. (1979). *The skills of helping: An introduction to counseling skills*. Amherst, MA: Human Resources Development Press.

Carkhuff, R. R., & Berenson, B. G. (1967). *Beyond counseling and psychotherapy*. New York: Holt, Rinehart, & Winston.

Carroll, L. (1962). *Alice's adventures in wonderland*. Harmondsworth, Middlesex, England: Penguin Books. (Original work published 1865)

Cartwright, R. D. (1990). A network model of dreams. In R. Bootzin, J. Kihlstrom, & D. Schachter (Eds.), *Sleep and cognition* (pp. 179–189). Washington, DC: American Psychological Association.

Cartwright, R. D., & Lamberg, L. (1992). *Crisis dreaming: Using your dreams to solve your problems*. New York: HarperCollins.

Cashdan, S. (1988). *Object relations therapy*. New York: Norton.

Caspar, F., Rothenfluh, T., & Segal, Z. (1992). The appeal of connectionism for clinical psychology. *Clinical Psychology Review, 12,* 719–762.

Claiborn, C. D., & Dowd, E. T. (1985). Attributional interpretations in counseling: Content versus discrepancy. *Journal of Counseling Psychology, 32,* 188–192.

Claiborn, C. D., Ward, S. R., & Strong, S. (1981). Effect of congruence between counselor interpretations and client beliefs. *Journal of Counseling Psychology, 28,* 101–109.

Cohen, J. (1960). A coefficient of agreement for nominal scales. *Educational and Psychological Measurement, 20,* 37–46.

Colby, K. M. (1961). On the greater amplifying power of causal–correlative over interrogative inputs on free association in an experimental psychoanalytic situation. *Behavioral Science, 10,* 233–239.

Condon, W. S., & Ogston, W. D. (1966). Sound film analysis of normal and pathological behavior patterns. *Journal of Nervous and Mental Diseases, 143,* 338–347.

Conoley, C. W., Padula, M. A., Payton, D. S., & Daniels, J. A. (1994). Predictors of client implementation of counselor recommendations: Match with problem, difficulty level, and building on client strengths. *Journal of Counseling Psychology, 41,* 3–7.

Conte, H. R., Plutchik, R., Picard, S., & Karasu, T. B. (1989). Ethics in the practice of psychotherapy: A survey. *American Journal of Psychotherapy, 43,* 32–42.

Cornett, C. (1991). The "risky" intervention: Twinship self–object impasses and therapist self-disclosure in psychodynamic psychotherapy. *Clinical Social Work Journal, 19*, 49–61.

Cournoyer, R. J., & Mahalik, J. R. (1995). Cross-sectional study of gender role conflict examining college-aged and middle-aged men. *Journal of Counseling Psychology, 42*, 11–19.

Crits-Christoph, P., Barber, J. P., & Kurcias, J. S. (1991). Introduction and historical background. In P. Crits-Christoph & J. P. Barber (Eds.), *Handbook of short-term dynamic psychotherapy* (pp. 1–16). New York: Basic Books.

Crits-Christoph, P., Cooper, A., & Luborsky, L. (1988). The accuracy of therapists' interpretations and the outcome of dynamic psychotherapy. *Journal of Counsulting and Clinical Psychology, 56*, 490–495.

Curtis, J. M. (1981). Indications and contraindications in the use of therapist's self-disclosure. *Psychological Reports, 49*, 499–507.

Curtis, J. M. (1982). Principles and techniques of non-disclosure by the therapist during psychotherapy. *Psychological Reports, 51*, 907–914.

Darwin, C. R. (1872). *The expression of the emotions in man and animals* (1st ed.). London: John Murray.

Delaney, D. J., & Heimann, R. A. (1966). Effectiveness of sensitivity training on the perception of non-verbal communications. *Journal of Counseling Psychology, 4*, 436–440.

Dewald, P. A. (1971). *Psychotherapy: A dynamic approach*. New York: Basic Books.

Duan, C., & Hill, C. E. (1996). Theoretical confusions in the construct of empathy: A review of the literature. *Journal of Counseling Psychology, 43*, 261–274.

Edwards, C. E., & Murdock, N. L. (1994). Characteristics of therapist self-disclosure in the counseling process. *Journal of Counseling and Development, 72*, 384–389.

Egan, G. (1994). *The skilled helper* (5th ed.). Monterey, CA: Brooks/Cole.

Eibl-Eibesfeldt, I. (1971). *Love and hate: The natural history of behavior patterns*. New York: Holt, Rinehart, & Winston.

Ekman, P., & Friesen, W. V. (1969). Non-verbal leakage and clues to deception. *Psychiatry, 32*, 88–106.

Ekman, P., & Friesen, W. V. (1984). *Unmasking the face* (reprint ed.). Palo Alto, CA: Consulting Psychologists Press.

Ekman, P., Friesen, W. V., & Ellsworth, P. (1972). *Emotion in the human face: Guidelines for research and an integration of the findings*. New York: Pergamon Press.

Elkind, S. N. (1992). *Resolving impasses in therapeutic relationships*. New York: Guilford Press.

Elliott, R. (1985). Helpful and nonhelpful events in brief counseling interviews: An empirical taxonomy. *Journal of Counseling Psychology, 32*, 307–322.

Elliott, R., Barker, C. B., Caskey, N., & Pistrang, N. (1982). Differential helpfulness of counselor verbal response modes. *Journal of Counseling Psychology, 29*, 354–361.

Elliott, R., Hill, C. E., Stiles, W. B., Friedlander, M. L., Mahrer, A. R., & Margison, F. R. (1987). Primary therapist response modes: Comparison of six rating systems. *Journal of Consulting and Clinical Psychology, 55*, 218–223.

Elliott, R., Shapiro, D. A., Firth-Cozens, J., Stiles, W. B., Hardy, G. E., Llewelyn, S. P., & Margison, F. R. (1994). Comprehensive process analysis of insight events in cognitive–behavioral and psychodynamic–interpersonal psychotherapies. *Journal of Counseling Psychology, 41*, 449–463.

Ellis, A. (1962). *Reason and emotion in psychotherapy*. New York: Lyle Stuart.

Ellis, A. (1973). *Humanistic psychotherapy: The rational–emotive approach*. New York: McGraw-Hill.

Ellis, A. (1995). Rational emotive behavior therapy. In R. Corsini & D. Wedding (Eds.), *Current psychotherapies* (5th ed., pp. 161–196). Itasca, IL: Peacock.

Epstein, R. S., Simon, R. I., & Kay, G. G. (1992). Assessing boundary violations in psychotherapy: Survey results with the Exploitation Index. *Bulletin of the Menninger Clinic, 54,* 150–166.

Erikson, E. H. (1963). *Childhood and society* (2nd ed.). New York: Norton.

Eysenck, H. J. (1952). The effects of psychotherapy: An evaluation. *Journal of Consulting Psychology, 16,* 319–324.

Falk, D., & Hill, C. E. (1992). Counselor interventions preceding client laughter in brief therapy. *Journal of Counseling Psychology, 39,* 39–45.

Farber, B. A., & Geller, J. D. (1994). Gender and representation in psychotherapy. *Psychotherapy, 31,* 318–326.

Fenichel, O. (1941). *The psychoanalytic theory of neurosis*. New York: Norton.

Ferenczi, S., & Rank, O. (1956). *The development of psycho-analysis* (C. Newton, Trans.). New York: Dover. (Original work published 1925)

Festinger, L. (1957). *A theory of cognitive dissonance*. Evanston, IL: Row, Peterson.

Forsyth, N. L., & Forsyth, D. R. (1982). Internality, controllability, and the effectiveness of attributional interpretations in counseling. *Journal of Counseling Psychology, 29,* 140–150.

Frank, J. D., & Frank, J. B. (1991). *Persuasion and healing: A comparative study of psychotherapy* (3rd ed.). Baltimore: Johns Hopkins University Press.

Frankl, V. (1959). *Man's search for meaning*. New York: Simon & Shuster.

Freud, S. (1933). *New introductory lectures on psychoanalysis* (J. H. Sprott, Trans.). New York: Norton.

Freud, S. (1943). *A general introduction to psychoanalysis* (J. Riviere, Trans.). New York: Garden City. (Original work published 1920)

Freud, S. (1949). *An outline of psychoanalysis* (J. Strachey, Trans.). New York: Norton. (Original work published 1940)

Freud, S. (1953). Fragment of an analysis of a case of hysteria. In J. Strachey (Ed.), *Standard edition of the complete psychological works of Sigmund Freud* (Vol. 7, pp. 15–122). London: Hogarth Press. (Original work published 1905)

Freud, S. (1953). Remembering, repeating, and working through. In J. Strachey (Ed.), *Standard edition of the complete psychological works of Sigmund Freud* (Vol. 12, pp. 147–156). London: Hogarth Press. (Original work published 1914)

Freud, S. (1959). The dynamics of transference. In E. Jones (Ed.) & J. Riviere (Trans.), *Collected papers* (pp. 312–322). New York: Basic Books. (Original work published 1912)

Freud, S. (1961). The ego and the id. In J. Strachey (Ed. and Trans.), *Standard edition of the complete psychological works of Sigmund Freud* (Vol. 19, pp. 3–66). London: Hogarth Press. (Original work published 1923)

Freud, S. (1963). Psychoanalysis. In P. Reiff (Ed.), *Character and culture* (pp. 230–251). New York: Collier. (Original work published 1923)

Friedman, E. H. (1990). *Friedman's fables*. New York: Guilford Press.

Fromm-Reichmann, F. (1950). *Principles of intensive psychotherapy*. Chicago: University of Chicago Press.

Geller, J. D., Cooley, R. S., & Hartley, D. (1981). Images of the psychotherapist: A theoretical and methodological perspective. *Imagination, Cognition, and Personality, 1,* 123–146.

Geller, J. D., & Farber, B. A. (1993). Factors influencing the process of internalization in psychotherapy. *Psychotherapy Research, 3,* 166–180.

Geller, J. D., & Farber, B. A. (1997, August). *Why therapists do and don't self-disclose*. Paper presented at the 105th Annual Convention of the American Psychological Association, Chicago, IL.

Gelso, C. J., & Carter, J. A. (1985). The relationship in counseling and psychotherapy. *Counseling Psychologist, 13,* 155–243.

Gelso, C. J., & Carter, J. A. (1994). Components of the psychotherapy relationship: Their interaction and unfolding during treatment. *Journal of Counseling Psychology, 41,* 296–306.

Gelso, C. J., & Fretz, B. R. (1992). *Counseling psychology*. Orlando, FL: Holt, Rinehart & Winston.

Gelso, C. J., & Hayes, J. (1998). *The psychotherapy relationship: Theory, research, and practice*. New York: Wiley.

Gelso, C. J., Hill, C. E., Mohr, J., Rochlen, A., & Zack, J. (in press). The face of transference in successful long-term therapy. *Journal of Counseling Psychology*.

Gillespie, J. F., Jr. (1951). Verbal signs of resistance in client-centered therapy. *Dissertation Abstracts International, 5*(01), 454B. (University Microfilms No. AAI000305)

Glass, A. L., & Holyoak, L. J. (1986). *Cognition* (2nd ed.). New York: Random House.

Goldfried, M. R., & Davison, G. C. (1994). *Clinical behavior therapy* (2nd ed.). New York: Wiley.

Goldfried, M. R., & Trier, C. S. (1974). Effectiveness of relaxation as an active coping skill. *Journal of Abnormal Psychology, 83,* 348–355.

Good, G. E., Robertson, J. M., O'Neil, J. M., Fitzgerald, L. F., Stevens, M., DeBrod, K. A., Bartels, K. M., & Braverman, D. G. (1995). Male gender role conflict: Psychometric issues and relations to psychological distress. *Journal of Counseling Psychology, 42,* 3–10.

Gourash, N. (1978). Help-seeking: A review of the literature. *American Journal of Community Psychology, 6,* 413–423.

Grace, M., Kivlighan, D. M., & Kunce, J. (1995). The effect of nonverbal skills training on counselor trainee nonverbal sensitivity and responsiveness and on session impact and working alliance ratings. *Journal of Counseling and Development, 73,* 547–552.

Greenberg, L. S. (1979). Resolving splits: The two-chair technique. *Psychotherapy: Theory, Research, and Practice, 16,* 310–318.

Greenberg, L. S., & Clarke, K. (1979). The differential effects of the two-chair experiment and empathic reflections at a conflict marker. *Journal of Counseling Psychology, 26,* 1–8.

Greenberg, L. S., & Dompierre, L. (1981). Differential effects of gestalt two-chair dialogue and empathic reflection at a split in counseling. *Journal of Counseling Psychology, 24,* 288–294.

Greenberg, L. S., Elliott, R., & Lietaer, G. (1994). Research on experiential psychotherapies. In A. E. Bergin & S. L. Garfield (Eds.), *Handbook of psychotherapy and behavior change* (4th ed., pp. 509–539). New York: Wiley.

Greenberg, L. S., Rice, L. N., & Elliott, R. (1993). *Facilitating emotional change*. New York: Guilford Press.

Greenberg, L. S., & Webster, M. C. (1982). Resolving decisional conflict by gestalt two-chair dialogue: Relating process to outcome. *Journal of Counseling Psychology, 29*, 468–477.

Greenson, R. R. (1967). *The technique and practice of psychoanalysis* (Vol. 1). Madison, CT: International Universities Press.

Gross, A. E., & McMullen, P. A. (1983). Models of the help-seeking process. In B. DePaulo, A. Nadler, & D. Fisher (Eds.), *New directions in helping* (Vol. 2, pp. 45–70). New York: Academic Press.

Haase, R. F., & Tepper, D. T., Jr. (1972). Nonverbal components of empathic communication. *Journal of Counseling Psychology, 19*, 417–426.

Hackett, G. (1993). Career counseling and psychotherapy: False dichotomies and recommended remedies. *Journal of Career Assessment, 1*, 105–117.

Haley, J. (1987). *Problem-solving therapy*. San Francisco: Jossey-Bass.

Hall, E. T. (1968). Proxemics. *Current Anthropology, 9*, 83–108.

Hall, J. A., Rosenthal, R., Archer, D., DiMatteo, M. R., & Rogers, P. L. (1978). Profile of nonverbal sensitivity. In P. McReynolds (Ed.), *Advances in psychological assessment* (Vol. 4, pp. 179–221). San Francisco: Jossey-Bass.

Hanson, W. E., Claiborn, C. D., & Kerr, B. (1997). Differential effects of two test interpretation styles in counseling: A field study. *Journal of Counseling Psychology, 44*, 400–405.

Harper, R. G., Wiens, A. N., & Matarazzo, J. D. (1978). *Nonverbal communication: The state of the art*. New York: Wiley.

Hayes, J. A., McCracken, J. E., McClanahan, M. K., Hill, C. E., Harp, J. S., & Carozzoni, P. (1998). Therapist perspectives on countertransference: Qualitative data in search of a theory. *Journal of Counseling Psychology, 45*, 468–482.

Helms, J. E., & Cook, D. A. (1999). *Using race and culture in counseling and psychotherapy: Theory and practice*. Needham, MA: Allyn & Bacon.

Heppner, P. P., Kivlighan, D. M., & Wampold, B. E. (1999). *Research designs in counseling* (2nd ed.). Pacific Grove, CA: Brooks/Cole.

Herr, E. L. (1989). Career development and mental health. *Journal of Career Development, 16*, 5–18.

Highlen, P. S., & Hill, C. E. (1984). Factors affecting client change in individual counseling: Current status and theoretical speculations. In S. D. Brown & R. W. Lent (Eds.), *Handbook of counseling psychology* (pp. 334–398). New York: Wiley.

Hill, C. E. (1978). Development of a counselor verbal response category system. *Journal of Counseling Psychology, 25*, 461–468.

Hill, C. E. (1985). *Manual for the Hill counselor verbal response modes category system* (rev.). Unpublished manuscript, University of Maryland at College Park.

Hill, C. E. (1986). An overview of the Hill Counselor and Client Verbal Response Modes Category Systems. In L. S. Greenberg & W. M. Pinsof (Eds.), *The psychotherapeutic process: A research handbook* (pp. 131–160). New York: Guilford Press.

Hill, C. E. (1989). *Therapist techniques and client outcomes: Eight cases of brief psychotherapy*. Newbury Park, CA: Sage.

Hill, C. E. (1990). A review of exploratory in-session process research. *Journal of Consulting and Clinical Psychology, 58*, 288–294.

Hill, C. E. (1991). Almost everything you ever wanted to know about how to do process research on counseling and psychotherapy but didn't know who to ask. In C. E. Watkins & L. J. Schneider (Eds.), *Research in counseling* (pp. 85–118). Hillsdale, NJ: Erlbaum.

Hill, C. E. (1992). An overview of four measures developed to test the Hill process model: Therapist intentions, therapist response modes, client reactions, and client behaviors. *Journal of Counseling and Development, 70,* 729–737.

Hill, C. E. (1996). *Working with dreams in psychotherapy.* New York: Guilford Press.

Hill, C. E., Carter, J. A., & O'Farrell, M. K. (1983). A case study of the process and outcome of time-limited counseling. *Journal of Counseling Psychology, 30,* 3–18.

Hill, C. E., & Corbett, M. M. (1993). A perspective on the history of process and outcome research in counseling psychology. *Journal of Counseling Psychology, 40,* 3–24.

Hill, C. E., Corbett, M. M., Kanitz, B., Rios, P., Lightsey, R., & Gomez, M. (1992). Client behavior in counseling and therapy sessions: Development of a pantheoretical measure. *Journal of Counseling Psychology, 39,* 539–549.

Hill, C. E., & Gormally, J. (1977). Effect of reflection, restatement, probe, and nonverbal behaviors on client affect. *Journal of Counseling Psychology, 24,* 92–97.

Hill, C. E., Helms, J. E., Spiegel, S. B., & Tichenor, V. (1988). Development of a system for categorizing client reactions to therapist interventions. *Journal of Counseling Psychology, 35,* 27–36.

Hill, C. E., Helms, J. E., Tichenor, V., Spiegel, S. B., O'Grady, K. E., & Perry, E. S. (1988). The effects of therapist response modes in brief psychotherapy. *Journal of Counseling Psychology, 35,* 222–233.

Hill, C. E., Mahalik, J. R., & Thompson, B. J. (1989). Therapist self-disclosure. *Psychotherapy, 26,* 290–295.

Hill, C. E., Nutt-Williams, E., Heaton, K. J., Thompson, B. J., & Rhodes, R. H. (1996). Therapist retrospective recall of impasses in long-term psychotherapy: A qualitative analysis. *Journal of Counseling Psychology, 43,* 207–217.

Hill, C. E., O'Brien, K. M., Kolchakian, M. R., Quimby, J. L., Kellums, I. S., & Zack, J. S. (1998). *Training undergraduate students in helping skills.* Unpublished manuscript, University of Maryland.

Hill, C. E., & O'Grady, K. E. (1985). List of therapist intentions illustrated in a case study and with therapists of varying theoretical orientations. *Journal of Counseling Psychology, 32,* 3–22.

Hill, C. E., Siegelman, L., Gronsky, B., Sturniolo, F., & Fretz, B. R. (1981). Nonverbal communication and counseling outcome. *Journal of Counseling Psychology, 28,* 203–212.

Hill, C. E., & Stephany, A. (1990). The relationship of nonverbal behaviors to client reactions. *Journal of Counseling Psychology, 37,* 22–26.

Hill, C. E., Thames, T. B., & Rardin, D. (1979). A comparison of Rogers, Perls, and Ellis on the Hill counselor verbal response category system. *Journal of Counseling Psychology, 26,* 198–203.

Hill, C. E., Thompson, B. J., Cogar, M. M., & Denman, D. W., III. (1993). Beneath the surface of long-term therapy: Client and therapist report of their own and each other's covert processes. *Journal of Counseling Psychology, 40,* 278–288.

Hill, C. E., Thompson, B. J., & Corbett, M. M. (1992). The impact of therapist ability to perceive displayed and hidden client reactions on immediate outcome in first sessions of brief therapy. *Psychotherapy Research, 2,* 143–155.

Hill, C. E., Thompson, B. J., & Mahalik, J. R. (1989). Therapist interpretation. In C. E. Hill, *Therapist techniques and client outcomes: Eight cases of brief psychotherapy* (pp. 284–310), Newbury Park, CA: Sage.

Hill, C. E., Thompson, B. J., & Williams, E. N. (1997). A guide to conducting consensual qualitative research. *The Counseling Psychologist, 25,* 517–572.

Hill, C. E., Zack, J. S., Wonnell, T. L., Hoffman, M. A., Rochlen, A. B., Goldberg, J. L., Nakayama, E. Y., Heaton, K. J., Kelley, F. A., Eiche, K., Tomlinson, M. J., & Hess, S. (1999). *A structured brief therapy with a focus on dreams or loss.* Manuscript in preparation, University of Maryland.

Hoglend, P. (1996). Long-term effects of transference interpretations: Comparing results from a quasiexperimental and a naturalistic long-term follow-up study of brief dynamic psychotherapy. *Acta Psychiatrica Scandinavica, 93,* 205–211.

Holroyd, J. C., & Brodsky, A. (1977). Psychologists' attitudes and practices regarding erotic and nonerotic physical contact with patients. *American Psychologist, 32,* 843–849.

Horvath, A. O., & Symonds, B. D. (1991). Relation between working alliance and outcome in psychotherapy: A meta-analysis. *Journal of Counseling Psychology, 38,* 139–149.

Howard, K. I., Lueger, R. J., Maling, M. S., & Martinovich, Z. (1993). A phase model of psychotherapy outcome: Causal mediation of change. *Journal of Consulting and Clinical Psychology, 59,* 12–19.

Hunter, M., & Struve, J. (1998). *The ethical use of touch in psychotherapy.* Thousand Oaks, CA: Sage.

Ivey, A. E. (1994). *Intentional interviewing and counseling: Facilitating client development in a multicultural society* (3rd ed.). Pacific Grove, CA: Brooks/Cole.

Izard, C. E. (1977). *Human emotions.* New York: Plenum.

Jacobson, E. (1929). *Progressive relaxation.* Chicago: University of Chicago Press.

Jourard, S. M. (1971). *The transparent self.* New York: Van Nostrand Reinhold.

Jung, C. G. (1984). *Dream analysis.* Princeton, NJ: Princeton University Press.

Kazdin, A. E. (1994). *Behavior modification in applied settings* (5th ed.). Pacific Grove, CA: Brooks/Cole.

Kelly, A. E. (1998). Clients' secret keeping in outpatient therapy. *Journal of Counseling Psychology, 45,* 50–57.

Kendon, A. (1967). Some functions of gaze-direction in social interaction. *Acta Psychologica, 26,* 22–63.

Kestenbaum, R. (1992). Feeling happy versus feeling good: The processing of discrete and global categories of emotional expressions by children and adults. *Developmental Psychology, 28,* 1132–1142.

Kiesler, D. J. (1988). *Therapeutic metacommunication: Therapist impact disclosure as feedback in psychotherapy.* Palo Alto, CA: Consulting Psychologist Press.

Kitchener, K. S. (1984). Intuition, critical evaluation and ethical principles: The foundation for ethical decisions for counseling psychology. *The Counseling Psychologist, 12,* 43–55.

Kleinke, C. L. (1986). Gaze and eye contact: A research review. *Psychological Bulletin, 100,* 78–100.

Knox, S., Goldberg, J. L., Woodhouse, S., & Hill, C. E. (in press). Clients' internal representations of their therapists. *Journal of Counseling Psychology.*

Knox, S., Hess, S., Petersen, D., & Hill, C. E. (1997). A qualitative analysis of client perceptions of the effects of helpful therapist self-disclosure in long-term therapy. *Journal of Counseling Psychology, 44,* 274–283.

Kohut, H. (1971). *The analysis of the self.* New York: International Universities Press.

Kohut, H. (1977). *The restoration of the self.* New York: International Universities Press.

Kohut, H. (1984). *How does analysis cure?* Chicago: University of Chicago Press.

Kopta, S. M., Howard, K. I., Lowry, J. L., & Beutler, L. E. (1994). Patterns of symptomatic recovery in psychotherapy. *Journal of Consulting and Clinical Psychology, 62,* 1009–1016.

Ladany, N., Hill, C. E., Thompson, B. J., & O'Brien, K. M. (1998). *Therapist use of silence in psychotherapy.* Manuscript in preparation, LeHigh University.

Ladany, N., O'Brien, K. M., Hill, C. E., Melincoff, D. S., Knox, S., & Petersen, D. A. (1997). Sexual attraction toward clients, use of supervision, and prior training: A qualitative study of psychotherapy predoctoral interns. *Journal of Counseling Psychology, 44,* 413–424.

LaFrance, M., & Mayo, C. (1976). Racial differences in gaze behavior during conversations: Two systematic observational studies. *Journal of Personality and Social Psychology, 33,* 547–552.

Laing, R. D., & Esterson, A. (1970). *Sanity, madness, and the family.* Middlesex, England: Penguin.

Lamb, M. E., Hershkowitz, I., Sternberg, K. J., Esplin, P. W., Hovav, M., Manor, T., & Yudilevitch, L. (1996). Effects of investigative utterance types on Israeli children's responses. *International Journal of Behavioral Development, 19,* 627–637.

Lambert, M. J., & Hill, C. E. (1994). Assessing psychotherapy outcomes and processes. In A. E. Bergin & S. L. Garfield (Eds.), *Handbook of psychotherapy and behavior change* (4th ed., pp. 72–113). New York: Wiley.

Lang, P. J., Melamed, B. G., & Hart, J. (1970). A psychophysiological analysis of fear modification using an automated desensitization procedure. *Journal of Abnormal Psychology, 76,* 220–234.

Leong, F. T. L., Wagner, N. S., & Tata, S. P. (1995). Racial and ethnic variations in help-seeking attitudes. In J. G. Ponterotto, J. M. Casas, L. A. Suzuki, & C. M. Alexander (Eds.), *Handbook of multicultural counseling* (pp. 415–438). Thousand Oaks, CA: Sage.

Levy, A. (1989). Social support and the media: Analysis of responses by radio psychology talk show hosts. *Professional Psychology: Research and Practice, 20,* 73–78.

Levy, L. H. (1963). *Psychological interpretation.* New York: Holt, Rinehart, & Winston.

Lin, M., Kelly, K. R., & Nelson, R. C. (1996). A comparative analysis of the interpersonal process in school-based counseling and consultation. *Journal of Counseling Psychology, 43,* 389–393.

Loftus, E. (1988). *Memory.* New York: Ardsley House.

Luborsky, L., & Crits-Christoph, P. (1990). *Understanding transference: The CCRT method.* New York: Basic Books.

Mahalik, J. R. (1994). Development of the Client Resistance Scale. *Journal of Counseling Psychology, 41,* 58–68.

Mahler, M. S. (1968). *On human symbiosis of the vicissitudes of individuation*. New York: International Universities Press.

Mahler, M. S., Pine, F., & Bergman, A. (1975). *The psychological birth of the human infant: Symbiosis and individuation*. New York: Basic Books.

Mahoney, M. J. (1991). *Human change processes: The scientific foundations of psychotherapy*. New York: Basic Books.

Mahrer, A. R., Sterner, I., Lawson, K. C., & Dessaulles, A. (1986). Microstrategies: Distinctively patterned sequences of therapist statements. *Psychotherapy, 23,* 50–56.

Malan, D. H. (1963). *A study of brief psychotherapy*. London: Tavistock.

Malan, D. H. (1976a). *The frontier of brief psychotherapy*. New York: Plenum.

Malan, D. H. (1976b). *Toward a validation of dynamic psychotherapy: A replication*. New York: Plenum.

Mallinckrodt, B., Gantt, D. L., & Coble, H. M. (1995). Attachment patterns in the psychotherapy relationship: Development of the Client Attachment to Therapist Scale. *Journal of Counseling Psychology, 42,* 307–317.

Mann, J. (1973). *Time-limited psychotherapy*. Cambridge, MA: Harvard University Press.

Markus, H., & Kitayama, S. (1991). Culture and the self: Implications for cognition, emotion, and motivation. *Psychological Review, 98,* 224–253.

Marx, J. A., & Gelso, C. J. (1987). Termination of individual counseling in a university counseling center. *Journal of Counseling Psychology, 34,* 3–9.

Marziali, E. A. (1984). Prediction of outcome of brief psychotherapy from therapist interpretive interventions. *Archives of General Psychiatry, 41,* 301–304.

Marziali, E. A., & Sullivan, J. H. (1980). Methodological issues in the context analyses of brief psychotherapy. *British Journal of Medical Psychology, 53,* 19–27.

Maslow, A. (1970). *Motivation and personality* (rev. ed.). New York: Harper & Row.

Matsumoto, D., Kudoh, T., Sherer, K., & Wallbott, H. (1988). Antecedents of and reactions to emotions in the United States and Japan. *Journal of Cross-Cultural Psychology, 19,* 267–286.

McCullough, L., Winston, A., Farber, B., Porter, F., Pollack, J., Laikin, M., Vingiano, W., & Trujillo, M. (1991). The relationship of patient–therapist interaction to outcome in brief psychotherapy. *Psychotherapy, 28,* 525–533.

McWhirter, E. H. (1994). *Counseling for empowerment*. Alexandria, VA: American Counseling Association.

Meador, B. D., & Rogers, C. R. (1973). Client-centered therapy. In R. Corsini (Ed.), *Current psychotherapies* (pp. 119–166). Itasca, IL: Peacock.

Meara, N. M., Schmidt, L. D., & Day, J. D. (1996). Principles and virtues: A foundation for ethical decisions, policies, and character. *The Counseling Psychologist, 24,* 4–77.

Medin, D. L., & Ross, B. H. (1992). *Cognitive psychology*. New York: Harcourt Brace Jovanovich.

Meichenbaum, D., & Turk, D. C. (1987). *Facilitating treatment adherence: A practitioner's handbook*. New York: Plenum.

Mendel, W. M. (1964). The phenomenon of interpretation. *American Journal of Psychoanalysis. 24,* 184–189.

Messer, S. B., Tishby, O., & Spillman, A. (1992). Taking context seriously in psychotherapy research: Relating therapist interventions to patient progress in brief psyhodynamic therapy. *Journal of Consulting and Clinical Psychology, 60,* 678–688.

Mickelson, D., & Stevic, R. (1971). Differential effects of facilitative and nonfacilitative behavioral counselors. *Journal of Counseling Psychology, 18,* 314–319.

Miller, J. B. (1976). *Toward a new psychology of women.* Boston: Beacon Press.

Miller, W. R., Benefield, R. G., & Tonigan, J. S. (1993). Enhancing motivation for change in problem drinking: A controlled comparison of two therapist styles. *Journal of Consulting and Clinical Psychology, 61,* 455–461.

Minuchin, S. (1974). *Families and family therapy.* Cambridge: Harvard University Press.

Montagu, A. (Ed.). (1971). *Touching: The significance of the human skin.* New York: Columbia University Press.

Murray, I. (Ed.). (1989). *Oscar Wilde.* Oxford, England: Oxford University Press.

Nagel, D. P., Hoffman, M. A., & Hill, C. E. (1995). A comparison of verbal response modes by master's-level career counselor and other helpers. *Journal of Counseling and Development, 74,* 101–104.

Nakayama, E. Y., Thompson, K., Knox, S., & Hill, C. E. (1998). *Psychodynamic therapists' boundaries: A qualitative study.* Manuscript in preparation, University of Maryland.

Natterson, J. M. (1993). Dreams: The gateway to consciousness. In G. Delaney (Ed.), *New directions in dream interpretation* (pp. 41–76). Albany: State University of New York Press.

Nichols, M., & Schwartz, R. (1991). *Family therapy: Concepts and methods* (2nd ed.). Boston: Allyn & Bacon.

Nisbett, R. E., & Wilson, T. D. (1977). Telling more than we can know. *Psychological Review, 83,* 231–259.

Nutt-Williams, E., & Hill, C. E. (1996). The relationship between self-talk and therapy process variables for novice therapists. *Journal of Counseling Psychology, 43,* 170–177.

O'Farrell, M. K., Hill, C. E., & Patton, S. (1986). Comparison to two cases of counseling with the same counselor. *Journal of Counseling and Development, 65,* 141–145.

Olson, D. H., & Claiborn, C. D. (1990). Interpretation and arousal in the counseling process. *Journal of Counseling Psychology, 37,* 131–137.

O'Neil, J. M. (1981). Male sex-role conflicts, sexism, and masculinity: Psychological implications for men, women, and the counseling psychologist. *The Counseling Psychologist, 9,* 61–81.

Orlinsky, D. E., & Geller, J. D. (1993). Patients' representations of their therapists and therapy: New measures. In N. E. Miller, L. Luborsky, J. P. Barber, & J. P. Docherty (Eds.), *Psychodynamic treatment research: A handbook for psychodynamic research* (pp. 423–466). New York: Basic Books.

Orlinsky, D. E., Grawe, K., & Parks, B. K. (1994). Process and outcome in psychotherapy—Noch einmal. In A. E. Bergin & S. L. Garfield (Eds.), *Handbook of psychotherapy and behavior change* (4th ed., pp. 270–376). New York: Wiley.

Patterson, G. R., & Forgatch, M. S. (1985). Therapist behavior as a determinant for client noncompliance: A paradox for the behavior modifier. *Journal of Consulting and Clinical Psychology, 53,* 846–851.

Patton, M. J., & Meara, N. M. (1992). *Psychoanalytic counseling.* New York: Wiley.

Paul, G. L. (1969). Outcome of systematic desensitization: II. Controlled investigations of individual treatment, technique variations, and current status. In C. M. Franks (Ed.), *Behavior therapy: Appraisal and status* (pp. 105–159). New York: McGraw-Hill.

Pavlov, I. P. (1927). *Conditioned reflex: An investigation of the physiological activity of the cerebral cortex* (G. V. Anrep, Trans.). London: Oxford University Press.

Petersen, D., Friedman, S., Geshmay, S., & Hill, C. E. (1998). *Client perspectives on impasses.* Manuscript in preparation, University of Maryland.

Petty, R. E., & Cacioppo, J. T. (1986). The elaboration likelihood model of persuasion. *Advances in Experimental Social Psychology, 19*, 123–205.

Piper, W. E., Azim, H. F., Joyce, A. S., & McCallum, M. (1991). Transference interpretations, therapeutic alliance, and outcome in short-term individual psychotherapy. *Archives of General Psychiatry, 48*, 946–953.

Piper, W. E., Debbane, E. G., Bienvenu, J. P., de-Carufel, F. F., & Garant, J. (1986). Relationships between the object focus of therapist interventions and outcome in short-term individual psychotherapy. *British Journal of Medical Psychology, 59*, 1–11.

Ponterotto, J. G., Casas, J. M., Suzuki, L. A., & Alexander, C. M. (Eds.). (1995). *Handbook of multicultural counseling.* Thousand Oaks, CA: Sage.

Pope, K. S. (1994). *Sexual involvement with therapists: Patient assessment, subsequent therapy, forensics.* Washington, DC: American Psychological Association.

Pope, K. S., Keith-Spiegel, P., & Tabachnick, B. (1986). Sexual attraction to clients: The human therapist and the (sometimes) inhuman training system. *American Psychologist, 41*, 147–158.

Pope, K. S., Sonne, J. L., & Holyroyd, J. (1993). *Sexual feelings in psychotherapy: Explorations for therapists and therapists-in-training.* Washington, DC: American Psychological Association.

Prochaska, J. O., DiClemente, C. C., & Norcross, J. C. (1992). In search of how people change: Applications to addictive behavior. *American Psychologist, 47*, 1102–1114.

Prochaska, J. O., Norcross, J. C., & DiClemente, C. C. (1994). *Changing for good.* New York: Guilford Press.

Regan, A. M., & Hill, C. E. (1992). Investigation of what clients and counselors do not say in brief therapy. *Journal of Counseling Psychology, 39*, 168–174.

Reid, J. R., & Finesinger, J. E. (1952). The role of insight in psychotherapy. *American Journal of Psychiatry, 108*, 726–734.

Reik, T. (1935). *Surprise and the psychoanalyst.* London: Routledge.

Reik, T. (1948). *Listening with the third ear.* New York: Grove Press.

Rennie, D. L. (1994). Clients' deference in psychotherapy. *Journal of Counseling Psychology, 41*, 427–437.

Rhodes, R. H., Hill, C. E., Thompson, B. J., & Elliott, R. (1994). Client retrospective recall of resolved and unresolved misunderstanding events. *Journal of Counseling Psychology, 41*, 473–483.

Richardson, M. S. (1993). Work in people's lives: A location for counseling psychologists. *Journal of Counseling Psychology, 40*, 425–433.

Rimm, D. C., & Masters, J. C. (1979). *Behavior therapy: Techniques and empirical findings.* New York: Academic Press.

Robitschek, C. G., & McCarthy, P. R. (1991). Prevalence of counselor self-reference in the therapeutic dyad. *Journal of Counseling and Development, 69*, 218–221.

Rogers, C. R. (1942). *Counseling and psychotherapy.* Boston: Houghton-Mifflin.

Rogers, C. R. (1951). *Client-centered therapy: Its current practice, implications, and theory.* Boston: Houghton-Mifflin.

Rogers, C. R. (1957). The necessary and sufficient conditions of therapeutic personality change. *Journal of Consulting Psychology, 21,* 95–103.

Rogers, C. R. (1959). A theory of therapy, personality, and interpersonal relationships, as developed in the client-centered framework. In S. Koch (Ed.), *Psychology: A study of a science: Vol. 3. Formulations of the person and the social context* (pp. 184–256). New York: McGraw-Hill.

Rogers, C. R. (Ed.). (1967). *The therapeutic relationship and its impact: A study of psychotherapy with schizophrenics.* Madison: University of Wisconsin Press.

Rogers, C. R. (1980). *A way of being.* Boston: Houghton-Mifflin.

Rogers, C. R., & Dymond, R. (1954). *Psychotherapy and personality change.* Chicago, IL: University of Chicago Press.

Rosenthal, R., Hall, J. A., DiMatteo, M. R., Rogers, P. L., & Archer, D. (1979). *Sensitivity to nonverbal communication: The PONS Test.* Baltimore: Johns Hopkins University Press.

Rummelhart, D. E., & McClelland, J. L. (Eds.). (1986). *Parallel distributing processing. Explorations in the microstructure of cognition: Vol. 1. Foundations.* Cambridge, MA: MIT Press.

Safran, J. D., & Muran, J. C. (1996). The resolution of ruptures in the therapeutic alliance. *Journal of Consulting and Clinical Psychology, 64,* 447–458.

Salerno, M., Farber, B. A., McCullough, L., Winston, A., & Trujillo, M. (1992). The effects of confrontation and clarification on patient affective and defensive responding. *Psychotherapy Research, 2,* 181–192.

Salter, A. (1949). *Conditioned reflex therapy.* New York: Creative Age.

Sarason, I. G., Sarason, B. R., & Pierce, G. R. (1990). Social support: The search for theory. *Journal of Social and Clinical Psychology, 9,* 133–147.

Satir, V. M. (1988). *The new peoplemaking.* Palo Alto, CA: Science and Behavior Books.

Savickas, M. L. (1994). Vocational psychology in the postmodern era: Comment on Richardson (1993). *Journal of Counseling Psychology, 41,* 105–107.

Shakespeare, W. (1980). *Macbeth* [Play]. New York: Bantam. (Original work published 1603)

Shapiro, E. G. (1984). Help-seeking: Why people don't. *Research in the Sociology of Organizations, 3,* 213–236.

Silberschatz, G., Fretter, P. B., & Curtis, J. T. (1986). How do interpretations influence the process of therapy? *Journal of Consulting and Clinical Psychology, 54,* 646–652.

Sileo, F. J., & Kopala, M. (1993). An A-B-C-D-E worksheet for promoting beneficence when considering ethical values. *Counseling and Values, 37,* 89–95.

Simon, J. C. (1988). Criteria for therapist self-disclosure. *American Journal of Psychotherapy, 42,* 404–415.

Singer, E. (1970). *New concepts in psychotherapy.* New York: Basic Books.

Skinner, B. F. (1953). *Science and human behavior.* New York: Macmillan.

Smith, M. L., Glass, G. V., & Miller, T. J. (1980). *The benefits of psychotherapy.* Baltimore: Johns Hopkins University Press.

Speisman, J. C. (1959). Depth of interpretation and verbal resistance in psychotherapy. *Journal of Consulting Psychology, 23,* 93–99.

Spence, D. P., Dahl, H., & Jones, E. E. (1993). Impact of interpretation on associative freedom. *Journal of Consulting and Clinical Psychology, 61,* 395–402.

Spiegel, S. B., & Hill, C. E. (1989). Guidelines for research on therapist interpretation: Toward greater methodological rigor and relevance to practice. *Journal of Counseling Psychology, 36,* 121–129.

Spokane, A. R. (1989). Are there psychological and mental health consequences of difficult career decisions? *Journal of Career Development, 16,* 19–23.

Stein, D. J. (1992). Schemas in the cognitive and clinical sciences: An integrative construct. *Journal of Psychotherapy Integration, 2,* 207–210.

Sternberg, K. J., Lamb, M. E., Hershkowitz, I., Esplin, P. W., Redlich, A., & Sunshine, N. (1996). The relationship between investigative utterance types and the informativeness of child witnesses. *Journal of Applied Developmental Psychology, 17,* 439–451.

Sternberg, K. J., Lamb, M. E., Hershkowitz, I., Yudilevitch, L., Orbach, Y., Esplin, P. W., & Hovav, M. (1997). Effects of introductory style on children's abilities to describe experiences of sexual abuse. *Child Abuse and Neglect, 21,* 1133–1146.

Stiles, W. B. (1979). Verbal response modes and psychotherapeutic technique. *Psychiatry, 42,* 49–62.

Stiles, W. B., & Shapiro, D. A. (1995). Verbal exchange structure of brief psychodynamic–interpersonal and cognitive–behavioral psychotherapy. *Journal of Consulting and Clinical Psychology, 63,* 15–27.

Stiles, W. B., Shapiro, D. A., & Firth-Cozens, J. (1988). Verbal response mode use in contrasting psychotherapies: A within-subjects comparison. *Journal of Consulting and Clinical Psychology, 56,* 727–733.

Stiles, W. B., Startup, M., Hardy, G. E., Barkham, M., Rees, A., Shapiro, D. A., & Reynolds, S. (1996). Therapist session intentions in cognitive–behavioral and psychodynamic–interpersonal psychotherapy. *Journal of Counseling Psychology, 43,* 402–414.

Strachey, J. (1934). The nature of therapeutic action of psychoanalysis. *International Journal of Psychoanalysis, 15,* 127–159.

Strupp, H. H. (1955). An objective comparison of Rogerian and psychoanalytic techniques. *Journal of Consulting Psychology, 19,* 1–7.

Strupp, H. H. (1957). A multidimensional analysis of therapist activity in analytic and client-centered therapy. *Journal of Consulting Psychology, 21,* 301–308.

Strupp, H. H. (1996). The tripartite model and the *Consumer Reports* Study. *American Psychologist, 51,* 1017–1024.

Strupp, H. H., & Binder, J. L. (1984). *Psychotherapy in a new key: A guide to time-limited dynamic psychotherapy.* New York: Basic Books.

Strupp, H. H., & Hadley, S. W. (1977). A tripartite model of mental health and therapeutic outcomes: With special reference to negative effects in psychotherapy. *American Psychologist, 32,* 187–196.

Sue, D., & Sue, D. (1999). *Counseling the culturally different: Theory and practice* (3rd ed.). New York: Wiley.

Sue, D., Sue, D., & Sue, S. (1994). *Understanding abnormal behavior* (4th ed.). Princeton, NJ: Houghton-Mifflin.

Suinn, R. M. (1988). Imagery rehearsal applications to performance enhancement. *Behavior Therapist, 8,* 155–159.

Teyber, E. (1997). *Interpersonal process in psychotherapy: A relational approach.* Pacific Grove, CA: Brooks/Cole.

Thompson, B. J., & Hill, C. E. (1991). Therapist perceptions of client reactions. *Journal of Counseling and Development, 69,* 261–265.

Tinsley, H. E. A., de St. Aubin, T. M., & Brown, M. T. (1982). College students' help-seeking preferences. *Journal of Counseling Psychology, 29,* 523–533.

Tinsley, H. E. A., & Weiss, D. J. (1975). Interrater reliability and agreement of subjective judgments. *Journal of Counseling Psychology, 22,* 358–376.

Toro, P. A. (1986). A comparison of natural and professional help. *American Journal of Community Psychology, 14,* 147–159.

Torrey, E. F. (1986). *Witchdoctors and psychiatrists: The common roots of psychotherapy and its future.* New York: Harper & Row.

Truax, C. B., & Carkhuff, R. R. (1967). *Toward effective counseling and psychotherapy.* Chicago: Aldine.

Wampold, B. E., Mondin, G. W., Moody, M., Stich, F., Benson, K., & Ahn, H. (1997). A meta-analysis of outcome studies comparing bona fide psychotherapies: Empirically "all must have prizes." *Psychological Bulletin, 122,* 203–215.

Ward, D. E. (1984). Termination of individual counseling: Concepts and strategies. *Journal of Counseling and Development, 63,* 21–25.

Waters, D. B., & Lawrence, E. C. (1993). *Competence, courage, and change: An approach to family therapy.* New York: Norton.

Watkins, C. E., Jr. (1990). The effects of counselor self-disclosure: A research review. *Counseling Psychologist, 18,* 477–500.

Watson, J. B., & Rayner, R. (1920). Conditioned emotional reactions. *Journal of Experimental Psychology, 3,* 1–14.

Watzlawick, P., Weakland, J. H., & Fisch, R. (1974). *Change: Principles of problem formation and problem resolution.* New York: Norton.

Webster, D. W., & Fretz, B. R. (1978). Asian-American, Black and White college students' preference for help-giving sources. *Journal of Counseling Psychology, 25,* 124–130.

Williams, E., Judge, A., Hill, C. E., & Hoffman, M. A. (1997). Experiences of novice therapists in prepracticum: Trainees', clients', and supervisees' perceptions of therapists' personal reactions and management strategies. *Journal of Counseling Psychology, 44,* 390–399.

Wolpe, J. (1958). *Psychotherapy by reciprocal inhibition.* Palo Alto, CA: Stanford University Press.

Yalom, I. D. (1980). *Existential psychotherapy.* New York: Basic Books.

Yalom, I. D. (1990). *Love's executioner.* New York: Basic Books.

Yalom, I. D. (1995). *Theory and practice of group psychotherapy* (4th ed.). New York: Basic Books.

Yalom, I. D., & Lieberman, M. A. (1971). A study of encounter group casualties. *Archives of General Psychiatry, 25,* 16–30.

Zunker, V. G. (1994). *Career counseling: Applied concepts and life planning* (4th ed.). Pacific Grove, CA: Brooks/Cole.

Appendix A:
Helper Intentions List

Intention	Definition
1. Set limits	To structure, make arrangements, establish goals and objectives of helping, outline methods to attain goals, correct expectations about helping, or establish rules or parameters of relationship (e.g., time, fees, cancellation policies, homework)
2. Get information	To find out specific facts about history, client functioning, future plans, and so on
3. Give information	To educate, give facts, correct misperceptions or misinformation, give reasons for helper's behavior or procedures
4. Support	To provide a warm, supportive, empathic environment; increase trust and rapport and build relationship; help client feel accepted, understood, comfortable, reassured, and less anxious; help establish a person-to-person relationship
5. Focus	To help client get back on the track, change subject, channel or structure the discussion if she or he is unable to begin or has been diffuse or rambling
6. Clarify	To provide or solicit more elaboration, emphasis, or specification when client or helper has been vague, incomplete, confusing, contradictory, or inaudible
7. Instill hope	To convey the expectation that change is possible and likely to occur, convey that the helper can help the client, restore morale, build up the client's confidence to make changes
8. Encourage catharsis	To promote relief from tension or unhappy feelings, allow the client a chance to let go of or talk through feelings and problems
9. Identify maladaptive cognitions	To identify maladaptive, illogical, or irrational thoughts or attitudes (e.g., "I must be perfect")

(Continues)

Intention	Definition
10. Identify maladaptive behaviors	To identify and give feedback about the client's inappropriate behaviors and their consequences, do a behavioral analysis, point out games
11. Encourage self-control	To encourage client to own or gain a sense of mastery or control over her or his thoughts, feelings, behaviors, or impulses; help client become more appropriately internal rather than inappropriately external in assigning responsibility for her or his role
12. Identify and intensify feelings	To identify, intensify, and enable acceptance of feelings; encourage or provoke the client to become aware of or deepen underlying or hidden feelings or affect or experience feelings at a deeper level
13. Promote insight	To encourage understanding of the underlying reasons, dynamics, assumptions, or unconscious motivations for cognitions, behaviors, attitudes, or feelings (may include an understanding of the client's reactions to others' behaviors)
14. Promote change	To build and develop new and more adaptive skills, behaviors, or cognitions in dealing with self and others; to instill new, more adaptive assumptive models, frameworks, explanations, or conceptualizations; to give an assessment or opinion about client functioning that helps client see self in new way
15. Reinforce change	To give positive reinforcement or feedback about behavioral, cognitive, or affective attempts at change to enhance the probability that the change is continued or maintained; encourage risk taking and new ways of behaving
16. Deal with resistance	To overcome obstacles to change or progress (may discuss failure to adhere to procedures in helping, either in past or to prevent possibility of such failure in future)
17. Challenge	To jolt the client out of a present state; shake up current beliefs or feelings; test validity, adequacy, reality, or appropriateness of beliefs, thoughts, feelings, or behaviors; help client question the necessity of maintaining old patterns
18. Deal with the therapeutic relationship	To resolve problems as they arise in the relationship in order to build or maintain a smooth working alliance; heal ruptures in the alliance; deal with dependency issues appropriate to stage in helping; uncover and resolve distortions in client's thinking about the relationship that are based on past experiences rather than current reality

Intention	Definition
19. Relieve helper's needs	To protect, relieve, or defend the helper; alleviate anxiety (may try unduly to persuade, argue, or feel good or superior at the expense of the client)

Note. The terms *helper* and *helping* are used here instead of *therapist* and *therapy* as in the original system. From "List of Therapist Intentions Illustrated in a Case Study and With Therapists of Varying Theoretical Orientations," by C. E. Hill and K. E. O'Grady, 1985, *Journal of Counseling Psychology, 32,* p. 8. Copyright 1985 by the American Psychological Association. Adapted with permission.

Appendix B: Helping Skills System

Introduction: The helping skills system (HSS) includes verbal helping skills, which refer to what helpers say during sessions to help clients. One (and only one) skill is judged as occurring in every grammatical sentence (a unit that includes at least a subject and a verb) of the helper's speech (instructions for dividing speech into grammatical sentences can be found in Appendix C). Note that this judgment is a description of the presence or absence of the helping skill, but it is not an indication of the intensity or quality of the helping skill. In this appendix, we present each skill and its definition followed by examples. In Appendix C, we present guidelines for using the HSS in research.

1. *Approval and Reassurance:* Provides emotional support, reassurance, encouragement, reinforcement. It might indicate that the helper empathizes with or understands the client. It might suggest that what the client is feeling is normal or to be expected. It might imply sympathy or attempt to alleviate anxiety by minimizing the client's problems. It might imply approval of the client's behavior.

   "I'm concerned about you."
   "That's hard."
   "I understand what you're going through."
   "I can't believe he said that."
   "I think you did the right thing."
   "That's really good that you were able to speak up to him."
   "You're right."

2. *Closed Question:* Requests limited or specific information or data, usually a one- or two-word answer, a "yes" or "no," or a confirmation. Closed questions can be used to gain information, to ask a client to repeat, or to ask if the helper's intervention was accurate.

   Client: "I went away for the weekend."

   Helper: "Did you like it?"

   Client: "My husband thinks I'm too fat."

   Helper: "Do you think you're too fat?"

   Helper: "What did you say?"

   Helper: "Right?"

   Helper: "Does this fit for you?"

3. *Open Question:* Asks client to clarify or to explore thoughts or feelings. The helper does not ask for specific information and does not purposely limit the nature of the client's response to a "yes" or "no" or a one- or two-word response, even though the client may respond that way. Note that open questions can be phrased as directives as long as the intent is to facilitate clarification or exploration.

> **Helper:** "What would you like to talk about today?"
> **Client:** "Everything is awful right now."

> **Helper:** "What kind of hassles are you experiencing?"
> **Client:** "I've had a backache for days."

> **Helper:** "I'm wondering if you can tell me what's making you tense?"
> **Client:** "I'm surprised at what she did."

> **Helper:** "Tell me more about that."
> **Client:** "I get so angry at my boss."

> **Helper:** "Tell me about the last time that happened."
> **Client:** "I don't know how to respond when my boss criticizes me."

> **Helper:** "What is a specific example of what he says, and how you respond?"
> **Client:** "My sister got all the attention in the family."

> **Helper:** "How does that make you feel?"
> **Client:** "What should I talk about?"

> **Helper:** "How are you feeling right now?"

4. *Restatement:* A simple repeating or rephrasing of the content or meaning of the client's statement(s) that typically contains fewer but similar words and usually is more concrete and clear than the client's statement. The restatement may be phrased either tentatively or as a direct statement. The restatement may be a paraphrase of either immediately preceding material or material from earlier in session or treatment.

> **Client:** "My father thinks I should earn my own money."
> **Helper:** "You're saying your father doesn't want to support you anymore."

> **Client:** "Since I got into trouble, no one will talk to me."
> **Helper:** "Everyone seems to be ignoring you."

> **Client:** "I'm finally getting my life in order. I've been feeling good most of the time. My job is getting easier."
> **Helper:** "Things are going well for you."

> **Client:** (talks for a long time about his reactions to his parents aging)
> **Helper:** "Your parents are not as able to take care of themselves as they get older, and you're wondering whether you should step in and start making some decisions for them."

> **Helper:** "Last session you talked about your problems with anger and you wondered where it came from."

5. *Reflection of Feelings:* A repeating or rephrasing of the client's statements, including an explicit identification of the client's feelings. The feelings may have been stated by the client (in either exactly the same words or in similar words) or the helper may infer the feelings from the client's nonverbal behavior, the context, or the content of the client's message. The reflection may be phrased either tentatively or as a statement.

> **Client:** "I did better than I've done before."
>
> **Helper:** "You're pleased with your performance."
>
> **Client:** "My best friend went out with my boyfriend."
>
> **Helper:** "You feel hurt that she did that?"
>
> **Client:** "I don't know if I could handle this problem by myself. It feels like it's too much for me right now."
>
> **Helper:** "You feel uncertain of yourself and overwhelmed by this problem."

6. *Challenge:* Points out discrepancies, contradictions, defenses, or irrational beliefs of which the client is unaware, unable to deal with, or unwilling to change. Challenges can be said with either a tentative or confrontational tone.

> **Client:** "I know Jannelle really likes me."
>
> **Helper:** "From what you've said, she seems to be hostile to you and maybe even jealous. That doesn't sound to me like she likes you."
>
> **Client:** "I feel so worthless. Nothing's going right. I'd be better off dropping out of school."
>
> **Helper:** "You did poorly on one test, so you want to drop out of school?"
>
> **Client:** "I don't have any problems. Everything in my life is going really well right now."
>
> **Helper:** "You say everything is going well, but you keep getting sick. I wonder if it's difficult for you to look at your situation?"
>
> **Client:** "If I don't get into graduate school, I couldn't stand it. It would mean the end of everything."
>
> **Helper:** "I doubt that you couldn't stand it. I wonder how you might really react?"

7. *Interpretation:* Goes beyond what the client has overtly stated or recognized and gives a new meaning, reason, or explanation for behaviors, thoughts, or feelings so that the client can see problems in a new way. Makes connections between seemingly isolated statements or events; points out themes or patterns in client's behavior or feelings; explicates defenses, resistances, or transferences; gives a new framework to behaviors, thoughts, feelings, or problems.

> **Client:** "I'm doing badly in school. I just can't seem to study. Another problem is that my husband and I have been arguing constantly."
>
> **Helper:** "Perhaps you're unable to concentrate in school because you're preoccupied with the problems with your husband."
>
> **Client:** "I can't seem to get close to anyone."

Helper: "Since your father died, you have had a hard time trusting anyone. Maybe you're afraid that if you get close to someone, she or he will die."

Client: "I have just been incredibly mean and nasty to everyone this week."

Helper: "I wonder if you use your anger as a protection to keep you from getting too close to anyone."

Client: "He never does anything around the house, just goes out drinking with the guys. I get stuck taking care of the kids and all the housework."

Helper: "He seems to be saving you from any decision about what you are going to do with your life and your career."

8. *Self-Disclosure:* Reveals something personal about the helper's nonimmediate experiences or feelings. These statements typically start with an "I." However, not all helper statements that start with an "I" are self-disclosures (e.g., "I can understand that" or "I don't know" are not self-disclosures). Self-disclosures can be of history and credentials, feelings, personal experiences, or strategies.

Client: "Where did you go to school?"

Helper: "I got my degree from University of Podunck."

Client: "What kind of degree do you have?"

Helper: "I am a counseling psychologist."

Client: "I just don't really know how I feel."

Helper: "When I have been in your situation, I felt angry when someone stood me up."

Client: "I've got to meet his mother tomorrow. I've never met any boyfriend's mother."

Helper: "If I were you, I would feel nervous about meeting his mother."

Client: "I get so anxious at parties that I just don't want to go to any."

Helper: "I have a hard time at parties too. I never know what to say to strangers."

Client: "I have been feeling down lately, but I should be feeling happy because I just got married."

Helper: "I just recently got married so I know what a hard transition that can be."

Client: "I just don't know how to get a job in the department."

Helper: "One strategy that I tried when I was your age was to go and talk to all the professors about their interests, and then if I liked the professor I asked if she or he had any openings for assistants."

9. *Immediacy:* Discloses helper's immediate feelings about self in relation to the client, about the client, or about the therapeutic relationship.

Client: "Everything has been going great in helping."

Helper: "It's interesting that you say that now because I've been feeling anxious and stressed in our relationship."

Client: "Do you like me?"

Helper: "I feel very close to you."

Client: (cutting helper off) "No, that's not it. You're wrong. I feel fine."

Helper: "I am feeling annoyed that you keep interrupting me."

10. *Information:* Supplies information in the form of data, facts, opinions, resources, or answers to questions.

   a. *Information About the Process of Helping*

   Client: "Will I be meeting with you weekly?"

   Helper: "We will meet twice a week."

   Client: "Should I start?"

   Helper: "Mmhmm."

   b. *Facts, Data, or Opinions*

   Client: "What were the results of the test?"

   Helper: "The test indicates that you share interests with people happily employed in forestry."

   Client: "I think I want to major in biology."

   Helper: "Biology requires several additional laboratory courses."

   Client: "I got really upset but I didn't say anything to her."

   Helper: "It is my opinion that when people bottle up their anger, they are more prone to blowing up at some point."

   Helper: "Students tend to do better on tests after they have gotten a full night of sleep."

   c. *Feedback About the Client*

   Client: "Am I depressed?"

   Helper: "You seem more anxious than depressed."

   Client: "He didn't even know what hit him."

   Helper: "Are you aware that you smiled when you said that?"

11. *Direct Guidance:* Provides suggestions, directives, instructions, or advice for what the client should do to change (goes beyond directing the client to explore thoughts or feelings in session).

   a. *Process Advisement*

   "Play the part of the firefighter in your fantasy."
   "Try and relax your muscles right now."
   "Rate your level of relaxation now."

   b. *Directives*

   "I want you to try to talk to your father during the week and tell him about your feelings about his not calling you."
   "Take the test tomorrow before you forget the material."
   "For homework, I would like you to complete this record of your automatic thoughts."
   "You should take charge of your life."

12. *Other:* Includes helper statements that are unrelated to the client's problems, such as small talk, salutations, and comments about the weather or events.
    "Excuse me"
    "Goodbye. See you next week."
    "The Redskins game was terrific, wasn't it?"
    "That's a pretty blouse that you're wearing."

Note. The helping skills system was first developed by Clara Hill (1978) as the Hill counselor verbal response category system and has been modified several times (Hill, 1985, 1986, 1992; Hill et al., 1981). This present version has been modified once again in several major ways.

Appendix C: Using the Helping Skills System for Research

In this section, we include materials that can be helpful to researchers who would like to use the helping skills system in research. This material is adapted from previous manuals of the Hill counselor verbal response category system (Hill, 1985, 1992; Hill et al., 1981). In this appendix, we discuss collecting data, unitizing transcripts, training judges, and determining interjudge agreement. At the end, we provide a practice transcript that judges can use for training. In this appendix, we do not discuss using the helper intentions list, client reactions system, or client behavior system, nor do we discuss coding attending or nonverbal skills. For more details about coding and process research, see Hill (1986, 1992) and Lambert and Hill (1994). We have been experimenting with judging the quality of interventions in addition to helping skills, and interested researchers can contact us about our work in this area.

METHOD

Collecting Data

We have found that transcripts are necessary for making judgments about helping skills. Although it is possible to code helping skills from listening just to tapes, it is difficult to ensure that judges are responding to the same segment of the session and judges often hear different things, which lowers the agreement levels. Hence, a verbatim transcript must first be created (which typically requires that one person type the transcript and another proofread by listening to the tape).

Unitizing Transcripts

Once a transcript is created, it must be unitized because people do not typically talk in neat sentences. Therefore, to code speech, we have to first force what people have said into some kind of unit. This system requires that speech be broken into response units, which are essentially grammatical sentences. The rules that we use have been adapted from Auld and White (1956). A unit is indicated in a transcript by a slash (/). Two judges first code all transcripts independently (without consulting each other). Agreement should be computed for the independent codings; agreement should be above 90% because codings are relatively easy if judges follow the rules listed below. Judges should discuss all discrepancies and agree on final judgments. The rules are as follows.

1. A grammatical sentence consists minimally of a subject and a verb. More specifi-cally, the unit consists of an independent or main clause, standing by itself or occurring with one or more dependent or subordinate clauses. A clause is a state-ment containing a subject and a predicate, with or without complements or mod-ifiers. Judges should be careful not to try to interpret what the sentence means, but should attend carefully to clauses and conjunctions.

    We define an *independent or main clause* as a clause that expresses a completed thought and can stand alone as a sentence. When two independent clauses are joined together by *coordinating conjunctions* (i.e., and, or, nor, but), or by *conjunc-tive adverbs* (i.e., accordingly, also, besides, consequently, hence, however, more-over, nevertheless, otherwise, then, therefore, thus, still, yet), they are considered separate units.

    We define a *dependent or subordinate clause* as a clause that does not express a complete thought and cannot stand alone as a sentence. There are several types of dependent clauses: (a) an adjective clause—acts as an adjective; modi-fies a noun or a pronoun (e.g., The report *that he submitted* was well-documented); (b) a relative pronoun clause—begins with relative pronouns (who, whom, what, whose, which, that) that act as either subject or object of the verb in the clause (e.g., He got *what he wanted*); (c) a noun clause—acts as a noun within the sentence (e.g., *Exercising at night* helped her sleep better); and (d) an adverbial clause—acts as an adverb in the sentence (e.g., I was astonished *when I heard the news*).

    Independent and dependent clauses are joined together by conjunctions. There are several types of conjunctions: (a) Subordinating conjunctions (after, although, as, as is, as long as, as though, because, before, if, so that, then, unless, when, whenever, where, wherever, while, and whereas) always introduce an adverbial clause, joining it to the rest of the sentence. Subordinating conjunctions generally confer meaning to the subsequent clause, whereas coordinating conjunctions do not. Therefore, subordinating conjunctions can join dependent clauses (usually adverb clauses) or fragments. (b) Coordinating conjunctions (and, or, but, nor) can join independent clauses or fragments. (c) Correlative conjunctions (either–or, neither–nor, both–and, not only–but [also], whether–or) precede dependent clauses or fragments and are always used in pairs.

2. Independent clauses can be distinguished from dependent clauses: (a) when two independent clauses are connected, the second is introduced by a coordinating conjunction or a conjunctive adverb; and (b) dependent clauses are introduced by subordinating conjunctions or by pronouns such as *who, which,* or *that*.

3. Some combinations of words without an expressed subject and predicate can make complete sentences (and therefore units). These are called elliptical sentences. Examples: "Speak"/ (a command), "Good"/ (an exclamatory sentence), "What?"/ (a question), a response to a question. Helper: "What room did they give you?"/ Client: "The same as before."/

4. False starts do not count as separate units. For example "And Wednesday night, uh, I more or less . . . I didn't high pressure him"/ counts as one unit. "And Wednesday night, uh, I more or less . . ." is not scored as a separate unit.

5. Utterances lacking some essential feature of a complete sentence because of an interruption by the other speaker or a lapsing into silence are considered separate units whenever the meaning is clear. Example: "And he would ask her to write the . . ."/ (the meaning in this sentence is clear even though the last word or two is

not spoken). However, when the speaker has not said enough to make his or her meaning clear, we consider the utterance a false start rather than a unit (e.g., "The little girl ..." would not be considered a unit).

6. Minimal verbal encouragers (e.g., "mmhmm") and silences are not counted as separate units unless they are responses to direct questions.

7. Phrases such as "you know" and "I guess" are not usually considered separate units. Example: "Some, you know, very serious thing may be, you know, happening."/ (all one unit). Similarly, stutters, uhs, ahs, etc. are not separate units. However, the phrase "right?"/ or "is that right?"/ at the end of a sentence is considered a separate unit because it asks for confirmation and is typically a separate action.

8. If one independent clause is interrupted parenthetically by another independent clause, each is scored as a separate unit. Example: "I decided to go ... well, really what happened was she asked me ... to the concert." In this case, the clause "well, really what happened was she asked me" is a separate unit which interrupts the other unit "I decided to go to the concert." Hence, in this case there are two units.

Selecting and Training Judges

At least three and preferably four or five judges should be used for coding transcripts into helping skills. The reason for using more judges is that these judgments are difficult to make and having more opinions typically leads to better final judgments. We typically select upper level undergraduates or graduate students who have high grade-point averages, are motivated to learn about helping skills, and are detail oriented so that they are more likely to be able to do and enjoy the task.

To train, judges should read through this book to get an overview of the skills, reread the helping skills system (Appendix B) to learn the definitions of the skills, and then code the practice transcript and discuss discrepancies in codings. Each response unit should be coded into one and only one helping skill. After they have completed the practice transcript, judges should go through several real transcripts independently and code each helper response unit into one of the 12 helping skills (the transcripts in chapters 21 and 22 could be used). After independent coding, judges should come together and discuss their codings and resolve discrepancies. Judges should continue training until they reach high rates of agreement (two of the three judges, three of the four judges, or four of the five judges agree on 80% of the codings for all the response units within a 1-hr transcript). Training (not including reading this book) usually requires about 20 hr.

The judges are now ready to code actual transcripts. The judges should do all codings independently, preferably apart, so that they do not influence one another. Judges should meet frequently during the judgment process to discuss and resolve discrepancies. Frequent meetings can build morale and prevent drift of judgments. Judgments that the majority of the judges agree on during the independent judgments (2 of 3, 3 of 4, or 4 of 5) are considered the consensus judgment—those for which there is no consensus must be discussed and resolved. During discussions, make sure that one person does not dominate and persuade others. Every participant should have a chance to talk openly and have her or his opinions heard.

Determining Agreement Levels Among Judges

Judgments about the helping skills are nominal (yes or no) and hence the most appropriate statistic for agreement is a kappa statistic because it reflects percentage agreement corrected for chance agreement (Cohen, 1960; Tinsley & Weiss, 1975). Kappas should be calculated for each pair of judges, so you end up with three kappas if you use three judges (report the average kappa). You should compute the kappas on all the data or a large representative sample of the data used for the study. You can determine kappas for the 12 major categories (e.g., 1, 2, 3, 4, 5, etc.), or including all the subdivisions within the categories (e.g., 10a, 10b, 10c, 11a, 11b, which would yield 15 categories). Please note, however, that it is harder to obtain adequate kappas (> .60) when using 15 categories. You need kappas to be above .60, so if you obtain above .60 for the 12 categories but not for the 15 categories, report the data using 12 categories. Note that when categories occur infrequently, it is more difficult to obtain high kappas. You can also obtain kappas for individual categories by comparing it to all other categories combined.

To compile the data to calculate kappas, you first need to create a table that summarizes the co-occurrences of categories used by the two judges. To do this, make a table that has the number of columns and rows representing the number of categories that you are using. Then go through the codings and make hash marks (/) in the relevant boxes (e.g., if Judge 1 coded the first response unit as Category 1 and Judge 2 coded it as Category 3, you would put a hash mark in the box formed by column 1 and row 3).

Calculate a percentage for each box by dividing the number of hash marks in the box by the total number of categorizations in the table. Table C1 shows the hypothetical data for two judges who each categorized 100 response units into 4 categories. The formula for kappa (Tinsley & Weiss, 1975) is

$$K = P_o - P_c/1 - P_c,$$

where P_p = the proportion of ratings in which the two judges agree, and P_c = the proportion of ratings for which agreement is expected by chance. The total proportion of agreement (P_o) is obtained by adding the figures in the diagonal (.18 + .18 + .24 + .10 = .70). The expected change agreement (P_c) is obtained by summing the product of multiplying the rows by their respective columns.

$$(.20 \times .30) + (.30 \times .20) + (.30 \times .40) + (.20 \times .10) = .26$$

Hence, by filling the numbers into the formula, we get

$$(.70 - .26)/(1 - .26) \text{ or } .44/.74 = .59.$$

Kappa can vary from −1.00 to 1.00. A kappa of 0 indicates that the observed agreement is exactly equal to the agreement that could be observed by chance. A negative kappa indicates that the observed agreement is less than the expected chance agreement. A kappa of 1.00 indicates perfect agreement between judges.

TABLE C1. Hypothetical Proportions of Categorizations by Two Judges to Determine Kappa

Judge 2 scores	Judge 1 scores				
	Category 1	Category 2	Category 3	Category 4	Row total
Category 1	.18	.00	.02	.00	.20
Category 2	.00	.18	.12	.00	.30
Category 3	.06	.00	.24	.00	.30
Category 4	.06	.02	.02	.10	.20
Column total	.30	.20	.40	.10	

PRACTICE TRANSCRIPT

Instructions for Unitizing

The transcript is presented first with no punctuation so that you can practice unitizing. Put a slash (/) after each grammatical sentence (see earlier directions) for the helper's statements. Check your unitizing against the transcript shown later. For every slash shown in the transcript, you should mark whether or not you have one. Considering that there are 57 slashes in the transcript, you should agree on at least 51 before you proceed further. For each instance that you disagree with the transcript, go back to the rules and try to understand the discrepancy.

Transcript

1. **Helper:** Thanks for coming today my name is Judy I am beginning to learn helping skills we have 20 minutes to talk today the task here is for you to talk about whatever is on your mind.

   Client: I've been feeling down lately. I'm having a lot of trouble getting motivated. I haven't felt like going to class. Nothing really interests me.

2. **Helper:** Give me an example of what happened the last time you didn't go to class oh but first what is your major?

   Client: I haven't really decided on a major because I haven't found anything that interests me.

3. **Helper:** So you haven't decided yet are you living on campus?

   Client: I'm living at home and I feel a lot of pressure on me. I would like to live in the dorm but my parents won't pay for it and I don't have the money myself. I mean my parents live right near campus and they say why should you live in a dorm when we live so close that you can easily walk. You might as well save money.

4. **Helper:** It seems to you like your parents are forcing you to live at home.

   Client: Yeah, it sure does and I really resent it. I think I would feel so much freer in a dorm. I feel restricted at home like they're watching every move I make and I don't feel free to come and go as I please.

5. **Helper:** You feel stifled it sounds like you also feel uncomfortable because your parents are so restrictive.

   Client: Right, but I'm not sure how to deal with it. They do provide me with a place to sleep and help me out a little with school. I feel like I ought to be grateful to them.

6. **Helper:** You started fidgeting a lot just then and your voice got real soft I wonder if you feel a little upset did I get that feeling right?

   Client: Well I guess I feel bad like I'm not a good son. I feel like they're giving me so much and all I do is want more.

7. **Helper:** Can you give me an example of the last time that your parents said anything to you about staying home?

   Client: It was just last night. They told me that they really didn't want me to leave. They got all upset when I even brought up the topic, especially my mom.

8. **Helper:** I wonder if both you and your parents are having trouble separating because of your changing role as you're growing up maybe they're not quite ready

for you to leave home because they're anxious about having an empty nest and I wonder if you have a hard time leaving because you're afraid you'll hurt them does that sound right to you?

Client: That could be true. You know, I'm an only child and my parents are older. They built their whole world around me.

9. **Helper:** On the one hand, it's hard to leave them; but on the other hand, you want to go out and lead your own life.

Client: Well I want to move out, but I don't want to hurt them.

10. **Helper:** I had a similar situation when I left home my parents were quite upset at first I felt terrible and guilty. What is it like for you?

Client: Yeah, well, I don't know. It seems so difficult to figure all this out.

11. **Helper:** How do you feel about the situation?

Client: I feel guilty about wanting to leave them. But I also feel angry that they don't want to let me grow up. I know they've got problems, but they should work them out on their own. What do you think I should do?

12. **Helper:** You should move out you could have a talk with your parents and tell them how you feel.

Client: Well I could try it. I if I wanted to get into the dorms, do you know how I'd go about it?

13. **Helper:** The housing office on campus would have all that information they're located on the other side of campus.

Client: I should call them I guess. Do you really think I should move out?

14. **Helper:** I can see that you would like me to tell you what to do but I'm a little anxious about giving you advice because I don't know enough about you and your situation you are the one who has to decide whether to move out.

Client: I'm afraid of making a mistake, so I'd like to hear what you think.

15. **Helper:** I feel a bit surprised that you want me to tell you what to do do you suppose you also rely on your parents to tell you what to do too and then get angry at them?

Client: I never thought of that before. You might be right. I do get passive and then they tell me what to do. And I certainly do get angry at them. I guess we have some bad patterns that have been established over the years. I'll think about that. But I would still like to know whether you think I should move out?

16. **Helper:** I can tell you that when I had problems with my parents I talked to them and then I moved out it was important for me to talk to them to keep our relationship good but I felt really scared when I first sat down to talk with them because I was afraid they would get angry in my opinion, it will probably be hard on all of you at first but most young people need to leave home and strike out on their own even if it is hard.

Client: Well, thanks for your help.

17. **Helper:** What do you think you'll do?

Client: Maybe I'll talk with my parents.

18. **Helper:** Let's try it right now the research shows that it is easier to do it outside once you have practiced doing it in a helping session what I'd like you to do is pretend that your parents are right here and tell them that you want to move out.

Client: Okay. Mom and dad. I just want to tell you that, well, I guess I would like to move out maybe sometime soon.

19. **Helper:** That was a good start but you hesitated several times and your voice got real soft try to say it louder and state exactly what you want.

    Client: Mom and Dad: I have decided to move out.

20. **Helper:** That sounds real good your voice was loud and clear and you stated exactly what you wanted try doing that when you talk to them you know I want to tell you that I am really enjoying working with you because you are so eager to change how do you feel about the work we did today?

    Client: I feel really good. You gave me a lot to think about. I'm not sure yet what I'll do, but I feel more confident that I'll be able to work it out with my parents.

21. **Helper:** Terrific bye now I hope you enjoy the rest of the day.

    Client: You too. Bye.

Instructions for Judging Helping Skills

Place each response unit (indicated by a slash) in the following practice transcripts into one and only one of the helping skills (use the spaces in front of the helper statements to indicate your judgment). After you have judged every response unit, look at the correct responses at the end. Please note that we are trying to illustrate all the skills here rather than trying to present a transcript where the helper is particularly effective. Use the following numbers for the helping skills (note that we do not code attending skills in this transcript):

  1 = approval and reassurance
  2 = closed question
  3 = open question
  4 = restatement
  5 = reflection of feelings
  6 = challenge
  7 = interpretation
  8 = self-disclosure
  9 = immediacy
10a = information about the process of helping, **10b** = data, facts, or opinions, **10c** = feedback about client
11a = process advisement, **11b** = directives
 12 = other

Scoring

1. __/__/__/__/__/ **Helper:** Thanks for coming today./ My name is Judy./ I am beginning to learn helping skills./ We have 20 minutes to talk today./ The task here is for you to talk about whatever is on your mind./
   Client: I've been feeling down lately. I'm having a lot of trouble getting motivated. I haven't felt like going to class. Nothing really interests me.

2. __/__/ **Helper:** Give me an exmaple of what happened the last time you didn't go to class./ Oh, but first, what is your major?/

Client: I haven't really decided on a major because I haven't found anything that interests me.

3. __/__/ **Helper:** So you haven't decided yet./ Are you living on campus?/

Client: I'm living at home and I feel a lot of pressure on me. I would like to live in the dorm but my parents won't pay for it and I don't have the money myself. I mean my parents live right near campus and they say why should you live in a dorm when we live so close that you can easily walk. You might as well save money.

4. __/ **Helper:** It seems to you like your parents are forcing you to live at home./

Client: Yeah, it sure does and I really resent it. I think I would feel so much freer in a dorm. I feel restricted at home like they're watching every move I make and I don't feel free to come and go as I please.

5. __/__/ **Helper:** You feel stifled./ It sounds like you also feel uncomfortable because your parents are so restrictive./

Client: Right, but I'm not sure how to deal with it. They do provide me with a place to sleep and help me out a little with school. I feel like I ought to be grateful to them.

6. __/__/__/ **Helper:** You started fidgeting a lot just then and your voice got real soft./ I wonder if you feel a little upset./ Did I get that feeling right?/

Client: Well I guess I feel bad like I'm not a good son. I feel like they're giving me so much and all I do is want more.

7. __/ **Helper:** Can you give me an example of the last time that your parents said anything to you about staying home?/

Client: It was just last night. They told me that they really didn't want me to leave. They got all upset when I even brought up the topic, especially my mom.

8. __/__/__/__/ **Helper:** I wonder if both you and your parents are having trouble separating because of your changing role as you're growing up./ Maybe they're not quite ready for you to leave home because they're anxious about having an empty nest./ I wonder if you have a hard time leaving because you're afraid you'll hurt them./ Does that sound right to you?/

Client: That could be true. You know I'm an only child and my parents are older. They built their whole world around me.

9. __/__/ **Helper:** On the one hand, it's hard to leave them,/ but on the other hand, you want to go out and lead your own life./

Client: Well, I want to move out, but I don't want to hurt them.

10. __/__/__/__/ **Helper:** I had a similar situation when I left home./ My parents were quite upset at first./ I felt terrible and guilty./ What is it like for you?/

Client: Yeah, well, I don't know. It seems so difficult to figure all this out.

11. __/ **Helper:** How do you feel about the situation?/

Client: I feel guilty about wanting to leave them. But I also feel angry that they don't want to let me grow up. I know they've got problems, but they should work them out on their own. What do you think I should do?

12. __/__/ **Helper:** You should move out./ You could have a talk with your parents and tell them how you feel./

Client: Well, I could try it. I if I wanted to get into the dorms, do you know how I'd go about it?

13. __/__/ **Helper:** The housing office on campus would have all that information./ They're located on the other side of campus./
Client: I should call them I guess. Do you really think I should move out?

14. __/__/__/ **Helper:** I can see that you would like me to tell you what to do,/ but I'm a little anxious about giving you advice because I don't know enough about you and your situation/you are the one who has to decide whether to move out./
Client: I'm afraid of making a mistake, so I'd like to hear what you think.

15. __/__/ **Helper:** I feel a bit surprised that you want me to tell you what to do./ Do you suppose you also rely on your parents to tell you what to do too and then get angry at them?/
Client: I never thought of that before. You might be right. I do get passive and then they tell me what to do. And I certainly do get angry at them. I guess we have some bad patterns that have been established over the years. I'll think about that. But I would still like to know whether you think I should move out?

16. __/__/__/__/__/ **Helper:** I can tell you that when I had problems with my parents, I talked to them and then I moved out./ It was important for me to talk to them to keep our relationship good./ But I felt really scared when I first sat down to talk with them because I was afraid they would get angry./ In my opinion, it will probably be hard on all of you at first./ But most young people need to leave home and strike out on their own even if it is hard./
Client: Well, thanks for your help.

17. __/ **Helper:** What do you think you'll do?/
Client: Maybe I'll talk with my parents.

18. __/__/__/ **Helper:** Let's try it right now./ The research shows that it is easier to do it outside once you have practiced doing it in a helping session./ What I'd like you to do is pretend that your parents are right here and tell them that you want to move out./
Client: Okay. Mom and dad. I just want to tell you that, well, I guess I would like to move out maybe sometime soon.

19. __/__/__/ **Helper:** That was a good start./ But you hesitated several times and your voice got real soft./ Try to say it louder and state exactly what you want./
Client: Mom and Dad: I have decided to move out.

20. __/__/__/__/__/__/ **Helper:** That sounds real good./ Your voice was loud and clear,/ and you stated exactly what you wanted./ Try doing that when you talk to them./ You know, I want to tell you that I am really enjoying working with you because you are so eager to change./ How do you feel about the work we did today?/
Client: I feel really good. You gave me a lot to think about. I'm not sure yet what I'll do, but I feel more confident that I'll be able to work it out with my parents.

21. __/__/__/ **Helper:** Terrific./ Bye now,/ I hope you enjoy the rest of the day./
Client: You too. Bye.

Answers to Practice Transcript

1 = 12, 8, 8, 10a, 10a

2 = 3, 2

$3 = 4, 2$

$4 = 4$

$5 = 5, 5$

$6 = 10c, 5, 2$

$7 = 3$

$8 = 7, 7, 7, 2$

$9 = 4, 6$ (Note that although the whole intervention is a challenge, two separate codes are necessary because there are two separate units; by itself, the first unit is a restatement and the second is a challenge.)

$10 = 8, 8, 8, 3$

$11 = 3$

$12 = 11b, 11b$

$13 = 10b, 10b$

$14 = 9, 9, 6$ (see note for response 9)

$15 = 9, 7$

$16 = 8, 8, 8, 10b, 10b$

$17 = 3$

$18 = 11a, 10b, 11a$

$19 = 1, 10c, 11a$

$20 = 1, 10c, 10c, 11b, 9, 3$

$21 = 1, 12, 12$

Note. Two (if there are three) or three (if there are four) judges should agree with at least 51 of the 57 judgments shown above, and you should understand the reasons for your lack of agreement with every response before you go on to the next stage (judging helping skills in transcripts of real sessions). (We expect higher agreement levels on this practice transcript than we would on transcripts of real sessions because these helper responses were created to be easier to judge.)

Appendix D:
Client Reactions
System

Reaction	Definition
	Positive
1. Understood	I felt that my helper really understood me and knew what I was saying or what was going on with me.
2. Supported	I felt accepted, reassured, liked, cared for, or safe. I felt like my helper was on my side or I came to trust, like, respect, or admire my helper more. This may have involved a change in my relationship with my helper, such that we resolved a problem between us.
3. Hopeful	I felt confident, encouraged, optimistic, strong, pleased, or happy and felt that I could change.
4. Relieved	I felt less depressed, anxious, guilty, or angry or had fewer uncomfortable or painful feelings.
5. Negative thoughts or behaviors	I became aware of specific negative thoughts or behaviors that cause problems for me or others.
6. Better self-understanding	I gained new insight about myself, saw new connections, or began to understand why I behaved or felt a certain new way. This new understanding helped me accept and like myself.
7. Clear	I got more focused about what I was really trying to say, what areas I need to change, what my goals are, or what I want to work on in helping.
8. Feelings	I felt a greater awareness or deepening of feelings or could express my emotions better.
9. Responsibility	I accepted my role in events and blamed others less.
10. Unstuck	I overcame a block and felt freed up and more involved in what I have to do in helping.
11. New perspective	I gained a new understanding of another person, situation, or the world. I understand why people or things are as they are.
12. Educated	I gained greater knowledge or information. I learned something I had not known.

Reaction	Definition
13. New ways to behave	I learned specific ideas about what I can do differently to cope with particular situations or problems. I solved a problem, made a choice or decision, or decided to take a risk.
14. Challenged	I felt shook up or forced to question myself or to look at issues I had been avoiding.

Negative

15. Scared	I felt overwhelmed or afraid and wanted to avoid admitting having some feeling or problem. I may have felt that my helper was too pushy or would disapprove of me or would not like me.
16. Worse	I felt less hopeful, out of control, dumb, incompetent, ashamed, or ready to give up. Perhaps my helper ignored me, criticized me, hurt me, pitied me, or treated me as weak and helpless. I may have felt jealous of or competitive with my helper.
17. Stuck	I felt blocked, impatient, or bored. I did not know what to do next or how to get out of the situation. I felt dissatisfied with the progress of helping or having to go over the same things again.
18. Lacking direction	I felt angry or upset that my helper did not give me enough guidance or direction.
19. Confused	I did not know how I was feeling or felt distracted from what I wanted to say. I was puzzled or could not understand what my helper was trying to say. I was not sure I agreed with my helper.
20. Misunderstood	I felt that my helper did not really hear what I was trying to say, misjudged me, or made assumptions about me that were incorrect.
21. No reaction	I had no particular reaction. My helper may have been making social conversation, gathering information, or was unclear.

Note. The term *helper* is used here instead of *therapist* as in the original system. From "Development of a System for Categorizing Client Reactions to Therapist Interventions," by C. E. Hill, J. E. Helms, S. B. Spiegel, and V. Tichenor, 1988, *Journal of Counseling Psychology, 35*, p. 36. Copyright 1988 by the American Psychological Association. Adapted with permission.

Appendix E: Client Behavior System

Client behavior	Definition
1. Resistance	Includes complaining or blaming others inappropriately, defenses (e.g., projection, dissociation, intellectualization, avoidance, denial), sidetracking (changing the topic), and inappropriate requests (reflecting excessive helplessness or dependency); resistant behavior tends to block progress in helping and is often used by clients to suggest that they cannot change or to protect themselves from a perceived abusive or hostile helper; the client's tone of voice is often defensive, whiny, defeated, abusive, or hostile
2. Agreement	Indicates understanding or approval of what the helper has said without adding substantially to the helper's statement; must be more than a simple response that serves to maintain conversation (e.g., "mmhmm" or "yeah")
3. Appropriate request	An attempt to obtain clarification, understanding, information, or advice from the helper; if client acts helpless or overly dependent, code as resistance
4. Recounting	Includes small talk, answers to questions, or factual information about past events; client reports in a storytelling style (e.g., "I said ..., he said ...") rather than actively exploring current feelings and thoughts or interacting with the helper; tone of voice tends to be monotonous or conversational, with minimal immediate involvement
5. Cognitive–behavioral exploration	Indicates that the client is currently involved and exploring significant thoughts or behaviors; clients are actively thinking about their issues, although they do not have all the answers and are exploring to understand more; voice tone tends to have a lot of energy and to be irregular, with pauses and thoughtfulness; disagreeing with or challenging the helper would be coded here if clients are actively exploring their own thoughts or behaviors; this category is not coded when a client is talking about another person

Client behavior	Definition
	person unless understanding that person's behavior has significant implications for the client
6. Affective exploration	Statements that indicate that the client is currently involved and exploring feelings about therapeutically significant material; specific feeling words must be stated (e.g., happy, sad, anxious), or clearly visible nonverbal behavior (e.g., audible sighs, clenched fists, lowering of the head, crying, or shifting body position) must accompany affective material; the client's voice must sound as if feelings are being experienced in the present moment; discussion of past feelings would be coded as recounting unless the client is reexperiencing the feelings in the present moment; disagreeing with or challenging the helper would be coded here if clients are actively exploring their feelings
7. Insight	Client expresses an understanding of something about himself or herself and can articulate patterns or reasons for behaviors, thoughts, or feelings. Insight usually involves an "aha" experience, in which the client perceives himself or herself or the world in a new way; the client takes appropriate responsibility rather than blaming others, using "shoulds" imposed from the outside world, or rationalizing (note that these latter behaviors would be coded as resistance)
8. Therapeutic changes	Client expresses changes in her or his behaviors, thoughts, and feelings in therapeutically significant areas; changes can be increases in positive target areas, decreases in negative areas, or indications of action-oriented plans or decisions; if client reports changes but no change is apparent to judges, code as resistance

Note. The terms *helper* and *helping* are used here instead of *therapist* and *therapy* as in the original system. From "Client Behavior in Counseling and Therapy Sessions," by C. E. Hill, M. M. Corbett, B. Kanitz, P. Rios, R. Lightsey, and M. Gomez, 1992, *Journal of Counseling Psychology, 39,* pp. 548–549. Copyright 1992 by the American Psychological Association. Adapted with permission.

Appendix F:
Process Notes

Helper's name: _____

Instructions: Please complete these process notes as soon as possible after your session. Answer as honestly as possible. Give the completed form to your supervisor, so that you can discuss your reactions to the session.

1. *Manifest content*: What did the client talk about?
   _____
   _____
   _____

2. *Underlying content*: What were the unspoken meanings in what the client talked about?
   _____
   _____
   _____

3. *Defenses and barriers to change*: How does the client avoid anxiety?
   _____
   _____
   _____

4. *Client distortions or transference*: In what ways does the client respond to you as she or he has to other significant people in her or his life?
   _____
   _____
   _____

5. *Countertransference*: In what ways were your emotional, attitudinal, and behavioral responses stimulated by your interactions with the client?
   _____
   _____
   _____

6. *Personal reactions*: How would you evaluate your interventions? What would you do differently if you could? Why?
   _____
   _____
   _____

Author Index

Subject Index

About the Authors

Clara E. Hill, PhD, is a professor in the Department of Psychology at the University of Maryland. She received her PhD in 1974 from Southern Illinois University in Carbondale and has been at the University of Maryland, College Park, since then. Her major areas of research are the process of counseling and psychotherapy, training students in how to do counseling and psychotherapy, dream interpretation, and supervision. She is past president of the North American Society for Psychotherapy Research and past president of the International Society for Psychotherapy Research. She served as an associate editor and then editor of the *Journal of Counseling Psychology* from 1991 to 1999.

Karen M. O'Brien, PhD, is an assistant professor in the Department of Psychology at the University of Maryland. She received her PhD in 1993 from Loyola University Chicago. Her research interests include investigating the career and life development of women and people of color, with special attention to the influence of psychodynamic (e.g., attachment) and social-cognitive (e.g., self-efficacy) variables. She is also interested in examining training issues in psychology (e.g., graduate research training and supervision, counseling skills training for crisis workers). She serves on the editorial boards of the *Journal of Counseling Psychology* and the *Career Development Quarterly* and is an ad hoc reviewer for the *Journal of Vocational Behavior.* She is a licensed psychologist in Maryland and maintains a small private practice in psychotherapy.

Feedback Form

To the reader of this book:

We hope that *Helping Skills: Facilitating Exploration, Insight, and Action* has been useful to you in learning the helping skills. We would like to hear your feedback, so that we can improve future editions of the book. Please complete this sheet and send it to us. Thank you for your help.

Name (optional):_____

School and address:_____

_____

Department:_____

Instructor's name:_____

Name of course for which this book was used:_____

_____

Were all the chapters assigned to you to read?   Yes ☐ No ☐
If not, which ones were assigned?

1. What did you like most about this book?

2. What did you like least about this book?

3. In the space below or on a separate sheet of paper, please write specific suggestions for improving this book and anything else that you would like to write about your experience using this book and trying to learn the helping skills.

Please return this form to APA Books, 750 First Street NE, Washington, DC 20002-4242.